HOLT *Tradition*
Fourth Course

M000276327

Language and Sentence Skills Practice
Support for *Warriner's Handbook*

▶ **Lesson Worksheets**
▶ **Chapter Reviews**
▶ **"Choices" Activities**
▶ **Literary Models**
▶ **Proofreading Applications**

FOR
■ **Grammar**
■ **Usage**
■ **Mechanics**
■ **Sentences**

HOLT, RINEHART AND WINSTON

ISBN 0-03-099705-4
ISBN 978-0-03-099705-1

9 10 1689 15
4500519819

Contents

Language and Sentence Skills Practice

Chapter 1

PARTS OF SPEECH OVERVIEW: IDENTIFICATION AND FUNCTION

Chapter 2

THE PARTS OF A SENTENCE: SUBJECTS, PREDICATES, AND COMPLEMENTS

Chapter 3

THE PHRASE: PREPOSITIONAL, VERBAL, AND APPOSITIVE PHRASES

Contents

Chapter 4

THE CLAUSE:
INDEPENDENT CLAUSES AND SUBORDINATE CLAUSES

Chapter 5

AGREEMENT:
SUBJECT AND VERB, PRONOUN AND ANTECEDENT

Contents

v

Contents

Chapter 9

A GLOSSARY OF USAGE: COMMON USAGE PROBLEMS

Chapter 10

CAPITALIZATION: STANDARD USES OF CAPITALIZATION

Chapter 11

PUNCTUATION: END MARKS AND COMMAS

Contents

Contents

Chapter 16

CORRECTING COMMON ERRORS: KEY LANGUAGE SKILLS REVIEW

Chapter 17

WRITING COMPLETE SENTENCES

Contents

Chapter 18
WRITING EFFECTIVE SENTENCES

Resources
MANUSCRIPT FORM

Using This Workbook

The worksheets in this workbook provide practice, reinforcement, and extension for *Warriner's Handbook.*

Most of the worksheets you will find in this workbook are **traditional worksheets** providing practice and reinforcement activities on every rule and on all major instructional topics in the grammar, usage, and mechanics chapters in *Warriner's Handbook.*

You will also find in the workbook several kinds of **Language in Context worksheets,** which have been developed to expand the exploration and study of grammar, usage, and mechanics. The Language in Context worksheets include Choices worksheets, Proofreading Applications, Literary Model worksheets, and Writing Applications.

- **Choices** worksheets offer up to ten activities that provide new ways of approaching grammar, usage, and mechanics. Students can choose and complete one independent or group activity per worksheet. Choices activities stimulate learning through research, creative writing, nonfiction writing, discussion, drama, art, games, interviews, music, cross-curricular activities, technology, and other kinds of projects, including some designed entirely by students.

- **Proofreading Application** worksheets help students apply what they learn in class to contexts in the real world. Students use proofreading symbols to correct errors in grammar, usage, and mechanics in practical documents such as letters, applications, brochures, and reports. A chart of proofreading symbols is provided on page xi of this workbook.

- **Literary Model** worksheets provide literary models that demonstrate how published authors use various grammatical forms to create style or meaning. Students identify and analyze each author's linguistic choices and then use grammatical forms to create style or meaning in their own literary creations. Students are asked to reflect on their own linguistic choices and to draw connections between the choices they make and the style or meaning of their work.

- **Writing Application** worksheets are similar to the Writing Application activities in the grammar, usage, and mechanics chapters in *Warriner's Handbook.* Following the writing process, students use specific grammatical forms as they create a publishable document such as a letter, report, script, or pamphlet.

The Teaching Resources include the **Answer Key** in a separate booklet titled *Language and Sentence Skills Practice Answer Key.*

Symbols for Revising and Proofreading

Symbol	Example	Meaning of Symbol
≡	Fifty-first street	Capitalize a lowercase letter.
/	Jerry's Aunt	Lowercase a capital letter.
∧	differant (e)	Change a letter.
∧	The capital (of) Ohio	Insert a missing word, letter, or punctuation mark.
⌐	beside the ~~river~~ (lake)	Replace a word.
℘	Where's the ~~the~~ key?	Leave out a word, letter, or punctuation mark.
℘	an invisibile guest	Leave out and close up.
⌣	a close friend ship	Close up space.
∾	thier	Change the order of letters.
(tr)	Avoid having too many corrections (of your paper) in the final version.	Transfer the circled words. (Write *tr* in nearby margin.)
¶	¶"Hi," he smiled.	Begin a new paragraph.
⊙	Stay well ⊙	Add a period.
∧	Of course you may be wrong.	Add a comma.
#	ice#hockey	Add a space.
⊙	one of the following ⊙	Add a colon.
∧	Maria Simmons, M.D. Jim Fiorello, Ph.D.	Add a semicolon.
=	a great=grandmother	Add a hyphen.
∨	Pauls car	Add an apostrophe.
(stet)	On the fifteenth of July	Keep the crossed-out material. (Write *stet* in nearby margin.)

Choices: Exploring Parts of Speech

The following activities challenge you to find a connection between parts of speech and the world around you. Do the activity below that suits your personality best and then share your discoveries with your class.

RESEARCH

Is That All There Is?

No, the list of prepositions that you have in your book is not a complete list, but it is a good start. Double the size of this list. Then, make one master alphabetical list of prepositions and give copies of the list to your classmates.

DICTION

Lions and Tigers and Bears, Oh, My!

Interjections are the scene stealers of grammar. They set the tone of all that follows. But why, oh, why do people only use five or six interjections? They can be so boring. Give your classmates some other interjections to choose from. Compile a list (make it a long one) of alternative interjections. When were these expressions popular? What are their meanings? For what, if any, situations are they appropriate? You can shorten your work if you search an electronic dictionary for the label *interjection*. The plays of William Shakespeare are also a good source. Be sure to pass out copies of your list to all your classmates.

SIGN LANGUAGE

Words Without Letters

Interview a person who is skilled in sign language. Does sign language use parts of speech? If so, which ones? How are signs strung together? Report back to your classmates. Be ready to demonstrate appropriate signs.

CARTOONS

Look Out, Charlie Brown!

Be the next syndicated cartoonist! Make up several cartoons using parts of speech as characters or as subject matter. Better yet, design a short comic book. Is there a superhero or heroine of parts of speech? Answer this burning question, and post your cartoon in the classroom.

HISTORY/ETYMOLOGY

Mackintoshes and Watts

Proper nouns and adjectives taken from people's names are constantly being added to our language. A few of these even enter the mainstream of English and lose their capitalization. Consequently, most people are not aware of the person behind the word. Investigate some of these words. Write short biographies about the people memorialized in these words. With your teacher's permission, post your biographies in your classroom.

RESEARCH/FOREIGN LANGUAGES

Me Gusta

Why do we need pronouns anyway? Do other languages use them? How does Spanish use pronouns? German? Japanese? Find out about at least one other language. Interview someone who speaks another language or conduct a library search. Then, write an essay explaining how another language uses pronouns and comparing the other language's use and English's use. Read your essay to the class.

LINGUISTICS

Every Word Counts

What is the longest verb phrase (no compound verbs!) that you can think of? Challenge your classmates to a duel. To the victor goes the snack.

MATHEMATICS

The X Factor

Answer the following question: In mathematics, what elements of formulas function as parts of speech? For instance, what part of speech would a number be? What elements of formulas are not like parts of speech? What parts of speech have no function in mathematical formulas? Explain your comparisons to the class.

Common, Proper, Concrete, and Abstract Nouns

1a. A *noun* names a person, a place, a thing, or an idea.

A *common noun* names any one of a group of persons, places, things, or ideas. A *proper noun* names a particular person, place, thing, or idea.

	PERSON	PLACE	THING	IDEA
COMMON NOUN	woman	city	car	belief
PROPER NOUN	Alice Walker	Memphis	Toyota	Marxism

A *concrete noun* names a person, a place, or a thing that can be perceived by one or more of the senses. An *abstract noun* names an idea, a feeling, a quality, or a characteristic.

CONCRETE NOUNS   tree, child, bicycle, mountain, computer

ABSTRACT NOUNS   confusion, thought, bravery, charm, triumph

EXERCISE For each of the following sentences, decide whether the underlined word or word group is a common noun or a proper noun and also whether it is a concrete noun or an abstract noun. Above the word, write *Com* for *common noun* or *P* for *proper noun* and *Con* for *concrete noun* or *A* for *abstract noun*.

> Com, Con
Example 1. After the American Revolution, the country's <u>founders</u> wrote a constitution.

1. A <u>constitution</u> may have a bill of rights.

2. The Constitution of the United States guarantees <u>freedom</u> of speech.

3. The <u>Works Progress Administration</u> existed during the Great Depression.

4. That candidate is a staunch supporter of a republican form of <u>government</u>.

5. The <u>Articles of Confederation</u> were approved in 1781.

6. This document established "a firm league of <u>friendship</u>" among the states.

7. The editorial in today's <u>newspaper</u> defended the proposed amendment.

8. The <u>Supreme Court</u> can decide cases involving public officials.

9. Have you read the most recent book about the trial of <u>Aaron Burr</u>?

10. He was tried for <u>treason</u>.

Compound Nouns and Collective Nouns

1a.	A *noun* names a person, a place, a thing, or an idea.

A *compound noun* consists of two or more words that together name a person, a place, a thing, or an idea. The parts of a compound noun may be written as one word, as separate words, or as a hyphenated word.

   EXAMPLES   highway, Bill of Rights, brother-in-law

A *collective noun* names a group of people, animals, or things.

   EXAMPLES   committee, crew, family, group, herd

EXERCISE A   Identify each of the following words as a compound noun or a collective noun. On the line provided, write *comp* for *compound* or *coll* for *collective*.

Example 1. _____*comp*_____ firehouse

1. _____ community
2. _____ fighter pilot
3. _____ seafood
4. _____ council
5. _____ public

6. _____ Congress
7. _____ girlfriend
8. _____ fund-raiser
9. _____ herd
10. _____ username

EXERCISE B   In the following sentences, underline each compound noun once and each collective noun twice.

Example 1. A <u>swarm</u> of bees hovered around the <u>beehive</u>.

11. How many players are on a team in baseball?

12. My sister-in-law plays the oboe in the local orchestra.

13. The crowd had already sat through a two-hour speech when President Lincoln rose to read the Gettysburg Address.

14. Leslie always lapses into baby talk when she sees a litter of kittens.

15. The band included one song that sounded as if it had been recorded in an echo chamber.

16. The class presented Ms. Stockdale with a bouquet of baby's breath.

17. The TV weatherperson explained to the audience how a barometer works.

18. In order to get a good batch of cookies, you need to use the best oatmeal available.

19. A school of killer whales followed in the wake of the ship.

20. The bird-watchers were awe-struck as the flock of geese lifted into the sky.

Language and Sentence Skills Practice

Pronouns and Antecedents

| **1b.** | A *pronoun* takes the place of one or more nouns or pronouns. |

> **EXAMPLE** Lian showed **her** dad how to use the computer program. Computers had always baffled **him.**

The word or word group that a pronoun stands for is called the *antecedent* of the pronoun. In the sentences above, *Lian* is the antecedent of *her*, and *dad* is the antecedent of *him*.

EXERCISE A Underline each pronoun in the following sentences.

Example 1. Did you tell Dr. Garza that his special order has arrived?

2. Who wants to eat something?

1. If you didn't tell Mr. Attansio about his car, and I didn't, then who did?

2. That pie has a nice flavor to it.

3. What did she say about your new haircut?

4. Nobody knows me as well as I know myself.

5. All of us in the class wondered if anyone else was as amused by the film as we were.

6. Neither of them has a question about the project.

7. They repaired the truck themselves.

8. Although only some of the students admitted it to themselves, everyone in the class enjoyed reading the stories.

9. "These pumpkins," he said, "aren't nearly as large as those."

10. One piece of fruit will be enough for me, thank you.

EXERCISE B In the following sentences, underline each pronoun. Then, draw an arrow from each pronoun to its antecedent.

Example 1. Anna showed Victor her new bicycle.

11. The sound from the stereo was too loud, and it woke up the neighbors.

12. Sometimes Virgil will eat asparagus; sometimes he won't.

13. First, Juan washed the car; then he waxed it.

14. Uncle Bart could never bring himself to praise his sister's cooking, no matter how good it was.

15. Debra handed the baby to her husband, John, who put him in the crib.

Personal, Reflexive, and Intensive Pronouns

A *personal pronoun* refers to the one(s) speaking (*first person*), the one(s) spoken to (*second person*), or the one(s) spoken about (*third person*).

    EXAMPLE   Did Dad tell **you** about **my** plans?

A *reflexive pronoun* refers to the subject of a sentence and functions as a complement or as an object of a preposition.

    EXAMPLES   She bought **herself** a new dress. He finished the test by **himself.**

An *intensive pronoun* emphasizes its antecedent and has no grammatical function in the sentence.

    EXAMPLE   They worked the puzzle **themselves.**

EXERCISE A   Underline all the personal pronouns in the following sentences.

Example 1. <u>He</u> bought a CD for <u>his</u> father but kept the receipt in case <u>he</u> had to return <u>it</u>.

1. I hope that the skates are worth the money that you paid for them.

2. Jared offered me a free ticket to his uncle's play.

3. Mike and Zahara played their guitars, and then Ethel got her guitar and joined them.

4. Our coats look so much alike that I can't tell which coat is mine and which is yours.

5. Angie wrote to me and explained why she couldn't visit us this summer.

6. If you ask me, Carla, I think you should take the class in lifesaving.

7. After he passed the pilot's exam, he took us for a ride in his new airplane.

8. Isn't she the person whose athletic prowess dazzled us during the soccer game last Sunday?

9. My father loves that CD of chanting monks, but it drives me crazy.

10. He blocked the pass and caught the ball himself, but as he ran down the field with it, he was

     brought down by a running back.

EXERCISE B   Underline each intensive and reflexive pronoun in the following sentences. Then, above the word, identify each underlined pronoun as *intensive* or *reflexive*.

intensive
Example 1. Andy baked the bread <u>himself</u>.

11. He poured himself a glass of milk.

12. Somebody said that Terry designed all of the costumes herself.

13. You take care of yourself, okay?

14. The cat pulled itself up the side of the sofa.

15. The homeowners painted their house themselves.

Language and Sentence Skills Practice

Demonstrative, Interrogative, and Relative Pronouns

A *demonstrative pronoun* points out a person, a place, a thing, or an idea.

EXAMPLE All of the paintings were good, but **those** were the best.

An *interrogative pronoun* introduces a question.

EXAMPLE **What** are you doing for your birthday?

A *relative pronoun* introduces a subordinate clause.

EXAMPLE The coat **that** I just bought is green.

EXERCISE A In each of the following sentences, identify the underlined pronouns. Above each, write *DEM* for *demonstrative, INT* for *interrogative,* or *REL* for *relative.*

Example 1. This is the friend _whom_ Marcia invited to dinner.

1. _What_ is the question?

2. _This_ is the last of the paint.

3. _Which_ of the videos does Ben want to rent, this one or that?

4. Those are the shoes _that_ Lainie bought for the dance.

5. Whose books are _these_?

6. Mary Ellen asked the same question _that_ Padgett did.

7. The casserole that Dad made last week tasted much better than _this_.

8. To _whom_ did Dave give the birthday card?

9. That is a problem _which_ has troubled the community for many years.

10. Take _that_, you scoundrel!

EXERCISE B In each of the following sentences, underline the pronoun. Identify each by writing above it *DEM* for *demonstrative, INT* for *interrogative,* or *REL* for *relative.*

Example 1. The book _that_ Jane is reading is very entertaining.

11. Tom is the person that Cheryl had in mind for the job.

12. Those will do quite nicely.

13. Neil is the student whose photograph was in the paper during the science fair.

14. Which of the flowers would work best on the homecoming float?

15. This is the song performed by the choir in last night's performance.

HOLT HANDBOOK | Fourth Course

Indefinite Pronouns

An *indefinite pronoun* refers to a person, place, idea, or thing that may or may not be specifically named. Some common indefinite pronouns are *all, any, anybody, both, each, everyone, everything, few, many, more, neither, nobody, none, no one, one, other, several, some,* and *somebody.*

> **EXAMPLE** A **few** of the sandwiches are left if **anyone** would like **more** to eat.

EXERCISE A Underline the indefinite pronouns in the following sentences.

Example 1. After last night's game, everyone had something to say about him.

1. Much is promised to someone who is willing to risk everything.

2. Knock on their door and see if anybody is home.

3. The twins rely on themselves more than they rely on anyone else.

4. Many tried out for the play, and the drama teacher chose almost everyone.

5. Jared forgot about everything but his science fair project.

6. Several of us are meeting her for lunch in the cafeteria.

7. Doesn't anybody here besides you speak Spanish?

8. Nobody forgot to bring a backpack on the field trip.

9. All of the members of the chess club wondered who would win the tournament this year.

10. Neither of the brothers was willing to ask someone for help.

EXERCISE B Fill in the gaps in the following sentences with an appropriate indefinite pronoun.

Example 1. Please don't tell ____*anybody*____ about the surprise party.

11. Did _____ remember to put yeast in the bread?

12. Derek has enjoyed _____ he has read in English class.

13. _____ except Tracy brought a raincoat to school today.

14. _____ of us like romantic comedies than you might think.

15. If you get lost on the way to my house, ask _____ for directions; _____ knows where I live.

Language and Sentence Skills Practice

Identifying Pronouns

1b. A *pronoun* takes the place of one or more nouns or pronouns.

The kinds of pronouns are *personal pronouns, reflexive pronouns, intensive pronouns, demonstrative pronouns, interrogative pronouns, relative pronouns,* and *indefinite pronouns.*

EXERCISE A Underline all the pronouns in each of the following sentences.

Example 1. This weekend Beth and Bryan painted <u>several</u> of the rooms in <u>their</u> house.

1. Before painting, they went to the hardware store to buy paint.

2. The paint that Bryan had originally wanted for the living room was no longer available.

3. Beth suggested two alternative colors, but neither matched their furniture.

4. After searching for an hour, Beth found a shade of green that both of them liked.

5. They returned home and quickly began preparing to paint.

6. "What should we do first?" asked Bryan.

7. "You can stir the paint while I put drop cloths over the furniture."

8. "That is a good idea," he replied.

9. Then Bryan realized he would also need to move some furniture in the bedroom that they intended to paint.

10. As a result, Beth had to paint the entire living room herself.

EXERCISE B Identify the underlined pronoun in each of the following sentences by writing *personal, reflexive, intensive, demonstrative, interrogative, relative,* or *indefinite* on the line provided.

_____ 11. Does <u>anyone</u> know whose books these are lying in the middle of the floor?

_____ 12. Our new foreign exchange student will be addressing the Lions Club at <u>its</u> lunch meeting today.

_____ 13. David was careful to ask to whom the canoe belonged before he borrowed <u>it</u>.

_____ 14. <u>That</u> was clearly our best performance so far.

_____ 15. Shouting for anyone <u>who</u> can help you will get people's attention quickly.

_____ 16. I gave <u>myself</u> a pat on the back for a job well done.

_____ 17. You'll have to choose another topic because someone is already researching <u>this</u>.

_____ 18. <u>Who</u> arrived first for the drama club auditions?

_____ 19. Kathryn will finish typing the report <u>herself</u>.

_____ 20. Have Josette and <u>I</u> been the only ones interested in the tutoring program?

Adjectives and the Words They Modify

1c.	An *adjective* modifies a noun or a pronoun.

To modify means "to describe" or "to make the meaning of a noun or a pronoun more specific" by telling *what kind, which one, how many,* or *how much.* The most frequently used adjectives—*a, an,* and *the*—are usually called *articles.*

> **EXAMPLES**   **A** storm that is approaching **the** coast is very **dangerous**. **Every** resident in **that** area should evacuate immediately. [*A* and *the* are articles. *Dangerous* modifies *storm* and tells what kind. *Every* modifies *resident* and tells how many. *That* modifies *area* and tells which one.]

EXERCISE A   Underline the adjectives in the following sentences. Be sure to include all articles.

Example 1. How cloudy and dark the sky looks!

1. The little electric car chugged over the steep hill and into the valley.

2. A bitter wind was blowing off the ocean the night that Keith heard the eerie howling.

3. The unpublished story revealed a new side of Faulkner to the scholar.

4. The clear view of the distant ocean was slowly obstructed by the new skyscraper.

5. The gray cat stretched itself out in the warm sunshine pouring through the window.

EXERCISE B   In the following sentences, underline each adjective. Then, draw an arrow from the adjective to the word it modifies. Do not include the articles *a, an,* and *the.*

Example 1. The yellow balloon soared over the steep roof of the house.

6. I heard a lovely piece of music on the portable radio this morning.

7. The red telephone on the desk rang loudly, startling the maintenance worker.

8. The sky is often clear this time of the year.

9. The kitten playfully dug its sharp claws into the old dog, who snapped at the kitten.

10. Tony can bring fifteen chairs to the graduation party, if you need them.

11. Hang the apron on the little hook inside the pantry door and put the oven mitt back in the left-hand drawer.

12. Many people don't understand that a snowstorm can be dangerous.

13. This recipe makes a delicious pie, but it does call for ten apples.

14. Out of the bedroom window, Nils could see a young deer.

15. Why does Mr. Ecklund always use a red pencil to mark homework assignments?

Pronoun or Adjective?

Some words may be used either as adjectives or as pronouns. Demonstrative, interrogative, and indefinite terms are called pronouns when they stand for other nouns or pronouns and are called adjectives when they modify nouns or pronouns.

PRONOUNS	ADJECTIVES
Whose is the black jacket?	**Whose** black jacket is this?
Please save **some** for me.	Please save **some** pasta for me.
This is my favorite.	**This** poem is my favorite.

EXERCISE Identify each underlined word in the following sentences by writing above it *P* for *pronoun* or *A* for *adjective*.

Examples 1. $\overset{P}{\underline{Some}}$ of you have already received your assignments.

2. $\overset{A}{\underline{Some}}$ students are still waiting for their assignments.

1. <u>Many</u> of the houses in this neighborhood were built by the same contractor.

2. The freshest fruits in the store are the apples and pears, <u>which</u> were picked only yesterday.

3. <u>These</u> are not the books I ordered.

4. A <u>few</u> days from now, we'll be able to laugh about the situation.

5. <u>Which</u> play are we going to see?

6. Remember to seat <u>those</u> who come late at the back of the church.

7. Katya enjoys <u>most</u> movies, though she prefers comedies.

8. <u>These</u> old photographs were left to me by my grandmother.

9. <u>Some</u> prefer a cold meal to a hot one.

10. <u>Those</u> rosebushes are lovely!

11. <u>Some</u> children are naturally talented at singing and playing an instrument.

12. Of all the items on display, <u>which</u> do you prefer?

13. <u>Most</u> of us have already been swimming today.

14. Mai enjoys being out in nature more than <u>most</u> people do.

15. <u>Many</u> people will be coming from out of town for the wedding.

16. The symphony has three movements; <u>each</u> has a different tempo.

17. Will <u>all</u> members of the squadron please report to the ready room?

18. The doctor will try to see <u>all</u> of you today.

19. <u>This</u> sort of painting is best seen in natural light.

20. <u>This</u> is my final offer.

HOLT HANDBOOK | Fourth Course

Noun or Adjective?

When a word that can be used as a noun modifies a noun or pronoun, it is called an adjective.

    ADJECTIVE   **Hurricane** winds battered the coast.

        NOUN   During the **hurricane** several houses were washed out to sea.

Some word groups are considered compound nouns.

    EXAMPLES   paper clip   bird dog   garter snake

To avoid mistaking a word that is part of a compound noun for a word that is considered a separate adjective, check an up-to-date dictionary.

EXERCISE   Identify each underlined word by writing above it *N* for *noun* or *A* for *adjective*.

    Examples 1. This picture frame is made of pure <u>silver</u>. *(N)*

             2. This <u>silver</u> saltshaker is very valuable. *(A)*

1. My mother writes a <u>newspaper</u> column once a week.

2. Originally, Mike's family came from <u>Los Angeles</u>.

3. Jamal's older brother is a successful <u>record</u> producer.

4. Tish has switched to a diet rich in grains, vegetables, and <u>fruit</u>.

5. Colin likes all sorts of <u>music</u>, but his favorite is opera.

6. Who answered the <u>telephone</u> when you called?

7. Are those <u>storm</u> clouds along the horizon?

8. The <u>Los Angeles</u> freeways are some of the most crowded roads in the world.

9. Please refold the <u>newspaper</u> when you're finished with it.

10. My older sister just received her degree in <u>music</u> education.

11. The lecturer found a <u>fruit</u> basket in his hotel room.

12. That recording of the <u>Duke Ellington</u> song "Don't Get Around Much Anymore" is classic.

13. Aunt Mimi still has a lot of her old rock 'n' roll <u>records</u> on vinyl.

14. The gale force winds of the <u>storm</u> caused a great deal of damage along the coast.

15. The <u>launch</u> controller decided to proceed with the countdown.

16. The author of my favorite <u>book</u> came to town to give a lecture.

17. He did a <u>book</u> signing at the local bookstore.

18. <u>Duke Ellington</u> was one of the founders of the big-band sound in jazz.

19. The <u>launch</u> of a space shuttle is always spectacular.

20. If you have a complaint about your service, you should call the <u>telephone</u> company.

Language and Sentence Skills Practice

GRAMMAR

Main and Helping Verbs

1d. A *verb* expresses action or a state of being.

A *verb phrase* consists of one *main verb* and one or more *helping verbs* (also called *auxiliary verbs*).

EXAMPLES We **should**n't **have been** so late. [*Should* and *have* are helping verbs. *Been* is the main verb. *N't*, the contraction of *not*, is an adverb and is not part of the verb phrase.]

EXERCISE In the following sentences, underline the main verb once and the helping verb or verbs twice. Some main verbs do not have a helping verb.

Example 1. We would have seen the movie if we had arrived at the theater on time.

1. Mr. Okagi was working in his garden.

2. I have known Gabrielle for many years.

3. The Baxters are building a swimming pool in their backyard.

4. If you had been wearing the mask, I might not have recognized you.

5. Where did she say the ladder should go?

6. Some friends of Caitlin's are having a party next Saturday night.

7. Would you like an invitation?

8. Had I known about the concert earlier, I would have gone with you.

9. Randall should know that his supervisor might ask him for an explanation of his absences.

10. Will you or will you not join the dance?

11. Can a dog that small jump that high?

12. Rafiq had known about the change in schedule as early as last week.

13. I would help you carry the sofa, but as you can see, my hands are full already.

14. After they had been eliminated in the first round of the championship, the team's ride home

    on the bus was very quiet.

15. He should have written his answers to the assignment yesterday.

16. We are always singing Nedra's praises.

17. Have they lived in the house very long?

18. While the carpenter is working in one room of the new house, the plumber is finishing up in

    another room.

19. If Mozart had only lived longer, he might have composed even greater works.

20. Mr. Boylan will sign copies of his book after he has given a reading from it.

12

for **CHAPTER 1: PARTS OF SPEECH OVERVIEW** *page 15*

Verb Phrases

A *verb phrase* consists of one *main verb* and one or more *helping verbs* (also called *auxiliary verbs*). Some commonly used helping verbs are *have, has, had, do, does, did, may, might, must, can, will, shall, could, would, should,* and forms of the verb *be.*

EXAMPLES   The United States **had purchased** the Louisiana Territory from Napoleon. [The helping verb *had* and the main verb *purchased* make up a verb phrase.]

Didn't the Louisiana Purchase **double** the size of the United States? [The helping verb *did* and the main verb *double* make up a verb phrase. *N't*, the contraction of *not*, is an adverb and is not part of the verb phrase.]

EXERCISE A   Underline the verb phrase in each of the following sentences.

Example 1. The Louisiana Purchase was completed by President Thomas Jefferson.

1. Before the Louisiana Purchase, the Louisiana Territory was owned by France.

2. President Jefferson must have wanted information about these interior lands.

3. Meriwether Lewis, Jefferson's private secretary, and William Clark were chosen as the leaders of the expedition into the Louisiana Territory.

4. A young Shoshone woman, Sacagawea, was living in a Mandan village near Lewis and Clark's camp.

5. Didn't she accompany them on their expedition as an interpreter and guide?

EXERCISE B   Underline the verb phrases in the following paragraph. Be sure to include all the helping verbs.

Example Sacagawea's husband, a French Canadian trader, had been hired as an interpreter.

The Lewis and Clark expedition had followed a trail that led to the Rocky Mountains. Those high mountain peaks must have appeared impassable to the members of the expedition. How could they ever get to the other side? Fortunately, Sacagawea knew these mountain passes. This was the land that she had traveled through as a youngster with the Shoshone before she had been captured by enemies. The expedition eventually encountered Sacagawea's own Shoshone people. Her brother had become a chief of the Shoshone, and Sacagawea convinced him that he should provide the explorers with horses, food, and canoes so that the expedition could continue through the mountains to the ocean. On November 7, 1805, the explorers reached the Pacific Ocean. Sacagawea has not been forgotten. Two mountain peaks, two lakes, and a state park have been named in honor of the young Shoshone woman who came to the aid of Lewis and Clark.

Language and Sentence Skills Practice

Action Verbs and Linking Verbs A

An *action verb* expresses either physical or mental activity.

EXAMPLES   I **raked** the lawn yesterday. [*Raked* expresses physical activity.]

Can you **remember** the numbers? [*Can remember* expresses mental activity.]

A *linking verb* connects the subject to a word or word group that identifies or describes the subject. Such a word or word group is called a *subject complement*.

EXAMPLES   Mr. Chavez **is** my art teacher. [*Teacher* identifies the subject *Mr. Chavez*.]

The road **feels** bumpy. [*Bumpy* describes the subject *road*.]

Some verbs can be used as action verbs or as linking verbs.

ACTION   The boy **tastes** his soup.

LINKING   This soup **tastes** good.

EXERCISE A   Underline the verb in each sentence. Then, above the verb, write *AV* if the verb is an action verb or *LV* if it is a linking verb.

Example 1. The tree grew tall and sturdy.

1. The crowd remained spellbound throughout the magician's performance.

2. Estelle turned the page of her science book.

3. Marcus should have arrived by now.

4. The solution to that problem remains a mystery to me.

5. I smell the aroma of a freshly mowed lawn.

6. The stone felt smooth and velvety.

7. The tomato turned red on the vine.

8. That vegetable soup smells delicious.

9. Cory felt a few raindrops on his head.

10. Is Samantha older than Jessica?

EXERCISE B   Underline the linking verb in each of the following sentences. Then, circle the subject and the subject complement.

Example 1. Don't those (children) seem (happy)?

11. The ocean is too calm for surfing.

12. Josh feels disappointed by the absence of surf.

13. The surf had been rough only one week ago.

14. Tomorrow the wind may become stronger.

15. Then the waves should be higher.

HOLT HANDBOOK | Fourth Course

Action Verbs and Linking Verbs B

An *action verb* expresses either physical or mental activity.

EXAMPLES   John **cooked** dinner last night. [physical activity]

Have you **considered** all the possibilities? [mental activity]

A *linking verb* connects the subject to a word or word group that identifies or describes the subject. Such a word or word group is called a **subject complement**.

EXAMPLES   Green **is** my favorite color. [*Color* identifies the subject *Green*.]

The sky **looks** beautiful. [*Beautiful* describes the subject *sky*.]

EXERCISE   Identify each underlined verb by writing above it *AV* for *action verb* or *LV* for *linking verb*.

Example 1. I feel sleepy.

1. Although most of the tour group went to the museum, Ms. Ruiz remained behind at the hotel.

2. The Hanson brothers are the best hockey players in the state.

3. In Madrid, Jody stayed in a youth hostel.

4. The project looks intimidating, but it really isn't.

5. In spite of his advancing years, our dog Tadger remains a handsome animal.

6. Taste this stew and tell me if you think it's spicy enough.

7. The detective looked carefully at the footprint in the dirt.

8. The storm yesterday blew down an old maple tree in our yard.

9. Was the delivery service prompt with the package?

10. Suzanne's casserole tastes delicious, just like the casserole mother used to make.

11. By the first of next month, Eric will have been a champion bicyclist for seven years.

12. If Steve isn't careful, he may injure himself while rock climbing.

13. Does this movie seem boring to you?

14. Please tell me again how much you liked my story.

15. When Charlie finished the book, he recommended it to his older brother.

16. The cows appear unhurt by the hailstorm.

17. Curt often impresses people with his knowledge of movie trivia.

18. Are most of the shoes in the shop this expensive?

19. The letter just appeared on my desk one morning.

20. Ms. Lindenmayer's plan for the debate tournament sounded good to the faculty committee.

Transitive and Intransitive Verbs

A *transitive verb* has an *object*—a word that tells who or what receives the action of the verb.

> **EXAMPLE**   In the seventeenth century, French colonists **founded** the region of Acadia in Canada. [The object *region* receives the action of the verb *founded*.]

An *intransitive* verb does not have an object.

> **EXAMPLE**   Several thousand Acadians **migrated** to Louisiana.

The same verb may be transitive in one sentence and intransitive in another.

> **TRANSITIVE**   The British **fought** the French for control of Acadia.
>
> **INTRANSITIVE**   The British and the French **fought** for control of the land.

EXERCISE A   Identify the verb in each of the following sentences and decide if it is transitive or intransitive. Draw a line under the verb, and then above it write *T* if it is *transitive* or *I* if it is *intransitive*.

Example 1. The British won control of Acadia in 1713.

1. In the 1700s, the British expelled thousands of Acadians from Canada.

2. Many of these Acadians moved to Louisiana.

3. In Louisiana the name "Acadian" evolved into "Cajun."

4. Cajun settlements spread across the southern part of Louisiana.

5. The paintings of Cajun artist George Rodrigue capture the flavor of Cajun life.

EXERCISE B   The same action verb is used in each pair of sentences, once as a transitive verb and once as an intransitive verb. Underline the verb in each sentence. Then, above the verb write *T* if the verb is *transitive* or *I* if it is *intransitive*.

Example 1. Longfellow wrote the poem *Evangeline* about the Acadians.

Longfellow wrote about the Acadians.

6. The people of New Orleans assembled along the streets for the Mardi Gras parade.

   The Cajun chef assembled the ingredients for gumbo on the counter.

7. The cars in the Louisiana Sugarcane Festival parade moved slowly down the street.

   The workers quickly moved the shrimp off the boat to the waiting trucks.

8. Marc Savoy, a Cajun musician, plays the accordion.

   The Cajun band plays every Saturday morning.

9. The tourists met Justin Wilson, the host of a popular Cajun cooking show.

   The two families met for a fishing trip on the bayou.

10. My favorite author has written a new novel.

    Karen has written in her journal every day for three years.

Adverbs and the Words They Modify

1e. An *adverb* modifies a verb, an adjective, or another adverb.

An adverb tells *how, when, where,* or *to what extent* (*how much, how long,* or *how often*).

EXAMPLES   We stayed **inside**. [The adverb *inside* modifies the verb *stayed* and tells *where*.]

It was an **unusually** quiet morning. [The adverb *unusually* modifies the adjective *quiet* and tells *how*.]

The dog barked **quite** loudly. [The adverb *quite* modifies the adverb *loudly* and tells *to what extent*.]

EXERCISE   Underline the adverbs in the following sentences. Then, draw a line from each adverb to the word or words it modifies.

Example 1. The animals stirred restlessly in the forest.

1. In the morning, the campers carefully built a fire and quickly began preparing breakfast.

2. The magician deftly pulled one colorful scarf after another from the hat.

3. The third baseman easily caught the pop fly.

4. Professor Losoya never had heard such a racket in his laboratory.

5. Yesterday I received an e-mail from my friend in Tokyo.

6. This very useful device will be a great addition to any household.

7. At the end of the recital, the audience applauded enthusiastically.

8. The extremely eager young actors gathered early at the door of the audition hall.

9. Will Cousin Bruce be arriving today or tomorrow?

10. Aunt Marta gave Carlie an uncommonly generous helping of mashed potatoes.

11. My father gives overly detailed directions.

12. The bus will leave for St. Louis early tomorrow.

13. The demolition crew very carefully placed the explosive charges in the old building.

14. At the stroke of midnight, the crowd in Times Square noisily greeted the new year.

15. The juggler's ridiculously red shirt distracted the audience from his juggling.

16. The coach explained the play especially carefully to the rookies on the team.

17. This thoroughly hilarious film will be playing at a theater soon.

18. The extremely cranky child cried loudly when his rattle was taken away.

19. The cleverly modified car easily won the road rally.

20. Occasionally an immensely patient farmer can become frustrated by the pace of farming.

Language and Sentence Skills Practice

GRAMMAR

Noun or Adverb?

Some words may be used as either nouns or adverbs. When identifying parts of speech, classify words that are used to modify verbs, adjectives, and adverbs as adverbs.

NOUN	I was at **home** all weekend.
ADVERB	Last weekend I stayed **home**. [The adverb *home* modifies the verb *stayed*.]

EXERCISE A Identify the underlined word in each of the following sentences by writing above it *N* for *noun* or *ADV* for *adverb*. For any adverbs, draw two lines under the word or words the adverb modifies.

Example 1. Will you go to the boxing match Friday?

1. Edwina takes a personal interest in the match on Friday.

2. She hopes Teresa will not be knocked down.

3. In addition to ups, everyone experiences a down now and then.

4. Teresa is strong but doesn't move very fast.

5. She has been able to maintain her weight without having to go on a fast.

6. Her opponent, Gabriella, will train tonight.

7. Tonight will be her first opportunity to use the new ring.

8. Although she is small, she boxes well.

9. Teresa will have to draw upon her deep well of pugilistic skill.

10. Teresa trains days and works nights.

EXERCISE B Write a pair of sentences for each word. First, use the word as a noun, then, as an adverb.

Example 1. right *The actor suddenly appeared on the right of the stage.*

Remember to turn right when you get to Cedar Lane.

11. downtown _____

_____

12. last _____

_____

13. Tuesday _____

_____

14. first _____

_____

15. outside _____

_____

Prepositions

| **1f.** | A *preposition* is a word that shows the relationship of a noun or a pronoun, called the *object of the preposition,* to another word. |

A preposition, its object, and any modifiers of the object form a *prepositional phrase*.

> **EXAMPLE**   The expedition traveled **to a foreign land.** [The preposition *to* shows the relationship of *land*, the object of the preposition, to *traveled*.]

A preposition that consists of two or more words is called a *compound preposition*.

> **EXAMPLE**   I'll take the red one **instead of** the blue one.

EXERCISE A   Underline the prepositions in each of the following sentences.

Example   1. The cat scampered up the tree.

1. Joe found a mouse underneath the kitchen table.

2. If it rains, the picnic will be moved inside the house.

3. If we don't get the supplies in time for the trip, we can do without them.

4. Jack and Jill tumbled down the hill.

5. The first mate took command of the ship when the captain went below deck.

EXERCISE B   Underline the prepositional phrases in the following sentences and circle the prepositions.

Example   1. After Cortés's military triumphs, Mexico and Central America were ruled by Spain.

6. In 1519, Hernando Cortés led an expedition to Mexico.

7. Under his command were 508 soldiers and 110 sailors.

8. After a long voyage he reached Mexico, where a mighty empire had been established by the Aztecs.

9. According to historians, Cortés and his small army had trouble seizing control of the empire because of the Aztecs' sophisticated military organization.

10. However, with the help of many enemies of the Aztecs, Cortés conquered the Aztec empire in 1521.

11. Cortés gathered his troops and dismantled every ship except one.

12. He then marched toward the Aztec capital, Tenochtitlan.

13. Several hundred Aztec chiefs escorted Cortés and his forces into the city.

14. An Aztec delegation carrying splendid gifts walked behind Emperor Montezuma II.

15. An Aztec chief set gifts of golden ornaments before Cortés.

Preposition or Adverb?

Some words may be used as either prepositions or adverbs. Remember that an adverb is a modifier and does not have an object.

ADVERB	When they reached the bridge, they marched **across.**
PREPOSITION	They marched **across** the bridge.
ADVERB	May I come **along**?
PREPOSTION	I followed her **along** the path.

EXERCISE Identify the underlined word in each of the following sentences by writing above it either *PREP* for *preposition* or *ADV* for *adverb*. Then, on the line provided, write a sentence using the word as the other part of speech.

Example 1. Don't just stand <u>around</u> gawking. *(ADV)*

    Carry those buckets of water around the house to the firefighters.

1. You knocked my hat <u>off</u>!

_____

2. It rolled <u>under</u> the porch.

_____

3. There are all sorts of bugs <u>underneath</u>.

_____

4. We were happy that Sam decided to come <u>along</u>.

_____

5. I'm going <u>inside</u> to tell everyone what you did.

_____

6. Go <u>ahead</u>.

_____

7. That hat never fit <u>on</u> my head very well, anyway.

_____

8. You can see the barn right <u>past</u> those trees.

_____

9. Will your hand fit <u>through</u> there?

_____

10. The rabbit quickly scampered <u>over</u> the hill.

_____

Conjunctions

1g. A *conjunction* joins words or word groups.

Coordinating conjunctions—*and, but, for, nor, or, so,* and *yet*—join words or word groups that are used in the same way.

> **EXAMPLES**   My mom **and** dad said that I can go.
>
> He can go, **but** I can't.

Correlative conjunctions—*both . . . and, not only . . . but also, either . . . or, neither . . . nor,* and *whether . . . or*—are pairs of conjunctions that join words or word groups that are used in the same way.

> **EXAMPLES**   **Neither** Yoko **nor** Evan had read the book.
>
> **Both** Marcus **and** I will be going.

EXERCISE   Identify the conjunctions in the following sentences by drawing one line under the coordinating conjunctions and two lines under the correlative conjunctions.

Example 1. Polar animals find food both in water and on land.

1. The polar bear is a carnivore and lives almost solely by hunting.

2. Polar bears are wonderfully equipped to exist in the wild, for a dense, white fur covers them completely.

3. Not only does fur grow between the pads on their feet, but also several inches of fat cover much of their bodies.

4. Polar bears can both gallop at a speed of up to twenty-five miles per hour and swim six miles an hour.

5. Female polar bears can breed every three years, and they give birth in snow-covered dens.

6. A den is warmer than the outside air, for the female bear seals the entry with snow.

7. The sleeping bear's heart rate, respiration, and metabolism drop, and this sleep is a form of hibernation.

8. Unlike that of a deep hibernator, though, the polar bear's temperature remains constant, so the bear can spring into action almost immediately.

9. Polar bears have a highly developed sense of smell and can detect food up to ten miles away.

10. They are well known for their swimming abilities, but they can also run on land at high speeds.

Language and Sentence Skills Practice

GRAMMAR

Interjections

1h. An *interjection* expresses emotion. An interjection has no grammatical relation to the rest of the sentence.

An interjection is generally set off from the rest of the sentence by an exclamation point or by a comma or commas. Exclamation points indicate strong emotion. Commas indicate mild emotion.

> **EXAMPLES**   **Wow!** I can't believe we won that game in the final second!
>
> **Well,** it certainly was an exciting game, wasn't it?
>
> It was, **uh,** my fault, I think.

EXERCISE A   Underline the interjections in the following sentences.

Example   1. <u>Goodness!</u> You startled me!

1. Hooray! Our soccer team is in the finals.

2. Ugh! The field is so muddy.

3. I don't mind playing in the rain, but, yuck, I don't like getting covered with mud.

4. Oh, I think it will be fun.

5. Oops! I slipped.

6. Luther, wow, you've got mud all over you.

7. Would you, ah, help me get up, please?

8. Hey! Watch out, or you'll fall, too.

9. Yikes! Your warning came too late.

10. Well, there's the whistle, so I guess the game is about to begin.

EXERCISE B   For each of the following words, write a sentence that uses the word as an interjection. Remember to use the correct punctuation to set off the interjection from the rest of the sentence.

11. ouch _____

12. aha _____

13. wow _____

14. sh _____

15. um _____

for **CHAPTER 1: PARTS OF SPEECH OVERVIEW** | page 28

Determining Parts of Speech

1i.	The way a word is used in a sentence determines what part of speech the word is.

EXAMPLES Tina has a small **cut** on her finger. [noun]

Cut some logs for the fire. [verb]

Save a sandwich **for** me. [preposition]

We lost our way, **for** we couldn't see the sun. [conjunction]

EXERCISE In each of the following sentences, determine how the underlined word is used. Above the underlined word, write *N* for *noun*, *PRON* for *pronoun*, *ADJ* for *adjective*, *V* for *verb*, *ADV* for *adverb*, *PREP* for *preposition*, or *C* for *conjunction*.

                              ADJ

Example 1. That is an unusual <u>book</u> bag.

1. Some friends went <u>downtown</u> to see the latest movie.

2. <u>Others</u> went roller-skating at a nearby rink.

3. Is <u>that</u> the rink with all the expensive stereo equipment?

4. Another friend has invited us back to his house <u>for</u> a party.

5. What should we have for a <u>midnight</u> snack?

6. Do you think that we will still be up at <u>midnight</u>?

7. The casserole, <u>which</u> is left over from dinner, tastes better cold than hot.

8. <u>Which</u> sandwich do you prefer?

9. Do you want American or Swiss <u>cheese</u> on your sandwich?

10. Any kind of cheese sandwich is fine <u>with</u> me.

11. <u>Tonight</u> is my favorite night of the week.

12. I volunteer at the nursing home <u>tonight</u>.

13. He let the dog <u>out</u> an hour ago.

14. <u>Call</u> me tomorrow night.

15. Do you have a <u>call</u> button beside your bed at the hospital?

16. Give him orchids, <u>for</u> they are his favorite.

17. <u>Which</u> do you prefer?

18. One dancer <u>mirrors</u> the other in a striking duet.

19. We still need more supplies, <u>so</u> we'll make one more trip to the store.

20. Of course, he refused to look in a <u>mirror</u>.

Language and Sentence Skills Practice

Review A: Identifying Parts of Speech

EXERCISE A Above each underlined word in the following paragraphs, indicate which part of speech it is by writing *N* for *noun,* PRON for *pronoun,* ADJ for *adjective,* V for *verb,* ADV for *adverb,* PREP for *preposition,* C for *conjunction,* or *I* for *interjection.*

Example All of [1] us have heard of Robert Louis Stevenson.

PRON

While yet an obscure young [1] writer, Robert Louis Stevenson traveled through Belgium and France by canoe and donkey. His [2] account of this trip was his [3] first book, *An Inland Voyage.* Although Stevenson wrote a number of plays, articles, [4] and short stories, he is probably best remembered [5] for the works that children love. *Treasure Island, Kidnapped,* and *A Child's Garden of Verses* have been [6] popular since they were first published.

Stevenson, who [7] became a writer after studying [8] engineering and law, suffered from [9] ill health all his life. [10] Well, he and his wife searched for a [11] healthful climate for the ailing writer. [12] Eventually, [13] they settled in the South Seas, on the island of Samoa. [14] There the natives [15] revered him; they called him *Tusitala,* which means "teller of tales." Stevenson died [16] in Samoa at the age of forty-four. [17] At his request, he was buried high on a Samoan mountain. His famous poem "Requiem," [18] which is inscribed on his tomb, ends: "Home [19] is the sailor, home from sea, / [20] And the hunter home from the hill."

EXERCISE B Each of the following sentences contains at least one word that is the part of speech given before the sentence. Find each such word and underline it.

Example 1. *(verb)* Scientific theories often fascinate writers of fiction.

21. *(pronoun)* Jules Verne, a nineteenth-century novelist, was one of the first writers of science fiction.

22. *(preposition)* Tales of imaginary voyages and incredible exploits had been popular long before Verne's time.

23. *(verb)* Verne, however, combined fantastic adventures with scientific "explanations."

24. *(adverb)* Several of his novels, including *Around the World in Eighty Days,* are still read today.

25. *(conjunction)* Of course, it is now easy to circle the world in eighty days, but modern science has not yet duplicated the feats described in Verne's *Journey to the Center of the Earth* and his *Twenty Thousand Leagues Under the Sea.*

for **CHAPTER 1: PARTS OF SPEECH OVERVIEW**   pages 2–28

Review B: Identifying Parts of Speech

EXERCISE A Above each underlined word in the following paragraph, indicate which part of speech it is by writing *N* for *noun, PRON* for *pronoun, ADJ* for *adjective, V* for *verb, ADV* for *adverb, PREP* for *preposition, C* for *conjunction,* or *I* for *interjection.*

ADV
Example [1] Not all authors achieve fame during their lifetimes.

Before William Shakespeare **[1]** died in 1616, he had achieved **[2]** some degree of success as a popular **[3]** playwright and actor. However, **[4]** few would have predicted the **[5]** impact that he has had **[6]** on our language, literature, and culture. **[7]** Many of Shakespeare's **[8]** expressions have become part of **[9]** everyday speech. Many of his lines are quoted **[10]** extensively both on stage and off. The following lines are **[11]** among the many that have inspired readers **[12]** and theatergoers for the last **[13]** three centuries: "Neither a borrower nor a lender be." "Something is rotten in the state **[14]** of Denmark." " **[15]** This was the noblest Roman of them all." " **[16]** O, beware, my lord, of jealousy . . . the green-eyed monster. . . . " "A horse! A horse! My kingdom **[17]** for a horse!" "Uneasy lies the head that **[18]** wears a crown." "The course of **[19]** true love **[20]** never did run smooth."

EXERCISE B Each of the following items contains two underlined words. Above each underlined word, indicate which part of speech it is by writing *N* for *noun, PRON* for *pronoun, ADJ* for *adjective, V* for *verb, ADV* for *adverb, PREP* for *preposition,* or *C* for *conjunction.*

ADJ   N
Example 1. Marita's brown dress matches the brown of her eyes.

21. I waited uneasily in the outer office until the principal called, "Come in!"

22. In some folk dances, each participant dances separately, improvising steps to the rhythm of the music.

23. Most drivers stop before turning onto a highway, even if there is no stop signal at the intersection.

24. The hikers took the trail to the left when they left the campsite.

25. All but Joel went to the restaurant, but most did not eat.

26. I returned home early because I wanted to see who was at home.

27. As we looked around, we discovered a small shop around the corner.

28. Blue is my favorite color, so I'm going to order a blue sweater.

29. Those fell from those trees.

30. If you hand me that pen, I'll write the number in my own hand.

Review C: Identifying Parts of Speech

EXERCISE A Each of the following sentences contains two underlined words. Above each underlined word, indicate its part of speech by writing *N* for *noun*, *PRON* for *pronoun*, *ADJ* for *adjective*, *V* for *verb*, *ADV* for *adverb*, *PREP* for *preposition*, *C* for *conjunction*, or *I* for *interjection*.

Example 1. Right! Now, turn right at the next light.

1. Over a three-month period he was able to win her over to his point of view.

2. I believe that I left your book in the drawer on the left.

3. They hadn't expected so many people, so they had to bring in more chairs.

4. That is not the best place for that lamp.

5. When you chip away at that hard stone, make sure that you don't get a chip in your eye.

EXERCISE B Each of the following sentences contains at least one word that is the part of speech given before the sentence. Find each such word and underline it.

Example 1. *(verb)* The writer carefully considered several leads for an article.

6. *(pronoun)* No one knew the answer to the riddle posted on the Web site.

7. *(preposition)* According to the directions on the inside cover, only two players are needed.

8. *(verb)* The student hesitantly qualified his answer with a shrug.

9. *(adverb)* Hold on tightly as you climb to the top of the ladder!

10. *(conjunction)* I asked José and Lenora to meet me at the library, but they both decided to study at home.

11. *(adverb)* I am quite capable of doing it, thank you.

12. *(pronoun)* Errol is looking forward to excavating those.

13. *(preposition)* In the past, she has encouraged teamwork.

14. *(noun)* That orange suits you.

15. *(adjective)* Which orange do you mean?

Literary Model: Poetry

Same Song
by Pat Mora

While my sixteen-year-old son
  sleeps,
my twelve-year-old daughter
stumbles into the bathroom at
  six a.m.
plugs in the curling iron
squeezes into faded jeans
curls her hair carefully
strokes Aztec Blue shadow on
  her eyelids
smoothes Frosted Mauve
  blusher on her cheeks
outlines her mouth in
  Neon Pink
peers into the mirror, mirror on
  the wall
frowns at her face, her eyes,
  her skin,
not fair.

At night this daughter
stumbles off to bed at nine
eyes half-shut while my son
jogs a mile in the cold dark
then lifts weights in the garage
curls and bench presses
expanding biceps, triceps,
  pectorals,
one-handed push-ups, one
  hundred sit-ups
peers into that mirror, mirror
  and frowns too.

EXERCISE A Write each verb that appears in the above poem. For each verb that appears more than once, indicate the number of times it is used. Do not include verbals. (Hint: In the second stanza, *curls* is a noun and *bench presses* is a compound noun.)

_____

_____

EXERCISE B

1. Describe how the poet uses verbs in the first stanza.

_____

_____

_____

"Same Song" from *Borders* by Pat Mora. Copyright © 1986 by Pat Mora. Published by **Arte Público Press-University of Houston, Houston, TX, 1986.** Reprinted by permission of the publisher.

Literary Model (continued)

2. What effect is created by such a use of verbs?

_____

_____

_____

EXERCISE C Using Mora's first stanza as a model, write a poem about something you or another person does routinely. As Mora did, break down the routine into many steps and use descriptive and precise verbs.

_____

_____

_____

_____

_____

_____

_____

_____

_____

_____

EXERCISE D

1. Read your poem critically with the goal of replacing one verb for an even more precise, descriptive one. Write the original verb followed by the replacement.

_____

_____

2. How does your use of verbs contribute to the effect of your poem?

_____

_____

_____

_____

for **CHAPTER 1: PARTS OF SPEECH OVERVIEW** `pages 10–11`

Writing Application: Description

What is your reaction when you hear that you're having "steak and potatoes" for dinner? What is your reaction when you're told that you'll be eating "a grilled sirloin steak and a baked potato served with fresh chives, sharp Cheddar cheese, real bacon bits, and whipped butter"? The adjectives used in the second case certainly spice up both the language and your image of the upcoming meal. When you include lively, precise adjectives in your writing, you help readers to visualize what you're describing.

WITHOUT ADJECTIVES	The guitarist played a solo.
WITH ADJECTIVES	The **lead** guitarist, seemingly **entranced,** played an **intricate five-minute** solo.

The sentence with adjectives not only gives readers specific information about which guitarist but also helps them to imagine what the guitarist and his or her solo were like.

WRITING ACTIVITY

Your memories are an important part of what makes you you. Sometimes, however, you have to make an effort to bring a memory to the forefront. Think about a room that is a part of your past and that had great significance for you. It could be in your present or a previous house or apartment, your school, or a friend's house. It might be in a public place. Spend a few moments visualizing the room. Then, write a description of it. Include at least ten adjectives. The adjectives you use should be precise and vivid so that your memory of the room comes alive for your readers.

PREWRITING As you jot down ideas, think in terms of all five senses. In addition to what you see as you visualize the room, address the sensations of hearing, touch, smell, and taste. Use interesting adjectives to describe vivid sensory details; such details will enhance your writing.

WRITING Decide how you will arrange your ideas. You might want to use a spatial arrangement, perhaps moving in your mind's eye from one part of the room to another as you describe it.

REVISING Examine your draft to determine whether you can replace some of the adjectives with others that are more descriptive, precise, or lively. A thesaurus can help you with this step, but double-check a dictionary to make sure that the word suggested by the thesaurus is appropriate for the sentence. Read your draft aloud to get a "feel" for the language. Ask yourself how you could make the writing more appealing to readers and then revise accordingly. Be sure that you have included at least ten adjectives.

PUBLISHING Exchange drafts with a classmate. Each of you should read every word of the other's draft carefully, looking for errors in grammar, usage, spelling, capitalization, and punctuation. Next, present your description to your class.

EXTENDING YOUR WRITING

You could submit your description for publication on a Web site that publishes students' writing. Be sure to find out what the guidelines are for length and check submission dates.

Choices: Examining the Parts of a Sentence

The following activities challenge you to find a connection between the parts of a sentence and the world around you. Do the activity below that suits your personality best, and then share your discoveries with your class.

LINGUISTICS

Transformations

There are many different ways to analyze sentences. Find an example of another way of diagramming sentences. Then, with your teacher's permission, give a short description of the method and provide examples for the class.

OBSERVATION/LISTENING

Kid Talk

Do you know any children between ages two and six? If so, let them do the work for this project! All you have to do is tape-record a few examples of children's endless chattering and make a few observations. Bring your tape to class. Discuss your observations of the parts of speech favored by the children, the sentence structures mastered, their use of complements, and anything else you notice. If other students choose this project, gather your notes together and make a time line of them, arranging them in order of each child's age. What patterns do you notice?

ANIMATION

Cartoon Madness

Using either a computer program or a flip book, create an animation of a sentence being created, corrected, and edited. Since animation is known for its humor, add a few laughs to your footage. For instance, instead of just crossing out a word, have another word eat it! You might want to include sound effects or recordings for atmosphere.

ETYMOLOGY

Keep on the Subject

Investigate the words *subject* and *predicate*. What are their roots? How many meanings does each have? What are they? What other words have the same roots? Write a memo detailing your findings. Give everyone in the class a copy.

CREATIVE WRITING/DRAMA

Communication Gap

Write a dialogue for four characters. One character speaks only in declarative sentences, one only in interrogative sentences, one only in imperative sentences, and one only in exclamatory sentences. Find three or four friends to help you stage your skit for the class.

STYLE

K.I.S.

Those letters stand for "Keep it simple!" Some writers follow this advice by using the simple style. The simple style aims at keeping the subject, verb, and complement together. In the simple style, no adjectives, adverbs, or prepositional phrases come between these three basic elements of the sentence. Try it. Take a piece of your writing or a passage from a published work. Then, rewrite it in the simple style. Post both versions of the writing selection so that everyone in the class can have a chance to compare them.

DESIGN

Fine Form

Create forms for your classmates to use as they analyze the sentence structure of their own writings. Use all the categories that you have studied so far: subjects, verbs, prepositional phrases, and kinds of sentences. Also, make a column for the number of words in each sentence. Then, make copies of your chart for all your classmates.

ROLE PLAY

Love or Money?

With a partner, create and perform a skit in which a stern businessperson tries to explain business writing to a rather wild poet. The poet has a fixation on sentence fragments; however, the business person most decidedly does not harbor such idiosyncrasies. Create a somewhat friendly disagreement between the two.

Sentences and Sentence Fragments

2a. A *sentence* is a word group that contains a subject and a verb and that expresses a complete thought.

A *sentence fragment* is a word or word group that is capitalized and punctuated as a sentence but that does not contain both a subject and a verb or that does not express a complete thought.

FRAGMENT Tony, the outstanding baseball player on the team.

SENTENCE Tony, the outstanding baseball player on the team, is my brother.

SENTENCE Hurry! [*You* is the understood subject.]

EXERCISE A Identify each of the following groups of words as a sentence or a sentence fragment. On the line provided, write *S* if the group of words is a sentence or *F* if it is a fragment.

Example __*F*__ **1.** The lamp that tipped on its side and shattered.

_____ **1.** The delicately sculptured, alabaster Chinese statue.

_____ **2.** At Saint Croix in the Virgin Islands, where the water is warm.

_____ **3.** Glancing at the thick Sunday paper.

_____ **4.** The aircraft that just departed is headed toward Denver.

_____ **5.** Lois Lane, the *Daily Planet*'s star reporter, whom Superman loved.

_____ **6.** Before marching down the deck, the sailor saluted the captain.

_____ **7.** After the violent summer storm, we were content to stay at home.

_____ **8.** On a scorching summer day when children and adults enjoy cool, fresh fruit and sip icy lemonade.

_____ **9.** The painting of a little girl with somber brown eyes.

_____ **10.** Stretching for miles through barren and rocky terrain.

EXERCISE B Identify each of the following groups of words as a sentence or a sentence fragment. On the line provided, write *S* if the group of words is a sentence or *F* if it is a fragment.

Example __*F*__ **[1]** Six students who joined the chess club.

_____ **[11]** Campaigning to encourage more students to join the chess club. _____ **[12]** Several new students became members of the school's chess team. _____ **[13]** The important competition scheduled for next month. _____ **[14]** The team was both nervous and excited about the event.

_____ **[15]** Everyone studied the common strategies used to succeed.

Language and Sentence Skills Practice

Subjects and Predicates

2b. Sentences consist of two basic parts: subjects and predicates.

The *subject* tells whom or what the sentence or clause is about, and the *predicate* tells something about the subject.

          SUBJECT   PREDICATE

The police on the island of Tobago / once rode bicycles.

PREDICATE   SUBJECT   PREDICATE

  Now /   the police /   ride in air-conditioned sedans.

PREDICATE   SUBJECT   PREDICATE

When did / this change / take place?

EXERCISE In each sentence below, underline the subject once and the predicate twice.

Example 1. <u>The island of Bequia</u> <u>lies between the islands of Grenada and St. Vincent.</u>

1. Until recently, tourists could reach the tiny island only by boat.

2. The island of Bequia remains relatively untouched by the trappings of modern life.

3. A need for economic growth has led to the construction of an airport.

4. Some islanders are worried about the loss of the old way of life.

5. Six hundred species of butterfly have been recorded on Tobago and Trinidad.

6. The Tobago Forest Preserve has protected much of the island from tourism.

7. About a half mile offshore is beautiful Buccoo Reef.

8. Sun-drenched fishing villages dot the scenic coastline.

9. On Little Tobago Island, eager bird-watchers may spot several kinds of exotic birds.

10. The red-billed tropicbird is one of the magnificent birds inhabiting the forests of Tobago.

11. Many other birds migrate over the area.

12. Different kinds of trees, shrubs, and wildlife are abundant on the islands.

13. Tobagonians share their island with many types of snakes, lizards, and frogs.

14. Different kinds of bats, including the fish-eating bat, inhabit the island.

15. Four types of forests can be found in Tobago.

16. The mangrove forest occupies the wetlands.

17. The coastal edge of the island and the surrounding beaches are home to the littoral woodlands.

18 The seasonal deciduous forest extends to the lower level of the mountain range.

19. The evergreen rain forest covers the top of the mountain range.

20. The streams of Tobago also provide homes to many types of fish and crabs.

for **CHAPTER 2: THE PARTS OF A SENTENCE**   *pages 37–38*

Simple and Complete Subjects

2c. The main word or word group that tells whom or what the sentence is about is called the *simple subject*.

The *complete subject* consists of the simple subject and any words or word groups that modify the simple subject.

SENTENCE	The flowers in the vase are wilted.
COMPLETE SUBJECT	The flowers in the vase
SIMPLE SUBJECT	flowers

EXERCISE A In each sentence below, underline the simple subject.

Example 1. The last person out of the gym pulled the door shut.

1. Twenty people applied for the job.

2. Last year my mother traveled to China.

3. The cat's thick fur was soft to the touch.

4. Is *The Hobbit* your favorite book?

5. The wet, exhausted hiker was happy to see the shelter.

6. The long rain yesterday turned our yard green overnight.

7. Suddenly, the old bridge began to sag in the middle.

8. The large, orange ball bounced over my head.

9. The dog just had puppies.

10. Cool, fresh air blew through the open window.

EXERCISE B In each sentence below, underline the complete subject and circle the simple subject.

Example 1. The small child appeared to be lost.

11. A young boy was wandering alone through the large shopping mall.

12. The fearful child began to cry.

13. Several concerned shoppers tried to help him.

14. The frightened child, however, would not speak.

15. Finally, an elderly lady walked up to the child.

16. The kind lady began to tell the child a story.

17. Her long, funny story was about a prince.

18. The handsome prince had gotten lost on the way to see his lady.

19. A beautiful white horse helped the prince find his way.

20. After telling the story, the kindhearted lady helped the child find his mother.

GRAMMAR

Simple and Complete Predicates

2d. The *simple predicate,* or *verb,* is the main word or word group that tells something about the subject.

The *complete predicate* consists of the verb and all the words that modify the verb and complete its meaning.

> **SENTENCE** She has posted the notice.
>
> **COMPLETE PREDICATE** has posted the notice   **SIMPLE PREDICATE** has posted

EXERCISE A In each sentence below, underline the verb.

Example 1. The storm clouds <u>blew</u> over the mountains.

1. Nicci and Jackie sat on the porch swing for the photograph.

2. Carl lifted the lid of the pot.

3. The old barn leaned a little to one side.

4. The four cowboys walked down the street in a line.

5. One of the players brought her own soccer ball to the match.

6. The dog slept on the porch all afternoon.

7. The plumber shut off the water under the sink.

8. We have made our final selection from the menu.

9. Will Carter come to the party on Friday?

10. You need this book for class tomorrow.

EXERCISE B In each sentence below, underline the complete predicate and circle the verb.

Example 1. Magical flowers (grew) in the girl's garden.

11. Margarette designed a beautiful garden in the backyard.

12. She planted very special tulips along the edges of the garden.

13. One day Margarette went outside to water the garden.

14. Margarette heard an unusual noise coming from the edges of the garden.

15. The tulips were making a soft noise.

16. Margarette knelt down near one of the tulips.

17. The tulip talked to Margarette in a soft, delicate voice.

18. A small red tulip was thanking Margarette for watering it!

19. The voices of the tulips always amazed Margarette.

20. After all, not too many people have heard the gentle voice of a tulip.

HOLT HANDBOOK | Fourth Course

Complete and Simple Subjects and Predicates

2c. The main word or word group that tells whom or what the sentence is about is called the *simple subject.*

The *complete subject* consists of the simple subject and any words or word groups that modify the simple subject.

2d. The *simple predicate,* or *verb,* is the main word or word group that tells something about the subject.

The *complete predicate* consists of the verb and all the words that modify the verb and complete its meaning.

SENTENCE	That last dive qualified him for the finals.
COMPLETE SUBJECT	That last dive
SIMPLE SUBJECT	dive
COMPLETE PREDICATE	qualified him for the finals
SIMPLE PREDICATE	qualified

EXERCISE A In each sentence below, underline the complete subject and circle the simple subject.

Example 1. The entire family enjoys the nearby park.

1. The Gómez family goes to a nearby park almost every weekend.

2. The two youngest boys enjoy playing soccer with their friends.

3. The older girls prefer to go bird-watching through the park's beautiful trails.

4. Sometimes the entire family goes hiking together.

5. A long day at the park is a favorite pastime for the Gómez family.

EXERCISE B In each sentence below, underline the complete predicate and circle the simple predicate.

Example 1. Many composers of music have gained international fame.

6. Modern composer Dan Welcher was born in 1948.

7. Welcher earned degrees from the Eastman School of Music and Manhattan School of Music.

8. Dan Welcher is one of the most original and exciting modern American composers.

9. Dan Welcher has composed many types of music, including symphonies, operas, and chamber music.

10. The Chicago Symphony, the St. Louis Symphony, and many other orchestras have performed Welcher's music.

Finding the Subject

2e.   The subject of a verb is never in a prepositional phrase.

Do not mistake a noun or pronoun in a prepositional phrase for the subject of a sentence.

EXAMPLE   **Some** of the apples were rotten.

The word *there* or *here* may begin a sentence, but it is almost never the subject.

EXAMPLE   Here comes the **train.**

Questions usually begin with a verb, a helping verb, or a word such as *what, when, where, how,* or *why.* In most cases, the subject follows the verb or part of the verb phrase.

EXAMPLE   Is his **brother** coming with us?

EXERCISE   In the following sentences, underline the verb twice and the subject once.

Example 1.   Here is a painting by Diego Rivera.

1. The people of Mexico have a great appreciation of his work.

2. Is Rivera known for any particular style?

3. His murals of Mexico's social problems are famous.

4. We looked at that painting of two Mexican women with a baby.

5. How does the artist achieve the feeling of tranquillity in that picture?

6. What do you think of the muted colors?

7. Don't those soft pastel colors convey a sense of calm?

8. There is a copy of that picture in this brochure about the artist.

9. What is the title of that painting?

10. Here is an article about Rivera.

11. Which years was Rivera in the United States?

12. Have you seen photographs of his murals?

13. Some of the murals show different aspects of Mexican history.

14. Do you know about his wife, Frida Kahlo?

15. Wasn't Kahlo an accomplished artist, also?

16. There have been many great artists of the twentieth century.

17. What kinds of art influenced Rivera?

18. Several different styles of art influenced the artist.

19. Was he influenced by postmodernism and cubism?

20. There are significant moments in history reflected in Rivera's works.

The Understood Subject

In a request or a command, the subject is usually not stated. In such sentences, *you* is the
understood subject.

    REQUEST [*You*] Take this to the principal's office, please.

    COMMAND [*You*] Do your homework now, María.

EXERCISE On the line before each sentence, write the subject of the sentence. If the subject of the sentence is understood to be *you*, write *you* in the blank.

Example _____ *you* _____ **1.** Patricia, please hand me those maps.

_____ **1.** Jerome didn't hear your answer.

_____ **2.** Speak more clearly.

_____ **3.** Please help the children with their luggage.

_____ **4.** Constance is arriving at noon.

_____ **5.** Please tell me what time it is.

_____ **6.** Jaime, be careful on your trip.

_____ **7.** Karl is wearing his new suit.

_____ **8.** Ginger left the meeting early.

_____ **9.** Rogelio, please write me a list of what you'd like from the store.

_____ **10.** Be respectful of the students who have not finished their tests yet.

_____ **11.** Bring me the salad bowl, please.

_____ **12.** Is Teddy going to be at the track meet?

_____ **13.** Jim told Margaret to bring her bathing suit.

_____ **14.** Take the bread out of the oven.

_____ **15.** Please, Jeremy, don't laugh at me.

_____ **16.** While reading this poem, you should pay particular attention to the rhythm.

_____ **17.** Paolo seemed distracted by the radio.

_____ **18.** Sing the solo yourself.

_____ **19.** Clean your room as soon as possible, Martina.

_____ **20.** We will all take a look at the rings of Saturn.

Compound Subjects

2f. A *compound subject* consists of two or more subjects that are joined by a conjunction and that have the same verb.

The parts of a compound subject are generally joined by the coordinating conjunction *and* or *or*.

> **EXAMPLES** Many **flowers, shrubs,** and **fruit trees** began blooming early this spring.
>
> Either the **cups** or the **glasses** go in that cupboard.

EXERCISE Underline the compound subjects in the following sentences.

Example 1. Both Marvin and Abel are going on the trip.

1. Exercise, a healthful diet, and sufficient rest are essential for good health.

2. Either Raoul or Marty will win the election.

3. The oaks, the maples, and the sycamores have lost their leaves.

4. Greta or Sheila will water the garden this afternoon.

5. Sheep, goats, and chickens wandered around in the large yard.

6. The musicians, dancers, and actors met for a final dress rehearsal.

7. Either Jon or I will wash the dishes tonight.

8. Did the children and their parents enjoy the camping trip?

9. Randy, Martha, and Jennifer were the top three finishers in the math competition.

10. Will Monday or Tuesday be a good day for a meeting?

11. The police and the fire department responded to the alarm.

12. Planes, trains, and buses are all means of public transportation.

13. Will Victor or Elian answer the question?

14. The hippos and giraffes crowded around the water hole.

15. Either exercise or an extended vacation will help relieve your stress.

16. *The Grapes of Wrath* and *East of Eden* are two novels by John Steinbeck.

17. The barn and the front pasture were flooded during the storm.

18. In spite of Roger's objection, Kelly and Wilson painted the doghouse bright red.

19. John Lennon and Paul McCartney were the two chief songwriters for the Beatles.

20. Did Ross, Margaret, and Chen recognize the bicycle?

Compound Verbs

2g. A *compound verb* consists of two or more verbs that are joined by a conjunction and that have the same subject.

The parts of a compound verb are usually joined by the coordinating conjunction *and, but,* or *or.*

EXAMPLES The boys **cooked** dinner and also **washed** the dishes.
We **have finished** our project but **have** not yet **cleaned** up our mess.

EXERCISE Each of the sentences below contains a compound verb. Draw a line under each verb that is part of a compound verb.

Example 1. She will go early and get things ready for the ceremony.

1. The speech will be televised live at noon and rerun at six.

2. I have finished my research and can now write my report.

3. The teacher reviewed the material and asked each student a question.

4. I put the plants in the sunlight and watered them thoroughly.

5. We talked, laughed, and sang during the long bus ride.

6. Have the students researched the issue or discussed different possibilities yet?

7. I will go to the movies, see a play, or visit a museum this weekend.

8. The actress could sing and dance quite well.

9. Jack put on his coat and went out into the snow.

10. The entertainer juggled several balls and performed acrobatics.

11. Will you pack your bags and confirm your airline reservations today?

12. The audience rose to their feet and applauded loudly.

13. The picnickers gathered the leftovers, collected the trash, and cleaned the tables.

14. Next summer we will hike, climb mountains, and ride our bikes in Colorado.

15. Did Uncle William receive the package and examine it?

16. We read the papers, signed them, and mailed them back to the agency.

17. Will you come to my house and help me with some repairs?

18. After school, we exercise at the gym and then do our homework.

19. The customer looked at her receipt and asked about her change.

20. Our grandmother paints, sews, and plays flute quite well.

Compound Subjects and Verbs

2f.   A *compound subject* consists of two or more subjects that are joined by a conjunction and that have the same verb.

> **EXAMPLE**   Is there a **hammer** or a **screwdriver** in that toolbox?

2g.   A *compound verb* consists of two or more verbs that are joined by a conjunction and that have the same subject.

> **EXAMPLE**   The laundry **has been taken** out of the dryer and **folded.**

Both the subject and the verb of a sentence may be compound.

EXERCISE   In each of the following sentences, underline each part of the subject once and each part of the verb twice.

Example 1. The children and their parents lined up and waited for the contest to begin.

1. Will the players and their team captain introduce themselves?

2. The four boys ran to the line, picked up a stick, and raced back to the start.

3. Jeanette and her brother will be at choir practice early.

4. Did you feed the cats and change their water?

5. Are Maía and Paula rehearsing tonight?

6. The members of the committee discussed the proposition and then voted against it.

7. We washed the vegetables, sliced them, and then cooked them with spices.

8. Ducks, geese, and swans were swimming around the large lake.

9. Luigi doesn't swim, run, or cycle very often.

10. Florentine painted a picture of black doves and hung it in the living room.

11. The book and the movie were equally dull.

12. Bob and Geno put on their helmets and rode their bikes.

13. Dietrich studied hard for his exam and made a high grade.

14. Are the cardinals and blue jays visible from here?

15. Sasha and Boris played a hard game of tennis and then swam in the lake.

16. The tourists took photographs, asked questions, and looked around curiously.

17. Jacqui washed the clothes, hung them to dry, and folded them neatly.

18. We listened to the song and asked the singer many questions about it.

19. Will the coach teach us a new drill and practice it with us?

20. When will the crew and passengers board the plane?

HOLT HANDBOOK | Fourth Course

Complements

2h.	A *complement* is a word or word group that completes the meaning of a verb.

The complement may be a noun, a pronoun, or an adjective.

EXAMPLES

    S   V   C
We were feeling very **tired.** [adjective]

    S   V   C   C
Ms. Johnson found your **notebook** and your **glasses.** [nouns]

    S   V C   C
Shawna sent **me** an **invitation** to her party. [pronoun, noun]

    S   V   C
This lamp is an **antique.** [noun]

EXERCISE   Underline each complement in the following sentences.

Example 1. Mark sent his sister a birthday gift.

1. The pilot checked the gauges carefully.

2. Have you given your brother his lunch yet?

3. After a long day at work, the nurse felt exhausted.

4. Wanda became an engineer after graduation.

5. I read science fiction and mysteries most often.

6. After the concert, the musicians seemed satisfied.

7. Did you find a book about real estate yet?

8. The committee planned the construction and maintenance of roadways.

9. After the football game, Duane appeared tired.

10. Stephen mailed his grandmother a music box.

11. Send a birthday card to your uncle John.

12. The sweater looks green to me.

13. Has Richie submitted a college application yet?

14. The candidate sent the reporter a copy of his speech.

15. Bring me the bread knife, please.

16. Steve enjoys horror novels and action movies.

17. Will Moira send her poem to a magazine?

18. Errol is often late.

19. This book is not the one.

20. The babysitter gave little Nora her dinner.

Language and Sentence Skills Practice

The Subject Complement: Predicate Nominatives

2i. | A *subject complement* is a word or word group that completes the meaning of a linking verb and identifies or modifies the subject.

(1) A *predicate nominative* is a word or word group that is in the predicate and that identifies the subject or refers to it.

EXAMPLES   She had been my **friend.**   The class president will be **he.**

What **nonsense** that is!   My favorite colors are **turquoise** and **black.**

EXERCISE A   Underline each predicate nominative in the following sentences.

Example 1. Did Peter become the new captain of the team?

1. Louis is a mathematician and a teacher.

2. Were those two girls the winners?

3. After years of hard work, she became a superb ballerina.

4. Should Barney have been the leader of this team?

5. What an excellent singer she is!

6. The pianist is a composer, also.

7. Mrs. Woodward became an excellent nurse.

8. Her doves' names are Juliette, Musetta, and Luigi.

9. What a mistake that could have been!

10. My father has been an engineer, a scientist, and a professor.

EXERCISE B   On the blank provided in each of the following sentences, write an appropriate predicate nominative.

Example 1. After years of medical school, Tonya at last became a _____*doctor*_____ .

11. My favorite movie star is _____ .

12. The winner of the spelling bee is _____ .

13. Ms. Ozu had been a _____ before she became a teacher.

14. Is Chet the new _____ of the student council?

15. The best day to visit the museum is _____ .

The Subject Complement: Predicate Adjectives

2i. A *subject complement* is a word or word group that completes the meaning of a linking verb and identifies or modifies the subject.

(2) A *predicate adjective* is an adjective that is in the predicate and that modifies the subject of a sentence or a clause.

> **EXAMPLES** He is becoming **stronger.**   I heard that the joke you told was **humorous.**
>
> How **ridiculous** I felt!   The children seem **lively** and **mischievous.**

EXERCISE A Underline each predicate adjective in the following sentences.

Example 1. Did the baby seem restless and nervous this morning?

1. Carlos has grown much taller through the years.

2. Does the soup taste too salty to you?

3. How beautiful her voice is!

4. The seas appear calm this morning.

5. The kitten looked quite content in its new box.

6. The modern music sounded odd to us.

7. Does Jorge seem happy in his new home?

8. The roses from the bush outside smell sweet.

9. François is satisfied with his new job.

10. How soft and delicate the baby bird seems!

EXERCISE B On the blank provided in each of the following sentences, write an appropriate predicate adjective.

Example 1. The ending of the tragic play was very _____sad_____ .

11. How _____ the sunset is this evening!

12. Lin often feels _____ after soccer practice.

13. As the sky grew darker, the stars grew _____ .

14. Jennifer seems _____ about winning the award.

15. This ghost story is _____ than I remembered.

Subject Complements

2i. A *subject complement* is a word or word group that completes the meaning of a linking verb and identifies or modifies the subject.

There are two kinds of subject complements: the *predicate nominative* and the *predicate adjective*.

(1) A *predicate nominative* is a word or word group that is in the predicate and that identifies the subject or refers to it.

> **EXAMPLES** Grace is a **nurse.**   The team captain will be **she.**

(2) A *predicate adjective* is an adjective that is in the predicate and that modifies the subject of a sentence or a clause.

> **EXAMPLES** Joshua became **angry.**   Was the book very **interesting**?

EXERCISE Underline the subject complements in the following sentences. Identify each complement by writing above it *PN* for *predicate nominative* or *PA* for *predicate adjective*.

Example 1. Chico Mendes was a rubber tapper from Brazil.

1. Latex becomes rubbery when heated.

2. Rubber tappers from the Amazon sell latex, which they extract from rubber trees, to

   manufacturers; this substance is the basis for many rubber products.

3. The rubber tappers are mostly poor and uneducated, but they are hard workers.

4. The ranchers and farmers were greedy for land and began to burn the rain forest at an

   alarming rate.

5. These fires were dangerous not only to the thousands of species of plants and animals of the

   forest but also to the livelihood of the rubber tappers.

6. Chico Mendes was a rubber tapper and a member of a workers' union.

7. He became the spokesperson for and a hero to the poor rubber tappers.

8. He warned that the destruction of the Amazon rain forest was a threat to the world.

9. Environmentalists from around the world took notice of Mendes's message, but local ranchers

   and farmers became angry with Mendes.

10. It was a surprise to the world when two local ranchers assassinated Chico Mendes on

    December 22, 1988.

for **CHAPTER 2: THE PARTS OF A SENTENCE**   *pages 53–55*

Objects: Direct Objects

An *object of a verb* is a noun, pronoun, or word group that completes the meaning of a *transitive verb*—a verb that expresses an action directed toward a person, a place, a thing, or an idea.

2j. A *direct object* is a noun, pronoun, or word group that tells *who* or *what* receives the action of a transitive verb or shows the result of the action.

A direct object answers the question "Whom?" or "What?" after a transitive verb.

EXAMPLES   I gave the **books** to Harrison. [Gave what? *Books*.]

Don't forget **Hans** and **Kate**. [Forget whom? *Hans* and *Kate*.]

EXERCISE A   Decide whether the underlined words in the following sentences are direct objects. If the word is a direct object, write *DO* above the word. If it is not a direct object, write *NDO*.

                        DO
Example 1. Medieval knights often rescued people in danger.

1. The nobles wore steel armor and helmets.

2. He was a successful warrior thanks to his great war horse.

3. Women in splendid gowns attended the tournaments.

4. A knight would often throw a scarf to his lady during the events.

5. People of the Middle Ages respected chivalry, bravery, and honor.

6. Medieval students studied the craft of alchemy.

7. Travelers took shelter in a castle or monastery.

8. Educated nobles enjoyed the tales of Chaucer and the poetry of Petrarch.

9. King Edward III's son was the Black Prince.

10. King Edward III started a war with France.

EXERCISE B   Underline the direct objects in the following sentences.

Example 1. Knights endured dangerous Crusades to foreign lands.

11. In 1346, trading ships carried infected black rats into Italian ports.

12. Fleas on the rats spread a dangerous disease.

13. The bubonic plague killed thousands throughout Europe until 1352.

14. It attacked people of all ages.

15. Medieval doctors found no cure for the plague.

Language and Sentence Skills Practice

Objects: Indirect Objects

An *object of a verb* is a noun, pronoun, or word group that completes the meaning of a *transitive verb*—a verb that expresses an action directed toward a person, a place, a thing, or an idea.

2k. | An **indirect object** is a noun, pronoun, or word group that often appears in sentences containing direct objects. An indirect object tells *to whom* or *to what* (or *for whom* or *for what*) the action of a transitive verb is done.

EXAMPLES　Hand **her** the clean sheets, please. [Hand the sheets to whom? *Her.*]

Play **Kim** and **me** a tune. [Play a tune for whom? *Kim* and *me.*]

EXERCISE A　Decide whether the underlined words in the following sentences are direct objects or indirect objects. If the word is a direct object, write *DO* above the word. If it is an indirect object, write *IO*.

Example 1. Jill handed Jack the bucket.

1. Are you reading the book I gave you?

2. I mailed my brother the birthday gift.

3. Juanita sent her teacher an Easter card.

4. Would you like a drink with your sandwich?

5. Please send me a copy of the letter.

6. The flight attendant offered the passengers drinks and snacks.

7. Are you going to buy plates and napkins for the picnic?

8. The dog chased its tail for several minutes.

9. Please hand me the pitcher of orange juice, Franco.

10. Have you given Janice your answer yet?

EXERCISE B　Underline the indirect objects in the following sentences.

Example 1. Fred sent the college his application.

11. Why don't you tell us a story?

12. Aunt Maria brought me a souvenir from Thailand.

13. The driver told the officer his version of the accident.

14. Please offer cousin Tina my condolences.

15. Lester loaned Miranda a sweater.

Objects: Direct and Indirect Objects

| **2j.** | A *direct object* is a noun, pronoun, or word group that tells *who* or *what* receives the action of a transitive verb or shows the result of the action. |

A direct object answers the question "Whom?" or "What?" after a transitive verb.

EXAMPLE We sent some **flowers** to Aunt Grace. [Sent what? *Flowers.*]

| **2k.** | An *indirect object* is a noun, pronoun, or word group that often appears in sentences containing direct objects. An indirect object tells *to whom* or *to what* (or *for whom* or *for what*) the action of a transitive verb is done. |

EXAMPLE Russell offered **her** the tickets. [Offered the tickets to whom? *Her.*]

EXERCISE A Decide whether the underlined words in the following sentences are direct objects or indirect objects. Above each object, write *DO* for *direct object* or *IO* for *indirect object*.

                   IO

Example 1. Please take <u>him</u> these sandwiches.

1. The committee chairperson gave <u>her</u> the gavel.

2. Our pool's lifeguard left Manuelo the free <u>passes</u>.

3. The interview will give <u>Emily</u> a chance to visit the college.

4. The algebra teacher lent <u>her</u> a new ruler.

5. Aerobic dancing provided us an <u>opportunity</u> for vigorous exercise.

6. The track star jumped <u>hurdles</u> and ran <u>relays</u> during the meet.

7. The pet store owner gave the <u>puppy</u> a bone.

8. The doctor prescribed <u>penicillin</u> for the child's illness.

9. The counselor offered the students some <u>advice</u>.

10. Their discovery of radium and polonium earned <u>Pierre</u> and <u>Marie Curie</u> the Nobel Prize

    in physics.

EXERCISE B In the following sentences, underline the indirect objects once and the direct objects twice. Not every sentence contains an indirect object.

Example 1. She sent <u>me</u> a <u><u>book</u></u> about woodworking.

11. Kareem taught his sister an African American folk song.

12. The president signed the energy bill after the congressional vote.

13. The Lions Club awarded Mrs. Rosa a silver tray for community service.

14. The tree branch struck the car's windshield with a crash.

15. Toni Morrison read the audience an excerpt from her novel.

Language and Sentence Skills Practice

GRAMMAR

Parts of a Sentence

| **2a.** | A *sentence* is a word group that contains a subject and a verb and that expresses a complete thought. |

| **2b.** | Sentences consist of two basic parts: subjects and predicates. |

Sentences may contain *complements,* such as *subject complements: predicate nominatives* and *predicate adjectives;* or *objects of verbs: direct objects and indirect objects.*

EXERCISE   Decide whether the underlined words in the following sentences are predicate nominatives, predicate adjectives, direct objects, or indirect objects. Above each underlined word, write *PN* for *predicate nominative, PA* for *predicate adjective, DO* for *direct object,* or *IO* for *indirect object.*

                             IO   DO   PA
Example 1. After he gave her a rowing lesson, he felt tired.

1. Ruth became the new treasurer for the bicycle club.

2. Felix wrote Martha a long letter while she was away.

3. The students seemed tired after the long lecture.

4. We finished our geometry homework before dinner.

5. The principal offered the seniors some good advice about choosing a college.

6. Has the coach given the players their gloves?

7. The salad tasted better after you added the horseradish.

8. The winner of this year's poetry competition was Carlita.

9. The sophomores chose a new team name.

10. What a great leader he became!

11. The magician appeared nervous during the beginning of her performance.

12. Will Jacqueline be our new tutor?

13. Hear this beautiful poem by Emily Dickinson.

14. Are the counselors going to send us a list of recommended books?

15. We went to the shopping mall and bought some candles and a vase.

16. Ron gave me some paint, a few brushes, and a large pad to practice with.

17. The soup that my grandmother made smells spicy.

18. When will Trevor become a performer?

19. The snow felt cold, but we continued to play outside.

20. Are those black birds with yellow spots starlings?

Classifying Sentences by Purpose

2l. Depending on its purpose, a sentence may be classified as *declarative, imperative, interrogative,* or *exclamatory.*

(1) A *declarative sentence* makes a statement and ends with a period.

EXAMPLE   I wonder how the fans will react to our victory.

(2) An *imperative sentence* gives a command or makes a request. Most imperative sentences end with a period. A strong command ends with an exclamation point.

EXAMPLES   Please tell the coach that I'll be a little late. Look at that score!

(3) An *interrogative sentence* asks a question and ends with a question mark.

EXAMPLE   Are you coming to the celebration at the coach's house tonight?

(4) An *exclamatory sentence* shows excitement or expresses strong feeling and ends with an exclamation point.

EXAMPLE   We finally beat the Cougars!

EXERCISE   Punctuate each of the following sentences with an appropriate end mark. Then, on the line provided, classify each sentence by writing *DECL* for *declarative, IMP* for *imperative, INT* for *interrogative,* or *EXCL* for *exclamatory.*

Example   *IMP*   **1.** What a great team!

_____ **1.** How were we able to win

_____ **2.** We won by using our superior skill and stamina

_____ **3.** Stop gloating

_____ **4.** Oh, why shouldn't we brag just a bit

_____ **5.** It's never becoming to brag

_____ **6.** I can't believe we won

_____ **7.** Keep your excitement to yourself

_____ **8.** Do you hear that applause

_____ **9.** It's so loud

_____ **10.** Let's go accept our trophy

Review A: Sentences and Sentence Fragments

EXERCISE Identify each of the following groups of words as a sentence or a sentence fragment. On the line provided, write *S* if the group of words is a sentence or *F* if it is a fragment.

Example _____F____ **1.** The students who won blue ribbons in the contest.

_____ **1.** Jeffrey will graduate from high school next year.

_____ **2.** Trying to decide which college to go to.

_____ **3.** It's a good idea to apply to several colleges.

_____ **4.** Sent requests to seven colleges that looked interesting.

_____ **5.** The colleges sent information packets.

_____ **6.** Looking at the tuition expenses, majors offered, and location.

_____ **7.** Jeffrey was interested in five of the colleges.

_____ **8.** He requested applications to the five colleges he preferred.

_____ **9.** Takes some time for the applications to be processed.

_____ **10.** A good idea to start looking for colleges early.

_____ **11.** Very important to keep good grades.

_____ **12.** Jeffrey's high school maintains his grade-point average.

_____ **13.** An A is worth four points.

_____ **14.** Maintaining above a 3.5 grade-point average.

_____ **15.** The colleges will consider his test scores and high school grades.

_____ **16.** Offering better programs than other colleges.

_____ **17.** The reputation of the colleges that Jeffrey is interested in.

_____ **18.** All five of the colleges offer advanced degrees in electrical engineering.

_____ **19.** A lot of math and science courses.

_____ **20.** An advisor will help Jeffrey plan out his schedule each semester.

Review B: **Sentence Parts**

EXERCISE A In each of the following sentences, underline the simple subject once and the verb twice. If the subject is understood, write it in parentheses before the sentence. Be sure to include all parts of a verb phrase and all parts of a compound subject or verb.

Example *(You)* **1.** Listen carefully and write each word on the line provided.

1. Do many of us worry about the future?

2. To most of us, the future probably seems uncertain.

3. Will we go to college?

4. What kinds of jobs will we have?

5. Some of us are wondering about marriage and children.

6. Even very young boys and girls sometimes worry about world conditions.

7. We surely cannot predict the future with any certainty.

8. In my opinion, one should not waste time and fret about the future.

9. One should plan ahead but should also enjoy the present.

10. Tell me your thoughts about the future.

EXERCISE B Each of the following sentences contains at least one complement. Underline each complement, and above the complement, indicate the type of complement it is by writing *PA* for *predicate adjective, PN* for *predicate nominative, DO* for *direct object,* or *IO* for *indirect object.*

Example 1. Did I ever tell you the story about my friends' night in jail?

11. Several years ago my family bought a new place in Arizona.

12. At that time my friends were college students in Texas.

13. We sent them an invitation for a weekend visit.

14. They were happy and accepted the invitation immediately.

15. Our home was a ranch about thirty miles from the nearest town.

16. We sent them detailed directions for getting to the ranch.

17. A bus was the only link between the ranch and the town.

18. Unfortunately, my friends arrived in town after 6:00 P.M. and missed the last bus.

19. The only hotel in town was full.

20. The friendly police chief gave my friends a room for the night in the local jail.

Language and Sentence Skills Practice

Review C: **Sentence Parts**

EXERCISE A In each of the following sentences, underline the simple subject once and the verb twice. If the subject is understood, write it in parentheses before the sentence. Be sure to include all parts of a verb phrase and all parts of a compound subject or verb.

Example *(You)* **1.** Come with me to buy Mother's birthday present, please.

1. How far in advance do you usually shop for birthday presents?

2. In my opinion, birthdays are very important occasions.

3. Gifts for others should reflect their tastes, not yours.

4. One must consider the recipients' interests carefully.

5. Not many of my relatives share my sister's interests or like her taste.

6. Her choice of gift for a grandparent or an aunt or an uncle is often inappropriate.

7. Neither subtle hints nor candid suggestions penetrate her consciousness.

8. Fortunately, all of us recognize the thought behind the present.

9. Tell me your opinions about birthday gifts.

10. Would you consider a job as a personal shopper?

EXERCISE B Each of the following sentences contains at least one complement. Underline each complement, and above the complement, indicate the type of complement it is by writing *PA* for *predicate adjective*, *PN* for *predicate nominative*, *DO* for *direct object*, or *IO* for *indirect object*.

Example **1.** Did you send Flora a thank-you note?
                        IO   DO

11. The reading assignment was an informative article about medical ethics.

12. The haiku is a major form of Japanese verse.

13. The last mile of a ten-mile hike always seems longest.

14. Do you give your pets enough water during the summer?

15. The jurors carefully considered the allegations of the defense counsel.

16. The audience at the awards dinner grew restless during the long speeches and fidgeted uncomfortably.

17. To the playwright's surprise, his work became the talk of the town.

18. I gave my brother a book for his birthday last year.

19. The group improvised and sang the song without accompaniment.

20. They sent us a detailed list of suggestions for the camping trip.

Review D: **Kinds of Sentences**

EXERCISE Punctuate each of the following sentences with an appropriate end mark. Then, on the line provided, classify each sentence by writing *DECL* for *declarative*, *IMP* for *imperative*, *INT* for *interrogative*, or *EXCL* for *exclamatory*.

Example ___*IMP*___ **1.** Please call us as soon as possible.

_____ **1.** What fantastic weather we had on our vacation

_____ **2.** Where is the nearest fire station

_____ **3.** How we will raise the money is a good question

_____ **4.** Ask the owner's permission before feeding the animals

_____ **5.** Stop making all that noise

_____ **6.** Can you recommend anyone for the job

_____ **7.** If necessary, may we call on you for help

_____ **8.** At what time do you get off work

_____ **9.** I have a job at the local supermarket this summer

_____ **10.** Would you mind helping me with my homework

_____ **11.** What an exciting trip that was

_____ **12.** When did the first settlers arrive in Australia

_____ **13.** Where the meeting will be held is anybody's guess

_____ **14.** Does the University of Washington have a medical school

_____ **15.** How pleased your parents must be

_____ **16.** Go to Mrs. Panico's office and give her this note

_____ **17.** A noted chemist has been invited to speak at the next assembly

_____ **18.** In case of emergency, dial this number

_____ **19.** What is the correct English translation of that Latin expression

_____ **20.** If you have any questions, be sure to ask your teacher

Literary Model: Short Story

There was a summer in my life when the only creature that seemed lovelier to me than a largemouth bass was Sheila Mant. I was fourteen. The Mants had rented the cottage next to ours on the river; with their parties, their frantic games of softball, their constant comings and goings, they appeared to me denizens of a brilliant existence. "Too noisy by half," my mother quickly decided, but I would have given anything to be invited to one of their parties. . . .

Sheila was the middle daughter—at seventeen, all but out of reach. She would spend her days sunbathing on a float my Uncle Sierbert had moored in their cove, and before July was over I had learned all her moods. If she lay flat on the diving board with her hand trailing idly in the water, she was pensive, not to be disturbed. On her side, her head propped up by her arm, she was observant, considering those around her with a look that seemed queenly and severe. Sitting up, arms tucked around her long, suntanned legs, she was approachable, but barely, and it was only in those glorious moments when she stretched herself prior to entering the water that her various suitors found the courage to come near.

—from *"The Bass, the River, and Sheila Mant"* by W. D. Wetherell

EXERCISE A   List the predicate nominatives and predicate adjectives that appear in the above passage. After each one, write the subject (of a sentence or clause) that is being explained or identified.

Predicate Nominatives	**Predicate Adjectives**
_____	_____
_____	_____
_____	_____
_____	_____
_____	_____

EXERCISE B   What function do these predicate nominatives and predicate adjectives have in the passage?

_____

_____

_____

From "The Bass, the River, and Sheila Mant" from *The Man Who Loved Levittown* by W. D. Wetherell. Copyright © 1985 by W. D. Wetherell. All rights controlled by the **University of Pittsburgh Press, Pittsburg, PA 15261.** Reprint and electronic format by permission of the publisher.

Literary Model (continued)

EXERCISE C   Using the passage as a model, write one or two paragraphs using the first-person point of view in which a character is being introduced. Use several predicate nominatives and predicate adjectives. In addition to the verb *be*, use other linking verbs such as *appear, become, remain,* and *seem.*

_____

_____

_____

_____

_____

_____

_____

_____

_____

EXERCISE D

1. Make a list of the predicate nominatives and predicate adjectives that appear in your paragraph(s). After each one, write the subject (of a sentence or clause) that is being explained or identified.

Predicate Nominatives	Predicate Adjectives
_____	_____
_____	_____
_____	_____
_____	_____

2. Analyze your use of predicate nominatives and predicate adjectives in the paragraph(s).

_____

_____

_____

_____

_____

_____

Language and Sentence Skills Practice

Writing Application: Letter

A friend whispers to you, "That guy is." Undoubtedly, you'll be waiting for your friend to complete the sentence, since the group of words does not express a complete thought—despite the presence of a subject and verb. To make sense, the group of words needs a predicate nominative or predicate adjective that identifies or describes the subject *guy*.

PREDICATE NOMINATIVE   That guy is **captain** of the basketball team.

PREDICATE ADJECTIVE   That guy is absolutely **amazing** on the court.

Remember that *be* is only one of several verbs that can link a subject and a predicate adjective or predicate nominative. Other linking verbs include *appear, become, feel, look, remain,* and *seem.*

WRITING ACTIVITY

You have just been told that an eccentric aunt is giving away her fortune to relatives she considers deserving of her money. You've never met this aunt. You decide to write a detailed letter describing yourself, hoping that she will consider you worthy of a financial gift. Your letter should include at least five predicate nominatives, five predicate adjectives, and two linking verbs other than *be.*

PREWRITING   You're quite an expert on the letter's topic: *yourself.* However, it may still help you to brainstorm for points you want to make about the topic. Jot down all the ideas that come to your mind without stopping to evaluate them. Then, choose the most significant points that you will develop and prioritize them from most important to least important.

WRITING   Write a draft of the letter with the framework for a persuasive essay in mind. Begin with an attention-grabbing statement of your opinion that you're worthy of the financial gift. Discuss the reasons, accompanied by explanations and evidence, that you think yourself worthy. Conclude the letter with a restatement of your opinion.

REVISING   Read the draft to a friend. Ask him or her whether there are enough reasons to convince your audience (the aunt) and whether any of the reasons could be made stronger. Check that you have used at least five predicate nominatives, five predicate adjectives, and two linking verbs other than *be.* Ask yourself whether any of the adjectives in the draft could be replaced with a more descriptive or precise word.

PUBLISHING   When you're trying to impress someone, your writing should be completely error-free. Read your draft slowly to identify errors in grammar, usage, spelling, capitalization, and punctuation. Finally, check to make sure that you have followed the proper format for a personal letter. Continue revising this personal letter until you consider it completely polished.

EXTENDING YOUR WRITING

Add your final letter to an anthology of letters you've written. You will probably find these letters quite interesting to read one or two years from now, as they are written records of how you viewed yourself at this present stage of your life. Gather the letters into a booklet and, if appropriate, share them with your classmates.

for **CHAPTER 3: THE PHRASE** | _pages 65–82_

Choices: Investigating Phrases

The following activities challenge you to find a connection between phrases and the world around you. Do the activity below that suits your personality best, and then share your discoveries with your class.

MATHEMATICS/SCIENCE

It's the Law

Mathematics and science function according to a number of laws and principles. These laws and principles are usually stated by a noun modified by an adjective phrase. Do some research. Make a list of these laws and principles. Start with the law of association and work your way toward the principles of thermodynamics. Publish your list of laws on the class Web site, or design a bulletin board to display your findings.

ETYMOLOGY

Side by Side

What is the root word of _appositive_? What other words contain this root? Find out. Then, make a graphic that shows the relationship of these words to the root word. After putting the final touches on your project, ask for permission to post it in the classroom.

CONTEST

Dare You

Challenge your classmates to a contest that will last five minutes. Pick a verb, any verb. Then, write as many adverb phrases as you can about it. For instance, if you chose _run_, you might write _run in place, run to school_, or _run like the wind_. Pick a common verb so that you will be able to generate many phrases. You will get more ideas if you keep a list of prepositions in front of you. The person or team with the most adverb phrases wins. Make sure your word is not used as some other part of speech, as in _run of the mill._

RESEARCH

Bringing up Baby

When movie producers and directors choose a title for a film, they must choose very carefully. They have to pack a lot of information, excitement, and emotion in only a few words. Verbals are often just the tools for such a job. Visit the library and find a good book about film. Then, make a list of famous movie titles that include verbals. Yes, you can use television series titles if you wish. Divide your list into each type of verbal. Try to include a few of each type. Make copies of your list for your classmates.

CREATIVE WRITING

To Dream the Possible Dream

Write a poem in which each line or each stanza begins with an infinitive or an infinitive phrase. Perhaps write about something you would like to do or be in your lifetime. Send your poem to the school newspaper or to a Web site that publishes poetry.

DISCUSSION

I Don't Want To!

Have you ever been advised not to end a sentence with a preposition? Many people believe that doing so is slipshod. Do you? What is the basis for their opinion and for yours? Research this question. (While you are at it, check out a dictionary to find out what Winston Churchill had to say about this injunction.) Create a few examples, each written two ways. One possible pair is _What is that for?_ and _For what is that?_ Then, with your teacher's approval, lead the class in a discussion of this issue. Does this rule apply to prepositions used as adverbs? Or to sentences that end with _to_, the sign of the infinitive? Should the prohibition against ending sentences with prepositions stand? What can you gain or lose by following or breaking this custom?

Phrases

3a. A *phrase* is a group of related words that is used as a single part of speech and that does not contain both a verb and its subject.

PREPOSITIONAL PHRASE	under the bed
PARTICIPIAL PHRASE	discarded needlessly
GERUND PHRASE	painting the house
INFINITIVE PHRASE	to go quickly
APPOSITIVE PHRASE	a well-known poet

EXERCISE   If the underlined word group in each of the following sentences is a phrase, write *phrase* on the line. If the word group is not a phrase, write *no* on the line.

Example _____*phrase*_____ **1.** Some people love <u>working in the kitchen</u>, while others don't.

_____ **1.** Many devices help <u>to make a cook's work</u> easier.

_____ **2.** <u>Mincing onions</u> in a food processor takes only a minute.

_____ **3.** Even simple tools like a good knife, a utensil <u>used for centuries</u>, speed up the cook's task.

_____ **4.** Baking, <u>considered a time-consuming task</u>, can also be simple because of bread machines.

_____ **5.** Even fancy food processors can't touch <u>what is coming in the future</u>, however.

_____ **6.** Researchers <u>at top labs</u> dream of kitchens equipped with sensors and computer chips.

_____ **7.** Refrigerators and storage cabinets will be able to order foodstuffs online <u>before the cook knows</u> the supply is low.

_____ **8.** Talking countertops will be able to weigh ingredients and guide cooks <u>through difficult recipes</u>.

_____ **9.** Even oven mitts programmed <u>to tell cooks</u> when foods have cooked long enough, will get in on the action.

_____ **10.** Sadly, there is no help yet for most cooks' least enjoyed task, <u>kitchen clean-up</u>.

Prepositional Phrases

3b. A *prepositional phrase* includes a preposition, the object of the preposition, and any modifiers of that object.

> **EXAMPLES** Arlene climbed **up the ladder.** [The preposition is *up,* and the object of the preposition is *ladder.*]
>
> The picture **on the cover** is mine. [The preposition is *on,* and the object of the preposition is *cover.*]

EXERCISE A Underline the prepositional phrase in each of the following sentences.

Example 1. She found her jacket in the closet.

1. The bus drove by a large, red barn.

2. An enormous picture was painted on one wall.

3. The picture reached above the second story.

4. It showed an eighteenth-century man in a white shirt.

5. The picture was painted by a local artist.

EXERCISE B In each of the following sentences, underline the preposition once and the object of the preposition twice.

Example 1. Spike Lee is the director of the film.

6. Spike Lee was born in Georgia.

7. He studied at a New York university.

8. The video store near my house carries his films.

9. Lee appears in some films.

10. His father wrote the music for this movie.

11. Lee made a film about Malcolm X.

12. The director wore a hat with a large X.

13. During a recent newscast I heard Lee speak.

14. He talked about a film he had just finished.

15. The interviewer showed several scenes from the film.

Language and Sentence Skills Practice

GRAMMAR

Adjective Phrases

3c.   A prepositional phrase that modifies a noun or a pronoun is called an *adjective phrase.*

An adjective phrase tells *what kind* or *which one.*

> **EXAMPLES**   Everyone **on my soccer team** had experience. [*On my soccer team* modifies the pronoun *Everyone*, telling *which one.*]
>
> The snack **of leftovers** was delicious. [*Of leftovers* modifies the noun *snack*, telling *what kind.*]

Two or more adjective phrases may modify the same noun or pronoun.

> **EXAMPLE**   Our flight **from St. Louis to Atlanta** was delayed. [Both *from St. Louis* and *to Atlanta* modify the noun *flight.*]

An adjective phrase may also modify the object of another prepositional phrase.

> **EXAMPLE**   On the floor **of the rain forest** live many unusual plants. [*Of the rain forest* modifies *floor*, the object of the preposition *On.*]

EXERCISE A   In each of the following sentences, underline the prepositional phrase or phrases and circle the word that each phrase modifies.

Example 1. Alaska and Hawaii are the newest member (states) of the Union.

1. Both Alaska and Hawaii were once territories of the United States.

2. The name for the mainland portion of Alaska was once *Alákshak.*

3. The origin of the name *Hawaii* is unknown.

4. These are two of our most beautiful states.

5. Many people from all over enjoy these magical places.

EXERCISE B   Rewrite each of the following sentences, adding a prepositional phrase above the sentence in the place indicated by the caret (∧).

                in the driveway
Example 1. The red car ∧ is my brother's.

6. The early inhabitants ∧ drew hunting scenes on the walls.

7. No one ∧ spoke during the performance.

8. The magician called upon two people ∧.

9. A single fingerprint ∧ turned out to be a critical clue.

10. Erica lent me two magazines ∧.

Adverb Phrases

3d. A prepositional phrase that modifies a verb, an adjective, or an adverb is called an *adverb phrase.*

Adverb phrases tell *when, where, why, how,* or *to what extent.*

EXAMPLES The actor Sessue Hayakawa became famous **for his film roles.** [*For his film roles* modifies the adjective *famous* and tells *how.*]

We arrived too late **for the opening ceremonies.** [*For the opening ceremonies* modifies the adverb *late* and tells *to what extent.*]

In the final act, Macbeth dies **in battle.** [*In the final act* and *in battle* both modify the verb *dies. In the final act* tells *when* and *in battle* tells *where.*]

EXERCISE A In the following sentences, underline the prepositional phrases and circle the word that each phrase modifies. Then, draw an arrow from the prepositional phrase to the word it modifies.

Example 1. After the game we ate dinner at a restaurant.

1. Please return your books to the library shelves.

2. Harry is helpful in a crisis.

3. During the last century my ancestors came to this country.

4. Pete found some sesame oil on the top shelf.

5. Chinese food is well known for its delicious flavors.

6. Mother served dinner at the kitchen table.

7. After the holiday we put the ornaments away in the attic.

8. We ate fresh fruit for dessert.

9. For the first time I felt confident.

10. The kids remained quiet during the movie.

EXERCISE B Add a prepositional phrase to the end of each of the following sentences. Choose a phrase that will answer one of the questions in parentheses.

Example 1. The sleeping dog looked comfortable. (Where? How?) _in the sunny yard_

11. We fried the fish we had caught. (When? How?) _____

12. Do you enjoy playing the violin? (When? Where?) _____

13. The VCR seems to be broken. (To what extent? Why?) _____

14. Run as fast as you can! (Where? When?) _____

15. That actor is quite famous. (Why? How?) _____

Adjective and Adverb Phrases

3c. A prepositional phrase that modifies a noun or a pronoun is called an *adjective phrase*.

> **EXAMPLE** The bowl **of soup** was full. [*Of soup* is an adjective phrase modifying the noun *bowl*.]

3d. A prepositional phrase that modifies a verb, an adjective, or an adverb is called an *adverb phrase*.

> **EXAMPLE** The bowl was full **of soup**. [*Of soup* is an adverb phrase modifying the adjective *full*.]

EXERCISE A Each of the following sentences contains an underlined prepositional phrase. On the line provided, write *adverb* if the phrase modifies a verb, an adjective, or an adverb. Write *adjective* if the phrase modifies a noun or a pronoun. Circle the word or words modified by the phrase.

Example _____*adverb*_____ **1.** "He's such a chameleon," we might (say) about a friend who often seems to change personality.

_____ **1.** Chameleons are famous for their ability to change color to match their surroundings.

_____ **2.** However, true chameleons, which live mainly in Madagascar and Africa, do not change color to camouflage themselves.

_____ **3.** The chameleons of Madagascar do change color in response to light, temperature, and fear of attack.

_____ **4.** Chameleons change color by collecting or diluting pigmented cells called melanophore cells.

_____ **5.** They are funny-looking lizards with as many as three horns on their heads and bulging eyes that move separately from each other.

EXERCISE B Write a prepositional phrase to expand each of the following sentences. Draw a caret (∧) to show where the phrase should be inserted in the sentence. Then, identify the phrase as an *adjective phrase* or an *adverb phrase*.

Example 1. They run two miles∧each day. *by the river, adverb phrase* _____

6. Did she blow out all of the candles? _____

7. Be sure to sign your name. _____

8. I enjoy cooking fish. _____

9. The moviegoers' hearts pounded. _____

10. I counted at least twenty guests. _____

Participles

Verbals are formed from verbs and are used as adjectives, nouns, or adverbs. One kind of verbal is the *participle*.

3e.   A *participle* is a verb form that can be used as an adjective.

Two kinds of participles are *present participles* and *past participles*.

> **EXAMPLES**   **Smiling**, the winner accepted the trophy. [*Smiling*, the present participle form of the verb *smile*, modifies the noun *winner*.]
>
> The old, **dented** scooter was still reliable. [*Dented*, the past participle form of the verb *dent*, modifies the noun *scooter*.]

EXERCISE A   Underline the participle in each of the following sentences. Then, circle the noun it modifies.

Example   1. The thrashing winds of the tropical storm damaged our city park.

1. Our excited meteorologists told us that the storm's name was Clive.

2. It was the worst storm in recorded history to reach our town.

3. The worried townspeople hastily nailed up boards and filled sandbags.

4. My grandparents recalled a similarly chilling storm from their youth.

5. When the storm hit, everyone hunkered down in their mildewing basements.

6. Several hours later, the storm abated and relieved neighbors came up to see the damage.

7. The surprised townspeople found, to their delight, that only the city park needed repairs.

8. Uprooted trees had fallen on the playground.

9. Several dozen energized volunteers worked together to cut up and stack the branches.

10. Only a few days later, delighted children were once again playing on the swings and slides.

EXERCISE B   After each of the following sentences is a verb in parentheses. Revise each sentence by forming a present or past participle and inserting it above the caret next to the noun it modifies.

Example   1. Some ∧ performers really get an audience cheering. *(inspire)*
inspired

11. Long before Elvis and the Beatles, ∧ pianists were mesmerizing audiences. *(fascinate)*

12. Among pianist Franz Liszt's ∧ fans were half-swooning women. *(adore)*

13. ∧ women were not Ludwig von Beethoven's problem, however. *(Faint)*

14. This ∧ composer sometimes forgot that he was also the soloist, rose from the piano, and began to conduct in wild, extravagant gestures. *(rivet)*

15. Once, Beethoven became so involved in the music that he accidentally jostled a boy whose job was to hold a candle, knocking the candlestick out of the ∧ boy's hand. *(embarrass)*

Language and Sentence Skills Practice

GRAMMAR

Participial Phrases

3f. A *participial phrase* consists of a participle and any modifiers or complements the participle has. The entire phrase is used as an adjective.

EXAMPLES **Donning her mask,** the catcher prepared for the big game. [The participial phrase modifies the noun *catcher*. The noun *mask* is the direct object of the present participle *Donning*.]

News **reported by the tabloids** is often fictitious. [The participial phrase modifies the noun *News*. The adverb phrase *by the tabloids* modifies the past participle *reported*.]

EXERCISE A In the following sentences, circle the word that each underlined participial phrase modifies and draw an arrow from the participial phrase to the word it modifies.

Example 1. Standing at home plate, Jesús faced the pitcher.

1. This bowl, carved in the hills of Tennessee, is unique.

2. Chopping the carrots quickly, the chef finished the stew.

3. Given all the facts, we reached our decision quickly.

4. The power lines damaged by the storm needed repairs.

5. Fifteen men, clothed in military uniforms, presented the flags.

6. The hikers, exhausted by the long climb, slept soundly that night.

7. Stopping to tie my shoelace, I noticed an unusual insect on the sidewalk.

8. The cat, seeing movement in the bushes, crouched low in the grass.

9. Covered by a cloth napkin, the loaf of bread in the basket was still warm.

10. She returned to the house, remembering the keys and the book.

EXERCISE B Underline each participial phrase once and the word it modifies twice.

Example 1. Grown in most countries, the potato is popular.

11. The potato, first cultivated in South America, is a versatile food.

12. Discovered by the Spanish in Peru, the potato reached Europe in the 1550s.

13. This vegetable, once worshipped by the Incas, was first scorned by the Europeans.

14. Some people, confusing the potato with another plant, thought the vegetable was poisonous.

15. Actually, potatoes are quite nutritious, providing people with various vitamins and minerals.

Participles and Participial Phrases

Verbals are formed from verbs and are used as adjectives, nouns, or adverbs. One kind of verbal is the *participle*.

3e.   A *participle* is a verb form that can be used as an adjective.

Two kinds of participles are *present participles* and *past participles*.

3f.   A *participial phrase* consists of a participle and any modifiers or complements the participle has. The entire phrase is used as an adjective.

EXAMPLES   **Eating his cupcake,** the toddler sighed happily. [The participial phrase modifies the noun *toddler*. The noun *cupcake* is the direct object of the present participle *Eating.*]

Campfires **built with your own hands** give you a sense of accomplishment. [The participial phrase modifies the noun *Campfires*. The adverb phrase *with your own hands* modifies the past participle *built.*]

EXERCISE   Each of the following sentences contains a participial phrase. Underline the participial phrase once. Then, draw an arrow from the participial phrase to the word or words it modifies.

Example 1. Everyone has read stories of knights made famous for brave deeds.

1. Few people know about the process required to become a knight.

2. By the twelfth century, a program challenging to both mind and body had been developed.

3. Boys growing up in noble households began training for knighthood at a young age.

4. Leaving their family homes, they were fostered in the houses of influential friends or uncles.

5. The boys learned etiquette, cared for horses, and exercised to build the musculature needed to carry heavy arms.

6. Demonstrating his ability to hunt, fence, and ride, a fourteen-year-old became a squire.

7. At about the age of twenty-one, well-trained in arts of defense, the young man was ready to undergo initiation into knighthood.

8. The ritual usually began when the squire, freshly bathed, put on ceremonial robes of white and red.

9. He spent the night in the chapel and offered his sword, blessed by a priest, to the service of his lord.

10. Now called an *acolyte,* the young man put on his best clothes and went in to a breakfast feast.

GRAMMAR

Gerunds

Verbals are formed from verbs and are used as adjectives, nouns, or adverbs. One kind of verbal is the *gerund.*

| **3g.** | A *gerund* is a verb form that ends in *–ing* and that is used as a noun. |

EXAMPLES   **Swimming** exercises every major muscle. [*Swimming,* formed from the verb *swim,* is the subject of the verb *exercises.*]

Before **running** I like to do some stretches. [*Running,* formed from the verb *run,* is the object of the preposition *before.*]

EXERCISE   In the following sentences, underline the gerund. Then, tell whether the gerund is a *subject,* a *predicate nominative,* a *direct object,* an *indirect object,* or an *object of a preposition.*

Example _____*direct object*_____   **1.** Mario likes diving best of all sports.

_____ **1.** Swimming, another aquatic sport, demands physical endurance.

_____ **2.** A more leisurely form of exercise is walking.

_____ **3.** Although it may seem leisurely, sailing also requires strength.

_____ **4.** Petra prefers water-skiing and is quite good at it.

_____ **5.** For me, nothing beats the thrill of cycling!

_____ **6.** Was Olympian Babe Zaharias best known for her running?

_____ **7.** Wasn't her forte golfing?

_____ **8.** Which contestants won medals in tumbling?

_____ **9.** Figure skating is certainly a graceful sport!

_____ **10.** Every person should find a way of exercising for health and for pleasure.

_____ **11.** Some kinds of exercise require planning and expense.

_____ **12.** Sports, however, are not the only means of staying fit.

_____ **13.** Even bird-watching can offer opportunities for exercise.

_____ **14.** Avid bird-watchers often do a lot of hiking.

_____ **15.** On weekends, give gardening a try.

_____ **16.** Hoeing gives a person's arms and shoulders a real workout.

_____ **17.** In the fall, fallen leaves need raking.

_____ **18.** My least favorite kind of yardwork is mowing.

_____ **19.** For some people, of course, working provides exercise.

_____ **20.** Vacuuming and other household chores also require effort and energy.

Gerund Phrases

3h. A *gerund phrase* consists of a gerund and any modifiers or complements the gerund has. The entire phrase is used as a noun.

EXAMPLES My grandfather and his friends enjoy **swimming at the beach.** [The gerund phrase is the direct object of the verb *enjoy.*]

The **growling of the chained dogs** made me uneasy. [The gerund phrase is the subject of the verb *made.*]

EXERCISE Underline the gerund phrase in each of the following sentences. Then, identify its function in the sentence by writing above it *S* for *subject, PN* for *predicate nominative, DO* for *direct object,* or *OP* for *object of a preposition.*

Example 1. We eagerly anticipated <u>diving into the icy water.</u> *[DO]*

1. Jumping out of airplanes sounds scary to me.

2. Our reason for calling you is to invite you to our graduation.

3. I don't mind shoveling snow once in a while.

4. Skidding on wet pavement causes many accidents.

5. You will enjoy meeting Hatim.

6. Sweating over a hot stove in August is not fun.

7. My favorite weekend activity is singing with a local band.

8. Achieving a perfect score gave Molly a sense of pride.

9. Instead of subtracting the service charge, Chad added it.

10. Daydreaming about problems can be a source of creative solutions.

11. After dining at a nice restaurant, they went to a movie.

12. His idea of a pleasant Saturday is fishing from the bridge.

13. One service club's holiday project is caroling at the hospital.

14. Nicole's sisters enjoy skating in the park.

15. By shopping early in the morning, we will get the freshest produce.

16. My hobbies include reading mysteries and biographies.

17. His arms were sore after kneading the dough for ten pizzas.

18. Choosing a college to attend can be overwhelming.

19. Mike doesn't like waiting for the bus at night.

20. Her part-time job is packing computer components at the factory.

Language and Sentence Skills Practice **67**

Gerunds and Gerund Phrases

3g. A *gerund* is a verb form that ends in *–ing* and that is used as a noun.

3h. A *gerund phrase* consists of a gerund and any modifiers or complements the gerund has. The entire phrase is used as a noun.

> **EXAMPLES** I am responsible for **cooking dinner on Tuesdays.** [The gerund phrase is the object of the preposition *for*. The adverb phrase *on Tuesdays* modifies the gerund *cooking*.]
>
> **Smelling the kitchen aromas** always pleases me. [The gerund phrase is the subject of the verb *pleases. The kitchen aromas* is the direct object of *smelling*.]

EXERCISE A In the following sentences, underline the gerund or gerund phrase. Then, identify its function in the sentence by writing above it *S* for *subject,* *PN* for *predicate nominative,* *DO* for *direct object,* or *OP* for *object of a preposition.*

Example 1. Stargazing is a popular hobby among many people.

1. Buying a good telescope is a good way to get started.

2. Also, many colleges have a practice of opening their observatories to the public.

3. One other helpful activity is studying star charts to learn the layout of the sky.

4. Some amateur astronomers also invest time in photographing the stars.

5. Discovering a comet is the dream of a few persistent skywatchers.

6. The tradition of naming comets after the first person or people to sight them brings a kind of fame to these skywatchers.

7. For most stargazers, however, a night of lying out under the stars is pleasure enough.

8. Several times a year, people can enjoy viewing meteor showers.

9. Sometimes you can see up to forty meteors an hour, simply by being outside at the right time!

10. The sky is filled with the streaking of meteors among the stars.

EXERCISE B Compose five sentences of your own, using a gerund or gerund phrase in each. Use the verb in parentheses to form the gerund. Underline the gerund or gerund phrase in each sentence.

Example 1. *(breathe)* *Breathing deeply and slowly can help a nervous person relax.*

11. *(plant)* _____

12. *(debate)* _____

13. *(snooze)* _____

14. *(subscribe)* _____

15. *(taste)* _____

Participial Phrases and Gerund Phrases

Gerunds and present participles both end in *–ing*. Do not confuse a *gerund,* which is used as a noun, with a *present participle,* which may be used as an adjective or as part of a verb phrase.

EXAMPLES   I always love **skiing in Colorado.** [*Skiing in Colorado* is a gerund phrase used as the direct object of the verb *love.*]

I hurt my ankle last year **skiing in Colorado.** [*Skiing in Colorado* is a participial phrase modifying the pronoun *I.*]

This year we are **skiing** in Colorado during the winter holiday. [*Skiing* is used as part of the verb phrase *are skiing.*]

EXERCISE   Decide if the underlined word group in each sentence is a gerund phrase or a participial phrase. Then, above the underlined word or words, write *G* for *gerund phrase* or *P* for *participial phrase.*

Example 1. $\overset{G}{\underline{\text{Winning the drama award}}}$ thrilled my sister.

1. <u>Eating out in Tokyo</u> is fun.

2. The problem is <u>choosing among so many different restaurants.</u>

3. <u>Pointing at the puppy,</u> Jim said he really wanted to get one.

4. In botany class, we became quite good at <u>identifying types of flowers.</u>

5. After dinner, <u>feeling happy and full,</u> we thanked our hosts.

6. <u>Going to the beach this summer</u> will be a lot of fun.

7. <u>Searching for an answer,</u> I looked in a current dictionary.

8. <u>Smiling proudly,</u> the little boy pointed to his new toys.

9. I have always enjoyed <u>eating sushi.</u>

10. It's too bad that <u>preparing sushi</u> is Mom's least favorite thing to do!

11. <u>Buying a used car</u> requires research.

12. The little boy stomped into his room, <u>slamming the door behind him.</u>

13. The team has a slim chance of <u>finishing in the top four.</u>

14. The dog, <u>wagging its tail wildly,</u> bounded out to meet us.

15. <u>Quickly paying for the groceries,</u> she ran out of the store.

16. <u>Decorating this birthday cake</u> will take at least an hour.

17. My cousin actually enjoys <u>taking tests.</u>

18. <u>Sorting through the old photographs,</u> we found a portrait of our grandfather.

19. The alligator, <u>gliding silently through the dark water,</u> approached its prey.

20. My least favorite part of this job is <u>scraping the paint off the woodwork.</u>

Infinitives

Verbals are formed from verbs and are used as adjectives, nouns, or adverbs. One kind of verbal is the *infinitive*.

3i. | An *infinitive* is a verb form that can be used as a noun, an adjective, or an adverb. Most infinitives begin with *to*.

> **EXAMPLES** Often, the best strategy is **to forgive.** [*To forgive* is used as a noun, a predicate nominative identifying the subject *strategy*.]
>
> This is the chapter **to study.** [*To study* is used as an adjective modifying the noun *chapter*.]
>
> My sister is willing **to help.** [*To help* is used as an adverb modifying the adjective *willing*.]

EXERCISE A Underline the infinitives in each of the following sentences. Then, identify how the infinitive is used by writing above it *subject, direct object, adjective,* or *adverb.*

                                        direct object

Example 1. A well-equipped study area needs <u>to have</u> all supplies handy.

1. I like to keep my stapler and tape right at hand.

2. The dictionary is on the next shelf, ready to answer my questions about spelling.

3. To succeed in math is a special goal of mine.

4. I often use a calculator to check my work.

5. I intend to study for my next algebra exam.

6. I also need to complete an essay for my history class.

7. That's a project to begin early!

8. I keep an alarm clock on my desk to remind me of how much study time remains.

9. To concentrate for an hour is sometimes a challenge.

10. I am sure to excel in my classes if I stick with my study habits.

EXERCISE B Write five sentences, using an infinitive in each sentence. Use the verb in the parentheses, and underline the infinitive in your sentence.

Example 1. *(fly)* Why have people always wanted to <u>fly</u> like birds?

11. *(plan)* _____

12. *(describe)* _____

13. *(exhale)* _____

14. *(iron)* _____

15. *(build)* _____

Infinitive Phrases

| **3j.** | An *infinitive phrase* consists of an infinitive and any modifiers or complements the infinitive has. The entire phrase can be used as a noun, an adjective, or an adverb. |

EXAMPLES Ada May needs **to leave now.** [The infinitive phrase is used as a noun, the direct object of the verb *needs*. The infinitive *to leave* is modified by the adverb *now.*]

The night light is there **to calm the children.** [The infinitive phrase is used as an adverb modifying the adverb *there. Children* is the direct object of the infinitive *to calm.*]

EXERCISE A Underline the infinitive phrase in each sentence, and identify the phrase's function by writing above it *S* for *subject, PN* for *predicate nominative, DO* for *direct object, ADJ* for *adjective,* or *ADV* for *adverb.*

Example 1. Most high-school students have an opportunity to read Shakespeare.
                                                                    ADJ

1. For some, the attempt to understand his writing is a challenge.

2. They find it hard to understand the sixteenth-century expressions.

3. However, most people like to see the plays performed.

4. To prevent the audience from becoming bored, Shakespeare included comic scenes.

5. He also tried to include music and songs in many plays.

6. To see a play staged can be a great pleasure.

7. Many famous actors have wanted to play the part of Hamlet.

8. Scholars are still curious to learn more about Shakespeare's life.

9. He is known to have been the son of a glove maker in Stratford-on-Avon.

10. His goal was to be both a playwright and an actor.

EXERCISE B On the lines provided, write a sentence using the verb in parentheses to construct an infinitive phrase.

Example 1. (*memorize*) *My goal for this week is to memorize half of my lines for the play.*

11. (*forget*) _____

12. (*fasten*) _____

13. (*notice*) _____

14. (*sleep*) _____

15. (*read*) _____

Language and Sentence Skills Practice

GRAMMAR

Infinitives and Infinitive Phrases

3i. An *infinitive* is a verb form that can be used as a noun, an adjective, or an adverb. Most infinitives begin with *to*.

3j. An *infinitive phrase* consists of an infinitive and any modifiers or complements the infinitive has. The entire phrase can be used as a noun, an adjective, or an adverb.

EXAMPLES Jaime likes **to help** his little sister. [The infinitive phrase is used as a noun, the direct object of the verb *likes*. The infinitive *to help* takes the direct object *his little sister*.]

The dike is there **to hold back floodwaters**. [The infinitive phrase is used as an adverb modifying the adverb *there*. *Floodwaters* is the direct object of the infinitive *to hold*, and *back* is an adverb modifying the infinitive.]

EXERCISE Underline the infinitive or infinitive phrase in each sentence, and identify the phrase's use by writing above it *S* for *subject*, *PN* for *predicate nominative*, *DO* for *direct object*, *ADJ* for *adjective*, or *ADV* for *adverb*.

Example 1. In our house, we use the hall to display photos of our family. [*ADV* written above "display"]

1. The pictures to see are my family's baby pictures.

2. Of course, to call my own baby pictures anything but beautiful would be lying!

3. To record the growth of our family is another of our goals.

4. We keep many family pictures in our house to remind us of the importance of our past.

5. I like to study the old, crumbling photo of my great-grandparents.

6. The photographer chose to take the picture on my great-grandparents' porch.

7. I use looking at this picture as a way to imagine how hard they worked on their farm.

8. I never met them, but I am told that they managed to raise corn, potatoes, and other vegetables for the family's table.

9. My goal is to imitate their hard work and hopefulness.

10. I often pause to think about this brave and enterprising couple.

Verbal Phrases A

A *verbal phrase* consists of a verbal and its modifiers and complements. The three kinds of verbal phrases are the *participial phrase,* the *gerund phrase,* and the *infinitive phrase.*

PARTICIPIAL PHRASE	Is *Sunshine* the name **given to you at birth** or a nickname?
GERUND PHRASE	I hurt my shoulder by **throwing the ball too hard.**
INFINITIVE PHRASE	She is planning **to eat a vegan diet.**

EXERCISE A Underline the verbal phrases in the following sentences, and identify the phrase by writing *PP* (*participial phrase*), *GP* (*gerund phrase*), or *IP* (*infinitive phrase*) above the underlined words.

                                PP

Example 1. Consumed hot or cold by a third of the world's population, coffee is a drink with an

                 interesting history.

1. Learning about the history of coffee led me to the conclusion that coffee hasn't been

      around forever.

2. The story is that about 850 A.D., an Arab goatherd noticed his goats acting strangely.

3. Investigating the goats' behavior, Kaldi tasted the berries of a bush the goats had been eating.

4. The berries were coffee berries, and Kaldi, feeling the effects of the caffeine, told others of

      his discovery.

5. The newly discovered coffee was under production in Arabia by the fifteenth century.

6. Europe had to wait for coffee until the sixteenth and seventeenth centuries.

7. Some people started using coffee not only as a beverage but also as a medicine.

8. Drinking coffee in the new coffeehouses was a prime form of entertainment in the 1700s.

9. People sipped their coffee and read newspapers, talking about the latest news.

10. Some people's idea of a pleasant time is to drink coffee with friends.

EXERCISE B Write five sentences, using the verb in parentheses to form the type of verbal named. Underline the verbal phrase in each sentence.

Example 1. (*holler,* participial phrase)   <u>*Hearing my name hollered from the house, I took off for*</u>

              <u>*home right away.*</u>

11. (*spin,* infinitive phrase) _____

12. (*creep,* gerund phrase) _____

13. (*succeed,* gerund phrase) _____

14. (*acknowledge,* infinitive phrase) _____

15. (*enter,* participial phrase) _____

Verbal Phrases B

A *verbal phrase* consists of a verbal and its modifiers and complements. The three kinds of verbal phrases are the *participial phrase*, the *gerund phrase*, and the *infinitive phrase*.

PARTICIPIAL PHRASE	The beaver **loaded down with branches** managed to struggle up the bank.
GERUND PHRASE	Jofre convinced us to tour the museum by **describing the art we would see.**
INFINITIVE PHRASE	Do you intend **to get an early start**?

EXERCISE A Underline the verbal phrases in the following sentences, and identify the phrases by writing *PP (participial phrase)*, *GP (gerund phrase)*, or *IP (infinitive phrase)* above the underlined words.

Example 1. Choosing the right college takes time and consideration.

1. I started to think about the choice in my sophomore year of high school.

2. You can start by reading books that describe colleges.

3. You may want to narrow your choices to colleges in your state or to private colleges.

4. A college renowned for its strong academic program is always a good choice.

5. Some students, looking forward to making new friends at college, also examine social opportunities.

6. Of course, there is no harm in considering a school with a good sports program, too.

7. Cheering your team on until you are hoarse in the throat is fun.

8. The excitement of a good game helps students to blow off steam.

9. In the end, however, students considering their four years of college must focus on the education they will gain.

10. Another option is to take advantage of your school counselor's knowledge and assistance.

EXERCISE B Write five sentences, using the verb in parentheses to form the type of verbal named. Underline the verbal phrase in each sentence.

Example 1. (*call*, infinitive phrase) *Be sure to call home if you will be late.*

11. (*drive*, gerund phrase) _____

12. (*record*, participial phrase) _____

13. (*keep*, gerund phrase) _____

14. (*deny*, infinitive phrase) _____

15. (*pronounce*, participial phrase) _____

Appositives

3k. An *appositive* is a noun or pronoun placed beside another noun or pronoun to identify or describe it.

> **EXAMPLE** Haley, a math **genius,** helped me with my calculus. [The appositive *genius* describes the noun *Haley.*]

Appositives that are not essential to the meaning of the sentence are set off by commas. Essential appositives tell *which one of two or more* and should not be set off by commas.

> **NONESSENTIAL** My brother, **Franklin,** is a chess champion. [I have only one brother.]
>
> **ESSENTIAL** Cici's brother **Hamar** is a basketball player. [Cici has more than one brother.]

EXERCISE Underline the appositive in each sentence below, and draw an arrow from the appositive to the word or words it identifies or describes.

Example 1. Goro Hasegawa, a salesperson, invented the game called Othello.

1. The puppy, a Pomeranian, had long, wavy fur.

2. We gave the dry cleaner, Mr. Nowlin, our suits to press.

3. We especially wanted to hear the cellist Yo-Yo Ma.

4. The hottest months, June, July, and August, are my favorites.

5. The book details the activities of Timmy Roybal, a Pueblo.

6. Samuel Maverick, a cattle rancher, refused to brand his animals.

7. My mentor, Jane Galway, is helping me research colleges.

8. Terrill Park, my hometown, holds a parade each year for Independence Day.

9. My friend Anandi is learning to snowboard.

10. The last day of exams, Friday, is on our minds constantly.

11. The house, a turn-of-the-century mansion, is now a museum.

12. We've looked everywhere for our dog Jake.

13. Dr. Renwick, the violin teacher, also plays cello and viola.

14. Who wrote the poem "Ode on a Grecian Urn"?

15. The younger of the two boys in that family, Sam, looks like his grandfather.

16. The dessert, a magnificent chocolate cake, stood in the center of the table.

17. You should call your aunt Sarah this weekend.

18. He must take this medicine, an antibiotic, for ten days.

19. The addition to their house, an extra bedroom, took six months.

20. Mr. Galvan, the assistant principal, wants to see you in his office.

GRAMMAR

Appositive Phrases

3l. An *appositive phrase* consists of an appositive and any modifiers it has.

> **EXAMPLES** Estrella, **my best friend in the world,** is moving away. [The appositive phrase identifies the noun *Estrella*.]
>
> **An aviation student with lots of talent,** Moshe flew yesterday. [The appositive phrase describes the noun *Moshe*.]

EXERCISE Underline the appositive phrase in each of the following sentences, and draw an arrow from the phrase to the word or words it identifies or describes.

Example 1. A description of life on the frontier, the book became a bestseller.

1. Dorothy Parker, the poet and short-story writer, is remembered for her wit.

2. A college education, a dream of many, is a worthy pursuit.

3. The gold ring, a family heirloom, was given to my grandmother by her mother.

4. Our family car, a rusty 1981 station wagon , still runs well despite its age.

5. We traveled to Horseshoe City, a tiny town left over from the state's mining days.

6. Charon, the tiny moon of Pluto, is named for a character in Greek mythology.

7. Fear of walking under ladders, a superstition held by many people, is baseless.

8. A well-known folk tale, "Bean Soup" is a favorite story among children.

9. Oxalis, a clover-like plant, makes a colorful garden border.

10. The piano, a neglected old spinet, stood in the dusty corner.

11. This book, a collection of short stories, was due yesterday.

12. The essay contest, one of several sponsored by the newspaper, is open to all students.

13. My cousin, now a private pilot in Alaska, used to be afraid of flying.

14. Central Avenue, the main street of the town, is lined with shops and restaurants.

15. The magazine article, a feature story about hot-air balloonists, was fascinating.

16. Three bowls and a platter, examples of the potter's best work, are on display in the gallery.

17. Usually a slow, shallow stream, the creek now raged out of its banks.

18. That movie, one of the best I've ever seen, should win several awards.

19. My mother, the eighth of eleven children, grew up in North Dakota.

20. Jeremy, until recently an unexceptional student, is determined to excel in math.

for **CHAPTER 3: THE PHRASE**   *pages 81–82*

Appositives and Appositive Phrases

3k.	An *appositive* is a noun or a pronoun placed beside another noun or pronoun to identify or describe it.

3l.	An *appositive phrase* consists of an appositive and any modifiers it has.

EXAMPLES   The dog, **a brown and gold shepherd,** stood panting eagerly. [The appositive phrase identifies the noun *dog. Brown and gold* modifies the appositive *shepherd*.]

A breed with great intelligence, shepherds can be trained to help people in many ways. [The appositive phrase describes the noun *shepherds*. The adjective *A* and the prepositional phrase *with great intelligence* modify the appositive *breed*.]

EXERCISE   Underline the appositive or appositive phrase in each of the following sentences, and draw an arrow from the phrase to the word or words it identifies or describes.

Example 1. Pluto, the second-largest known dwarf planet in the solar system, is about two-thirds the size of Earth's moon.

1. Pluto is normally farther away than the eight planets in our solar system, but its steep orbit at times brings it inside the orbit of its nearest neighbor, the planet Neptune.

2. On this dwarf planet, a complete rotation, one day and night, takes 6.39 Earth days.

3. We have not known about Pluto, a very distant member of the solar system, for very long.

4. In fact, it was discovered by Clyde Tombaugh, an amateur astronomer at the Lowell Observatory.

5. Tombaugh located Pluto in Gemini, a well-known constellation, on February 18, 1930.

6. For a time, scientists wondered if Pluto were an escaped moon of Neptune, a planet with many moons.

7. The discovery of Charon, Pluto's tiny moon, brought this idea into question.

8. This dwarf planet is named after Pluto, Greco-Roman god of the underworld.

9. Fittingly, little Charon is named after a dreaded character in Greek myth, the ferryman who rowed the dead into the underworld.

10. Some Scientists have discovered other dwarf planets, such as Ceres, the closest known dwarf planet to Earth.

Language and Sentence Skills Practice

GRAMMAR

Review A: **Phrases**

EXERCISE A   Underline the prepositional phrase in each of the following sentences. Then, identify the phrase by writing above it *ADJ* for *adjective phrase* or *ADV* for *adverb phrase*.

Example 1. Have you ever been very nervous *ADV* before a test or an examination?

1. During a test I used to become nervous or upset.

2. My mother discussed this with me last spring.

3. I had become quite upset about my final exams.

4. I had become very tense, and I had lost much of my appetite.

5. One day my mother sat down and explained the value of a little anxiety.

6. Although she was concerned, she talked very calmly about test taking.

7. Too much worry, she told me, is unhealthy for anyone.

8. No one in that situation can perform well.

9. Too much worry about a test can prevent clear thinking.

10. Her explanation of stress and anxiety was very helpful.

EXERCISE B   In each of the following sentences, underline the verbal phrase. Then, identify the phrase by writing above it *PART* for *participial phrase*, *GER* for *gerund phrase*, or *INF* for *infinitive phrase*.

Example 1. *INF* Are you afraid to swim in deep water?

11. Many people never learn to stay afloat in the water.

12. Some of them, fearing the water, stay away from it.

13. Others, however, try again and again to become good swimmers.

14. Eventually some succeed in mastering the basic technique.

15. My sister, for instance, can now swim after spending many years in classes.

16. Undaunted by past failures, she would enroll in a new class each fall.

17. In class, she would cling to the side of the pool, kicking her feet.

18. Standing in shallow water, she would then practice her arm movements.

19. In deep water, though, she sometimes ended by paddling slowly to the side.

20. Then she would work up her nerve to begin again.

for **CHAPTER 3: THE PHRASE**   pages 65–82

Review B: **Phrases**

EXERCISE A Underline the prepositional phrase in each of the following sentences. Then, identify the phrase by writing above it *ADJ* for *adjective phrase* or *ADV* for *adverb phrase*.

                                                         ADV
Example 1. A bird built its nest in my attic.
                                          _____

1. At first I thought I heard kittens.

2. The cries I heard were loud enough for a whole litter.

3. I took a saucer of milk and went upstairs.

4. I began an extensive search and wasted most of the afternoon.

5. To my surprise, I did not find the kitten I had expected.

6. Instead, I spotted a nest with two little pigeons in it.

7. That was very surprising to me.

8. Using some wood from my workroom, I built the pigeons a snug house.

9. Few of the neighborhood birds can boast such luxury.

10. Unfortunately, they are skittish and flighty as pets.

EXERCISE B In each of the following sentences, underline the verbal phrase. Then, identify the phrase by writing above it *PART* for *participial phrase*, *GER* for *gerund phrase*, or *INF* for *infinitive phrase*.

                          GER
Example 1. Growing your own luffa gourds is both practical and fun.
                  _____

11. It is easy to grow luffa gourds.

12. Many people are quite successful at raising a large crop.

13. It takes about ten days for vines to sprout from seeds.

14. Plants nurtured by the sun flourish and produce many gourds.

15. Sun-ripened in about eighty days, the gourds may be harvested and eaten.

16. Left on the vines, the gourds eventually make sponges.

17. Consider the benefits of growing a single luffa crop.

18. Combining some of the luffas with apples and sweet potatoes, you can prepare a delicious treat.

19. You might use other luffas from the same crop to wash the dishes.

20. Giving luffas as gifts to your family and friends is another option.

Language and Sentence Skills Practice

Review C: **Phrases**

EXERCISE A In each of the following sentences, identify the underlined phrase by writing above it *PREP* for *prepositional phrase*, *PART* for *participial phrase*, *GER* for *gerund phrase*, *INF* for *infinitive phrase*, or *APP* for *appositive phrase*. Note: Do not label shorter phrases within the underlined phrase.

                                           INF

Example 1. I love to ride my bike.

1. Bicycling through the countryside is a favorite hobby of mine.

2. I enjoy the freedom to get around on my own.

3. I also ride my bike to school.

4. At 8:00 A.M., I am on my way, pedaling furiously.

5. Neither rain nor heat nor barking dogs keep me from riding my bike daily.

6. My current bike, an old three-speed model, is not well suited for long-distance riding.

7. Affectionately dubbed Wheels, it originally belonged to Carlos Ramirez.

8. Carlos, a former neighbor of mine, made me promise to keep Wheels clean and properly oiled.

9. Three years' worth of repairs attests to my good faith in the matter.

10. Nevertheless, I am trying to save enough money for an all-terrain bike.

EXERCISE B In each of the following sentences, identify the underlined phrase by writing above it *PREP* for *prepositional phrase*, *PART* for *participial phrase*, *GER* for *gerund phrase*, *INF* for *infinitive phrase*, or *APP* for *appositive phrase*. Note: Do not label shorter phrases within the underlined phrase.

                                                       INF

Example 1. At college, my sister tried again to master the art of swimming.

11. Swimming the length of the pool was one of the requirements for graduation.

12. This requirement, a longtime rule at the college, was easy for many students.

13. To my sister, it was a difficult challenge.

14. She would jump into the pool with her friends standing by to cheer her on.

15. Despite her intentions, she never got farther than ten feet from the edge of the pool.

16. Nevertheless, she would try again, advancing and improving each time.

17. The instructor, a sympathetic person, became interested in my sister's problem.

18. He convinced her that swimming did not mean risking her life.

19. My sister persisted, finally passing the swimming requirement.

20. In her case, swimming seemed to be a challenge that she accepted and met.

for **CHAPTER 3: THE PHRASE**   *pages 70–72*

Literary Model: Short Story

The platoon of twenty-six soldiers moved slowly in the dark, single file, not talking. One by one, like sheep in a dream, they passed through the hedgerow, crossed quietly over a meadow, and came down to the rice paddy. There they stopped. Their leader knelt down, motioning with his hand, and one by one the other soldiers squatted in the shadows, vanishing in the primitive stealth of warfare. For a long time they did not move. Except for the sounds of their breathing, the twenty-six men were very quiet: some of them excited by the adventure, some of them afraid, some of them exhausted from the long night march, some of them looking forward to reaching the sea, where they would be safe. At the rear of the column, Private First Class Paul Berlin lay quietly with his forehead resting on the black plastic stock of his rifle, his eyes closed. He was pretending he was not in the war, . . . pretending he was a boy again, camping with his father in the midnight summer along the Des Moines River. In the dark, with his eyes pinched shut, he pretended. . . .

—from "Where Have You Gone, Charming Billy?" by Tim O'Brien

EXERCISE A   Underline the ten participles in the passage above. Then, circle each noun that is being modified. (Hint: *Breathing* and *reaching* are gerunds.)

EXERCISE B   In general, participles express either action that occurs simultaneously with the main verb or a state of being. Of the ten participles you identified, write *SA* over those that appear to express simultaneous action with the main verb. Write *SB* over those participles that express a state of being.

From "Where Have You Gone, Charming Billy?" slightly adapted from *Going After Cacciato* by Tim O'Brien. Copyright © 1975, 1976, 1977, 1978 by **Tim O'Brien.** Reprinted by permission of the author.

GRAMMAR | Language in Context: Literary Model

Literary Model (continued)

EXERCISE C   This passage is from a short story that deals with a young soldier's initiation into combat. Use your imagination or personal experience to write a passage about a person's first-time experience of an important event that causes an emotional impact. Be sure to use several participles and participial phrases to express simultaneous action with the main verbs and to express the state of being of your character.

_____

_____

_____

_____

_____

_____

_____

_____

_____

_____

EXERCISE D

1. Rewrite at least half of your passage so that all participles and participial phrases are replaced by verbs (or verb phrases).

_____

_____

_____

_____

_____

_____

_____

2. Compare the use of verbs in your rewritten passage and the use of verbals in your original. How do the passages differ in their styles?

_____

_____

_____

_____

Writing Application: Restaurant Review

Question: What looks like a verb but doesn't act like a verb?
Answer: A verbal.

Verbals—participles, gerunds, and infinitives—are formed from verbs but are used as other parts of speech. They can be modified by adverbs and adjectives and can have complements. Look at these examples.

PARTICIPLE The pasta, **cooked** to perfection, rivals the sauce that covers it.

GERUND A dinner at Pino's is like **traveling** to Italy.

INFINITIVE **To eat** the fettucine is a truly divine experience.

In the first example, the participle *cooked* modifies the noun *pasta*. In the second example, the gerund *traveling* is the object of the preposition *like*. In the third example, the infinitive *to eat* is the subject of the sentence. Each of these verbals is part of a phrase.

Writing Activity

What is your favorite restaurant? Think for a moment about why it's your favorite restaurant. Do you think it's outstanding because of the food, the atmosphere, the service, or the prices? Imagine that the local newspaper has asked you to write a review of this restaurant. In your review, include at least four participles, two gerunds, and two infinitives.

PREWRITING Use a cluster diagram to break the topic—your favorite restaurant—into smaller parts. Add related ideas to the diagram as you think of them. Allow new ideas to lead to others. Determine the audience for whom the review is intended. Then, decide the appropriate level of language for that audience. Will you use short sentences, long sentences, or both? How complex do you want the vocabulary to be? In addition, consider the tone you will use in the review. Although the topic is the same, a restaurant review written in a serious tone will be quite different from one written in a light, casual tone.

WRITING Your topic sentence should be based on your own opinion of the restaurant. Be sure to include details that support your opinion. You may want to devote a paragraph to each reason that the restaurant is outstanding. Conclude your review with a sentence that will leave an impression on the reader.

REVISING Read your draft carefully to identify words or phrases you can replace with others that are more descriptive or lively. In particular, can you think of other participles that, because of their dual verb-adjective nature, might spice up your review as you describe the food? Check that your opinions are sufficiently supported by the details. Also, check that your choice of details and words, as well as the rhythms of the language you have used, are suitable for the tone you chose. Be sure that you have included at least four participles, two gerunds, and two infinitives.

PUBLISHING Put your draft aside for a while. When you return to it, look carefully for errors in grammar, usage, spelling, and punctuation. Pay special attention to the spelling of participles and gerunds. Have you followed the spelling rules for adding suffixes? Finally, with your teacher's permission, present your review to the class.

Extending Your Writing

Perhaps you could submit your restaurant review for publication in a local or school newspaper. First, find out what the guidelines are for length and submission dates.

Choices: Investigating Clauses

The following activities challenge you to find a connection between clauses and the world around you. Do the activity below that suits your personality best, and then share your discoveries with your class.

LITERATURE

If Wishes Were Horses

Many traditional proverbs begin with a subordinate clause. How many such proverbs can you find? Using a book of proverbs or some other reliable source, compile a collection of as many as you can find. Then, make copies and share your collection with your classmates.

CREATIVE WRITING

Mad Scientists

Have you got a sense of humor? Well, here's your opportunity to use it. Write a skit about mad scientists creating a "Frankensentence" out of independent and subordinate clauses. First, find several clauses from the novel or story your class is currently reading or has just finished reading. Then, write your skit and try to include a special effect or two. Your skit should involve two mad scientists piecing together a sentence from the clauses they found. Videotape or perform your skit in front of the class.

LAW

Legal Eagle

What is the legal definition of the word *clause*? How does the legal definition differ from the grammatical definition? Do a little research on this subject. Go beyond a simple dictionary definition, and consult a legal dictionary and a couple of other sources. Then, prepare and give a short oral presentation to the class.

ANALYSIS

Point by Point

A noun clause acts as a noun, but are they really the same? How does a noun clause differ from a noun? For instance, a noun can be modified by an adjective. Can a noun clause be so modified? What can a noun do that a clause can't? Nouns can name a specific person, place, or thing, but can a clause do so? Think about these questions.

Think, too, about the ways that a noun clause is like a noun. Both can be composed of a number of words. In what other ways are they similar? Then, make a chart that shows the similarities and differences between nouns and noun clauses. Present your chart to the class as you lead a point-by-point discussion of each of the items on your chart.

RESEARCH

And So It Goes

Have you been told never to begin a sentence with a conjunction such as *and, but, nor, for, so,* or *yet*? What reasons were you given? Did you agree with them? When did this principle begin? What is the reasoning behind it? Do a little research, and find out. Also, find some examples of sentences beginning with conjunctions in published writing. How do conjunctions affect a writer's tone? What words might a writer substitute for the conjunctions? In what ways might these substitutions change the tone? Write up a report of your findings, and share them with your class.

BUILDING WRITING SKILLS

Making the Transition

Complex sentences make fabulous transitions between paragraphs. With a complex sentence, you can touch on the point in the previous paragraph, begin making the next point, *and* establish a relationship between the two ideas. Find some examples of published complex sentences that function as transitions. Then, prepare a presentation to the class. You'll need copies of the two paragraphs that are being joined. You'll also want to highlight the transition sentence, its clauses, and their subjects and verbs. Be ready to identify how specific words in the transition sentence echo ideas and words in the adjoining paragraphs.

Clauses

4a. A *clause* is a word group that contains a verb and its subject and that is used as a sentence or as part of a sentence.

Clauses that express a complete thought are called *independent clauses*. Clauses that do not express a complete thought are called *subordinate clauses*.

SENTENCE	**We have some gardenias that are very fragrant.** [The sentence contains two clauses. *We* is the subject of the verb *have*, and *that* is the subject of the verb *are*.]
INDEPENDENT CLAUSE	**We have some gardenias** [The clause expresses a complete thought.]
SUBORDINATE CLAUSE	**that are very fragrant** [The clause does not express a complete thought.]

EXERCISE In the independent and subordinate clauses in the following sentences, underline the subjects once and the verbs twice.

Example 1. Harriet, a horticulturist, raises gardenias in her enclosed porch that she uses as a greenhouse.

1. Ever since she was a young girl, Harriet has loved flowers.

2. She is fond of all flowers, but she especially loves those with a beautiful fragrance.

3. Harriet's backyard is bordered by many different varieties of roses that bloom profusely all summer.

4. Her favorite rosebush, a red, climbing variety, grows from a fifty-year-old cutting that was taken from a rosebush in her mother's yard.

5. Did you know that she has taken cuttings from that bush and has given them to her daughter and granddaughter?

6. Since Harriet lives in Illinois, her garden is covered with snow during the winter and has no flowers for her to enjoy.

7. After reading an article about growing flowers in a greenhouse, Harriet turned her porch, which faces south, into a greenhouse.

8. Inspired by the beautiful gardenia bush that was a birthday gift, she fashioned a tabletop greenhouse of plant stakes and plastic.

9. Soon, the gardenia bush that had been the only plant in the greenhouse was joined by small cuttings.

10. The indoor and outdoor flowers add beauty to Harriet's house and to her neighborhood, and the fragrant plants bring joy to the woman who so carefully tends them.

Language and Sentence Skills Practice

GRAMMAR

Independent Clauses

4b. An *independent* (or *main*) *clause* expresses a complete thought and can stand by itself as a sentence.

EXAMPLES **The hurricane may hit here.**

The hurricane may hit here, so **we need to leave.** [Two independent clauses are linked by a comma and a coordinating conjunction.]

The hurricane may hit here; we need to leave. [Two independent clauses are linked by a semicolon.]

EXERCISE In each of the following sentences, underline the independent clauses.

Example 1. At the National Hurricane Center in Miami, Florida, which is part of the National Weather Service, meteorologists chart air pressure, temperature, and wind speed of storms over the oceans.

1. During the hurricane season, meteorologists keep a close eye on storm systems over oceans near the United States.

2. Hurricanes begin as easterly waves, which may grow and form an area of low pressure called a tropical depression.

3. When winds of a tropical depression reach 32 miles per hour, the depression officially becomes a tropical storm, and when the storm winds reach 74 miles per hour, the storm is classified as a hurricane.

4. Collecting data from the storms helps meteorologists because, from the data, they can forecast the size, strength, and timing of impending hurricanes.

5. Since hurricanes can have wind speeds of more than 200 miles per hour, they produce large waves, which are called storm surges.

6. Even if a hurricane's winds do not cause severe damage, a community lying in a low area along the waterfront may be flooded by the storm surge.

7. One of the benefits of hurricane forecasting is the time the warnings give to residents who live in flood-prone areas.

8. Residents can decide whether they will stay for the duration of the storm or evacuate.

9. Evacuating can be difficult because hurricanes can measure 300 miles across.

10. Pay attention to weather forecasts from June to November, the months during which most hurricanes occur in the United States.

Subordinate Clauses

4c. A *subordinate* (or *dependent*) *clause* does not express a complete thought and cannot stand alone as a sentence.

The thought expressed by a subordinate clause becomes part of a complete thought when the clause is combined with an independent clause.

EXAMPLES   **since I work after school** [not a complete thought]

Since I work after school, I value my study halls. [complete thought]

A subordinate clause may contain complements and modifiers.

EXAMPLE   before Holly threw **me** the **ball** [*Me* is the indirect object of the verb *threw,* and *ball* is the direct object of *threw.*]

EXERCISE A   For each of the following sentences, underline the subordinate clause.

Example 1. Before we went to the play, we invited our friends to our house for a party.

1. Samuel just finished reading the book that he bought last weekend at the beach.

2. We will introduce Madeleine to everyone as soon as she arrives from the airport.

3. Have you ever wondered when that tree in the backyard was originally planted?

4. Margaret, whose essay on indigenous North American birds was nominated for an award, will present her research to the class on Friday.

5. Do you know who in the class will attend the symphony concert on Saturday night?

EXERCISE B   Identify the subject and verb in the underlined subordinate clause by writing *S* for *subject* and *V* for *verb* above the words. Then, circle any complements in the clause and identify them by writing above them *DO* for *direct object, IO* for *indirect object, PN* for *predicate nominative,* or *PA* for *predicate adjective.*

Example 1. We know who she is.

6. Since the hour is late, let's postpone making our decision.

7. He is an artist who paints billboards.

8. The interview will go well if you remember one rule.

9. Because I had lent Julius my book, I had to borrow Melanie's.

10. I don't know who Carson McCullers is.

11. Here is the book that you want.

12. When the field is wet, we have to cancel the baseball game.

13. Dad wanted a car that used very little gas.

14. I couldn't remember what the answer was.

15. She draws the cartoons that are so weird.

Language and Sentence Skills Practice

Independent and Subordinate Clauses A

4b. An *independent* (or *main*) *clause* expresses a complete thought and can stand by itself as a sentence.

4c. A *subordinate* (or *dependent*) *clause* does not express a complete thought and cannot stand alone as a sentence.

INDEPENDENT CLAUSE **Some people find television boring.**

SUBORDINATE CLAUSE Some people **who enjoy reading** find television boring.

EXERCISE A In each of the following sentences, identify the underlined clause as independent or subordinate by writing above it *IND* for *independent* or *SUB* for *subordinate*.

Example 1. The Plains Indians decorated themselves <u>so that they could make themselves</u> <u>look fierce.</u>   *SUB*

1. After they rubbed deer fat on their bodies, <u>they painted designs on their skins.</u>

2. <u>You might wonder</u> how they created such vivid colors.

3. <u>They made their paints from natural minerals and plants.</u>

4. <u>If a warrior had been particularly brave,</u> he would wear an eagle feather on his shield.

5. <u>Sometimes warriors carried buffalo robes,</u> which might have battle scenes painted on them.

EXERCISE B Make each of the following subordinate clauses into a complete sentence. Write your revised sentences on the lines provided.

Example 1. If you buy that CD,

If you buy that CD, I'd like to listen to it.

6. Whenever you walk in the park,

_____

7. Although we are having spaghetti for dinner,

_____

8. Because I live in this town,

_____

9. What I wish for every day

_____

10. After I come back from spring break,

_____

HOLT HANDBOOK | Fourth Course

Independent and Subordinate Clauses B

| **4b.** | An *independent* (or *main*) *clause* expresses a complete thought and can stand by itself as a sentence. |

| **4c.** | A *subordinate* (or *dependent*) *clause* does not express a complete thought and cannot stand alone as a sentence. |

| INDEPENDENT CLAUSE | **The woman on the bench is my mother.** |
| SUBORDINATE CLAUSE | The woman **who is seated on the bench** is my mother. |

EXERCISE For each of the following sentences, identify the underlined clause as independent or subordinate by writing on the line before each sentence *IND* for *independent* or *SUB* for *subordinate*.

Example ___SUB___ **1.** Soccer, which is the national sport of many European and Latin American countries, is becoming more and more popular in the United States.

_____ **1.** During a career that spanned twenty years, Pelé was probably the most popular athlete in the world.

_____ **2.** He was named Edson Arantes do Nascimento, but hardly anyone recognizes that name.

_____ **3.** Soccer fans the world over, however, knew Pelé, who was considered to be the world's best soccer player.

_____ **4.** While he was still a teenager, he led his Brazilian teammates to the first of their three World Cup titles.

_____ **5.** Whenever he played, his skill and agility awed fans.

_____ **6.** Once, he juggled the ball on his foot for fifty yards, eluding four opponents who were trying to take the ball away from him.

_____ **7.** When he quickly became a superstar, no one was surprised.

_____ **8.** Even though soccer was less popular in the United States than elsewhere, Pelé managed to spark considerable interest in the game.

_____ **9.** After he signed with the New York Cosmos, people flocked to the stands to watch him play.

_____ **10.** They soon recognized that Pelé was an athlete who was also an entertainer.

GRAMMAR

The Adjective Clause A

4d. An *adjective clause* is a subordinate clause that modifies a noun or a pronoun.

An adjective clause tells *what kind* or *which one* and generally follows the word or words it modifies.

> **EXAMPLES**   The dog **that I found** was clearly someone's lost pet. [The clause modifies the noun *dog* and tells *which one*.]
>
> Mr. Shange's truck, **which was filled with eggs,** blocked the road. [The clause modifies the noun *truck* and tells *which one*.]

EXERCISE   Underline the adjective clause in each sentence below, and circle the word or words the clause modifies.

Example 1. I waited for my (friend,) who had to stay late.

1. The house that we bought needs work.

2. The band, which I had heard before, was wonderful.

3. Those people who already have tickets may go inside.

4. That crispy shrimp dish has a sauce that I like.

5. The weavers whom we met live in Cuzco.

6. Marcos, whose ambition is to become a restaurant chef, has enrolled at the Institute of Culinary Arts.

7. Have you met Emily, who is Greg's first cousin?

8. The airline ticket to Chicago that I bought last week is nonrefundable.

9. The subject on which Dr. Kolar will be speaking Thursday is the art and science of repairing computers.

10. This is the scenic overlook where you can see the rolling hills on the left, the flat prairie on the right, and our beautiful city straight ahead.

The Adjective Clause B

4d.   An *adjective clause* is a subordinate clause that modifies a noun or a pronoun.

An adjective clause tells *what kind* or *which one* and generally follows the word or words it modifies. An *essential* (or *restrictive*) *clause*, which contains information necessary to the sentence's meaning, is not set off by commas. A *nonessential* (or *nonrestrictive*) *clause*, which contains information that can be omitted without affecting the sentence's basic meaning, is set off by commas.

> **EXAMPLES**   The ring **that I lost** belonged to my grandmother. [The clause modifies the noun *ring* and tells *which one*. The clause is essential.]
>
> Marcella's backpack**, which split open at the seam,** lasted only one semester. [The clause modifies the noun *backpack* and tells *which one*. The clause is nonessential.]

EXERCISE   In the following sentences, underline any adjective clauses. Then, draw an arrow from each clause to the word that the clause modifies. Identify each clause by writing above it *E* for *essential* or *N* for *nonessential*.

Example 1. Do you know any people who would benefit from a hot meal delivery service?

1. Meals on Wheels, a volunteer organization, delivers hot, nutritious meals to people who are unable to shop and cook for themselves.

2. The nutrition programs that we know today can trace their roots back to World War II.

3. During the war, people in England whose homes were bombed often lost their kitchens.

4. The Women's Volunteer Service for Civil Defense cooked and delivered meals to people who no longer could cook at home for themselves.

5. The hot meals, which the women delivered to the people with no cooking facilities and also to military personnel, came to be known as Meals on Wheels.

6. Where did the first American program that delivered meals to homebound senior citizens begin?

7. Philadelphia, Pennsylvania, is the city where the home-delivered meal service was pioneered.

8. Who would have believed that the program, which began serving only seven senior citizens, would grow to serve so many?

9. The number of meals that are delivered every day is in the millions.

10. The recipients of the meals not only receive nutritious food, which helps to keep them healthy, but they also receive the benefit of human contact with the volunteers.

Relative Pronouns

An adjective clause is usually introduced by a *relative pronoun*. These pronouns are called *relative pronouns* because they relate an adjective clause to the word or word group the clause modifies. Each relative pronoun also serves a grammatical function within the sentence. Common relative pronouns are *who, whom, whose, which,* and *that*. Sometimes the relative pronoun is left out. In such a sentence, the pronoun is understood and still serves a grammatical function within the adjective clause. Occasionally, an adjective clause is introduced by the words *where* or *when*, called *relative adverbs* when used in this way.

EXAMPLES The film, **which I had seen before,** provides amazing insight into the life of the famous clogger. [The relative pronoun *which* relates the adjective clause to the noun *film* and also serves as the direct object of the verb *had seen*.]

The dancer **I wrote my paper about** was Isadora Duncan. [The relative pronoun *that* or *whom* is understood. The relative pronoun relates the adjective clause to the noun *dancer* and also serves as the object of the preposition *about* in the clause.]

This is the time **when I usually stop for a lunch break.** [The relative adverb *when* relates the adjective clause to the noun *time*.]

EXERCISE Underline the adjective clause in each sentence below and circle the relative pronoun or relative adverb that introduces it. Then, draw an arrow from the clause to the word the clause modifies. If the relative pronoun is understood, write it at the end of the sentence.

Example 1. Have you heard of Jesse Owens, (who) is one of the most well-known athletes in the world?

1. Jesse Owens, whose real name was James Owens, was a great athlete.

2. His birth, which was in 1913, took place on a farm in Alabama.

3. The place where he first showed indications of being a fast runner was junior high school.

4. One race, when he ran extraordinarily well, stands out.

5. People remember the 100-meter dash that he ran in 10.3 seconds.

6. At the 1936 Olympics, which were held in Germany, Owens won four gold medals.

7. Owens became the athlete every other athlete in track and field tried to emulate.

8. Owens had a stunt that he sometimes performed.

9. He would race against a racehorse, which was actually faster than he was.

10. Because the firing of the gun that was used to start the race usually caused the horse to balk, Owens would win many of the races.

The Adverb Clause A

4e.   An *adverb clause* is a subordinate clause that modifies a verb, an adjective, or an adverb.

An adverb clause tells *how, when, where, why, to what extent,* or *under what condition.*

EXAMPLES   **When you leave,** lock the door. [The adverb clause modifies the verb *lock*, telling *when*.]

The actor became nervous **because he couldn't remember his lines.** [The adverb clause modifies the adjective *nervous*, telling *why*.]

Don't run the water any longer **than you must.** [The adverb clause modifies the adverb *longer*, telling *to what extent*.]

EXERCISE   Underline the adverb clauses in the sentences below. Hint: There may be more than one adverb clause in a sentence.

Example 1. If they've been good, could you tell them a story before they go to bed?

1. When we got out of the traffic jam, we all relaxed.

2. According to Alexander Pope, "Fools rush in where angels fear to tread."

3. When you return from your trip, show us your pictures.

4. While Mr. Thundercloud read the poem, everyone listened.

5. Unless someone notifies you, you should be at the airport by noon.

6. They discussed the problem for almost an hour, but they could not resolve the issue because neither side was listening.

7. In preparation for her grandmother's arrival, Marissa emptied the two top drawers of the dresser so that her grandmother would have a place to put her clothes during the visit.

8. Even though John had read the chapter twice, he went over the material a third time.

9. My mother believes that you should do every task as well as you can, even if the job is very small.

10. You may go to the concert Saturday night provided that you have finished your homework for the weekend.

Language and Sentence Skills Practice

for **CHAPTER 4: THE CLAUSE**   *pages 96–97*

The Adverb Clause B

4e. | An *adverb clause* is a subordinate clause that modifies a verb, an adjective, or an adverb.

An adverb clause tells *how, when, where, why, to what extent,* or *under what condition.*

EXAMPLES   **When the bell rang,** I leapt from my seat and raced outside. [The adverb clause modifies the verb *rang,* telling *when.*]

Arthur played well **because he loved the game.** [The adverb clause modifies the adverb *well,* telling *why.*]

Provided that she gets enough sleep, she is very agile. [The adverb clause modifies the adjective *agile,* telling *under what condition.*]

EXERCISE   In each of the following sentences, underline the adverb clause.

Example   1. When you go on vacation this summer, will you go to Philadelphia?

1. When I was twelve, my family and I spent a week in Philadelphia, the City of Brotherly Love.

2. William Penn planned for the city that he founded to be a haven for religious freedom because he had been persecuted for practicing the Quaker religion.

3. Until it was abolished in 1984, a city regulation prohibited structures from being higher than Penn's statue, 548 feet atop city hall.

4. Philadelphia is considered the birthplace of the United States since both the Declaration of Independence and the Constitution were signed there.

5. Did you know that Philadelphia was the capital of the colonies while the patriots were rebelling against the British government?

6. If I am not mistaken, every year millions of tourists visit the Liberty Bell, Independence Hall, Carpenters' Hall, and Congress Hall.

7. Historians believe that in 1777 Betsy Ross sewed the first flag of the United States in the house on Arch Street, although they are not certain.

8. Wherever you go in the historic district, you will find such famous structures as Christ Church, which was built beginning in 1727.

9. Even though I have visited many historic sites, few compare to Elfreth's Alley, about thirty-five brick houses that have been occupied continuously since the early 1700s.

10. I believe the buildings in Southwark, which was settled by the Swedes in the early 1600s, are even older than the buildings in the downtown area are.

for **CHAPTER 4: THE CLAUSE**   *pages 96–97*

Subordinating Conjunctions

An adverb clause is introduced by a *subordinating conjunction*—a word that shows the relationship between the adverb clause and the word or words that the clause modifies. Common subordinating conjunctions include *after, as, as if, as long as, because, before, even though, if, in order that, since, so that, though, until, whenever, whether, while,* and *why.*

> **EXAMPLES**   The rain stopped **after we got home.** [The subordinating conjunction *after* relates the adverb clause to the verb *stopped.*]
>
> The speech lasted longer **than I had hoped.** [The subordinating conjunction *than* relates the adverb clause to the adverb *longer.*]

EXERCISE   In the sentences below, underline each adverb clause and circle each subordinating conjunction.

Example 1. I brought the tennis rackets (so that) we can play right after school.

1. After Kyle returned, he reported his findings.

2. Magdelena made an important announcement before the bell rang.

3. As soon as the weather warms up, let's go camping.

4. We visited my grandmother whenever we could.

5. We'll leave a light on until you return from the game.

6. Wherever I go, my dog follows.

7. The group sang while they waited for the school bus.

8. After we washed the car, we had a water fight.

9. Please answer every question if you can.

10. Michael ran as if someone were chasing him.

11. Although we planned to arrive early, the traffic was heavy and we were late.

12. We won't start dinner until you arrive.

13. I understood the situation better after we discussed it.

14. We will go shopping tomorrow whether it is snowing or not.

15. Unless we have a late freeze, the peaches should do very well this year.

16. Even though he had taken the day off, Eric still worked diligently at home.

17. The veterinarian said to keep the dog quiet so that its incision would have a chance to heal.

18. You can borrow the one hundred dollars provided that you pay it back in one month.

19. Please call me soon because I need to make plans for our trip.

20. As long as you are getting the car washed, would you please go to that station where we went last week and get five gallons of gas?

Language and Sentence Skills Practice

Adjective and Adverb Clauses

4d. An **adjective clause** is a subordinate clause that modifies a noun or a pronoun.

> **EXAMPLE** A picture of everyone **who graduated** was in the paper. [The adjective clause modifies the pronoun *everyone*.]

4e. An **adverb clause** is a subordinate clause that modifies a verb, an adjective, or an adverb.

> **EXAMPLE** I'm not going to the concert **unless you join us.** [The adverb clause modifies the verb *am going*.]

EXERCISE A   In each of the following sentences, identify the underlined subordinate clause by writing above it *ADJ* for *adjective clause* or *ADV* for *adverb clause*.

Example 1. Last summer we visited Niagara Falls, <u>which is on the border between New York and Ontario.</u> [ADJ]

1. The two waterfalls <u>that form Niagara Falls</u> are the Horseshoe Falls in Ontario and the American Falls in New York.

2. Niagara Falls was carved about twelve thousand years ago <u>when Lake Erie overflowed and formed the Niagara River.</u>

3. For centuries, <u>as the river flowed over the land to a high cliff,</u> the water cut through the earth and eventually formed the falls.

4. The falls have cut a gorge about two hundred feet deep <u>that extends for seven miles past the falls.</u>

5. The water continues to erode the soft rock under the falls <u>so that the ledges of the falls wear away at a rate of one inch to six feet per year,</u> depending on the volume of water.

EXERCISE B   In each of the following sentences, underline the adjective or adverb clause. Then, indicate what kind of clause it is by writing above it *ADJ* for *adjective clause* or *ADV* for *adverb clause*.

Example 1. Will you turn down the music <u>when your father gets home?</u> [ADV]

6. Josh's father, who works at the library, loves all types of music.

7. In fact, as long as I have known him, Mr. Redmond has played an acoustic guitar.

8. Even though he is very talented, Mr. Redmond plays only for his family and friends.

9. Unless you know him well, you might ask, "Why doesn't he become a professional musician?"

10. He explains that the noise level of the clubs is too loud for his hearing, which is very acute.

The Noun Clause A

4f.   A *noun clause* is a subordinate clause that is used as a noun.

A noun clause may be used as a subject, a predicate nominative, a direct object, an indirect object, or the object of a preposition.

> **EXAMPLES**   A glass of water is **what I need now.** [predicate nominative]
>
> She thinks **that I'll do well on the test.** [direct object]
>
> Chen will give **whoever is closest** the ball. [indirect object]

Words commonly used to introduce noun clauses are *how, that, what, whatever, when, where, whether, which, whichever, who, whoever, whom, whomever, whose,* and *why.*

EXERCISE A   Underline the noun clause in each sentence below.

Example 1. I said that I wanted to visit some temples on our trip.

1. This is what you should wear inside a temple.

2. Find out which parts of the temple can be visited.

3. We don't know whether we will see a temple elephant.

4. Whoever is offered fresh coconut is being honored.

5. I understand that I need permission to photograph people.

EXERCISE B   Underline the noun clause in each sentence, and then, identify its function by writing above it *S* for *subject, PN* for *predicate nominative, DO* for *direct object, IO* for *indirect object,* or *OP* for *object of a preposition.*

Example 1. I got a scholarship for *OP* what I did in my science project.

6. I have always believed that people like to laugh.

7. What you decide to do is completely up to you.

8. We'll give whoever is left the prize.

9. Whatever Ms. Wing wants is fine.

10. His fear is that he will forget his lines.

11. My parents are very impressed by what I know about computers.

12. I have forgotten where I left my keys.

13. The problem was that Aaron hadn't arrived yet.

14. I was very surprised by what happened in the race.

15. That the milk was sour was immediately obvious.

Language and Sentence Skills Practice

The Noun Clause B

4f. A *noun clause* is a subordinate clause that is used as a noun.

A noun clause may be used as a subject, a predicate nominative, a direct object, an indirect object, or the object of a preposition.

> **EXAMPLES** **Whoever gets the right answer** will receive a prize. [subject]
>
> She talked about **why she had chosen the college.** [object of a preposition]
>
> We will give **whoever is earliest** free tickets. [indirect object]

Words commonly used to introduce noun clauses are *how, that, what, whatever, when, where, whether, which, whichever, who, whoever, whom, whomever, whose,* and *why.*

EXERCISE Underline the noun clause in each sentence, and then, identify its function by writing above it *S* for *subject, PN* for *predicate nominative, DO* for *direct object, IO* for *indirect object,* or *OP* for *object of a preposition.*

Example 1. Do you know <u>who the first female prime minister of India was</u> ? [DO]

1. Although I don't agree with you, I can see how you would think that.

2. That the candidate for the Senate office was very conservative was not a widely known fact.

3. A steaming bowl of fish chowder, a slice of whole-wheat bread, and a glass of cold milk are what I want for lunch.

4. Mrs. Scovil told us to write our two-page persuasive essays on whatever controversial topics were most interesting to us.

5. Give whoever is the last to leave the keys to lock the door.

6. My parents chose where the family will spend its summer vacation.

7. That she looks so much younger than her years surprised me.

8. Whoever parked in the no-parking zone must move the car.

9. We did not realize that the information would not be available until next Saturday.

10. Gilbert taught whoever was interested the basic chess moves.

Subordinate Clauses A

4d. | An *adjective clause* is a subordinate clause that modifies a noun or a pronoun.

   EXAMPLE   This is the desk **that I told you about.** [The adjective clause modifies the noun *desk*.]

4e. | An *adverb clause* is a subordinate clause that modifies a verb, an adjective, or an adverb.

   EXAMPLE   Could you carry my bag **when we get there?** [The adverb clause modifies the verb *could carry*.]

4f. | A *noun clause* is a subordinate clause that is used as a noun.

   EXAMPLE   The weather report indicates **that it will freeze tonight.** [The noun clause is the direct object of the verb *indicates*.]

EXERCISE   Each of the following sentences contains a subordinate clause. Underline the subordinate clause, and identify it by writing above it *ADJ* for *adjective clause, ADV* for *adverb clause,* or *N* for *noun clause.*

          N

Example 1. How I am ever on time to school is a mystery to my family.

1. They cannot believe that anyone can travel five blocks in four minutes.

2. It all begins each morning when my alarm goes off.

3. The alarm buzzes noisily, but I pretend that I do not hear it.

4. My older brother, who is very conscientious, begins to prod me.

5. After I finally get out of bed, he continues to bother me.

6. When I arrive downstairs, my parents take over.

7. Every day, they worry that I'll be late.

8. The only member of the family who doesn't scold me is the dog.

9. I leave for school at the last possible minute that I can.

10. I've never yet been late; why everyone worries so is beyond me.

Subordinate Clauses B

| **4d.** | An *adjective clause* is a subordinate clause that modifies a noun or a pronoun. |

> **EXAMPLE**   Sean, **who gave me the green balloon,** has Irish ancestry. [The adjective clause modifies the noun *Sean*.]

| **4e.** | An *adverb clause* is a subordinate clause that modifies a verb, an adjective, or an adverb. |

> **EXAMPLE**   He gave me the balloon **because our ancestors come from the same county in Ireland.** [The adverb clause modifies the verb *gave*.]

| **4f.** | A *noun clause* is a subordinate clause that is used as a noun. |

> **EXAMPLE**   **Where both of our ancestors came from** is Limerick County. [The noun clause is the subject of the verb *is*.]

EXERCISE   Each of the following sentences contains a subordinate clause. Underline the subordinate clause, and identify it by writing above it *ADJ* for *adjective clause, ADV* for *adverb clause,* or *N* for *noun clause.*

Example 1. Dana told me <u>that the exam was postponed</u>.   *(N)*

1. That the Brittany spaniel is good-natured and obedient is obvious to the neighbors.

2. Do not take the job if you are not able to lift heavy packages.

3. Give the door prize to whoever sold the most tickets to the banquet.

4. A sea horse looks like a tiny horse that has been joined to a fish's body.

5. Before you decide on a career, consider carefully your abilities, interests, and opportunities.

6. I was looking for a book that has a poem by Emily Dickinson.

7. Did you know that the church's centennial celebration was last weekend?

8. When you have finished peeling the potatoes and carrots, add them to the soup on the stove.

9. We have included gymnastics, which is a popular sport, in our new athletics program.

10. My Persian cat leaps into the air whenever she sees a flying insect.

Sentences Classified According to Structure A

4g. A sentence can be classified, depending on its structure, as *simple, compound, complex,* or *compound-complex.*

(1) A *simple sentence* contains one independent clause and no subordinate clauses.
(2) A *compound sentence* contains two or more independent clauses and no subordinate clauses.
(3) A *complex sentence* contains one independent clause and at least one subordinate clause.
(4) A *compound-complex sentence* contains two or more independent clauses and at least one subordinate clause.

EXERCISE A Classify each of the following sentences according to its structure. On the line provided, write *S* for *simple, CD* for *compound, CX* for *complex,* or *CC* for *compound-complex.*

Example ___CC___ **1.** Holiday customs vary around the world, but wherever they are held, celebrations often include food and special decorations.

_____ **1.** A major festival in India is the Festival of the Lights (Diwali).

_____ **2.** This holiday is celebrated by making lamps, and it also includes a cooking spree.

_____ **3.** In addition to decorating their houses, the celebrants settle up their business affairs.

_____ **4.** Relatives exchange gifts; then at sunset they light lamps that have special significance.

_____ **5.** They light lamps to beckon Lakshmi, who is the Hindu goddess of wealth.

EXERCISE B Classify each of the following sentences according to its structure. On the line provided, write *S* for *simple, CD* for *compound, CX* for *complex,* or *CC* for *compound-complex.*

Example ___S___ **1.** Sally Ride is a role model for many girls and women.

_____ **6.** In June of 1983, Sally K. Ride became the first American woman to orbit the earth.

_____ **7.** When she was growing up in the Los Angeles suburb of Encino, Ride appeared to be headed for a career in tennis, not in space.

_____ **8.** She competed in local tournaments while she was still in high school, and she eventually became a nationally ranked amateur.

_____ **9.** Ride evidently found space travel more compelling than tennis, and she became a member of the space shuttle program.

_____ **10.** After the space shuttle *Challenger* exploded in 1986, Ride was appointed to the presidential commission that investigated the accident.

Language and Sentence Skills Practice

Sentences Classified According to Structure B

4g. A sentence can be classified, depending on its structure, as *simple, compound, complex,* or *compound-complex.*

(1) A *simple sentence* contains one independent clause and no subordinate clauses.
(2) A *compound sentence* contains two or more independent clauses and no subordinate clauses.
(3) A *complex sentence* contains one independent clause and at least one subordinate clause.
(4) A *compound-complex sentence* contains two or more independent clauses and at least one subordinate clause.

EXERCISE For each of the following sentences, underline any independent clauses once and any subordinate clauses twice. Then, classify each of the sentences according to its structure. On the line provided, write *S* for *simple, CD* for *compound, CX* for *complex,* or *CC* for *compound-complex.*

Example __*S*__ **1.** After dinner, we took a walk and tried out our new shoes.

_____ **1.** Before the contest began, the soloists were nervously pacing back and forth.

_____ **2.** Tired of studying, Diego closed his book and turned on his stereo.

_____ **3.** After the storm had uprooted the tree, some of the clean-up crew trimmed the branches, and others loaded them into trucks.

_____ **4.** Without saying another word, Harriet collected her belongings, jammed them into a bag, and marched out of the meeting.

_____ **5.** I waited impatiently as the postal worker approached our mailbox with my long-awaited package.

_____ **6.** Take your jacket, or wear a sweater.

_____ **7.** Jacques wished that he could go on the camping trip, but he couldn't convince his parents to let him go because he had come home late three nights the week before.

_____ **8.** The flowers that create the beautiful scene outside the courthouse window are cared for by a professional gardener.

_____ **9.** The arrival of the candidates had been anticipated for months; the city officials were waiting for them at the reception.

_____ **10.** The only person with a key was Mr. Pavarotti, the owner and operator of the store.

Review A: **The Clause**

EXERCISE A For each of the following sentences, identify the underlined clause as independent or subordinate by writing above it *IND* for *independent* or *SUB* for *subordinate*. Then, tell how each subordinate clause functions in the sentence by writing above the clause *ADJ* for *adjective clause*, *ADV* for *adverb clause*, or *N* for *noun clause*.

> **Example 1.** My aunt told me something strange that she saw on a trip.

1. Travelers who drive across the Great Plains during the summer are often surprised by the size of the bridges spanning the streams.

2. Sometimes a half-mile-long bridge has been built across a stream that is little more than a muddy trickle.

3. They may wonder why the bridge is there at all.

4. If they revisited the spot in the springtime, they would understand the need for the bridge.

5. The tiny stream is transformed into a huge river when the spring rains come.

EXERCISE B Each of the following sentences contains a subordinate clause. Underline this clause. Then, tell how the clause functions in the sentence by writing above it *ADJ* for *adjective clause*, *ADV* for *adverb clause*, or *N* for *noun clause*.

> **Example 1.** The Mississippi and Missouri Rivers, which flow through the Great Plains, flow year-round.

6. However, some of the rivers that drain the Great Plains dry up entirely during the summer.

7. If there is little rainfall during the autumn, the riverbeds may remain dry until March or April.

8. A spring thaw that is accompanied by heavy rains may lead to flood conditions.

9. Residents know that a small stream can become a wide river practically overnight.

10. The bridges crossing such a river have to be strongly constructed so that they can withstand the raging floodwaters.

11. The wooden bridges of earlier days were washed away or badly damaged whenever there was a rainy spring.

12. Construction teams would replace what the spring torrents had destroyed.

13. With steel and reinforced concrete, they built bridges that could withstand the spring floods.

14. That the new bridges would be needed only one or two weeks a year was obvious to the designers and the builders.

15. A Great Plains bridge is like a summer cottage that stands empty most of the year.

Review B: **The Clause**

EXERCISE A For each of the following sentences, identify the underlined clause as independent or subordinate by writing above it *IND* for *independent* or *SUB* for *subordinate*. Then, tell how each subordinate clause functions in the sentence by writing above the clause *ADJ* for *adjective clause*, *ADV* for *adverb clause*, or *N* for *noun clause*.

SUB, ADV
Example 1. <u>Because I was tired</u>, I went to bed early.

1. If you are in the neighborhood, <u>stop by for a Texas-style barbecue</u>.

2. <u>That Daphne could not attend Diego's party</u> is unfortunate.

3. Latwanda's cousins, <u>who have lived in London for the past eight years</u>, are in the United States for an extended visit.

4. <u>Did Henri find the path</u> that leads to the orchard?

5. Please let the phone ring at least ten times <u>whenever you call</u>.

EXERCISE B In each of the following sentences, underline the subordinate clause. Then, tell how the clause functions in the sentence by writing above the clause *ADJ* for *adjective clause*, *ADV* for *adverb clause*, or *N* for *noun clause*.

ADJ
Example 1. I usually make several New Year's resolutions, <u>which I end up breaking</u>.

6. One New Year's resolution that I plan to keep is to hand in my homework on time.

7. If I don't start writing my reports in advance, I am likely to be late in handing them in.

8. Few of my friends are as skilled at procrastinating as I am.

9. For me and others like me, the problem is not that the work is too difficult.

10. What is problematic for many of us is actually getting started.

11. Putting things off creates problems that can often be avoided.

12. For example, I nearly failed a Spanish course because I put off writing a paper on Cervantes.

13. After a little research, I knew exactly what I wanted to say.

14. I just wasn't willing to set aside the time that I needed to write it.

15. I now pretend that every project is due at least two weeks in advance.

for **CHAPTER 4: THE CLAUSE** pages 90–103

Review C: **The Clause**

EXERCISE In each of the following sentences, underline independent clauses once and subordinate clauses twice. Then, classify each of the sentences according to structure by writing on the line provided *S* for *simple,* *CD* for *compound,* *CX* for *complex,* or *CC* for *compound-complex.*

Example ___CX___ **1.** In my opinion, bridges are some of the most lovely structures that people build.

_____ **1.** Although bridges are built for practical purposes, many bridges are not only useful but also beautiful.

_____ **2.** Old-fashioned covered bridges can still be seen in some parts of the country, chiefly in New England.

_____ **3.** These bridges were not intended to be objects of art, but many people today consider them very lovely.

_____ **4.** The simple lines and the weathered wood of a covered bridge go well with its rustic surroundings.

_____ **5.** Those who design modern bridges take both usefulness and beauty into account.

_____ **6.** The Brooklyn Bridge, which was opened in 1883, was one of the first steel suspension bridges in the United States.

_____ **7.** Not only was the Brooklyn Bridge the longest suspension bridge of its time, but it was also one of the most artistically pleasing.

_____ **8.** The bridge was recognized as an artistic triumph even before it was completed, and it quickly became a favorite subject for painters and photographers.

_____ **9.** Many suspension bridges built during the twentieth century employ structural principles that were developed by the designer of the Brooklyn Bridge.

_____ **10.** Two of the best-known suspension bridges of recent times are San Francisco's Golden Gate Bridge and New York's Verrazzano-Narrows Bridge.

Review D: **The Clause**

EXERCISE Classify each of the following sentences according to structure by writing on the line provided *S* for *simple*, *CD* for *compound*, *CX* for *complex*, or *CC* for *compound-complex*. Then, underscore any subordinate clauses in the sentence.

Example _____CX_____ **1.** Tennis stars usually get their start <u>when they are fairly young</u>.

_____ **1.** Because tennis is so physically demanding, it's a sport in which strong young players can really shine.

_____ **2.** Steffi Graf of Germany began playing tennis professionally at the age of thirteen.

_____ **3.** Graf was still a teenager when she won four Grand Slam tennis championships and an Olympic gold medal.

_____ **4.** Another Olympic winner, Zina Garrison Jackson, began playing tennis in Houston at the age of ten, and at seventeen, she won the junior singles titles at Wimbledon and at the U.S. Open.

_____ **5.** The German tennis star Boris Becker won his first tournament competitions at the age of nine, but he didn't become a professional player until he graduated from high school.

_____ **6.** Michael Chang, who in 1989 became the youngest player to rank in the Top 5, won many national and international tennis competitions.

_____ **7.** Another American player, Andre Agassi, started serving on a tennis court at the age of two, and he, too, excelled at an early age.

_____ **8.** Agassi won six important tournaments when he was only eighteen.

_____ **9.** Tracy Austin and Chris Evert also started young; in fact, Tracy Austin was only sixteen years old when she made headlines by winning the women's title at the U.S. Open.

_____ **10.** In tennis, young players really can become big winners.

for **CHAPTER 4: THE CLAUSE**   pages 93–97

Literary Model: Narrative

> I went back to the Devon School not long ago, and found it looking oddly newer than when I was a student there fifteen years before. It seemed more sedate than I remembered it, more perpendicular and straight-laced, with narrower windows and shinier woodwork, as though a coat of varnish had been put over everything for better preservation. But, of course, fifteen years before there had been a war going on. . . .
>
> I didn't entirely like this glossy new surface, because it made the school look like a museum, and that's exactly what it was to me, and what I did not want it to be. In the deep, tacit way in which feeling becomes stronger than thought, I had always felt that the Devon School came into existence the day I entered it, was vibrantly real while I was a student there, and then blinked out like a candle the day I left.
>
> —from *A Separate Peace*, by John Knowles

EXERCISE A   In the passage above, underline the three adjective clauses once and underline the five adverb clauses twice. (Hint: The relative pronoun *that* has been omitted from some of the sentences.)

EXERCISE B

1. Rewrite one of the passages. Restructure each sentence so that, if at all possible, it no longer includes adjective or adverb clauses. Your rewritten passage may have a different number of sentences than the original.

_____

_____

_____

_____

_____

_____

_____

_____

From *A Separate Peace* by John Knowles. Copyright © 1960 by John Knowles.
Reprinted by permission of **Curtis Brown, Ltd.**

Literary Model (continued)

2. How does your rewritten passage compare with the original?

_____

_____

_____

_____

EXERCISE C Write a paragraph in which you describe a real or imagined visit to a place that is part of your past. Use adjective and adverb clauses in your paragraph. Underline each adverb clause once and each adjective clause twice.

_____

_____

_____

_____

_____

_____

_____

_____

_____

_____

_____

_____

_____

EXERCISE D What effect does the use of adjective and adverb clauses have on your paragraph?

_____

_____

_____

_____

_____

for **CHAPTER 4: THE CLAUSE** pages 93–97

Writing Application: Directions

Adjective and adverb clauses can really help you improve your writing by allowing you to combine related ideas into a single sentence. They also allow you to express details. An adjective clause typically gives additional information about a noun or a pronoun. Similarly, an adverb clause gives details about how, when, where, why, to what extent, or under what condition something occurs. If you use these clauses effectively, your writing will read more smoothly and won't seem choppy.

ADJECTIVE CLAUSE	The player **who reaches the black triangle first** wins the game.
ADVERB CLAUSE	**When neither player can advance,** each one draws a card from the center pile.

WRITING ACTIVITY

You are going to create a board game and write the directions that others will use to play the game. If you like, you may base your game on a board game that is familiar to you; however, the game you devise should have a different focus. You may prefer to create an entirely new game. In your directions, include at least three adjective clauses and three adverb clauses.

PREWRITING First, decide on the topic of your board game and what the objective of the game will be. Make a rough sketch of what the board will look like, and decide on the number of players, the necessary equipment, and the rules of the game.

WRITING As you write each part of the directions, imagine that you are a player who is about to play the game for the first time. Define terms that might be unknown to anyone playing the game. Consider using an informal, conversational tone for the directions.

REVISING Ask a classmate to look at the sketch you made and to read your game directions. Ask for feedback about how you can make the directions clearer. After revising the directions as needed, ask two or more classmates to play the game. Observe them as they play, noting any problems they have with the directions. Then, revise them again as needed. Be sure that you have included at least three adjective clauses and three adverb clauses in the directions.

PUBLISHING Proofread your game directions line by line for errors in grammar, usage, spelling, and punctuation. Pay special attention to your use of relative pronouns and to the punctuation of each subordinate clause. Finally, develop your rough sketch into a usable game that classmates, friends, and family can play.

EXTENDING YOUR WRITING

Present your game to a community organization that serves children or adolescents.

Language and Sentence Skills Practice

Choices: Exploring Agreement in the Real World

The following activities challenge you to find a connection between agreement and the world around you. Do the activity below that suits your personality best, and then share your discoveries with your class.

MUSIC
You Don't Say You Sing

Just about every musician keeps a few strange and funny songs in his or her hip pocket, ready to bring out at the proper moment. Write a humorous song featuring the linguistic problems of agreement. Then, with your teacher's permission, tape or play it for the class.

DRAMA
One, Not Two

Compound subjects joined by *or* can be confusing. After all, compound subjects name two or more nouns or pronouns, so these subjects seem plural, but they aren't always treated as such. Help your classmates see why compound subjects joined by *or* sometimes require a singular verb. Write four or five such sentences. Then, ask permission to act them out for the class. You'll need at least three people—a reader and two performers.

VIDEOGRAPHY
Crime Show

You are the host of a crime show. Your object is to show a dramatic reenactment of a vicious crime (or two or three) against the English language. The perpetrators come from all walks of life. They have but one thing in common—the abuse of our beloved language. Don't let them get away with it! Inform the public about their crimes. Videotape your show, and get approval to screen it for the class. Be sure to include mug shots of the suspects.

PHOTOGRAPHY
Credit Where Credit Is Due

Go on a photo scavenger hunt to find subjects and verbs that agree. Look on trucks, in newspaper ads, on signs and marquees, and in other public places. Take pictures of these agreeing subjects and verbs. Then, design a certificate of appreciation to award to the businesses that set such a good example.

REFLECTION
All for Nothing

What's the use of identifying your own usage errors if you don't learn from them? It's all for nothing! Turn your errors into opportunities! Keep a running list of the errors that you make in writing. After a while, you'll notice certain patterns. Then, formulate a checklist for proofreading for usage errors, and share it with your classmates.

ART HISTORY
Sunflowers

Many paintings and sculptures have a plural noun for their title. How many can you name? Go to the library and check out a few art books. Find a dozen or so paintings, sculptures, or other art forms that have titles that are plural in form. The title may be two or more nouns joined by a conjunction or a plural noun that may or may not be modified by a phrase. For each appropriate title, write a sentence in which you use a singular pronoun to refer to the title. For instance, you might write "Van Gogh's famous *Sunflowers* uses yellow as its primary color." While you still have the library books or prints, show the paintings and sculptures you chose to the class while you read the sentences you wrote.

WRITING
People People

People people like people. More or less, everyone is a people person. Think about a few people in your life. Make a list of the things each does. Then, compare these people by writing fifteen sentences. Each one will have a compound subject. Five of your sentences will use *and* to join the subjects. Five will use *or*. The last five will use *nor*. For example, you might write "Mom and Dad like to jog" or "Neither Mom nor Dad enjoys gardening." You get the picture.

Number

A word that refers to one person, place, thing, or idea is *singular* in number. A word that refers to more than one is *plural* in number. In general, nouns ending in –*s* are plural, and verbs ending in –*s* are singular.

SINGULAR	sandwich	she	wolf	family	makes	is	goes
PLURAL	sandwiches	they	wolves	families	make	are	go

EXERCISE A   On the lines provided, write *S* if the noun or pronoun is singular or write *P* if it is plural.

Examples __P__ **1.** catalogs

__S__ **2.** it

_____ **1.** country

_____ **2.** building

_____ **3.** raspberries

_____ **4.** radio

_____ **5.** him

_____ **6.** geese

_____ **7.** valley

_____ **8.** both

_____ **9.** neighborhood

_____ **10.** women

_____ **11.** address

_____ **12.** benches

_____ **13.** children

_____ **14.** speech

_____ **15.** courage

_____ **16.** us

_____ **17.** donkeys

_____ **18.** himself

_____ **19.** boxes

_____ **20.** press

EXERCISE B   Above the underlined verb, write *S* if the verb is singular or *P* if it is plural.

Example 1. The Morris brothers have <u>become</u> talented tennis players.

21. Many of the citizens <u>agree</u> with the platform of the candidate.

22. Someone <u>has suggested</u> several good ideas for new uses of the old factory.

23. A print of a painting by Picasso <u>hangs</u> in the city library.

24. All of the women on the panel <u>were given</u> equal time to speak.

25. Theodore von Kármán, a leading aeronautics engineer, <u>was born</u> in Hungary.

26. Two senators from every state <u>serve</u> in the U.S. Congress.

27. Lukas and I <u>have</u> tickets to the Seurat exhibit at the Metropolitan Museum.

28. One of the gases in the earth's atmosphere <u>is</u> argon.

29. The President <u>was scheduling</u> another trip to Japan.

30. Salt and sand on the roadways often <u>damage</u> the undersides of cars.

Language and Sentence Skills Practice

USAGE

Subject-Verb Agreement A

5a.	A verb should agree in number with its subject.

(1) Singular subjects take singular verbs.
(2) Plural subjects take plural verbs.

SINGULAR SUBJECT AND VERB   **Spike Lee is** a talented movie director.
    PLURAL SUBJECT AND VERB   His **films are** noteworthy.

(3) The number of a subject usually is not determined by a word in a phrase or clause following the subject.
(4) A negative construction following the subject does not change the number of the subject.

EXAMPLES   The **actors** in Lee's film **are rehearsing** a scene.
           Lee, not one of the acting coaches, **has been advising** them.

EXERCISE A   In each of the following sentences, the verb agrees with its subject. Next to each sentence number, write *S* if the subject and verb are singular. Write *P* if the subject and verb are plural.

Example   *S*   **1.** This book of poems is one of my favorite possessions.

1. Gwendolyn Brooks was an award-winning African American poet.

2. For several years she served as the poet laureate of Illinois.

3. Many poems by Brooks express anger for the injustice of racial discrimination.

4. Two volumes of her poetry are *Annie Allen* and *A Street in Bronzeville*.

5. One day I hope to be as eloquent a poet as Gwendolyn Brooks.

EXERCISE B   In the following sentences, underline the verb in parentheses that agrees with the subject.

Example   **1.** These maps, not the globe, (<u>contain</u>, contains) the needed details.

6. The city of Buenos Aires (*is, are*) the capital of Argentina.

7. Today, almost nine million citizens (*lives, live*) in the city and its environs.

8. When I (*visit, visits*) Buenos Aires, I will want to see Plaza de Mayo.

9. The historic building Casa Rosada (*stands, stand*) there.

10. The offices of Argentina's president (*is, are*) housed within.

11. The land area of Argentina (*cover, covers*) over a million square miles.

12. This country of scrubland, swamps, and plains (*stretch, stretches*) 2,360 miles from north to south.

13. The width of the country from east to west (*is, are*) only about 884 miles.

14. Some people who look at Argentina on a map (*see, sees*) a triangular-shaped country.

15. The widest part of Argentina, the longest of the triangle's sides, (*form, forms*) the northern part of the country.

Subject-Verb Agreement B

| **5a.** | A verb should agree in number with its subject. |

(1) Singular subjects take singular verbs.
(2) Plural subjects take plural verbs.

SINGULAR SUBJECT AND VERB An **article** about insecticides **is** in today's paper.

PLURAL SUBJECT AND VERB The **players** from Miami **compete** in our league.

(3) The number of a subject usually is not determined by a word in a phrase or clause following the subject.
(4) A negative construction following the subject does not change the number of the subject.

EXAMPLES **Danny Glover,** along with Kevin Kline, **appears** in this movie.

The **coach,** not the team members, **chooses** the captain.

EXERCISE A In each of the following sentences, underline the verb in parentheses that agrees with the subject.

Example 1. The front counter, in addition to the tables, *(is, are)* in need of a good cleaning.

1. The short stories in this collection *(is, are)* mysteries.

2. The star of the play, as well as the chorus members, *(was, were)* rehearsing.

3. Three letters by Thomas Edison *(was, were)* donated to the museum.

4. The daffodils, not the dogwood tree, *(is, are)* in full bloom now.

5. A survey of the voters *(indicates, indicate)* their opinions on the issue.

6. Crushed leaves from the verbena plant *(makes, make)* a flavorful tea.

7. Lake Erie, along with Lake Superior and Lake Huron, *(is, are)* very deep.

8. A tax on both income and property *(was, were)* debated by the city council.

9. Immigrants from China *(was, were)* a major force in the building of the railroad.

10. Several dogs, but not one cat, *(was, were)* inoculated against rabies at the clinic.

EXERCISE B Most of the sentences in the following paragraph contain errors in the agreement between subject and verb. Cross out each incorrect verb. Above the error, write the correct form of the verb.

Example Ella Fitzgerald, not Janet Jackson or Jewel, ~~are~~ *is* my favorite female singer.

The late Ella Fitzgerald, of all American jazz singers, are perhaps the most popular. Her remarkable abilities at improvisation were the source of her worldwide acclaim. Her first record-ings of jazz music was made in 1938. Fitzgerald, along with such other African American female singers as Billie Holiday, were at that time the source of fame for Big Bands. Fitzgerald, more than all other singers, have inspired me to pursue a career in music.

Language and Sentence Skills Practice

USAGE

USAGE

Indefinite Pronouns A

An *indefinite pronoun* refers to a person, a place, a thing, or an idea that may or may not be specifically named.

| **5b.** | Some indefinite pronouns are singular; others are plural. Certain indefinite pronouns may be either singular or plural, depending on how they are used. |

> SINGULAR   **No one knows** the answer.   **Most** of the article **is** interesting.
>
> PLURAL   **Several have submitted** paintings.   **Most** of his articles **are** interesting.

EXERCISE   Above the indefinite pronoun in each sentence, write *S* if it is singular or *P* if it is plural. Then, underline the correct form of the verb in parentheses.

Example **1.** Everyone who likes vegetables *(enjoy, enjoys)* this meal.

1. Neither of the candidates *(has, have)* run for office before.

2. Most of the soup *(was, were)* gone.

3. None of the athletes *(was, were)* tired after the tournament.

4. A few of the volunteers for the job *(was, were)* selected.

5. *(Have, Has)* all of the cheese been eaten?

6. Someone from your fan club *(is, are)* waiting at the stage door.

7. None of the rain *(has, have)* seeped into the basement.

8. *(Is, Are)* either of the movies available on video?

9. Everyone, including the movie critics, *(raves, rave)* about her latest movie.

10. Everybody in the meeting *(agrees, agree)* with your position.

11. Some of the cookies *(has, have)* a filling of strawberry jam.

12. *(Has, Have)* anyone calculated the circumference of this circle?

13. Few of the items on the shelf *(was, were)* marked with prices.

14. *(Do, Does)* many of Jason's friends know about the surprise party?

15. All of the students in tenth grade *(was, were)* invited to the job fair.

16. *(Was, Were)* any of the varnish spilled on the carpet?

17. Somebody *(have, has)* already borrowed the camera from the equipment room.

18. Nothing *(surprise, surprises)* me anymore.

19. Each of the contest entries *(is, are)* evaluated by a panel of trained judges.

20. Everything in my locker *(smell, smells)* like the cologne I spilled in there.

Indefinite Pronouns B

An *indefinite pronoun* refers to a person, a place, a thing, or an idea that may or may not be specifically named.

5b. Some indefinite pronouns are singular; others are plural. Certain indefinite pronouns may be either singular or plural, depending on how they are used.

SINGULAR	**Everybody likes** Coach Wynn.	**None** of the song **was** familiar.
PLURAL	**Few know** of the job opening.	**None** of the songs **were** familiar.

EXERCISE A Complete each of the following sentences by adding an indefinite pronoun that agrees with the verb.

Example 1. Unfortunately, _____*none*_____ of the quiche is left.

1. _____ of the children was interested in swimming.

2. Does _____ want my peanut butter sandwich?

3. _____ of the students were surprised at the results of the experiment.

4. Has _____ submitted a vote for class officers?

5. _____ of Terry's friends know how to sculpt with clay.

6. _____ in the backyard has been rattling in the wind.

7. _____ of the sisters have taken flute lessons for years.

8. Do _____ of you know when the pep rally starts?

9. During the basketball game, _____ of the snacks and drinks were sold.

10. _____ of my research is finished now, but I haven't begun writing the paper.

EXERCISE B Some of the following sentences contain errors in the agreement between indefinite pronouns and verbs. Cross out each incorrect verb form. Above it, write the correct form of the verb. If a sentence is already correct, write *C* after it.

Example 1. I looked for my contact lenses, but both ~~is~~ *are* lost.

11. Is any of these CDs by Natalie Cole?

12. Several of us is going to the dance together in a limousine.

13. Neither of the horses are available to ride.

14. None of the runners were on the track yet.

15. One of the large pieces of cantaloupe are enough to satisfy my sweet tooth.

USAGE

USAGE

Compound Subjects A

5c.	Subjects joined by *and* generally take a plural verb.
5d.	Singular subjects joined by *or* or *nor* take a singular verb. Plural subjects joined by *or* or *nor* take a plural verb.
5e.	When a singular subject and a plural subject are joined by *or* or *nor*, the verb agrees with the subject nearer the verb.

> **EXAMPLES** **Peru** and **Chile are** South American countries.
>
> Either the **battery** or the **starter needs** replacement.
>
> Neither the **Hendersons** nor the **Chongs want** to attend the concert.
>
> Neither the **players** nor the **coach agrees** with the referee's call.
>
> Neither the **coach** nor the **players agree** with the referee's call.

EXERCISE A Underline the verb in parentheses that agrees with the compound subject of the sentence.

Example 1. Neither Sandy nor John *(appear, appears)* in this skit.

1. The producer and director of *Schindler's List (was, were)* Steven Spielberg.

2. Eight crew members and a captain *(was, were)* hired for the cruise.

3. Neither her manuscript nor her research notes *(was, were)* lost in the fire.

4. Coach Anderson or Ms. Teele *(is, are)* presenting the next award.

5. Rice and beans *(are, is)* her favorite meal.

EXERCISE B Some of these sentences contain subjects and verbs that do not agree in number. Other sentences are awkward constructions. Revise the sentences to make them clear and correct.

Example 1. Neither steak nor pasta are on my grocery list. *Neither steak nor pasta is on my*
grocery list.

6. Either Elena or one of her sisters are entering tomorrow's marathon. _____

_____

7. Neither the tools nor the lumber fits into the back of the van. _____

_____

8. My voice coach and greatest supporter are Miriam Goldstein. _____

_____

9. Neither the rain nor the music were a great addition to our picnic. _____

_____

10. Does the juniors or the seniors share your lunch period? _____

_____

Compound Subjects B

5c.	Subjects joined by *and* generally take a plural verb.
5d.	Singular subjects joined by *or* or *nor* take a singular verb. Plural subjects joined by *or* or *nor* take a plural verb.
5e.	When a singular subject and a plural subject are joined by *or* or *nor,* the verb agrees with the subject nearer the verb.

EXAMPLES **Baseball** and **soccer are** Simon's favorite sports.

Neither the **president** nor the **vice president** is at the press conference.

Either **bobcats** or **wild boars appear** in the new documentary.

Either **pizza** or **sandwiches are** served at the study group.

Either **sandwiches** or **pizza is** served at the study group.

EXERCISE A Underline the verb in parentheses that agrees with the compound subject of the sentence.

Example 1. Natural disasters and shipwrecks (*fascinate, fascinates*) many people.

1. Facts and a good photograph (*teach, teaches*) us about disasters.

2. In science class, my friends and I (*is, are*) reading about disasters.

3. Each day either Mr. Simms or students (*present, presents*) information on a disaster.

4. A tornado and a tidal wave (*is, are*) classified as natural disasters.

5. Earthquakes and floods (*fall, falls*) into the same category.

6. Either an avalanche or a rock slide (*make, makes*) a good research topic.

7. A shipwreck or a plane crash (*is, are*) a disaster, but not a natural disaster.

8. Neither the captain nor the passengers (*expect, expects*) a shipwreck.

9. Watery graves and underwater treasure (*is, are*) discussed in this book.

10. The book's writer and photographer (*is, are*) Dr. Jimenez.

EXERCISE B In the following sentences, cross out any verb that does not agree with its subject. Above the verb, write the correct verb form. Write *C* above the verb if it already agrees with its compound subject.

Example 1. Either a ticket or a season pass ~~are~~ needed for admittance.
is

11. Thrilling rides and a tall roller coaster makes this amusement park enjoyable.

12. Either the water rides or the new roller coaster are down that path.

13. Neither Roger nor the twins want to ride the tallest roller coaster.

14. Ted and Natalie is going to the food court.

15. Two drinks or a sandwich cost about the same.

Language and Sentence Skills Practice

USAGE

USAGE

Other Problems in Agreement A

5f. Collective nouns may be either singular or plural, depending on their meaning in a sentence.

> **SINGULAR** The **jury** has reached a verdict.
>
> **PLURAL** The **jury are** in agreement.

EXERCISE A In the following sentences, underline the verb in parentheses that agrees with the collective noun.

Example 1. The audience *(is, are)* slowly finding their seats in the theater.

1. A troop of Boy Scouts *(is, are)* a welcome sight to a lost hiker.

2. During the past month, the army *(has, have)* run advertisements on television.

3. A swarm of bees *(is, are)* in the hollow log over there.

4. The visiting band *(is, are)* staying with families of our own band.

5. The choir *(meet, meets)* for practice at seven o'clock.

6. Beside the pond in the pasture, the herd of cows *(is, are)* waiting for the rancher to bring them hay.

7. The class *(was, were)* introduced to its state representative.

8. In dance class the group *(divide, divides)* into pairs for the warm-up exercise.

9. The assembly *(is, are)* invited to cast their votes for treasurer.

10. The public *(voice, voices)* its opinion by voting in elections.

EXERCISE B In the following sentences, cross out each incorrect verb form and write the correct verb form above it. If a sentence is already correct, write *C* above the verb.

Example 1. ~~Is~~ *Are* the choir selling their raffle tickets as a fund-raiser?

11. The faculty is in their classrooms.

12. My whole family were eager to meet its new neighbors.

13. A large number has received their rebates in the mail.

14. The softball team is working in pairs during today's practice.

15. The jury is silently filing one by one into the jury box.

16. The club welcome Ms. Perez, our guest speaker.

17. Is staff given discounts on supplies?

18. A majority of the students have met with their guidance counselors.

19. A flock of geese are flying overhead.

20. The local police squad protects the entire neighborhood.

for **CHAPTER 5: AGREEMENT**   page 122

Other Problems in Agreement B

5g. A verb agrees with its subject but not necessarily with a predicate nominative.

                                S   PN

    EXAMPLE   Our leading **crop is blueberries.**

5h. When the subject follows the verb, find the subject and make sure that the verb agrees with it.

    EXAMPLE   Here **is** a **bowl** of soup.

EXERCISE A   In the following sentences, underline the subject. If the subject and verb do not agree, cross out the incorrect verb form and write the correct form above it. If the verb already agrees with the subject, write *C* above the verb.

                                     are

Example 1. There ~~is~~ four place <u>settings</u> on the dining table.

1. Chelsea and Juan was the favorite couple at the dance.

2. Here is the beads for the handmade bracelet.

3. The winners are a secret until the ceremony.

4. When is the times for the school play auditions?

5. There are several reasons for my admiration of my mom.

6. The walls of the house is adobe.

7. What's the results of your talk with Joey?

8. The late-night "intruder" were only Dave and Phillip.

9. Where are my box of oil paints?

10. The doctor's first priority was the patients in the waiting room.

EXERCISE B   In the following sentences, cross out any verb that does not agree with its subject. Then, write the correct form of the verb above the incorrect form.

                         are

Example   Where ~~is~~ the hills where the treasure is buried?

    There's rumors about treasure buried in the hills behind my house. Long ago in the Old West, when bandits on horseback was a part of life, bandits rode through this area. Here are a book of stories about events from that time. The stories in the book is fiction, of course, but they are inspired by rumors of actual events. There is three hills behind my house—do you see them out the window? A chest of gold and gems are what I believe is hidden there. Here's maps of the area, and they show a cave in the tallest hill. As the rumor goes, this cave were the living quarters for three bandits. They hid their treasure chest in the cave one night. Unfortunately for them, jail cells was their home the next night! The bandits were captured, but there were no evidence of their treasure. It has never been found.

Language and Sentence Skills Practice

Other Problems in Agreement C

5i. An expression of an amount (a measurement, a percentage, or a fraction, for example) may be singular or plural, depending on how it is used.

> **EXAMPLES** **Ten dollars was** the price. Ten **dollars were** scattered across the room.
> **Fifteen percent** of the check **is** a fair tip. **Fifteen percent** of the members **are** in agreement.

EXERCISE A Underline the verb in parentheses that agrees with the expression of an amount.

Example 1. Three dollars (*was*, *were*) lying on the table.

1. Fifty percent of the tables (*is*, *are*) occupied.

2. Two years (*is*, *are*) the length of time I saved up for my car.

3. Three fourths of the painting (*was*, *were*) completed yesterday.

4. Four quarts (*make*, *makes*) a gallon.

5. Forty-five minutes (*is*, *are*) the length of one class period.

6. During the sale, thirty percent (*is*, *are*) marked off the prices.

7. Five gallons of paint (*is*, *are*) the right amount for painting my room.

8. Two cups of peeled, sliced apples (*fill*, *fills*) the bowl.

9. Three days (*is*, *are*) plenty of time to finish the work.

10. Seventy percent of the students (*want*, *wants*) a longer lunch period.

EXERCISE B Cross out any verb that does not agree with the expression of an amount. Write the correct verb form above the incorrect form. If the verb is already correct, write *C* above the verb.

Example 1. Ninety minutes ~~are~~ the length of the movie.
is

11. Three quarters of the flour have been added to the cake batter.

12. Around four years are needed to earn a typical college degree.

13. Five kilometers is the distance between your ranch and the nearest town.

14. Two pints fill a one-quart jar.

15. Two months of her vacation was quite warm: June and July.

16. Two thirds of the fruit salad are eaten already.

17. Three hours are enough time for test preparation.

18. The number of candidates for class president is surprisingly large.

19. Six dollars is neatly arranged on the table.

20. Sixteen ounces equal one pound.

Other Problems in Agreement D

| **5j.** | When the relative pronoun *that, which,* or *who* is the subject in an adjective clause, the verb in the clause agrees with the word to which the relative pronoun refers. |

EXAMPLES The actors from our school **who are performing** today are Mattie and Phoebe.

The actors from a school **that is** across town are Carlos and Ronny.

| **5k.** | A subject preceded by *every* or *many a(n)* takes a singular verb. |

EXAMPLES **Every** student and teacher **was applauding.**

Many a cheer **was heard.**

EXERCISE A In the following sentences, underline the correct verb in parentheses.

Example 1. Mimes are a type of entertainer who (*perform, performs*) without speaking.

1. Many a young person (*enjoy, enjoys*) the charming performance of mimes.

2. Kevin is the only one of my friends who (*have, has*) not seen a live performance.

3. Every act and skit of the mime (*centers, center*) on gesture, movement, and expression.

4. Actors from the silent film era who (*was, were*) mimes include Charlie Chaplin and Ben Turpin.

5. Entertainers such as the circus clown, who (*is, are*) known for nonverbal performance, are a kind of mime.

6. Emmett Kelly is one of those circus clowns who (*is, are*) hard to forget.

7. Many a child and parent (*has, have*) seen Emmett Kelly or a clown like him.

8. Television entertainers, who (*is, are*) generally quite vocal, can also be mimes.

9. The entertainer Sid Caesar, who (*was, were*) a master mime, had a television show in the 1950s.

10. Every student and practitioner of mime (*is, are*) sure to know about Marcel Marceau.

EXERCISE B In the following sentences if the verb does not agree with its subject, cross out the incorrect verb form and write the correct form above it. If the verb already agrees with the subject, write *C* above the verb.

Example 1. The films in the class that ~~are~~ *is* on film history included a clip of Marceau.

11. The French mime Marcel Marceau, who was born in 1923, performs with graceful simplicity.

12. He studied at the School of Dramatic Art of the Sarah Bernhardt Theatre, which are in Paris.

13. Every fan and film student surely recognize his much-loved character Bip.

14. A group of mimes and Marceau, who were their leader, formed a mime troupe.

15. In the 1950s, many a country around the world were host to Marceau's mime group.

Other Problems in Agreement E

5l. The contractions *don't* and *doesn't* should agree with their subjects.

> **EXAMPLES** **You don't** enjoy wrestling matches.
> **He doesn't** have a ticket.

EXERCISE A In the following sentences, underline the correct contraction in parentheses.

Example 1. You (<u>*don't*</u>, *doesn't*) know much about the Holocaust either, do you?

1. Maria (*don't*, *doesn't*) know much about the Holocaust either.

2. Many teenagers (*don't*, *doesn't*) read or learn about this part of history.

3. I (*don't*, *doesn't*) want to be uninformed about crucial historical events.

4. A curious person (*don't*, *doesn't*) have to learn from history books alone.

5. People who (*don't*, *doesn't*) read textbooks may enjoy reading historical fiction or biography.

6. Skillful authors (*don't*, *doesn't*) include information that is not factual.

7. (*Don't*, *Doesn't*) miss *The Devil's Arithmetic* by Jane Yolen.

8. Readers of *We Are Witnesses,* a collection of teenagers' diary entries, (*don't*, *doesn't*) want to put the book down.

9. My friend Andrew (*don't*, *doesn't*) often read about history, but he enjoyed these two books.

10. Sometimes on a Saturday afternoon, we (*don't*, *doesn't*) go outside; we read instead.

EXERCISE B In the following sentences, if the form of *don't/doesn't* does not agree with its subject, cross it out and write the correct form above the error. If the sentence is already correct, write *C* above the contraction.

Example 1. Why ~~doesn't~~ ^{don't} you take the day off work?

11. "Friends doesn't keep secrets from one another," said Matthew.

12. Rainy days don't depress me in the least.

13. Fortunately, Mom don't suspect the surprise birthday party.

14. You doesn't have to drive; I will.

15. The football players doesn't have another game until next Friday.

16. Mr. Rodriguez, I doesn't mind mowing your lawn along with my own.

17. Why doesn't clocks run counterclockwise?

18. Some birds don't fly south for the winter.

19. For the party tonight, Antoine don't have any rap CDs.

20. The newspaper don't have a report of the fire at the waffle house.

for **CHAPTER 5: AGREEMENT**   pages 126–27

Other Problems in Agreement F

| **5m.** | Some nouns that are plural in form take singular verbs. |

> **EXAMPLES**   **Genetics teaches** us about heredity. **Is** the **news** on yet?

| **5n.** | Even when plural in form, the title of a creative work (such as a book, song, movie, or painting) generally takes a singular verb. |

| **5o.** | Even when plural in form, the name of a country, a city, or an organization generally takes a singular verb. |

> **EXAMPLES**   *Star Wars* **was directed** by George Lucas. **Computer Works is** on Main Street.

EXERCISE   In the following sentences, cross out any verb that does not agree with its subject. Above the verb, write the correct form of the verb. If the sentence is already correct, write *C* above the verb.

Example 1. ~~Is~~ *Are* your new pants marked "dry clean only"?

1. *Lord of the Flies* were my favorite book last year.

2. New Braunfels are a town on the Guadalupe River in Texas.

3. Molasses are delicious in homemade gingerbread.

4. "Free Fantasia: Tiger Flowers" contain memorable phrases such as "paradise of ironies."

5. *The Birds* are a 1963 film directed by Alfred Hitchcock.

6. Mathematics challenge me to think creatively about solving problems.

7. My eyeglasses are smudged from the dog's enthusiastic greeting.

8. Is electronics Mike's specialty?

9. Copies and Parcels are advertising student rates on photocopies.

10. The United States is part of North America.

11. Global news are on at 6:00 each morning and at 10:00 each night.

12. *Buffaloes in Combat* was painted in India in the late sixteenth century.

13. Are civics being offered in this high school every term?

14. Of all sporting events, the Olympics is the most exciting to watch.

15. "The Hills," by George Oppen, are written in first and second person.

16. "Old Times" is one of the songs on a CD by Stevie Ray Vaughan and Albert King.

17. Gymnastics are my passion.

18. Are pliers the right tool for this project?

19. Diego Rivera's *The Riches of California* are quite large, measuring 22 by 13 feet.

20. Expensive binoculars hangs around the neck of the coast guard captain.

Language and Sentence Skills Practice

USAGE

Pronoun-Antecedent Agreement: Number and Gender

5p.   A pronoun should agree in both number and gender with its antecedent.

(1) Use singular pronouns to refer to singular antecedents. Use plural pronouns to refer to plural antecedents.

> **EXAMPLES**   **Henry Aaron** ended **his** remarkable career in baseball in 1976.
>
> The **players** on the field celebrated **their** victory.

(2) Some singular pronouns indicate *gender*—*masculine, feminine,* or *neuter* (neither masculine nor feminine).

> **EXAMPLES**   Did **Jenny** leave **her** basketball in the gym? The **ball** has lost most of **its** air.

EXERCISE   Circle the antecedent in each sentence, and underline the pronoun in parentheses that agrees with it.

Example 1. Where did your (brothers) buy *(his, their)* new skis?

1. The volleyball players are getting *(her, their)* new jerseys today.

2. The maintenance worker swept the surface of the court and then polished *(it, him)*.

3. When Sandra decided to try out for cheerleader, *(she, it)* began practicing immediately.

4. Before practice began, the swimmers talked among *(himself, themselves)*.

5. The soccer team's bus has messages written in shoe polish on *(their, its)* windows.

6. I spoke to Aaron, and *(he, they)* will be happy to be the team's pitcher.

7. At the sporting goods store, Megan selected new tennis balls and a hat for *(itself, herself)*.

8. Leon and Marcos committed *(themselves, himself)* to a daily three-mile run.

9. When I saw Oscar and Phina near the soccer field, I called out to *(it, them)*.

10. After the rock climbers checked the equipment, *(he, they)* began the steep ascent.

11. The basketball hoop outside has icicles hanging from *(its, their)* rim.

12. When I last saw Katrina, *(they, she)* was over by the batting cages.

13. During the game the girls on the other team looked to *(their, her)* coach for direction.

14. Centerville High's students have dedicated *(itself, themselves)* to preserving the environment.

15. Kyle has made a good reputation for *(itself, himself)* as team captain.

16. Eric decided not to play football this year; instead, *(he, they)* will play golf.

17. Because the scoreboard wasn't working properly, Mr. Ruiz repaired *(them, it)*.

18. If you want to borrow Mindy's tennis racket, you'll have to ask *(her, it)* yourself.

19. Jamal was proud that *(it, he)* made the tie-breaking point.

20. The team's mascot, an articulate parrot, often talks to *(themselves, itself)*.

Pronoun-Antecedent Agreement: Indefinite Pronouns

5q. Indefinite pronouns agree with their antecedents according to the following rules.

(1) The indefinite pronouns *anybody, anyone, anything, each, either, everybody, everyone, everything, neither, nobody, no one, nothing, one, somebody, someone,* and *something* are singular.

> **EXAMPLE** **Each** of the police officers has received **his** or **her** duty assignment.

(2) The indefinite pronouns *both, few, many,* and *several* are plural.

(3) The indefinite pronouns *all, any, more, most, none,* and *some* may be singular or plural, depending on how they are used in a sentence.

> **EXAMPLES** **Many** of the students turned **their** reports in early.
>
> **All** of the paint is new; do you like **it**?   **All** of the rugs are new; do you like **them**?

EXERCISE Circle the indefinite pronoun in each sentence. Then, underline the pronoun or pronoun group in parentheses that agrees with it.

Example 1. (Some) of the employees planned a birthday party for (*his or her,* _their_) boss.

1. Everything in the bargain bin should have (*its, their*) original price tag removed.

2. Some of the cookies had tooth marks on (*it, them*).

3. One of the campers on the father-son camping trip shared (*his, their*) food with me.

4. All of the flower bed was overgrown, so I bent down to weed (*it, them*).

5. Something lay on the sidewalk near the mailboxes, and (*it, they*) sparkled in the sun.

6. Either of the girls in our carpool could have left (*her, their*) backpack in our car.

7. Since some of the music sounded familiar, I knew I had heard (*it, them*) before.

8. I saw that most of the sodas and sports drinks listed sugar in (*its, their*) ingredients.

9. Few of the boxes in the supply closet have labels on (*them, it*).

10. Many of the pipes were not protected from the cold weather, so (*it, they*) froze.

11. Most of the stones had unique patterns and textures on (*their, its*) surfaces.

12. Everybody voted for (*his or her, their*) favorite performer in the talent show.

13. Both of the trees in front of the school have begun losing (*its, their*) leaves for the winter.

14. Some of the pastries are homemade by Jitu, who delivers (*it, them*) each morning.

15. All of the bookcases in the library have Dewey decimal numbers marked on (*it, them*).

16. None of the volunteers at the hospital had met (*his or her, their*) new director yet.

17. Most of the money had writing on (*them, it*).

18. Any of my friends could have given me the note during (*their, his or her*) break.

19. Several of the authors were available to autograph copies of (*their, his or her*) books.

20. Neither of my cats will let (*itself, themselves*) be petted by strangers.

Language and Sentence Skills Practice

USAGE

Pronoun-Antecedent Agreement: Compound Subjects

5r. Pronouns agree with compound antecedents according to the following rules.

(1) Use a plural pronoun to refer to two or more antecedents joined by *and*.

Note that antecedents joined by *and* that name only one person, place, thing, or idea take singular pronouns.

(2) Use a singular pronoun to refer to two or more singular antecedents joined by *or* or *nor*.

EXAMPLES **Carmen** and **Janet** have not memorized **their** lines yet.

The **writer** and **director** of the play offered **his** suggestions.

Neither **Carmen** nor **Janet** has memorized **her** lines for the play.

EXERCISE A Circle the antecedent in each sentence. Then, underline the pronoun or pronoun group in parentheses that agrees with the antecedent.

Example 1. Either (John) or (Dylan) will spend (*their*, *his*) afternoon posting playbills.

1. The sofa and lamp should be placed in (*its*, *their*) proper positions on stage.

2. The stagehand and the carpenter worked carefully on (*his or her*, *their*) assignments.

3. The director or assistant director left (*his or her*, *their*) notes on the refreshment table.

4. A parent or sibling of an actor will be given a discount on (*his or her*, *their*) ticket.

5. The musicians and dancers prepared (*himself or herself*, *themselves*) for opening night.

6. The second spotlight or the third spotlight needs (*their*, *its*) bulb replaced.

7. Neither Wendy nor Margaret had considered (*herself*, *themselves*) an actor until now.

8. The lead character and the supporting character delivered (*his or her*, *their*) lines flawlessly.

9. Cheese and crackers will be served at the cast party; (*it*, *they*) will be provided by a caterer.

10. Actors and stagehands posed for (*their*, *his or her*) photograph.

EXERCISE B Circle the antecedent in each sentence. Then, decide whether the pronoun agrees with the antecedent. If the pronoun does not agree, cross it out and write the correct pronoun above it. If the pronoun already agrees, write *C* above it.

Example (Carrie) and (Rowan) took ~~his or her~~ *their* cameras to the beach.

Crabs and sea gulls had made its homes in the sand, grass, and rocks by the water. A seashell or a starfish occasionally dotted the beach where the tide had left it. Swimmers and surfers entertained himself in the water. Near a large sand dune, a child and her grandmother built herself a sand castle. Neither Carrie nor Rowan remembered to eat their lunch. The sandwiches and cookies remained in its wrappings while the photographers enthusiastically roamed the beach looking for the next photographic scene.

126

Pronoun-Antecedent Agreement: Collective Nouns

5s. A collective noun is singular when the noun refers to the group as a unit and plural when the noun refers to the individual members or parts of the group.

EXAMPLES The **jury** serving in the courtroom are eating **their** lunches.

The **jury** has withdrawn into **its** conference room.

EXERCISE A Underline the pronoun in parentheses that agrees with the collective noun.

Example 1. The troop always waits near the barracks for (*its*, *their*) commander.

1. The committee discussed (*its*, *their*) personal goals for the coming year.

2. "The public should never take the law into (*its*, *their*) own hands," advised the officer.

3. The family carefully packed (*its*, *their*) suitcases for the trip.

4. After hearing a moving speech, the majority enthusiastically clapped (*its*, *their*) hands.

5. The club perceived (*itself*, *themselves*) as average people despite their famous achievements.

6. At halftime the band picked up (*its*, *their*) instruments and marched onto the field.

7. The faculty arrived in twos and threes to take (*its*, *their*) places for the ceremony.

8. A flock of sheep are roaming throughout this canyon without (*its*, *their*) shepherd.

9. Performing the challenging song, the choir outdid (*itself*, *themselves*).

10. A number of trophies sat in (*its*, *their*) designated places in the trophy case.

EXERCISE B In each of the following sentences, circle the collective noun. If the pronoun in each sentence does not agree with its antecedent, cross it out and write the correct pronoun above it. If the pronoun already agrees with its antecedent, write *C* above it.

Example 1. A (swarm) of bees hovered over ~~their~~ *its* nest.

11. The team would like to welcome their newest member, Chris.

12. An army of men and women are setting up its campsites.

13. The class applauded its guest lecturer.

14. The flock built its nests in some of the larger trees near the lake.

15. During the crisis the group remained loyal to its fellow members.

16. Beneath the surface of the water, a school of fish made its way toward shore.

17. After the team's victory, the cheerleading squad performed their final cheer.

18. After the dedication ceremony, the crowd made their way to the exits.

19. The assembly is holding its applause until the end of the show.

20. Before the audience had taken its seats, the film began to roll.

Language and Sentence Skills Practice

USAGE

Pronoun-Antecedent Agreement: Other Problems A

| **5t.** | An expression of an amount (a measurement, a percentage, or a fraction, for example) may take a singular or plural pronoun, depending on how it is used. |

> **EXAMPLES**   I spent **three weeks** at the lake, and I enjoyed **them.**
>
> **Three weeks** is not a long time to wait. **It** should pass quickly.

| **5u.** | Some nouns that are plural in form take singular pronouns. |

> **EXAMPLES**   **Genetics** interests me, and I intend to learn more about **it.**
>
> We'll discuss **Great Expectations** tomorrow. **It** was written by Charles Dickens.

EXERCISE   In each of the following sentences, underline the pronoun in parentheses that agrees with its antecedent.

Example 1. Three fourths of the casserole is gone; we ate *(them, it)* at lunch.

1. Two thirds of the answers are correct, and I gave you credit for *(them, it)*.

2. Where in the mall is Trendy Accessories? I've been looking for *(them, it)* for thirty minutes.

3. Timothy presented a report on the Falkland Islands. *(Their, Its)* population is around 2,000.

4. Measure two teaspoons of vanilla. The recipe requires *(them, it)*, along with brown sugar.

5. In college, my brother is majoring in linguistics, and he really enjoys *(it, them)*.

6. I hung the binoculars on *(their, its)* hook in the closet.

7. Thirty inches is the distance you should measure. Then, mark *(them, it)* with a pencil.

8. I bought a copy of *The Canterbury Tales*. Geoffrey Chaucer wrote *(them, it)*.

9. Did you read Taneesha's poem "Sunflowers"? She composed *(it, them)* for her mom.

10. Twenty-five percent of the price is marked off; *(this, these)* should equal five dollars.

11. Have you seen the British comedy *Fawlty Towers*? *(It, They)* used to air on Tuesday night.

12. I am reading about economics. *(These, It)* includes the production of wealth.

13. *Cornfields* was painted by Derek. *(Its, Their)* color scheme is mainly shades of gold.

14. I'm familiar with genetics because I studied *(them, it)* in college.

15. I set aside two hours to review for the exam. *(They, That)* should be sufficient.

16. I need to iron my blue shorts since I'm wearing *(it, them)* today.

17. One of my favorite songs is "Still Waters," and I'm learning to play *(it, them)* on the guitar.

18. The cloth measures one hundred forty-four square inches. *(That, These)* equals one square foot.

19. I only report the news; I don't invent *(them, it)*.

20. Have you been to Cedar Rapids? *(Those, That)* is my hometown.

Pronoun-Antecedent Agreement: Other Problems B

5v.	The number of a relative pronoun (such as *that, which,* or *who*) is determined by the number of its antecedent.

> **EXAMPLES**   Mehmet is an athlete **who** always does **his** best. [singular antecedent *athlete*]
>
> Our team has many players **who** always do **their** best. [plural antecedent *players*]

EXERCISE   Above the relative pronoun in each sentence, write *S* if it refers to a singular antecedent or *P* if it refers to a plural antecedent. Then, on the line provided, write a pronoun that agrees with the relative pronoun.

Example 1. Saint Bernards are dogs that are valued for ____*their*____ pleasant nature.

 1. These are the teenagers who spent _____ afternoon tutoring younger kids.

 2. The sandwiches that have the crusts still on _____ are made with rye bread.

 3. The sales associates who meet _____ sales quotas will receive a bonus.

 4. The fax machine, which is on _____ stand in the corner, needs a new ink cartridge.

 5. The running shoes that had reflective strips on _____ were the ones I bought.

 6. Several people who desperately wanted tickets took _____ place in line early.

 7. The next-door neighbors, who hired me to "house sit" _____ house, are on vacation.

 8. Lisa, who spent _____ winter break in Florida, came back to school with a tan.

 9. At the discount bookstore, I found several books that had authors' signatures in _____.

 10. The movie, which featured Tom Hanks in _____ leading role, was a success.

 11. Sheila's parents, who are proud of _____ daughter, usually attend her debate competitions.

 12. The envelopes that have stamps on _____ are ready to mail.

 13. The painting that needs _____ frame dusted is in the corner.

 14. The first poem that I memorized in _____ entirety is "Stopping by Woods on a Snowy Evening."

 15. These posters, which have important information on _____, will be hung in the halls.

 16. The flowers that have thorns on _____ should be trimmed carefully.

 17. The keys, which normally hung from _____ hook in the kitchen, were nowhere to be found.

 18. Musicians who aren't afraid to take _____ seriously usually excel.

 19. A brown spider, which spun _____ web in a corner, lay in wait for passing insects.

 20. Brandon, who takes _____ dog for a run each morning before school, invited me to come along.

Review A: Subject-Verb Agreement

EXERCISE A Change each sentence according to the directions given in parentheses. Then, change the forms of verbs so that they agree with their subjects.

Example 1. ~~Every farm~~ *All farms* in this part of the country ~~has~~ *have* at least one tractor. (Change *Every farm* to *All farms.*)

1. Today very few farm children know how to harness a team of horses. (Change *very few farm children* to *almost no farm child.*)

2. Sixty years ago, horses or mules were essential for farming. (Change *horses or mules* to *a horse or a mule.*)

3. Most farm machinery at that time was literally "horsepowered." (Change *machinery* to *machines.*)

4. Only about a tenth of the farms were equipped with tractors. (Change *a tenth of the farms* to *one farm in ten.*)

5. The farmers in this part of the country were proud of their horses. (Change *The farmers* to *Each farmer* and *their* to *his or her.*)

EXERCISE B In each of the following sentences, underline the correct verb in parentheses.

Example 1. Where (<u>do</u>, does) you practice basketball?

6. The study of foreign languages in the lower grades (*is, are*) becoming increasingly common.

7. Each student in the biology classes (*has, have*) visited the medical lab.

8. There (*is, are*) only a few more sandwiches left.

9. Forty-five dollars (*is, are*) the price of the new bike.

10. (*Is, Are*) each of the pictures painted by the same artist?

11. Every one of the club members (*is, are*) invited to the party.

12. Neither of the chairs (*was, were*) badly damaged in the fire.

13. Here (*is, are*) the books that you ordered.

14. Neither you nor he (*was, were*) ready to speak.

15. There (*is, are*) many more like this one.

Review B: **Pronoun-Antecedent Agreement**

EXERCISE A Change each sentence according to the directions given in parentheses. Then, change the forms of pronouns and verbs in the sentence if necessary.

Example 1. ~~All of the students~~ *Every student* in the school district ~~have~~ *has* received ~~their~~ *his or her* fall schedules. (Change *All of the students* to *Every student*.)

1. The boys in Troop 95 spend some of their free time working at the recycling center. (Change *The boys* to *Each boy*.)

2. Rudi and one of her sisters are responsible for washing the dishes. (Change *and* to *or*.)

3. This green butterfly and that blue one make their home primarily in South America. (Change *This green butterfly and that blue one* to *This green butterfly, like that blue one,*.)

4. Stray cats or dogs frequently find their way to my door. (Change *Stray cats or dogs* to *A stray cat or dog*.)

5. All of the contestants who answered their questions correctly won prizes. (Change *All of the contestants* to *Each contestant*.)

EXERCISE B Circle the antecedent in each sentence. Then, underline the pronoun or pronoun group in parentheses that agrees with the antecedent.

Example 1. (Everybody) in the chemistry lab must wear *(their, his or her)* safety goggles.

6. Many of the citizens have already paid *(his or her, their)* taxes.

7. Each of the committee members has voiced *(his or her, their)* opinion.

8. Alonzo and I planted the seeds and watered *(it, them)* carefully.

9. Neither Darlene nor Naomi has finished *(her, their)* term paper yet.

10. Because Luis is allergic to eggs, he avoids eating *(it, them)*.

11. Each of the lost animals was returned to *(its, their)* owner.

12. Someone in the stands started stamping *(his or her, their)* feet loudly.

13. All of the workers were satisfied with *(his or her, their)* pay raises.

14. Evergreens are trees that do not shed *(its, their)* foliage in the fall.

15. Neither of the co-captains of the women's tennis team won *(her, their)* match.

Language and Sentence Skills Practice

Review C: **Agreement**

EXERCISE In most of the following sentences, a verb does not agree with its subject, or a pronoun does not agree with its antecedent. Cross out any incorrect verb or pronoun. Then, above it, write the correct form. If the sentence is already correct, write *C* next to its number.

Examples 1. Most were satisfied with ~~his or her~~ *their* grade.

         2. A squirrel or a bird ~~have~~ *has* been eating the blackberries off the vine.

1. Neither potatoes nor rice were my favorite dish.

2. One of your answers was incorrect.

3. Either Marisa or he are going to be the delegate to the conference.

4. One of the boys left their raincoat on the bus.

5. Where is the gifts you bought?

6. Neither her brothers nor she expects the team to win.

7. His feelings after the defeat was a combination of anger and disbelief.

8. Each of the delegates will pay their own expenses.

9. There was large quantities of surplus wheat in the grain elevators.

10. Two thirds of the day were spent getting the car repaired.

11. Neither Marco nor Lisette want to go fishing this afternoon.

12. Most of the games at the fair are intended for very young children.

13. Their hopes for a successful play was shattered by poor reviews.

14. Each of the students chose their own project.

15. A large crowd of people was clapping their hands and cheering.

16. There is always at least two librarians at the reference desk.

17. Every understudy who plan to succeed must be ready to perform at a moment's notice.

18. Not one of my classmates were prepared for the surprise quiz.

19. Some of the coins on the table belongs to me.

20. One quarter of the students want to join the drama club.

for **CHAPTER 5: AGREEMENT** `pages 110–36`

Review D: **Agreement**

EXERCISE In each of these sentences, underline the correct word or words in parentheses.

Examples 1. My brother or one of my sisters (*is, are*) responsible for the daily care of the horses.

   2. The soccer player who has the number *12* on (*their, her*) jersey is my sister.

1. Our family is proud of (*their, its*) ethnic traditions.

2. The crosstown bus (*don't, doesn't*) stop at Columbus Circle anymore.

3. The most valuable ingredient in any cook's soup is (*their, his or her*) secret spices.

4. (*There's, There are*) several candidates on the primary ballot.

5. (*Don't, Doesn't*) she have a cousin who writes scripts for television dramas?

6. Karen is one of the students who (*enjoy, enjoys*) swimming.

7. Every student and faculty member took (*their, his or her*) seat at the symposium.

8. *The Lower Depths* (*was, were*) written by the Russian playwright Maxim Gorki.

9. Two thousand dollars (*is, are*) the monthly rent for Dr. Simon's office.

10. My favorite team (*has, have*) never won the World Series.

11. Not one of the students turned in (*his or her, their*) assignment early.

12. The table that has a pile of books on (*its, their*) surface should be cleared.

13. Neither of the books (*is, are*) on the reading list.

14. Most of the students ate lunches that (*they, he or she*) had packed that morning.

15. The gleeful shrieking of the children (*was, were*) becoming annoying.

16. The horses that have (*its, their*) saddles on are ready for the rodeo.

17. My grandfather and his neighbors have formed (*his, their*) own neighborhood crime watch committee.

18. There (*is, are*) always several puppies and kittens at the shelter.

19. The computer that has (*their, its*) screensaver on is available for your use.

20. Neither a book nor a video movie (*was, were*) able to hold my attention last night.

Proofreading Application: Personal Essay

Good writers are generally good proofreaders. Readers tend to admire and trust writing that is error-free. Make sure that you correct all errors in grammar, usage, spelling, and punctuation in your writing. Your readers will have more confidence in your words if you have done your best to proofread carefully.

In everyday conversation, you quite possibly hear examples of nonstandard English usage. However, when you create a formal piece of writing, including personal essays, you should follow the rules of standard English.

PROOFREADING ACTIVITY

The following excerpt from a personal essay contains errors in subject-verb agreement. Find the errors and correct them using proofreading symbols to replace incorrect words.

Example Each of my friends ~~seem~~ *seems* concerned about the future.

A number of twelfth-grade students is presently in the throes of deciding which type of postsecondary education they will pursue. I think that at least nine tenths of the graduating class are undecided, including me. There's a few seniors who have decided not to continue studying once they graduate from high school. However, the majority has decided that they need a degree from a two- or four-year college to be financially successful. Either of these types of postsecondary institutions offer worthwhile degrees.

I, along with several of my friends, are planning to attend a career seminar. "Your Future Options" are the title of the seminar. Our desire to explore all possibilities have motivated us to attend. The planners of the event has assured us that at its conclusion we will feel more comfortable about making decisions. One thing is for sure: None of us wants to leave our futures up to chance.

for **CHAPTER 5: AGREEMENT** | pages 100–17

Literary Model: Dialogue in a Novel

I derived . . . that Joe's education, like steam, was yet in its infancy. Pursuing the subject, I [Pip] inquired:

'Didn't you ever go to school, Joe, when you were as little as me?'

'No, Pip.'

'Why didn't you ever go to school, Joe, when you were as little as me?'

'Well, Pip, . . . I'll tell you. My father, Pip, he were given to drink, and when he were overtook with drink, he hammered away at my mother, most onmerciful. It were a'most the only hammering he did, indeed, 'xcepting at myself. . . .'

'Consequence, my mother and me we ran away from my father. . . . But my father were that good in his hart that he couldn't abear to be without us. So, he'd come with a most tremenjous crowd and make such a row at the doors of the houses where we was, that they used to be obligated to have no more to do with us and to give us up to him. And then he took us home and hammered us. Which, you see, Pip,' said Joe, . . . 'were a drawback on my learning.' . . .

'Consequence, my father didn't make objections to my going to work; so I went to work to work at my present calling, which were his too, if he would have followed it. . . . In time I were able to keep him. . . .'

—from *Great Expectations* by Charles Dickens

EXERCISE A Identify each error in subject-verb agreement found in the passage above. Write the subject, followed by the verb that does not agree in number with it. (Some are repeated.)

_____   _____

_____   _____

_____   _____

_____   _____

EXERCISE B In terms of subject-verb agreement errors, contrast Joe's manner of speaking with the way Pip, the narrator, speaks. Why do you think the author has Joe speak in such a manner?

_____

_____

_____

_____

_____

_____

Language and Sentence Skills Practice

for **CHAPTER 5: AGREEMENT**   *pages 100–17*

Literary Model (continued)

EXERCISE C   Write a dialogue between two characters: the first, a person who has a mastery of standard English; the second, a person who has not fully mastered it. Have the second character use some verbs that do not agree with their subjects. Underline each verb that does not agree with its subject.

_____

_____

_____

_____

_____

_____

_____

_____

_____

_____

_____

_____

_____

EXERCISE D

1. How do the second character's errors in subject-verb agreement help to characterize him or her?

_____

_____

_____

_____

2. How was writing your dialogue challenging?

_____

_____

_____

_____

_____

for **CHAPTER 5: AGREEMENT**   *pages 100–17*

Writing Application: Descriptive Essay

It's possible that in informal conversation you say and hear instances of nonstandard subject-verb agreement such as "Neither of them want to sell magazines" or "Here's your missing gym shoes." However, when you create a formal piece of writing you should avoid such instances.

STANDARD   **Neither** of them **wants** to sell magazines.

STANDARD   Here **are** your missing gym **shoes.**

STANDARD   Here **is** your missing gym **shoe.**

In formal writing, standard usage, including correct subject-verb agreement, helps you make a good impression on your audience.

WRITING ACTIVITY

Write a descriptive essay about an athletic event at your school or at another school in your community. Provide descriptive details about the event as well as about individual team members. In your essay, include at least ten instances of standard subject-verb agreement.

PREWRITING   Freewrite about your topic for three to five minutes, jotting down ideas, images, and details that come to you. Do not stop to think about possible agreement errors. During the freewriting process, you may want to choose one word or phrase to use as a starting point for additional freewriting. Also, since any discussion of an athletic event is sure to mention actions, and actions are often expressed by verbs, brainstorm a list of verbs you can use that are particularly descriptive and lively.

WRITING   Decide how you will arrange your ideas. Will you devote the first part of the essay to the event in general and the second part to outstanding individuals? Will you discuss a few topics—such as strengths, weaknesses, or season predictions—and address both the event and players under each topic? Use the results of your freewriting and the list of verbs you brainstormed to begin writing.

REVISING   Read your draft aloud. Will the opening sentence make readers want to continue reading the essay? Have you used any weak words or clichés that could be replaced with more exciting words or phrases? Be sure you have included at least ten instances of standard subject-verb agreement.

PUBLISHING   Proofread your draft, beginning with the bottom line and moving to the top. Look for errors in spelling, grammar, and punctuation. In particular, be sure that each verb agrees with its subject. Once you have polished your essay, ask for permission to read it to your class.

EXTENDING YOUR WRITING

You may want to develop this writing exercise further. You could use your essay as the basis for a sports article intended for publication in your local or school newspaper. Since an essay and an article are two different forms of writing, you may need to make many changes to your writing before submitting it as an article. Start by comparing the tone and organizational structure of your writing to that found in published sports articles. Then, adjust your writing so that it looks and sounds like something that would be in a newspaper. Before submitting your article, be sure to find out what the newspaper's requirements for article publication are.

Choices: Exploring Pronoun Usage

The following activities challenge you to find a connection between pronouns and the world around you. Do the activity below that suits your personality best, and then share your discoveries with your class.

DISCUSSION

Family Reunion

You have a long-lost cousin that you have never met. Write a short letter to your cousin and say that you are coming to his or her town and would like to meet. In your letter, use every type of clear reference error at least once. Then, pass out copies to all your classmates. After they've read the letter, ask them what kind of an impression this letter is likely to make. Then, with the advice of your classmates, revise your letter, taking care to eliminate all clear reference errors.

ETYMOLOGY

Of He-Men and He-Mice

So, you think that you know what the pronoun *he* means, do you? You're in for a big surprise. Look up the word *he* in the *Oxford English Dictionary*. Read the entire entry. Make a list of each meaning, and post your list in the classroom.

LINGUISTIC HISTORY

Up Close and Personal

Look up each of the personal pronouns in a good dictionary. Don't settle for just a definition; get as full an etymology as you can find. Then, get a world map and note the languages and places where a form of each word has been used.

RESEARCH

Rasta Talk

The Rastafarian community, which has spread out from the Caribbean to a number of countries, has developed a unique brand of English. One of the ways that Rastafarians made their language special was by focusing on the personal pronoun *I*. In fact, they have created a new form of first-person pronoun—*I and I*. This pronoun has many uses. It may be used in both nominative and objective cases, merely for emphasis, or as a plural. Do some research on this interesting linguistic phenomenon. Report back to the class with a number of examples of how pronouns function in Rasta Talk.

DISCUSSION

A *Herm* of an Idea

The task of pairing indefinite pronouns with both third-person singular pronouns (*she/he* and *him/her*) proved so annoying to some people that a singular solution was offered a few years back. The word *herm* was suggested as an all-purpose alternative. Writers and speakers could just use *herm* instead of *him or her*. What do you think of this idea? Lead a discussion of this term.

ART

In Black and White

Those elliptical clauses can be tricky. Consider, for instance, the sentence *He liked the movie more than her.* Does this sentence mean that she didn't like the movie as much as he did, or that he liked the movie more than he liked her? Oops. These elliptical clauses can mean exactly what they were not intended to mean. Find or create at least five of these ambiguous sentences. Then, draw cartoons illustrating the two possible situations that each sentence describes. With your teacher's permission, post your illustrations in your class so that everyone can enjoy them.

LANGUAGE ACQUISITION

Me Hungry!

Have you ever noticed that toddlers often use objective case pronouns instead of nominative case pronouns? Do some research on language acquisition or development. When do children begin to use both objective and nominative cases? Which pronouns tend to be used first? When your research is done, write a report on what you have discovered, and share it with your class.

USAGE

Case Forms of Personal Pronouns

Case is the form that a noun or pronoun takes to show its relationship to other words in a sentence. In English, there are three cases: *nominative*, *objective*, and *possessive*. Personal pronouns have different forms for the different cases.

	SINGULAR	**PLURAL**
NOMINATIVE CASE	**He** bought it yesterday.	**We** are glad that **they** could come.
OBJECTIVE CASE	Give the job to **her** and **me**.	Todd gave **us** a message for **you**.
POSSESSIVE CASE	**My** bike is next to **yours**.	**Our** house is near **their** house.

EXERCISE A Above each underlined personal pronoun, write *1st* for *first person, 2nd* for *second person,* or *3rd* for *third person.* Then, write *N* for *nominative case, O* for *objective case,* or *P* for *possessive case.* Finally, write *S* for *singular* or *PL* for *plural.*

Examples 1. Senator Specter sent us a campaign newsletter. *[1st-O-PL over "us"]*

2. The newsletter interested her in its content. *[3rd-P-S over "its"]*

1. Cokie Roberts began her career in broadcasting over thirty years ago.

2. We recently saw her on a panel discussion regarding election procedures.

3. Several candidates gave their opinions concerning the primaries.

4. Ms. Roberts posed questions to each of them.

5. I was extremely impressed with her ability to focus on the issues.

6. Our state has scheduled its primary for March 10.

7. The program helped me understand the importance of primaries.

8. I've made up my mind regarding the candidates, too.

9. Our current senator has served for two terms.

10. Will you be giving him your support, Gina?

EXERCISE B On the line provided, add the pronoun described in parentheses to complete each sentence.

Example 1. Is this _____*your*_____ car, Brady? *(second person singular, possessive)*

11. I will read this poem aloud to _____. *(second person plural, objective)*

12. Have the artists finished _____ murals yet? *(third person plural, possessive)*

13. We have made up _____ minds on the issue. *(first person plural, possessive)*

14. After the movie, _____ ordered a pizza. *(third person plural, nominative)*

15. The sudden, loud clap of thunder startled _____. *(first person singular, objective)*

Language and Sentence Skills Practice

The Nominative Case A

6a.   A subject of a verb should be in the nominative case.

> **EXAMPLES**   **She** plays the guitar.
>
> **He** and **I** had never been to a game at the Spectrum.

6b.   A predicate nominative should be in the nominative case.

> **EXAMPLES**   It was **he** who called and left a message.
>
> The mysterious visitors might have been **they.**

EXERCISE A   For each sentence, if the underlined pronoun is correct write *C* above it. If it is not correct, cross it out and write the correct form of the pronoun above it.

Example 1. My choice for the student delegate will be ~~her~~. *she*

1. The man who sponsored the radio marathon was <u>him</u>.

2. My brother and <u>me</u> went on a camping trip.

3. Both her aunt and <u>she</u> speak fluent Chinese.

4. The junior class and <u>us</u> will sponsor the annual book fair.

5. Jim and <u>them</u> received scholarships from the Rotary Club.

6. The panelists selected for the quiz show may have been Luis and <u>her</u>.

7. It wasn't <u>I</u> who left the baseball equipment out on the field.

8. Was the winner of the tournament Augusta or <u>him</u>?

9. Raul and <u>her</u> have read almost every novel by Ernest Hemingway.

10. After the concert, Pia and <u>them</u> want to meet in the parking lot.

EXERCISE B   The following paragraph contains errors in the case forms of personal pronouns. Cross out each incorrect pronoun, and write the correct form of the pronoun above it.

Example ~~Us~~ three students are working on a presentation on Dorothy Parker. *We*

Among fiction lovers who appreciate Dorothy Parker are we. Parker was a famous American writer and critic. Her and her colleagues formed a literary circle that met regularly at the Algonquin Hotel in New York City. It was them who became known as the Algonquin Round Table. They were a witty, extremely talented group. Parker was perhaps the wittiest of all. For example, it was her who wanted her gravestone to read, "Pardon my dust." While the three of us were researching Parker, we collected other witty comments. We discovered a comment Parker made regarding Katharine Hepburn's performance in a play. Parker said that Hepburn "ran the gamut of emotions from A to B." All in all, us lovers of sarcasm consider Parker a genius.

The Nominative Case B

6a. A subject of a verb should be in the nominative case.

> **EXAMPLES** **They** went to a lacrosse game yesterday.
> **She** has been playing the cello daily.

6b. A predicate nominative should be in the nominative case.

> **EXAMPLES** It is **we** who should baby-sit on Friday.
> The winners of the dance contest are **he** and **she**.

EXERCISE Write an appropriate personal pronoun on each blank in the following sentences.

Example The student who will speak next is ____*she*____.

Ms. Rosewood said, "Marcy, are _____ ready with your report? It is _____ who are

next, and _____ are interested in your topic."

Marcy stood before the class and said, "Most people enjoy listening to the radio, but _____

may not know who invented FM broadcasting. Are _____ curious? Well, _____ can tell

about this amazing inventor. Have _____ heard of Edwin H. Armstrong? It is _____ who

made the crucial discoveries and filed the patents that made FM broadcasting possible.

"First, _____ will tell you about Armstrong's background. While still a teenager, _____

decided to become an inventor and immediately began work in the attic of his house. In college,

_____ experimented with wireless transmission and earned a gold medal from the Institute of

Radio Engineers for the discovery of the feedback circuit in wireless transmission. Until _____

developed this circuit, wireless signals were barely audible using earphones; _____ were cer-

tainly not audible from across a room.

"In 1933, Armstrong filed four patents. _____ were for circuits that comprised a new radio

system. Because the system required changes in transmitters and receivers, _____ was not an

immediate success. Armstrong spent more than $300,000 of his own money building the first full-

scale FM station. The radio industry became interested, and _____ slowly accepted and imple-

mented Armstrong's technology.

"Throughout his life Armstrong was involved in patent suits brought by rival inventors.

_____ gradually consumed his money and his spirit, and in 1954, _____ passed away.

Despite this tragedy, you and _____ have benefited from Armstrong's work. It is _____

radio enthusiasts of the twenty-first century who enjoy Armstrong's twentieth-century invention."

Language and Sentence Skills Practice

USAGE

The Objective Case A

| **6c.** | A direct object should be in the objective case. |

EXAMPLE   We watched **them** from the window.

| **6d.** | An indirect object should be in the objective case. |

EXAMPLE   Mel Tormé gave **me** his autograph.

| **6e.** | An object of a preposition should be in the objective case. |

EXAMPLE   Please give these tickets to **him** and **her**.

EXERCISE A   Underline the correct pronoun in parentheses to complete each sentence.

Example 1. Dr. Masoaka has been treating Rafael and (I, *me*) for our colds.

1. Sean entertained Luisa and (*I, me*) with a tale of Irish folklore.

2. Shizuo's employer gave (*he, him*) the raise that he had requested.

3. The tour guide gave Elia and (*her, she*) free souvenirs.

4. The remaining tickets were awarded to Jim Bob and (*I, me*).

5. Nobody remembered the words of the song except Elena and (*he, him*).

6. A reporter interviewed (*we, us*) after the quiz show.

7. Please tell (*them, they*) about your plans for next summer.

8. For (*we, us*), the best part of the movie involved the underwater chase.

9. The singing dogs will perform with Consuela and (*I, me*).

10. In addition to (*I, me*), Howin will be joining the yearbook staff.

EXERCISE B   If the underlined pronoun is incorrect, cross it out and write the correct pronoun above it. If it is already correct, write *C*.

Example 1. I made Valentine cards for you and ~~they.~~ *them*

11. Fran sent Marlo and he a letter.

12. Ms. Bonetta told Sasha and I about the sale.

13. To us, the price of admission seems rather high.

14. Do Mom and Dad know that I'll be home after both of they?

15. The costume designer has finally given him his costume for the play.

The Objective Case B

| **6c.** | A direct object should be in the objective case. |

EXAMPLE Tell **us** about your new job.

| **6d.** | An indirect object should be in the objective case. |

EXAMPLE Shelby gave **her** the bag of potatoes.

| **6e.** | An object of a preposition should be in the objective case. |

EXAMPLE Do these boxes have anything inside **them?**

EXERCISE A On each blank provided, write a personal pronoun in the objective case that will complete the sentence correctly. Use a variety of pronouns, but do not use *you* or *it*.

Example 1. Because my younger brother asked nicely, I lent ____*him*____ my dirt bike.

1. This information will remain between you and _____.

2. If Mom or Grandma asks where I am, tell _____ I'm at Sophie's house.

3. Standing before the row of paintings, I studied each of _____ carefully.

4. The mail carrier brought letters for you and _____.

5. Karla is at the front desk; give your application form to _____.

6. Martina challenged _____ to a race around the track.

7. Casey bought _____ lunch.

8. Your pet rabbits are hungry; you should feed _____ these vegetable scraps.

9. Tell _____ your secret!

10. When you see Robert, please give _____ these two magazines.

EXERCISE B For each sentence below, if the underlined pronoun is incorrect, cross it out and write the correct pronoun above it. If the pronoun is correct, write *C* above it.

Example Patti made heirloom quilts for both Tamara and ~~I~~. *me*

Patti continually searches for interesting sewing projects and then sews <u>them</u> beautifully. For example, she not only sewed the curtains in her room, but she designed <u>they</u> and a matching quilt herself. Tell <u>she</u> or her dad your favorite colors, and Patti will use <u>them</u> in a project for <u>you</u>. Whenever my friends and I are at Patti's house, her dad proudly shows <u>they</u> and <u>I</u> her latest accomplishments. Patti may act embarrassed, but I know she appreciates the admiration from her dad and <u>we</u>. She is currently working on customized birthday gifts for you and <u>he</u>. Once, I gave Patti one of my favorite formal dresses, which I had outgrown. She made two fancy, decorative pillows out of <u>it</u>.

Language and Sentence Skills Practice

Nominative and Objective Case Pronouns

| **6a.** | A subject of a verb should be in the nominative case. |

| **6b.** | A predicate nominative should be in the nominative case. |

> **EXAMPLES**   **They** were surprised to learn that the winner was **she.**

| **6c.** | A direct object should be in the objective case. |

| **6d.** | An indirect object should be in the objective case. |

| **6e.** | An object of a preposition should be in the objective case. |

> **EXAMPLES**   Let's eat **them** right away.
> Kurt gave **her** the phone message.
> Please send any questions to **me.**

EXERCISE A   Underline the correct pronoun in parentheses in each sentence.

Example 1. (*Her*, <u>*She*</u>) and Mrs. Martin have been friends since childhood.

1. Ask Lorna and (*they, them*) about the outcome of the race.

2. (*Us, We*) have little time for watching television.

3. It was (*her, she*) who organized the new filing system.

4. Ramona was uncertain whether she would vote for (*he, him*) or not.

5. Between you and (*me, I*), that painting is worth more than the artist is asking for it.

6. We will help both you and (*she, her*) with your projects.

7. The clerk said the smaller size would fit you better than it would fit (*her, she*).

8. The school newspaper's front-page article is about (*us, we*).

9. The package was sent to Raj and (*me, I*).

10. The drama coaches are Mr. Rolando and (*them, they*).

EXERCISE B   In the following sentences, if a pronoun is incorrect, cross it out and write the correct form above it. If a sentence is correct, write *C* next to the number.

Example 1. You should give the watch to Josh and ~~she~~ *her* for safekeeping.

11. The basketball game between Tomás and he soon grew into a major contest.

12. If it had not been for Luis and she, the fund-raising project would have failed.

13. She is a better swimmer, but the coach said she needed both of us on the team.

14. It is not fair to let all the boys except they go on a holiday.

15. Before going on the trip, you need written permission from your parents and I.

The Possessive Case

| **6f.** | The possessive pronouns *mine, yours, his, hers, its, ours,* and *theirs* can be used in the same way that the personal pronouns in the nominative and objective cases are used. |

> **EXAMPLE**   **His** won first place, while they won second place for **theirs.**

| **6g.** | The possessive pronouns *my, your, his, her, its, our,* and *their* are used to modify nouns and pronouns. |

> **EXAMPLE**   **His** poem won first place. [*His* modifies *poem.*]

| **6h.** | A noun or pronoun preceding a gerund generally should be in the possessive case. |

> **EXAMPLE**   I was not surprised at **his** winning the contest.

EXERCISE   Write a pronoun in the possessive case to correctly complete each sentence.

Example 1. Will ____*my*____ playing the piano wake the baby?

1. "_____ needs more blue in it," said the art teacher.

2. Mick gave _____ room a thorough cleaning before his friends came over.

3. _____ running the store during my absence is a good idea.

4. _____ house is the third one from the corner.

5. The neighbors' car is not in _____ driveway.

6. The kitten sat in a patch of sunlight and daintily licked _____ paws.

7. _____ jogging through the neighborhood has become a routine.

8. The pleasure is _____ .

9. I'll ask _____ mom for directions to the animal shelter.

10. During the movie, _____ talking on the cell phone disturbed several people.

11. It is only two miles from my house to _____.

12. The newspaper will print _____ notice on Friday.

13. My secretary will call _____ lawyer and arrange the meeting.

14. _____ was purchased by an antique dealer.

15. Cynthia planted _____ in the garden plot behind the house.

16. At the archaeology meeting, we'll tell you about _____ discovery.

17. I'll give _____ careful consideration.

18. All students must get _____ parent's or guardian's permission for the field trip.

19. Over the years, _____ teaching has won awards several times.

20. The skis in the attic are _____ .

Language and Sentence Skills Practice

145

Case Forms A

6a.	A subject of a verb should be in the nominative case.
6b.	A predicate nominative should be in the nominative case.

> **EXAMPLES** **He** will conduct the interview.
>
> The photographer is **she.**

6c.	A direct object should be in the objective case.
6d.	An indirect object should be in the objective case.
6e.	An object of a preposition should be in the objective case.

> **EXAMPLES** Give **it** to Mary.
>
> I promised **them** a copy of the article.
>
> I gave the book to **him** yesterday.

6f.	The possessive pronouns *mine, yours, his, hers, its, ours,* and *theirs* can be used in the same way that the personal pronouns in the nominative and objective cases are used.
6g.	The possessive pronouns *my, your, his, her, its, our,* and *their* are used to modify nouns and pronouns.
6h.	A noun or pronoun preceding a gerund generally should be in the possessive case.

> **EXAMPLES** **His** wearing tinted contact lenses changes **his** eye color. **Mine** are blue.

EXERCISE On each blank, write a pronoun that will correctly and logically complete the sentence.

Example 1. Mom will give either you or _____*him*_____ the keys to the car.

1. The Japanese restaurant's new sushi chef is _____.

2. _____ told me about his dreams for the future.

3. Mr. Greeson gave Kimberly and _____ extra help on our geometry homework.

4. We'll work on our homework together at _____ house.

5. Call _____ when you're ready to go.

6. Without you and _____, the outing was boring.

7. When I outgrow clothing, I give it to Laura or _____.

8. Gina gave _____ the Web site's address.

9. _____ is the trophy in the middle of the second shelf.

10. _____ cooking the meal was a great help.

Case Forms B

| **6a.** | A subject of a verb should be in the nominative case. |

| **6b.** | A predicate nominative should be in the nominative case. |

> **EXAMPLES** **They** arrived late.
>
> My manager is **he.**

| **6c.** | A direct object should be in the objective case. |

| **6d.** | An indirect object should be in the objective case. |

| **6e.** | An object of a preposition should be in the objective case. |

> **EXAMPLES** Describe **them** to the group.
>
> Send **her** your résumé.
>
> The lake has a bridge across **it.**

| **6f.** | The possessive pronouns *mine, yours, his, hers, its, ours,* and *theirs* can be used in the same way that the personal pronouns in the nominative and objective cases are used. |

| **6g.** | The possessive pronouns *my, your, his, her, its, our,* and *their* are used to modify nouns and pronouns. |

| **6h.** | A noun or pronoun preceding a gerund generally should be in the possessive case. |

> **EXAMPLES** **Yours** is the shovel near **my** truck. **Our** shoveling the snow was a help to Mark.

EXERCISE For each sentence below, if the underlined pronoun is incorrect, cross it out and write the correct pronoun above it. If the underlined pronoun is already correct, write C above it.

Example 1. You'll be riding to school each morning with ~~he~~ *him* and Shannon.

1. For science class, Polly and <u>me</u> read an article about swans.

2. The winners of the tournament will be either the Eagles or <u>we</u>.

3. <u>Him</u> hitting a home run was the highlight of the game.

4. The clay sculpture in the student art exhibit is <u>my</u>.

5. As they skated in the ice rink, Ken took Rhonda's hand in <u>his</u>.

6. Can you give the committee or <u>we</u> a hint about the outcome of the election?

7. The Carsons are working in <u>our</u> community garden.

8. The similarities between you and <u>I</u> are numerous.

9. Of all the sophomores, only Shane and <u>her</u> have lockers near the seniors.

10. Monique will be meeting Keller and <u>he</u> at the carnival on Saturday.

Language and Sentence Skills Practice

USAGE

Who and Whom

| **6i.** | The use of **who** (and *whoever*) or **whom** (and *whomever*) in a subordinate clause depends on how the pronoun functions in the clause. |

Who is in the nominative case, and *whom* is in the objective case.

NOMINATIVE CASE The person **who** wrote this poem is a great writer. [*Who* is the subject of the verb *wrote* in the clause *who wrote this poem*.]

OBJECTIVE CASE Did you see **whom** Mr. Burns selected? [*Whom* is the direct object of the verb *selected* in the clause *whom Mr. Burns selected*.]

EXERCISE A Underline the subordinate clause in each sentence. Then, above *who* or *whoever*, or *whom* or *whomever*, write *S* if the word is the subject of the clause, *PN* if it is the predicate nominative, *DO* if it is the direct object, or *OP* if it is the object of a preposition.

Examples 1. Do you know who the writer is? [*PN* above *who the writer is*]

2. The man to whom I was speaking is a great musician. [*OP* above *to whom I was speaking*]

1. I don't know to whom I should give my extra ticket.

2. Wasn't Charles Dickens the author who wrote *Oliver Twist*?

3. I've just figured out who the person in the gorilla costume is.

4. Mario is the student whom the committee selected for the award.

5. Billie Holiday, whom my parents greatly admire, was a famous singer.

6. Everyone wondered who the new cheerleader would be.

7. We will invite whomever Jane wants.

8. I wonder who gave the anonymous donation to the school.

9. Dad will lend the car to whoever will wash it this weekend.

10. I saw a car in my driveway, and wondered who was there.

EXERCISE B Underline the correct pronoun in parentheses in each sentence.

Example 1. Please give my compliments to (*whoever*, *whomever*) made the chili.

11. Was Henry Ford II the man (*who, whom*) designed the ill-fated Edsel?

12. The counselor (*who, whom*) she consulted gave her good advice.

13. William Faulkner was a novelist (*who, whom*) won the Nobel Prize.

14. Ms. Okimi would not tell us (*who, whom*) she preferred as a candidate.

15. Emily Dickinson, for (*who, whom*) we named this park, was a poet.

Appositives

6j. A pronoun used as an appositive should be in the same case as the word to which it refers.

An *appositive* appears next to another noun or pronoun to identify or describe that noun or pronoun.

> **EXAMPLES** The winners, **she** and **I**, received gold medals. [The appositives *she* and *I* are in the nominative case because they refer to the subject *winners*.]
>
> The awards committee gave the winners, **her** and **me**, gold medals. [The appositives *her* and *me* are both in the objective case because they refer to the indirect object *winners*.]

The pronouns *we* and *us* are sometimes used with noun appositives.

> **EXAMPLES** **We dancers** need frequent practice. The instructor taught **us dancers** a new step.

EXERCISE A Underline the correct pronoun in parentheses in each sentence.

Example 1. Henry gave the weary hikers, Sharon and (*he,* <u>him</u>), a ride home.

1. The party was planned by my two best friends, Alameda and (*she, her*).

2. For our guest speaker, (*we, us*) writers chose a famous poet.

3. Two foreign exchange students, José and (*I, me*), led the parade.

4. The top awards went to my favorite actors, Denzel Washington and (*he, him*).

5. The dancers in the final act were two professionals, Savion Glover and (*she, her*).

6. Often, (*we, us*) left-handers struggle with scissors designed for righties.

7. We gave the tennis players, Wolfgang and (*she, her*), more practice time.

8. Sometimes the fans are awfully rough on (*we, us*) referees.

9. The donors of the funds were prominent citizens, An Tsao and (*she, her*).

10. Pictures of the two teams, the Bobcats and (*they, them*), appeared in the paper.

EXERCISE B In each sentence below, if the appositive pronoun is incorrect, cross it out and write the correct form above it. If the pronoun is already correct, write *C* above it.

Example 1. The cartoonists, Alex and ~~her,~~ *she* delight their readers each week.

11. The two campers, Jill and him, found an abandoned mine shaft.

12. We sophomores and they are scheduled for yearbook pictures this week.

13. My relatives, Aunt Jessica and they, are helping me create a family tree.

14. The toddler sat happily between his sisters, Phoebe and she, at the circus.

15. Ask the recreation directors, Meredith and she, about the canoe outing.

Language and Sentence Skills Practice

USAGE

Reflexive and Intensive Pronouns

A *reflexive pronoun* refers to the subject of a verb and may serve as a direct object, an indirect object, a predicate nominative, or an object of a preposition.

EXAMPLES   You can teach **yourself** new habits.

An *intensive pronoun* has only one function: to emphasize its antecedent.

EXAMPLE   Jonathan **himself** will drive.

EXERCISE   For each blank in the following sentences, write a pronoun ending in –*self* or –*selves* that correctly completes the sentence. Then, identify the pronoun by writing above it *REF* for *reflexive* or *INT* for *intensive*. If neither a reflexive nor an intensive pronoun would be correct, give a personal pronoun.

Examples   1. I asked the kindergartner, "Did you tie your shoes _____*yourself*_____ ?" *(INT)*

   2. The winners of the cooking contest were Sonya and _____*I*_____.

1. Coach Woodard taught us to have confidence in _____.

2. Julie committed _____ to weekly piano lessons.

3. Bryan went straight to Ms. Ashok Mehta _____ with his question.

4. I pushed _____ an extra mile on the treadmill.

5. Have you ever said to _____, "Am I awake, or am I dreaming?"

6. I planned the entire Super Bowl party _____.

7. The mayor _____ visited my school during our seminar on city government.

8. Roy rebuilt a motorcycle for _____ and his brother.

9. My friends and _____ have plans for the evening.

10. We _____ are responsible for our own destiny.

11. Shaleen, Nick, and Juan frightened _____ with their own ghost stories.

12. It is they _____ who must pay for the trip.

13. Several of us promised _____ that we would always remain loyal to each other.

14. After recuperating from the flu, Josh was _____ again.

15. We sophomores congratulated _____ on winning the Spirit Contest at the pep rally.

16. Angie and _____ made a homemade vegetarian pizza.

17. Who said, "If you want something done right, do it _____"?

18. Rather than wait for someone else, Melinda cleaned the kitchen _____.

19. I said to Cheryl and James, "You _____ are responsible for catering the reception."

20. Our parents and _____ enjoyed the rafting trip.

Pronouns in Incomplete Constructions

6k. A pronoun following *than* or *as* in an incomplete construction should be in the same case as it would be if the construction were completed.

EXAMPLES Do you call Laura more than **me**? [Meaning: Do you call Laura more than *you call me*?]

Do you call Laura more than **I**? [Meaning: Do you call Laura more than *I call Laura*?]

EXERCISE The following sentences are incomplete constructions. On the lines provided, rewrite each sentence including the missing part of the construction. Use the pronoun in parentheses that is in the case specified.

Example 1. Sherri served the children before *(I, me)*. (objective)   *Sherri served the children*
before she served me.

1. Todd runs with the dog more than *(I, me)*. (nominative) _____

_____

2. The judges liked Meg's routine less than *(I, mine)*. (possessive) _____

_____

3. I waited on the elderly customer before *(she, her)*. (objective) _____

_____

4. We play more tournaments than *(they, them)*. (nominative) _____

_____

5. I love chocolate more than *(your, you)*. (nominative) _____

_____

6. The car pool picked up RayAnn before *(he, him)*. (objective) _____

_____

7. Kiki lives nearer the school than *(we, us)*. (nominative) _____

_____

8. Is Dan's pony in as many shows as *(her, hers)*? (possessive) _____

_____

9. You can wash our car after *(them, theirs)*. (possessive) _____

_____

10. I value friendship as much as *(he, him)*. (nominative) _____

_____

USAGE

Clear Pronoun Reference A

| **6l.** | A pronoun should refer clearly to its antecedent. |

(1) Avoid an *ambiguous reference,* which occurs when any one of two or more words can be a pronoun's antecedent.

> **AMBIGUOUS** Ludlow told Pete to wash his dirty socks. [Whose socks?]
>
> **CLEAR** Pete's socks were dirty, and Ludlow told him to wash them.

(2) Avoid a *general reference,* which is the use of a pronoun that refers to a general idea rather than to a specific antecedent.

> **GENERAL** The sky is black. That means rain is on its way. [no specific antecedent for *that*]
>
> **CLEAR** The black sky means rain is on its way.

EXERCISE On the lines provided, revise each sentence to make its meaning clear.

Example 1. I won the race. That made me proud.   *Winning the race made me proud.*

1. Jill saw Ida while she was in town. _____
_____

2. Hal told Milo that his brother was late. _____
_____

3. The streets are coated with ice. That is why everyone stayed home. _____
_____

4. We swam in the river, which is always fun. _____
_____

5. The last time Jerry saw Roberto, he didn't speak to him. _____
_____

6. Seeing the hat and coat in the window, I bought it. _____
_____

7. Today is payday. It means I go to the bank. _____
_____

8. I feed our parakeets. This is a daily responsibility. _____
_____

9. As soon as Mom and Jen arrived at the hotel, she called me. _____
_____

10. Dave saw Trent in the crowded diner when he stood up. _____
_____

Clear Pronoun Reference B

6l. A pronoun should refer clearly to its antecedent.

(3) Avoid a **weak reference,** which occurs when a pronoun refers to an antecedent that has been suggested but not expressed.

> **WEAK** In the last inning, Earl hit it out of the park! [Hit what?]
>
> **CLEAR** In the last inning, Earl hit the ball out of the park!

(4) Avoid an **indefinite reference,** which is the use of a pronoun that refers to no specific antecedent and that is unnecessary to the meaning of the sentence.

> **INDEFINITE** In Calaveras County, they hold a frog-jumping contest. [no specific antecedent]
>
> **CLEAR** Calaveras County holds an annual frog-jumping contest.

EXERCISE On the lines provided, revise each sentence to make its meaning clear.

Example 1. Chris sings well, and that one's my favorite. _Chris sings my favorite song well._

1. I scattered birdseed in the backyard, but they haven't eaten it yet. _____

_____

2. In Iowa they produce about ten percent of our nation's food supply. _____

_____

3. On my computer screen, it reflected the person standing behind me. _____

_____

4. Lloyd is a farmer. Some of the ones he grows are peanuts and potatoes. _____

_____

5. We are traveling to New Zealand. They speak English there. _____

_____

6. In the atlas, it confirmed my guess that Mississauga is a Canadian city. _____

_____

7. As President of the United States, you are guarded carefully. _____

_____

8. At the auto parts shop, they are having a sale. _____

_____

9. On the Web site, they guide you through the purchase process. _____

_____

10. Lee is a painter. He has won awards for some of them. _____

_____

Clear Pronoun Reference C

6l. | A pronoun should refer clearly to its antecedent.

(1) Avoid an *ambiguous reference,* which occurs when any one of two or more words can be a pronoun's antecedent.

(2) Avoid a *general reference,* which is the use of a pronoun that refers to a general idea rather than to a specific antecedent.

(3) Avoid a *weak reference,* which occurs when a pronoun refers to an antecedent that has been suggested but not expressed.

(4) Avoid an *indefinite reference,* which is the use of a pronoun that refers to no specific antecedent and that is unnecessary to the meaning of the sentence.

EXERCISE   On the lines provided, revise each sentence to make its meaning clear.

Example 1. Kristy met Holly after she got off work.   *After Kristy got off work, she met Holly.*

1. The bakery smells wonderful. Some of them are tarts and bread. _____
_____

2. Mel and I are flying kites this weekend, which should be fun. _____
_____

3. In the glossary, it said that a simile is a comparison using *like* or *as.* _____
_____

4. Before Bill met Chuck, he had never sky-dived. _____
_____

5. Eric can think of no one but Marcia. It must be love. _____
_____

6. Every summer in my town, they hold a rose festival. _____
_____

7. After seeing Faith's vases and Carola's bowls in pottery class, I bought one of her works. ____
_____

8. I'm taking a horseback riding class. They are gentle and friendly. _____
_____

9. Why do they interrupt regular TV news programs with commercials? _____
_____

10. Betsy and Kim worked in the store all weekend because her mom needed the help. _____
_____

for **CHAPTER 6: USING PRONOUNS CORRECTLY** | *pages 164–65*

Clear Pronoun Reference D

6l. A pronoun should refer clearly to its antecedent.

(1) Avoid an ***ambiguous reference,*** which occurs when any one of two or more words can be a pronoun's antecedent.

(2) Avoid a ***general reference,*** which is the use of a pronoun that refers to a general idea rather than to a specific antecedent.

(3) Avoid a ***weak reference,*** which occurs when a pronoun refers to an antecedent that has been suggested but not expressed.

(4) Avoid an ***indefinite reference,*** which is the use of a pronoun that refers to no specific antecedent and that is unnecessary to the meaning of the sentence.

EXERCISE On the lines provided, revise each sentence to make its meaning clear.

Example 1. Rita is a talented writer; this one is funny. *Rita is a talented writer; this story is funny.*

1. Larry called Trevor while he was at karate practice. _____

_____

2. I like it when I find really nice items at a flea market. _____

_____

3. Steven went fishing. This is his favorite pastime. _____

_____

4. I am always honest with my friends, but it isn't always easy. _____

_____

5. Before Lewis entered tenth grade with William, he went to a different school. _____

_____

6. Jeremy is replacing loose shingles on the roof. It should be finished soon. _____

_____

7. In pioneer times in America, you generally traveled by horse and buggy. _____

_____

8. My mom is a computer programmer. One of them that she knows is called Java. _____

_____

9. I filled the gas tank. This will allow us to reach Dallas with no problem. _____

_____

10. The jewelry box was full. One of the ones it held was a ruby ring. _____

_____

USAGE

Review A: Case Forms

EXERCISE A   Underline the correct pronoun in parentheses.

Example 1. (<u>We</u>, Us) stargazers enjoy a trip to the observatory.

1. Janice and (I, me) have always lived next door to each other.

2. Janice's father often takes (we, us) girls on trips.

3. Last month he took Janice and (I, me) to a nearby observatory to look at the stars.

4. The director of the observatory was a woman (who, whom) Janice's father knew.

5. She introduced us to a research assistant (who, whom) showed us the big telescope.

6. The research assistant asked whether (we, us) girls were amateur astronomers.

7. (She, Her) and Janice's father were both surprised when we admitted that we did not even know how to locate the North Star.

8. The two of them led Janice and (I, me) outside and showed us how to find the North Star by following the "pointers" in the Big Dipper.

9. Janice grasped the idea immediately, but I was a little slower than (she, her).

10. Ever since our trip to the observatory, the two most enthusiastic stargazers in town are my friend and (I, me).

EXERCISE B   In each sentence, cross out any pronoun that is used incorrectly and write the correct pronoun above it. If a sentence is correct, write *C* before the number.

Example 1. Courtney bought lunch for herself and ~~myself.~~ *me*

11. Where are Parvis and him?

12. Did you invite Liza Beth and she?

13. Mr. Arimitsu is confident that the editors were they.

14. He is a man who you can trust.

15. His sister is a better student than him.

16. There was no argument between Bianca and myself.

17. The committee has not decided whom should be in charge.

18. Angelo and him should have known better.

19. Did she prepare dinner for her friends and yourself?

20. We saw you and they at the game.

Review B: **Clear Reference**

EXERCISE The following sentences contain ambiguous, general, weak, and indefinite references. On the lines provided, revise each sentence to make its meaning clear.

Example 1. In the instructions, it shows how the parts fit together. *The instructions show how the parts fit together.*

1. Damon works at the YMCA. It is an interesting job. _____

_____

2. After seeing Trisha and Mindy in the mall, I called her. _____

_____

3. In modeling, they often must stand perfectly still. _____

_____

4. I'm planting a backyard garden, which is fun. _____

_____

5. Petra is at an audition; that is why she can't study with us. _____

_____

6. I did my math homework carefully; some of them were difficult. _____

_____

7. After reading Craig's mystery story and Bruce's science fiction story, the editor bought his work for the next issue. _____

_____

8. I live near a fruit orchard. They are apple. _____

_____

9. On the commercial, it said the sale continues through Friday. _____

_____

10. I relax by reading a magazine. They keep you updated on sports and fashion topics. _____

_____

Language and Sentence Skills Practice

Review C: Case Forms and Clear Reference

USAGE

EXERCISE A In each sentence below, cross out each pronoun that is used incorrectly. Then, write the correct form above it. If a sentence is already correct, write *C* next to the number.

Example 1. This is the new friend ~~who~~ *whom* I mentioned to you earlier.

1. You and him should come over after dinner.

2. Whom shall I say is calling?

3. You work more carefully than me.

4. Are Lanette and her in the same homeroom?

5. No one was surprised when both you and her made the team.

6. The one who asked for the newspaper was she.

7. Did the librarian give you and he a reading list?

8. You and him can bring in the groceries now, thank you.

9. Between you and I, we don't need their help.

10. I don't know who you should ask about the quiz.

EXERCISE B The following sentences contain ambiguous, general, weak, and indefinite references. On the lines provided, revise each sentence to make its meaning clear.

Example 1. I saw Ms. Martin making photocopies. This means we'll have a pop quiz.

I saw Ms. Martin making photocopies, so I think we'll have a pop quiz.

11. I eat a vegetarian diet. One of the those I like best is tofu with vegetables. _____

_____

12. Annette is performing in the talent show, which should be entertaining. _____

_____

13. If you are famous, the *paparazzi* may become intrusive. _____

_____

14. Darnell spoke to Tyrone before he began football practice. _____

_____

15. Cliff is ambidextrous. This means he can use both hands equally well. _____

_____

Review D: **Case Forms and Clear Reference**

EXERCISE A Each of the following sets of expressions is incorrect. Revise the incorrect expression on the line provided. Base your answer on standard formal usage.

Example 1. not for Ingrid or she _____*not for Ingrid or her*_____

1. to you and I _____

2. the girl who we saw _____

3. Max and him already left. _____

4. Ask him rather than I. _____

5. They like the same books as us. _____

EXERCISE B The following sentences contain ambiguous, general, weak, and indefinite references. On the lines provided, revise each sentence to make its meaning clear.

Example 1. Tate scuba dives. He took a course in it last summer. _____*Tate scuba dives. He took*_____
_____*a course in scuba diving last summer.*_____

6. Greg asked Frank if his paycheck had been left in the car. _____

7. In the article it describes a hurricane's destructive power. _____

8. Freddie is a talented painter; one of them hangs in the hall. _____

9. Phina creates mosaic tables. That is why she collects broken tiles. _____

10. I had no phone messages, which was a disappointment. _____

Proofreading Application: Letter

Good writers are generally good proofreaders. Readers tend to admire and trust writing that is error-free. Make sure that you correct all errors in grammar, usage, spelling, and punctuation in your writing. Your readers will have more confidence in your words if you have done your best to proofread carefully.

In informal conversation and writing, the nonstandard use of pronouns is acceptable. Few people frown upon your answering the phone with "This is me." However, when you talk and write for formal purposes, including nonpersonal letters, you should follow the rules of standard English.

PROOFREADING ACTIVITY

The following is from a thank-you note composed by a student council member and addressed to a speaker who recently gave a presentation to the council. It contains several errors in pronoun usage. Find the errors and correct them using proofreading symbols.

Dear Dr. Singh:

Us student council members of John F. Kennedy High School wish to express our sincere thanks for you having spoken to the group. We are aware of how precious your time is, and we are all the more appreciative that you came. The story of how you went from being a penniless immigrant with little knowledge of English to becoming the director of a medical facility was truly inspiring.

The beneficiaries of your valuable insight are both us, the council members, and our classmates with who we will share your experiences. They and ourselves will have a greater appreciation for what dedication and hard work can accomplish.

I feel compelled to conclude with a personal aside, since the one whom related most strongly to your talk was probably me. When my parents were younger, they were migrant farmworkers, which has greatly influenced myself. You, like them, bettered yourself through an incredible amount of personal effort.

Again, my peers and me greatly appreciated your presentation.

for **CHAPTER 6: USING PRONOUNS CORRECTLY**   *pages 145–66*

Literary Model: Poetry

He was a big man, says the size of his shoes
on a pile of broken dishes by the house;
a tall man too, says the length of the bed
in an upstairs room; and a good, God-fearing man,
says the Bible with a broken back
on the floor below the window, dusty with sun;
but not a man for farming, say the fields
cluttered with boulders and the leaky barn.

A woman lived with him, says the bedroom wall
papered with lilacs and the kitchen shelves
covered with oilcloth, and they had a child
says the sandbox made from a tractor tire.
Money was scarce, say the jars of plum preserves
and canned tomatoes sealed in the cellar-hole,
and the winters cold, say the rags in the window frames.
It was lonely here, says the narrow gravel road.

Something went wrong, says the empty house
in the weed-choked yard. Stones in the fields
say he was not a farmer; the still-sealed jars
in the cellar say she left in a nervous haste.
And the child? Its toys are strewn in the yard
Like branches after a storm—a rubber cow,
a rusty tractor with a broken plow,
a doll in overalls. Something went wrong, they say.

—from "Abandoned Farmhouse" by Ted Kooser

EXERCISE A Write all of the personal pronouns that appear at least once in the poem. After each pronoun, indicate its case (*nominative, objective,* or *possessive*).

_____

_____

_____

_____

EXERCISE B The author has included personal pronouns without ever actually identifying the people to whom those pronouns refer. Why do you think he used this technique?

_____

_____

From "Abandoned Farmhouse" from *Sure Signs: New and Selected Poems* by Ted Kooser. Copyright © 1980 by Ted Kooser.
Reprinted by permission of **University of Pittsburgh Press.**

Language and Sentence Skills Practice

Literary Model (continued)

EXERCISE C   Using Kooser's poem as a model, write a short poem about one or more people who have experienced life-altering events. As Kooser did, include personal pronouns without establishing their antecedents.

_____

_____

_____

_____

_____

_____

_____

_____

_____

_____

_____

_____

_____

_____

_____

_____

EXERCISE D

1. To whom or what do the personal pronouns in your poem refer?

_____

_____

_____

_____

2. Do you think it would be effective to use personal pronouns without antecedents in other forms of writing—for example, in book reports, essays, or business letters? Explain your answer.

_____

_____

_____

_____

Writing Application: Movie Review

Everyone uses pronouns frequently while speaking and writing. We use pronouns because they help to eliminate repetition, since their function is to take the place of nouns. "Mike likes his brother's room more than his own" is much more efficient than "Mike likes Mike's brother's room more than Mike's own." However, precisely because of a pronoun's function, it is up to you, the writer or speaker, to make sure that each one you use clearly refers to a specific antecedent.

AMBIGUOUS	Libby told Shanelle about the Kwanzaa celebration when she called.
CLEAR	When Libby called Shanelle, she told Shanelle about the Kwanzaa celebration.
GENERAL	The news anchorperson from KVEW is giving a speech tomorrow night, which should be interesting.
CLEAR	The speech that the news anchorperson from KVEW will give tomorrow night should be interesting.

WRITING ACTIVITY

A well-written movie review provides information—without giving too much away—that potential viewers can use to determine whether they want to see the movie. The movie critic discusses the strengths and weaknesses of various aspects of the movie, such as the acting, directing, dialogue, and plot. Usually, the critic includes his or her opinion of the movie, supporting the opinion with good reasons. Write a review of a movie you have seen recently. Since you will be mentioning events, individuals, and groups of people in your review, you will necessarily use pronouns. Include at least ten pronouns, and make sure that each one has a clear and specific antecedent.

PREWRITING Determine which aspects of the movie you will discuss in your review. Create a chart in which each column head is one of these aspects. Spend a few minutes evaluating each aspect and filling in the column with your evaluations. When the chart is complete, read over your evaluations of each aspect, and form your overall opinion of the movie. You may find that the opinion you previously held has changed slightly after having analyzed the movie.

WRITING Use the information in your chart to guide your draft. You may find that some of the points you included in the chart are not as strong as others. Don't hesitate to discard the weaker points. Make sure that you support each evaluation with reasons and evidence. As new details and ideas occur to you, incorporate them into your draft.

REVISING Read your draft several times. First, concentrate on the content. Next, read with the organization in mind. Finally, zero in on style (how you've used words and sentences). Ask yourself whether you have supported your opinion of the movie with sufficient reasons and evidence. Be sure you have included at least ten pronouns, each of which has a clear and specific antecedent.

PUBLISHING Re-read your review for spelling and punctuation errors. Also, look to see that pronouns are used correctly. Is each pronoun reference clear and specific? Does every pronoun agree with its antecedent in number and gender? After polishing your review, pass out copies to classmates who might be considering seeing the movie.

EXTENDING YOUR WRITING

You may want to submit your review for publication in your school newspaper or on a Web site that publishes movie reviews. Find out what the guidelines are for length and submission dates.

Choices: Exploring Verbs

The following activities challenge you to find a connection between verbs and the world around you. Do the activity below that suits your personality best, and then share your discoveries with your class.

MATHEMATICS

Easy as One, Two, Three

In a paragraph, describe how you solved an algebraic equation. Make sure your tenses are consistent and appropriate. When you make the final draft of your paper, write the equation at the top and highlight (write in red or use some other method) each verb or verb phrase.

MUSIC

If I Were a . . .

Apparently, singers often wish they were elsewhere or that things were different. Lots of songs use the subjunctive mood. Get together with a few friends, and brainstorm a list of these songs and the lines that use the subjunctive mood. Then, you guessed it, prepare a handout or poster to accompany your oral reading. And, yes, do sing (or play) a line or two where needed or requested.

DISCUSSION

May I, or Can I?

Has anyone ever asked you the question above? What did he or she mean? What's the difference between asking "Can I be excused?" and "May I be excused?" Explain the proper use of these auxiliary verbs that are called modals. Create a poster that illustrates the differences, and post it in the classroom.

COMPUTER ART

Play It as It Lies

Use a public-domain illustration library to create small posters illustrating the proper use of the troublesome verbs *lie/lay.* If you want to go wild, you could design a deck of playing cards, with each card illustrating a situation in which one form of these verbs is used correctly. Naturally, you'll need to include the sentence that each picture illustrates.

ART

Rise and Shine

Have you ever seen those posters with giant words that have dozens of tiny words inside each letter? That's the kind of poster that you're going to make. First, make a list of every idiom, saying, proverb, common use, or famous quotation you can think of that includes some form of the words *rise* or *raise.* Then, write *Rise/Raise* in giant open letters on your poster and write your list of sayings inside each letter. Display your poster in the classroom where everyone can read it.

CREATIVE WRITING

Director of Urban Culture

Are you planning to enter the business world, or does government service appeal to you? For either field, you might consider mastering the art of passive constructions. For a number of reasons, passive constructions are often used in business and government writings. Read a few business and government publications, and identify a few examples. Then, write your own. You are the chief executive officer of either a business or a new or old governmental office. Write a press release in which you use a number of passive constructions.

DRAMA

Opposites Attract

Show your classmates active and passive voices in practice. Working with a partner, write a dialogue in which one person speaks only in the active voice and the other speaks only in the passive voice. Then, perform your skit in front of the class or videotape it and show it to the class. After your performance, lead a discussion of the impact voice had on characterization.

The Principal Parts of Verbs

7a. The four principal parts of a verb are the **base form,** the **present participle,** the **past,** and the **past participle.**

BASE FORM	paint	catch	be	take
PRESENT PARTICIPLE	[is] painting	[is] catching	[is] being	[is] taking
PAST	painted	caught	was, were	took
PAST PARTICIPLE	[has] painted	[has] caught	[has] been	[has] taken

EXERCISE A   For each of the following sets of verbs, underline the form that is specified in italics.

Example   *past participle*   **1.** drive, (is) driving, drove, (has) <u>driven</u>

present participle   **1.** whisper, (was) whispering, whispered, (have) whispered

past participle   **2.** wear, (is) wearing, wore, (has) worn

base   **3.** enumerate, (is) enumerating, enumerated, (had) enumerated

present participle   **4.** make, (was) making, made, (has) made

past   **5.** announce, (is) announcing, announced, (have) announced

EXERCISE B   On the line provided, identify the form of each of the following verbs by writing *B* for *base,* *P-P* for *present participle,* *PT* for *past,* or *PT-P* for *past participle.*

Examples _*P-P*_ **1.** (were) laughing

     _*PT*_ **2.** sang

_____ **6.** (is) traveling   _____ **16.** (are) saving

_____ **7.** tore   _____ **17.** swim

_____ **8.** (have) spoken   _____ **18.** (have) surfed

_____ **9.** blink   _____ **19.** (is) grinning

_____ **10.** (had) scheduled   _____ **20.** took

_____ **11.** (is) walking   _____ **21.** (is) pouring

_____ **12.** saw   _____ **22.** (has) swung

_____ **13.** activate   _____ **23.** prepare

_____ **14.** (has) rung   _____ **24.** wrote

_____ **15.** was   _____ **25.** (was) taught

USAGE

Language and Sentence Skills Practice

Regular Verbs

7b. | A *regular verb* generally forms its past and past participle by adding *–d* or *–ed* to the base form.

A few regular verbs have alternate past and past participle forms that end in *–t.*

BASE FORM	save	enjoy	burn
PRESENT PARTICIPLE	[is] saving	[is] enjoying	[is] burning
PAST	saved	enjoyed	burned *or* burnt
PAST PARTICIPLE	[has] saved	[has] enjoyed	[has] burned *or* burnt

EXERCISE A   On the line provided, write the past or past participle of the verb in parentheses to complete each of the following sentences correctly.

Example 1. Before the trip, I had ___loaded___ film in my camera. *(load)*

1. The bus to Tulum _____ at noon. *(arrive)*

2. Lush jungle _____ us. *(surround)*

3. The ruins of Tulum _____ like a huge castle. *(look)*

4. Scholars have _____ about when the Mayans built it. *(argue)*

5. The builders had _____ beautiful feathered serpents. *(carve)*

6. They had also _____ many pictures on the walls. *(paint)*

7. A fortified area called the Castillo _____ the ocean. *(face)*

8. We _____ up on one of the lower platforms. *(climb)*

9. Everyone _____ the beautiful wall decorations. *(admire)*

10. Instead of taking the bus home, we _____ by boat. *(return)*

EXERCISE B   Revise each sentence below by crossing out the present tense verb and writing above it the form specified in parentheses. You may need to add *has, have,* or *had.*

Example 1. Carla ~~likes~~ her science teacher. *(past participle)*
              had liked

11. Frantically, they search the attic and basement. *(past)*

12. Unfortunately, the speaker strays from the main point. *(past)*

13. Chen answers Sue's letter within a week. *(past participle)*

14. Rebecca finally calms the frightened neighbor. *(past participle)*

15. Madeline gleefully leaps over puddles of melted snow. *(past)*

Irregular Verbs A

7c. An *irregular verb* forms its past and past participle in some way other than by adding *–d* or *–ed* to the base form.

Irregular verbs form the past and past participle in several ways.

CHANGING VOWELS	begin, began, [has] begun; drink, drank, [has] drunk
CHANGING CONSONANTS	send, sent, [has] sent; make, made, [has] made
CHANGING VOWELS AND CONSONANTS	teach, taught, [has] taught; fly, flew, [has] flown
MAKING NO CHANGE	let, let, [has] let; burst, burst, [has] burst

EXERCISE A On the line provided, write the past or past participle of the verb in parentheses to complete each of the following sentences correctly.

Example 1. Noel has ___*given*___ me some study tips. *(give)*

1. Laura has _____ in the chorus for two years. *(sing)*

2. Julio has _____ golf lessons since spring. *(take)*

3. The president has _____ the first ball of the season. *(throw)*

4. Velma has _____ two short stories. *(write)*

5. The pond behind the school has _____ solid. *(freeze)*

6. She had measured the piece of wood very carefully before she _____ it. *(cut)*

7. Second base was _____ twice in the first game. *(steal)*

8. The dealer _____ the vase by accident. *(break)*

9. Yesterday Harry _____ to school on his bike. *(come)*

10. Ruben and Nancy _____ in the Boston Marathon. *(run)*

EXERCISE B Many of the following sentences contain an error in verb form. Cross out each incorrect verb form. Then, write the correct verb form above it. If a verb is already correct, write *C* above it.

Example 1. Before the movie's end, I had ~~ate~~ *eaten* the entire bucket of popcorn.

11. During shipping, part of the package's wrapping was tore.

12. My best friend bringed me a souvenir from his summer travels in Europe.

13. After the election, I heard the results on the radio.

14. The priest had rang the bells just after daybreak.

15. On the fishing trip last weekend, Kenneth catched a perch and a catfish.

Irregular Verbs B

| **7c.** | An *irregular verb* forms its past and past participle in some way other than by adding *–d* or *–ed* to the base form. |

USAGE

EXERCISE A   On the line provided, write the past or past participle of the verb in parentheses to complete each of the following sentences correctly.

Example 1. Several CDs ___*fell*___ from the shelf and clattered to the floor. *(fall)*

1. After the movie we _____ to a nearby pizza parlor. *(go)*

2. Jorge already _____ me about your picnic in the park. *(tell)*

3. Paul had _____ the topic of his report by that evening. *(choose)*

4. I _____ it was you making that sound! *(know)*

5. The construction workers _____ a hotel on the empty lot. *(build)*

6. Felicia has never _____ in public before. *(sing)*

7. Morgan cheered when the dart _____ the bull's-eye. *(hit)*

8. The hardworking employee had _____ each of the tasks on the list by closing. *(do)*

9. I think I _____ my keys in the restaurant. *(leave)*

10. I trust Darla and often have _____ her borrow my books and jewelry. *(let)*

EXERCISE B   Many of the following sentences contain an error in verb form. Underline each incorrect verb form. Then, write the correct verb form above it. If a verb is already correct, write *C* above it.

Example 1. The thief had <u>went</u> by that time.
         gone

11. These shoes costed too much.

12. A flock of birds flied overhead just before sunset yesterday.

13. I have ate already.

14. Who put these muddy shoes on the carpet?

15. Both boxers fighted hard in the ring.

16. Vicky has wore the same hat two days in a row.

17. After an hour's worth of rock climbing, I had became thirsty.

18. Well before her birthday, I had send Grandmother a card.

19. No one has ever cut my hair this attractively before!

20. Final exams have began.

Irregular Verbs C

7c. An *irregular verb* forms its past and past participle in some way other than by adding *–d* or *–ed* to the base form.

EXERCISE A Underline the correct verb form in parentheses in each of the following sentences.

Example 1. Before the snow began, the cows (*come, came*) in from the pasture.

1. Barry forced the key into the lock and (*bended, bent*) it.

2. Will you stay for dinner? I (*maked, made*) taco salad.

3. When I saw the look on Toni's face, I knew I had (*said, say*) too much.

4. Lottie has (*finded, found*) her calling in life: working as a physical therapist.

5. Have you ever (*have, had*) a case of laryngitis?

6. When I got home, I sniffed the air and (*knew, known*) someone had let a wet dog into the house.

7. Unfortunately, we (*spended, spent*) all our money and couldn't afford a limousine.

8. I have (*seeked, sought*) you out to ask an important question.

9. Indira, exhausted from the day, (*slept, sleeped*) soundly.

10. Sue was sure she had (*hidden, hidded*) a spare house key in the flower bed.

EXERCISE B Many of the following sentences contain an error in verb form. Cross out each incorrect verb. Then, write the correct verb above it. If a sentence is already correct, write *C* before the numeral.

Example 1. Someone has ~~took~~ *taken* the oars from this rowboat.

11. After a brief appearance, the whale gone back out to sea.

12. The mother duck leaded her ducklings to the water.

13. By the end of my first day on the job, I had sell several jet skis and some snorkeling equipment.

14. For years a friendly manatee has swam in the bay behind my house.

15. During a sudden storm, a ship full of swords, armor, and other antiques had sank near those rocks.

16. I have dove with a team of professional divers many times.

17. Over time, water has wore all rough edges from these stones.

18. According to legend, mermaids sometimes have sung to fishermen in these waters.

19. Late in the evening, pelicans flew overhead.

20. The crew done all their duties according to the schedule.

Irregular Verbs D

USAGE

7c. | An *irregular verb* forms its past and past participle in some way other than by adding –*d* or –*ed* to the base form.

EXERCISE A   On the line provided, write the past or past participle of the verb in parentheses to complete each of the following sentences correctly.

Example 1. Last summer I ___*bought*___ some winter clothing at great prices. *(buy)*

1. After the storm we discovered that several tree branches had _____ across the road. *(fall)*

2. After they had _____ several miles in silence, they began to sing. *(ride)*

3. Hot and dusty from the long walk through the fields, the men seized the jugs of water and _____ every drop. *(drink)*

4. She _____ every opportunity to encourage us in our work. *(take)*

5. When heavy rains continued day after day, the water _____ through the dam. *(burst)*

6. During the hurricane, flying debris _____ most of the windows. *(break)*

7. Has everyone _____ the supplies back where they belong? *(put)*

8. Because I had _____ in advance, I skipped the ticket line. *(pay)*

9. At sunset, Martina _____ on the sea wall and gazed out to sea. *(stand)*

10. Justin would have made a home run if Raquel hadn't _____ the ball. *(catch)*

EXERCISE B   Underline the correct verb form in parentheses in each of the following sentences.

Example 1. I have *(chose, chosen)* the dessert for our candlelight dinner.

11. Carlos stopped at the store and *(buy, bought)* pens and paper.

12. Previously, we had *(dived, dove)* near this small coral reef.

13. Norma admired the Italian herbs I *(grown, grew)* in pots on the windowsill.

14. Ryan *(feeled, felt)* much stronger after working out for three months.

15. From deep in my beach bag, I *(got, gotten)* sunscreen and lip balm.

16. Sasha has never *(forgiven, forgave)* me for forgetting her birthday.

17. In the final game of the season, Sara *(broke, broken)* several school records.

18. Tabitha *(seen, saw)* a shy smile on Beth's face.

19. In yesterday's seminar, the lifeguards *(teached, taught)* us about riptides and other water dangers.

20. I am so excited! I have never *(won, winned)* a contest before!

170

Irregular Verbs E

| **7c.** | An *irregular verb* forms its past and past participle in some way other than by adding –*d* or –*ed* to the base form. |

EXERCISE A On the line provided, write the past or past participle of the verb in parentheses to complete each of the following sentences correctly.

Example 1. Because he _____*did*_____ his work so well, he got a raise. (*do*)

1. Although Emily Dickinson _____ poetry most of her life, very little of her work was published until after her death. (*write*)

2. The animals _____ all the water, so he gave them some more. (*drink*)

3. Regarding weeds as unwanted intruders, she pulled them from the ground and _____ them on the compost pile. (*throw*)

4. The water was cold and daylight was fading, so he _____ only a short distance before turning back to shore. (*swim*)

5. The dew _____ during the night, covering each twig and blade of grass with a crisp, silvery coating. (*freeze*)

6. After my brother had _____ his new puppy a bath, he seemed wetter than the dog. (*give*)

7. She _____ in such a hushed voice that the people in the audience strained to hear her. (*speak*)

8. Frightened by the traffic, the deer _____ back into the forest. (*run*)

9. Leading the parade was an officer who _____ a prancing black horse. (*ride*)

10. When the church bell _____ on Tuesday evening, the villagers became alarmed. (*ring*)

EXERCISE B Many of the following sentences contain an error in verb form. Underline each incorrect verb form. Then, write the correct verb above it. If a sentence is already correct, write *C* before the numeral.

Example 1. The athlete has <u>tore</u> a ligament in his leg.
                               torn

11. The players had feel the excitement of the crowd in the stands.

12. At one time I had went to school with one of the players on the opposing team.

13. In the blink of an eye, the player on second had stole third base.

14. An assistant brung water to the thirsty players.

15. Sadly, a single mistake had cost us the game.

Language and Sentence Skills Practice

Lie and *Lay*

The verb *lie* means "to rest," "to recline," or "to be in a place." *Lie* does not take a direct object.
The verb *lay* means "to put (something) in place." *Lay* generally takes a direct object.

EXAMPLES   Tori **is lying** on the sofa. She **has lain** there since lunch.

I **will lay** the baby in his crib. I **laid** his blanket down first.

EXERCISE A   In each sentence below, underline the correct verb form in parentheses.

Example 1. If you (*lie, lay*) your hand on the glass tabletop, you'll leave fingerprints.

1. While I am (*laying, lying*) the tablecloth on the table, you can get the plates.

2. The discarded clothing (*lay, laid*) on the floor where I had left it.

3. Eddie was (*lying, laying*) in the hammock when the rain began.

4. Yesterday, after washing it by hand, I (*lay, laid*) the sweater flat for drying.

5. A student who is ill may (*lay, lie*) down in the nurse's office.

6. Ouch! I had (*lain, laid*) my hand on the stove before I realized it was hot.

7. I was (*laying, lying*) in bed when the earthquake occurred.

8. The waiter (*laid, lay*) chopsticks beside my plate.

9. The faded newspaper had (*laid, lain*) in the sun too long.

10. Someone has (*lain, laid*) a wet towel on the sofa.

EXERCISE B   If a verb form in the following sentences is incorrect, cross it out and write the correct form above it. If the verb is already correct, write *C* above it.

Example 1. Monica ~~laid~~ ^{lay} on a quilt beneath the starry sky.

11. I could have lain the rug in Jessie's room.

12. May I lay in the hammock in your backyard?

13. The builder should lie the pane of glass gently across the table for now.

14. Our hosts are laying an assortment of snacks on the coffee table.

15. Those old wagon wheels have laid beside the fence for years.

16. My opponent lay all her cards on the table.

17. Several coins are laying beside the cash register.

18. Despite the thunder and lightning, Sandra lay peacefully asleep.

19. The clown laid his curly green wig beside the other pieces of his costume.

20. Thomas laid on the beach each morning during his vacation.

Sit and *Set*

The verb *sit* means "to rest in a seated, upright position" or "to be in place." *Sit* seldom takes a direct object. The verb *set* means "to put (something) in a place." *Set* generally takes a direct object.

EXAMPLES The new student **can sit** in this desk. No one **has been sitting** here.

I **set** the flowers on the table. I **had** already **set** candles on the table.

EXERCISE A In each sentence below, underline the correct verb form in parentheses.

Example 1. I became tired of walking and (*sat*, *set*) on a park bench.

1. Please (*set*, *sit*) the packages on the table in the kitchen.

2. I always (*sit*, *set*) in the recliner to watch television.

3. I have (*sat*, *set*) the sprinkler on the lawn; you can turn on the water now.

4. A pot of potato and leek soup is (*setting*, *sitting*) on the stove.

5. The gardener gently (*set*, *sat*) young plants in the holes in the dirt.

6. Steve is (*sitting*, *setting*) the new parts beside the malfunctioning computer.

7. When we went to the opera, we (*set*, *sat*) in a box above the regular seats.

8. Carol will be (*setting*, *sitting*) with Janet and Shanique in the movie.

9. I had (*set*, *sat*) on the bench before I realized the varnish was still wet.

10. My friends had (*set*, *sat*) their birthday gifts for me on the table near the cake.

EXERCISE B If a verb in the following sentences is incorrect, cross it out and write the correct form above it. If the verb is already correct, write *C* above it.

Example 1. The chef ~~sat~~ *set* an assortment of ingredients on the counter.

11. Beside the oven, a kitchen timer set.

12. An assistant chef sat a carving knife near the smoked ham.

13. She had set on a high stool at the work counter.

14. She is sitting cherry tomatoes around the border of the platter.

15. Eight individual spinach salads are setting on the top shelf of the refrigerator.

16. Tall glasses of ice water had sat on the serving tray for ten minutes.

17. The basket of sourdough bread and the bowl of butter can set here.

18. Earlier in the day, a pastry chef had sat a Key lime pie in the dessert case.

19. The asparagus and artichoke dip should not sit too long without refrigeration.

20. The raw potatoes have been setting in a marinade of spices and broth.

USAGE

Rise and *Raise*

The verb *rise* means "to go up" or "to get up." *Rise* does not take a direct object. The verb *raise* means "to lift" or "to cause (something) to rise." *Raise* generally takes a direct object.

EXAMPLES   Larry **has risen** early today. The sun **rose** at 5:55 A.M.

I **was raising** the flag on my mailbox when Nora **raised** her hand in greeting.

EXERCISE A   In each sentence below, underline the correct verb form in parentheses.

Example 1. The watchdog (rose, raised) when it heard a noise.

1. The grizzly bear was (raising, rising) on its hind legs in defense of its cubs.

2. On the sidelines of the game, Megan (raised, rose) to her feet and cheered enthusiastically.

3. When he discovered the theft, the security guard immediately (rose, raised) an alarm.

4. Only dough with a leavening agent such as yeast will (raise, rise).

5. Because the toy was so popular, the store owner (raised, rose) its price.

6. Brandy, the singer and actress, had (risen, raised) to stardom while still a teenager.

7. You (rise, raise) a good point in the third paragraph of your paper.

8. The students in the yoga class are (raising, rising) their hands high above their heads.

9. The man on the dock had (raised, risen) his hand as a shade against the sun.

10. All students in the assembly (raised, rose) to their feet.

EXERCISE B   On the blank in each of the following sentences, write the correct form of *rise* or *raise*.

Example 1. The helium-filled balloons have _____risen_____ higher in the breeze.

11. Timothy _____ a good point about the importance of recycling in our discussion about the environment.

12. Gwen has _____ ostriches on her ostrich farm for ten years.

13. At the sports awards banquet, Nicole _____ when her name was called.

14. Steam has _____ from these grates in the street ever since cold weather began.

15. Because I had _____ the windows, fresh air blew through the house.

16. Do not _____ while the boat is moving.

17. If you _____ the lid on that box, you'll find the surprise I have for you.

18. I _____ from the floor in front of the TV and stretched my legs.

19. The cheerleaders have _____ a banner above their heads.

20. Carlotta _____ from her chair and offered it to the man with a cast on his leg.

Six Troublesome Verbs

Six verbs that can be troublesome are *lie* and *lay*, *sit* and *set*, and *rise* and *raise*.

EXAMPLES   Claude **had lain** on his bed, and his mom **laid** a blanket over him.

We **will sit** here, and the caterers can **set** the buffet table over there.

A flock of birds **rose**, and I **raised** my binoculars to observe them.

EXERCISE A   In each sentence below, underline the correct verb form in parentheses.

Example 1. Your backpack is *(laying, <u>lying</u>)* on your desk.

1. We *(lay, laid)* on the white sandy beaches of Paradise Island.

2. The nobility *(sat, set)* in the balcony of the Globe Theater.

3. Kino, the main character, must *(raise, rise)* at dawn to dive for pearls.

4. Professor Jee *(lay, laid)* her final exams on the desk before she left.

5. Dr. Ceballos had *(sat, set)* his camera on a table.

6. The baby's voice *(rose, raised)* in a cry of hunger.

7. Has the wet newspaper *(lain, laid)* on the table all day?

8. The superintendent suddenly *(raised, rose)* her hand and asked for silence.

9. *(Lie, Lay)* down and rest before the next act.

10. Personal income has not *(risen, raised)* enough to keep up with inflation.

EXERCISE B   If a form of *lie, lay, sit, set, rise,* or *raise* in the following sentences is incorrect, cross it out and write the correct form above it. If the sentence is already correct, write *C* to the left of the numeral.

Example 1. I am ~~setting~~ *sitting* by the aisle.

11. The theater grew quiet when the curtain raised.

12. Julie had just sat something on the shelf.

13. When I set down, Julie brought over a black vase.

14. Gently, she lay the vase on the table.

15. A beautiful sienna vase by Popovi Da was laying in front of me.

16. We left our lawn furniture setting on the patio.

17. They lain the bricks in a pile next to where we sat the wood.

18. When the dough has risen for fifteen minutes, turn it out onto the floured board.

19. When we are rising from bed in the morning, people in China are laying down to sleep.

20. An hour ago he laid down to watch television, but he fell asleep.

Tense A

7d. | The *tense* of a verb indicates the time of the action or the state of being expressed by the verb.

Each tense has another form, called the *progressive form*, which is used to express continuing action or state of being. The progressive form consists of the appropriate tense of the verb *be* and the present participle of a verb.

7e. | Each of the six tenses has its own uses.

EXERCISE Above each underlined verb, identify its tense by writing *present, past, future, present perfect, past perfect*, or *future perfect*. Also, indicate if the tense is in the progressive form by writing *prog* above the verb.

Example 1. By the end of sophomore year, I shall have achieved many personal goals.
future perfect

1. We took the bike path through the woods.

2. By noon, they will have practiced for two hours.

3. Francine feels ill.

4. You will succeed if you try.

5. They had arrived before I got there.

6. She has visited China twice in the past three years.

7. Charo will be calling when she needs a ride.

8. You have talked on the telephone for two hours!

9. I will be glad to go to the movies with you tonight.

10. For a long time, I believed in good-luck charms.

11. The psychiatrist had been preparing carefully for her next patient.

12. Brandy watches cartoons on Saturday mornings.

13. As of next Friday, I shall have been employed here six months.

14. We will be happy with the results of our remodeling project.

15. Glenn is paying the final installment on his layaway purchase.

16. Your horse has gotten into the vegetable garden again.

17. If we keep up this pace, we will reach the campsite well before dark.

18. By midmorning, Nisha had given manicures to six clients.

19. The neighbors' Rottweiler has barked all night.

20. By spring break, I will have saved enough money for an airplane ticket to Florida.

USAGE

Tense B

7d. The *tense* of a verb indicates the time of the action or the state of being expressed by the verb.

Each tense has another form, called the *progressive form*, which is used to express continuing action or state of being. The progressive form consists of the appropriate tense of the verb *be* and the present participle of a verb.

7e. Each of the six tenses has its own uses.

EXERCISE On the line provided, write the form of the verb called for in parentheses.

Example 1. I _____*saw*_____ that show twice yesterday. (*see*, past)

1. Jess _____ as fast as he could. (*run*, past perfect progressive)

2. Takara _____ the class tomorrow. (*address*, future)

3. Mr. Saito _____ that the dog is friendly. (*conclude*, present perfect)

4. I _____ the chapter, but I have questions about one section. (*review*, past)

5. Rajesh _____ to band camp each summer. (*go*, present)

6. When I turn twenty-one, I _____ for six years. (*work*, future perfect)

7. This brisk wind _____ a cloud of dust. (*create*, present perfect)

8. I _____ a pack of gum, but I couldn't find it. (*buy*, past perfect)

9. Marisela _____ a serape on her wall. (*hang*, past progressive)

10. Marc _____ the design of the Web site when you arrive tomorrow. (*finish*, future perfect)

11. My mom cooks, and my dad _____ the dishes. (*wash*, present)

12. I _____ my mistake almost immediately. (*realize*, past)

13. Manuel _____ Leigh that he would be there. (*promise*, past perfect)

14. Grace's grandmother _____ for city council. (*run*, future progressive)

15. Finally! I _____ my ring! (*find*, present perfect)

16. By June, the book club _____ all the books on this list. (*read*, future perfect)

17. Mr. Patel _____ his son how to change gears. (*teach*, past)

18. Park rangers _____ the bridge across the stream. (*repair*, past perfect)

19. Ned _____ basketball practice by the time we arrive. (*finish*, future perfect)

20. The tailor _____ on that button after he hems these trousers. (*sew*, future)

Language and Sentence Skills Practice

177

Consistency of Tense

7f.   Do not change needlessly from one tense to another.

(1) When describing events that occur at the same time, use verbs in the same tense.

   EXAMPLE   Gail **loaded** film in the camera and **took** several pictures as the eagle **soared** overhead.

(2) When describing events that occur at different times, use verbs in different tenses to show the sequence of events.

   EXAMPLE   She **took** the film to the processor and **will enter** the pictures in a contest when they **come** back.

EXERCISE   In the sentences below, cross out any verb tense error and write the correct form above it. If a sentence is already correct, write *C* to the left of the numeral. (*Note:* There is more than one way to revise some sentences; give only one answer.)

Example **1.** Connie called her brother and ~~asks~~ *asked* him over for dinner.

1. Tomorrow night we will go to the concert, and Jane joined us.

2. If you have asked me earlier, I would have been able to give you an answer.

3. Ever since Marilu will have become president of the company, sales have increased.

4. My niece Claire had left before Harold arrives.

5. When you are at the store, did you pick up any onions?

6. I had decided to try out for the team even before the coach called me.

7. Pascal had been living in Italy for two months when he was meeting Rosa.

8. What happened to the box of cereal we have been buying yesterday?

9. Perhaps we will never know how it disappeared from the cupboard.

10. Joel lifted the suitcase and has set it in the overhead bin on the airplane.

Modals A

7g. | A *modal* is a helping (or auxiliary) verb that is joined with a main verb or an infinitive to express an attitude toward the action or state of being of the main verb.

(1) The modal *can* or *could* is used to express ability.

(2) The modal *may* is used to express permission or possibility.

> **EXAMPLES**   **Can** you **lift** that heavy box? I **could lift** it, but my wrist is sprained.
> You **may borrow** my new CD; however, you **may** not **like** the music.

(3) The modal *might,* like *may,* is used to express possibility. Often, the possibility expressed by *might* is less likely than the possibility expressed by *may.*

(4) The modal *must* is used most often to express a requirement. Sometimes, *must* is used to express an explanation.

> **EXAMPLES**   Brittany **might win** the race, but Cheryl is a faster runner.
> All contest entries **must be** postmarked by June 9, 2003.

EXERCISE   For each of the following sentences, write an appropriate modal on the blank provided. Choose your answer from the modals *can, could, may, might,* and *must.*

Example 1. "Dad, _____ may _____ I get a pet canary?" asked Hamid.

1. I _____ hear my neighbors through the thin walls of my apartment.

2. The scientist _____ have had a breakthrough in her search for an antidote.

3. Antonio thinks it _____ snow tomorrow although there is only a 25 percent chance of snow.

4. I _____ go out for track, but I should probably spend my afternoons studying.

5. Dorian _____ not read without glasses or contact lenses.

6. The tire _____ have been punctured by a nail.

7. Someone _____ have lost this bracelet while swimming here yesterday.

8. Each student _____ wear safety goggles in shop class.

9. I _____ have taken the bus home, but I preferred walking.

10. Brandon _____ know the Web site address.

Language and Sentence Skills Practice

Modals B

7g. | A *modal* is a helping (or auxiliary) verb that is joined with a main verb or an infinitive to express an attitude toward the action or state of being of the main verb.

(5) The modal *ought* is used to express an obligation or a likelihood.

(6) The modal *will* or *shall* is used to express future time.

EXAMPLES   Ryan **ought** to receive an award.

The ceremony **ought** to have started by now.

The package **will arrive** in three to five days.

(7) The modal *should* is used to express a recommendation, an obligation, or a possibility.

(8) The modal *would* is used to express the conditional form of a verb.

EXAMPLES   We **should place** new items in the display case.

If my uncle opened a bakery, he **would be fulfilling** a lifelong dream.

EXERCISE   For each of the following sentences, write an appropriate modal on the blank provided. Choose your answer from the modals *ought, will, shall, should,* and *would.*

Example 1. This gift _____*ought*_____ to make Joni very happy.

1. We _____ not say anything to Bahri-Gilani; it will be a surprise.

2. _____ anyone have questions about the test, I will gladly answer them.

3. If you exercised with me, I know you _____ enjoy it.

4. _____ you go to the dance with me?

5. We _____ overcome these difficulties and be stronger because of them.

6. Do you think I _____ get the job?

7. The director stated, "These lines _____ to be delivered tearfully."

8. Nelle _____ enter the art contest; she is sure to win.

9. _____ you excuse me for a moment? I need to make a phone call.

10. Customers _____ not come behind the counter.

Modals Review

7g. A *modal* is a helping (or auxiliary) verb that is joined with a main verb or an infinitive to express an attitude toward the action or state of being of the main verb.

The helping verbs *can, could, may, might, must, ought, shall, should, will,* and *would* are used as modals.

EXAMPLE Our study group **could meet** at my grandfather's coffee shop.

EXERCISE For each of the following sentences, write an appropriate modal on the blank provided. Choose your answer from the modals listed at the top of this page.

Example 1. You _____*should*_____ take the medicine exactly as the doctor prescribed.

1. When _____ I see you again?

2. Because the leaves of the mountain laurel are poisonous, children and pets _____ not be permitted to eat or chew on them.

3. You _____ borrow my cashmere sweater if you don't get it dirty.

4. The Greenville Rams _____ win the playoff, but odds are in favor of the Panthers.

5. In order to get a job there, you _____ have a social security number.

6. Sandra _____ have become a writer, but she studied medicine instead.

7. My younger sister _____ count to ten in four different languages.

8. If I had known you were there, I _____ have sat with you.

9. We _____ to have a party for our parents' anniversary.

10. The alarm system _____ sound if a window or door is opened.

11. This Chinese dish is very spicy, and you _____ not like it.

12. Intruders _____ beware of the guard dogs.

13. If I had a compass, I _____ tell you which way is north.

14. Jada _____ have forgotten our agreement to meet here at six o'clock.

15. _____ Angie cook?

16. Wesley _____ to be commended for his work on the set for the play.

17. If I knew the answer to the question, I _____ tell you.

18. When _____ I pick you up for dinner?

19. I _____ read that book, but I'd rather read this one about an adventure at sea.

20. Eric _____ change the oil in your car.

Active and Passive Voice

USAGE

| **7h.** | When the subject of a verb performs the action, the verb is in the ***active voice.*** When the subject of a verb receives the action, the verb is in the ***passive voice.*** |

> **ACTIVE**   Megan **played** the guitar.
> **PASSIVE**   The guitar **was played** by Megan.

EXERCISE A   In each of the following sentences, identify the voice of the verb by writing above it *A* for *active* or *P* for *passive.*

Example 1. The ballad was sung by Tiffany.   *[P marked above "was sung"]*

1. Janice was told by the doctor to rest.

2. At first, Alfredo was puzzled by the math problem.

3. Po Lan's mother and father encouraged her.

4. The dogwood blossoms were surrounded by bumblebees.

5. Helga's lost kitten was found by a neighbor.

6. Liona was hit by a fast-moving ball.

7. Robert Frost wrote "The Road Not Taken."

8. Grazing sheep covered the pasture.

9. The trapeze artist was watched closely by the crowd.

10. The bouquet of flowers was selected by Nahele.

EXERCISE B   On the line provided, revise each sentence below so that the verb is in the active voice.

Example 1. The books were carried by Leta.   *Leta carried the books.*

11. The leaves were blown from the trees by the winter winds.

_____

12. Michael was temporarily blinded by the sun.

_____

13. The amplifier was repaired by my cousin.

_____

14. The Kings' house was painted by college students last summer.

_____

15. The wedding cake was decorated with sugar roses by Angelica.

_____

Using and Revising the Passive Voice

7i.	The passive voice should be used sparingly.

Use the passive voice when you want to emphasize the receiver of the action or when you do not know, or do not want to reveal, the performer of the action.

EXAMPLES   A lifeboat full of sailors **was discovered** off the coast.

The museum **was robbed** yesterday.

EXERCISE   On the lines provided, revise any of the following sentences that contain awkward or unnecessary passive-voice constructions. If you think a sentence is best the way it is, write *C* and explain why.

Example 1. An ancient mummy was discovered in a secluded burial site.

C. Passive voice emphasizes the receiver of the action.

1. A body can be embalmed with preservatives for burial. _____

_____

2. Mummification was practiced by South American Incas, Egyptians, and others. _____

_____

3. Internal organs were removed by ancient Egyptian embalmers. _____

_____

4. At one point in history, the organs were treated and replaced by the embalmer. _____

_____

5. Linen bandages were wrapped around the body. _____

_____

6. In the Middle Ages, the embalming solution was considered medicinal. _____

_____

7. Mummified bodies were pounded into "mummy" by apothecaries and healers. _____

_____

8. Mummy was then given as medicine by apothecaries. _____

_____

9. Mummy was later made from the bodies of felons and suicides. _____

_____

10. The use of mummy was continued by Europeans until the 1700s. _____

_____

Mood

USAGE

7j. *Mood* is the form a verb takes to indicate the attitude of the person using the verb.

(1) The *indicative mood* is used to express a fact, an opinion, or a question.
(2) The *imperative mood* is used to express a direct command or request.
(3) The *subjunctive mood* is used to express a suggestion, a necessity, a condition contrary to fact, or a wish.

EXERCISE In each of the following sentences, identify the mood of the verb by writing above it *IND* for *indicative, IMP* for *imperative,* or *SUB* for *subjunctive.*

IND
Example 1. Do you <u>enjoy</u> compelling, realistic fiction?

1. If you <u>were</u> called a monster by a lawyer, how would you feel?

2. If the lawyer thought you had committed a crime, <u>would</u> people <u>believe</u> him?

3. <u>Keep</u> these questions in mind as you read *Monster.*

4. It is vital that sixteen-year-old Steve Harmon <u>remain</u> positive throughout his trial.

5. He <u>is accused</u> of playing a role in the fatal shooting of a convenience-store owner.

6. If I <u>were</u> in Steve's place, I would certainly panic.

7. <u>Listen</u> to what Steve does to remain calm during the trial.

8. He is an aspiring filmmaker, and he <u>chronicles</u> the trial in movie script format.

9. I recommend that you <u>try</u> this practice when you are in a stressful situation.

10. Many people <u>realize</u> the therapeutic value of writing about problems.

11. Steve <u>keeps</u> a journal in which he records thoughts about his life before and after the murder.

12. The movie script and journal entries <u>form</u> the book that you read.

13. During certain portions of the book, some readers may think that Steve <u>is</u> guilty.

14. Other readers <u>will be</u> sure that Steve is innocent.

15. Christopher Myers, son of the author Walter Dean Myers, <u>illustrated</u> *Monster.*

16. If I <u>were</u> Christopher, I would be proud of working on such a project with my dad.

17. <u>Consider</u> the Michael L. Printz Award.

18. The Young Adult Library Services Association (YALSA) believes that outstanding books for teenagers <u>should be honored</u>.

19. Someone suggested that YALSA <u>consider</u> *Monster* for its Michael L. Printz Award.

20. YALSA believed the suspenseful, realistic *Monster* <u>had earned</u> the award.

Review A: **The Principal Parts of Verbs**

EXERCISE A   One sentence in each of the following sets of sentences contains an error in verb form. Draw a line through the error. Then, write the correct form of the verb above the error.

Example 1. [a] He has written a poem. [b] They have ~~took~~ *taken* a break. [c] It had burst.

1. [a] The lake had frozen over. [b] The sweater has shrunk. [c] I have rode that horse.

2. [a] He begun the fight. [b] Who bought it? [c] They swam well.

3. [a] They have stolen apples. [b] You had chosen well. [c] He has drove the tractor.

4. [a] It had broke. [b] He has bought shoes. [c] They had fallen.

5. [a] The bell rung. [b] The boy ran. [c] The teacher saw him.

6. [a] You drank it. [b] We drived there. [c] She ran fast.

7. [a] He stole it. [b] The bell rang. [c] She had spoke.

8. [a] We have wrote. [b] She has fallen. [c] It was frozen.

9. [a] You had given. [b] He has went. [c] They have taken.

10. [a] We had ridden. [b] It had begun. [c] He has chose.

EXERCISE B   On the line provided, write the correct form (past or past participle) of the verb in parentheses.

Example 1. Has anyone ever ___*begun*___ dancing lessons willingly? *(begin)*

11. I think that most people have _____ to their first dancing lessons unwillingly. *(go)*

12. I _____ a fit before going to my first dancing lesson. *(throw)*

13. It was my mother who _____ me there. *(take)*

14. I _____ from the very start that there was no use arguing about it. *(see)*

15. The woman who _____ the dancing school was one of my mother's friends. *(run)*

16. She _____ over and welcomed us when we appeared for the first class. *(come)*

17. I _____ down in a corner and hoped no one would see me. *(sit)*

18. I stayed in my chair until an instructor had _____ to me firmly two or three times. *(speak)*

19. Soon she had _____ my hand and led me out on the floor. *(take)*

20. I _____ my best to follow the lesson, but I didn't learn very fast. *(do)*

Language and Sentence Skills Practice

USAGE

Review B: Troublesome Verbs and Tense

USAGE

EXERCISE A Some of the following sentences contain errors in verb usage. Draw a line through each incorrect verb. Then, write the correct verb above the error. If a sentence is already correct, write *C* to the left of the numeral.

Example 1. Ricardo ~~sat~~ *set* his catcher's mitt on the bench.

1. Those books have lain on the shelf for a long time.

2. By nine o'clock in the morning, the temperature had raised to ninety-five degrees.

3. A watchdog was laying at the front gate, ready to pounce on any unsuspecting stranger who might approach the house.

4. The man set in a comfortable chair near the fireplace.

5. After 6:00 P.M., the price of movie admission raises to eight dollars.

6. Before you leave, please straighten the newspapers that are laying all over the table.

7. Out of breath, the woman set the heavy package on the floor.

8. We rose the curtain to see if the sun had risen.

9. Having grown tired of wandering around the house, the sick child laid down to rest.

10. The lazy dog would just set there in its favorite spot for hours.

EXERCISE B The following passage contains needless changes in tense. Above each underlined verb, write the verb in the correct tense. If the tense is already correct, write *C*.

Example What [1] <u>is</u> *C* the most embarrassing accident that you [2] <u>will have</u> *have had*?

I [11] <u>had</u> a curious accident one day last summer. Late one afternoon I [12] <u>am riding</u> my bicycle down a busy street when someone suddenly [13] <u>opens</u> the door of a parked car right in front of me. The bicycle [14] <u>slammed</u> into the car door, and I [15] <u>am thrown</u> into the front seat, right next to the driver. When I [16] <u>realize</u> that the driver [17] <u>happens</u> to be one of the science teachers from the high school, I [18] <u>was overcome</u> with embarrassment. Much to my surprise, however, the teacher [19] <u>apologizes</u> to me at length and [20] <u>blames</u> himself for being careless. Do you think this incident proves that teachers know they make mistakes, too?

for **CHAPTER 7: USING VERBS CORRECTLY** *pages 172–202*

Review C: **Principal Parts, Tense, and Voice**

EXERCISE A On the line provided, write the correct form (past or past participle) of the verb in parentheses.

Example 1. The small, yapping Chihuahua has nearly ___driven___ me crazy. (*drive*)

1. After careful deliberation she _____ to run for office. (*choose*)

2. I am interested in reading the essay that you have _____. (*write*)

3. He had _____ the entire length of the pool. (*swim*)

4. My imagination had _____ away with me. (*run*)

5. Has the lake _____ over yet? (*freeze*)

EXERCISE B In the following sentences, cross out each verb that is in the wrong tense or that is in an awkward passive voice. Then, write a revision on the line provided. If a sentence is already correct, write *C* on the line.

Example 1. Although United States voters have never elected a female president, many women ~~had risen~~ to high government positions.

Although United States voters have never elected a female president, many women have risen to high government positions.

6. Katherine Davalos Ortega has worked in her family's restaurant and other businesses when she was a small child. _____

_____

7. She was told that being Hispanic might prevent her from getting a teaching position. _____

_____

8. As a result, a business career was pursued by her instead. _____

_____

9. By 1975, she will become the first woman president of a California bank. _____

_____

10. Ms. Ortega, in recognition of her professional abilities, was nominated by President Reagan to be Treasurer of the United States. _____

_____

Language and Sentence Skills Practice

Review D: Modals and Mood

USAGE

EXERCISE A In each of the following sentences, write an appropriate modal in the blank provided. Choose your answer from the modals *can, could, may, might, must, ought, shall, should, will,* and *would.*

Example 1. Most kindergartners _____*can*_____ memorize their own phone number.

1. I _____ have waved at you if I had seen you.

2. You and your friend _____ borrow my car on Saturday.

3. I _____ have spoken in his defense; unfortunately, I did not.

4. The substitute teacher _____ be back tomorrow, but Ms. Raign will probably be feeling better.

5. Computer files _____ be saved frequently to avoid loss in case of a crash.

6. No one _____ go without a coat in the winter.

7. _____ you tie the various knots taught in the Boy Scouts?

8. Tomorrow we _____ find out who the winner is.

9. My doctor said I _____ to eat vegetables every day.

10. When your photographs are developed, we _____ call you.

EXERCISE B In each of the following sentences, identify the mood of the underlined verb by writing above it *IND* for *indicative, IMP* for *imperative,* or *SUB* for *subjunctive.*

Example 1. Do you *count* objects when you cannot sleep? *(IND)*

11. Some people count sheep when they cannot sleep.

12. I think that clouds are more interesting to count.

13. Since I first saw them from an airplane window, clouds have fascinated me.

14. It is vital to my peace of mind that I watch clouds shifting shapes and traveling lazily across the sky.

15. Did you know that I have never seen two identical clouds?

16. Think of the shapes of clouds you have observed.

17. If I were a cloud, I would resemble misshapen cotton balls tossed at random into a pile.

18. Just as I do, you may wish you were as carefree as a cloud.

19. My father suggested that I become a meteorologist.

20. Please tell me what you think of my pursuing a career as a cloud sculptor.

Proofreading Application: Letter

Good writers are generally good proofreaders. Readers tend to admire and trust writing that is error-free. Make sure that you correct all errors in grammar, usage, spelling, and punctuation in your writing. Your readers will have more confidence in your words if you have done your best to proofread carefully.

When you write a letter to an elected official, you want to create a good impression as you express your opinion. Your verbs should be free of errors in form, usage, and tense.

PROOFREADING ACTIVITY

The following is a letter addressed to a state legislator. Find and correct the errors in verb form, usage, and tense. Use proofreading symbols to make your corrections.

Dear Ms. Barrera:

I was born and raised in the tiny town of Lawrenceville in the Panhandle of Texas. I plan to live here all my life and even to rise children here. It is a good community that sets in a beautiful prairie landscape. However, I am greatly concerned because this wonderful community has began to shrink in population. The problem was the lack of jobs; too many people are moving to places where they can find work. Even though a flour company is supposed to build a mill here last year, the owners changed their minds and builded it in the Valley instead.

Yesterday as I drive by the Canadian River, which is within walking distance of Lawrenceville, I imagine a state park on its banks. The recreation areas south of here have certainly help the economies of nearby towns. Lawrenceville citizens would be provided with work by the construction and maintenance of a state park.

Please give thoughtful attention to my proposal. To a certain extent, the future of Lawrenceville lays in your hands.

Sincerely,

Robert Ellington

Literary Model: Narrative

> I set down there on a log and looked out through the leaves. I see the moon go off watch and the darkness begin to blanket the river. But in a little while I see a pale streak over the tree-tops, and knowed the day was coming. So I . . . slipped off towards where I had run across that camp fire, stopping every minute or two to listen. But I hadn't no luck, somehow; I couldn't seem to find the place. But by-and-by, sure enough, I catched a glimpse of fire, away through the trees. I went for it, cautious and slow. By-and-by I was close enough to have a look, and there laid a man on the ground. . . . I set there behind a clump of bushes, in about six foot of him, and kept my eyes on him steady. It was getting gray daylight, now. Pretty soon he gapped, and stretched himself, and hove off the blanket, and it was Miss Watson's Jim! I bet I was glad to see him. I says:
>
> "Hello, Jim!" . . .
>
> —from *Adventures of Huckleberry Finn* by Mark Twain

EXERCISE A   In this excerpt, Huckleberry Finn makes errors in *verb form, verb tense,* and *verb choice.* For each of the underlined verbs in the excerpt, identify the kind of error made.

set _____   catched _____

see _____   laid _____

knowed _____

EXERCISE B   If the story were written in third person, using only standard verb forms, how would the characterization of Huck be different?

_____

_____

_____

_____

_____

_____

for **CHAPTER 7: USING VERBS CORRECTLY** *pages 172–204*

Literary Model (continued)

EXERCISE C Write a paragraph spoken by a character who is describing an event from his or her past. Have the character's speech include several incorrect verb forms.

_____

_____

_____

_____

_____

_____

_____

EXERCISE D

1. Rewrite the paragraph, correcting all verb forms.

_____

_____

_____

_____

_____

_____

_____

2. Compare the original and rewritten paragraphs in terms of a reader's impression about the character who is speaking.

_____

_____

_____

_____

Language and Sentence Skills Practice

Writing Application: Personal Essay

In English the tense of the verb indicates the time of the action or of the state of being that the verb is expressing. You, as a writer, by using verb tense correctly and consistently, can help your reader understand when the events in your writing occur. At times you will need to use different tenses in a paragraph or even in the same sentence, but be careful not to change needlessly from one tense to another.

EXAMPLE   Mrs. Santayana, our seventy-year-old neighbor, takes a stroll through the park every afternoon. I saw her yesterday as she was feeding the pigeons. I asked myself whether she'll be doing the same thing ten years from now.

WRITING ACTIVITY

Although you have many years to go before becoming an elder, it is a part of your life cycle. Write a personal essay in which you incorporate your vision of yourself as an elderly person, along with your opinions and ideas about the experience of being elderly in this country. In your essay, you will be addressing past, present, and future time frames. Use at least four different verb tenses correctly.

PREWRITING   Freewrite for several minutes on the topic of being elderly in this country. Next, freewrite about your personal experiences with, as well as observations of, elderly people—both those you know well and those you have observed in public places. Then, let your imagination loose as you freewrite in response to these questions: What will I be like, both physically and emotionally, when I'm seventy-five years old? Which abilities will I still retain, and which will I have lost? What will be the physical circumstances of my life?

WRITING   Write a draft of your ideas, arranging them in the order that seems most appropriate. Will you order them from those that are most important to you personally to those that are least important? Will you order them according to a classification scheme you have devised? You might consider devoting one paragraph to your observations and experiences, another to your thoughts on what it is like to be elderly in this country, and another to your vision of yourself as an elder.

REVISING   Ask a classmate to read your draft. Ask him or her to tell you its strengths and weaknesses, as well as a few suggestions for improving it. Furthermore, ask your peer evaluator whether the writing holds his or her attention and whether the ideas are smoothly connected and arranged in a sensible order. Check that you have used at least four verb tenses, that they are all used correctly, and that you have not introduced inconsistency of tense.

PUBLISHING   Proofread your essay for errors in grammar, usage, spelling, and punctuation. Prepare your essay for presentation in front of your classmates. Since your audience will be your peers, you may need to revise the essay. Check that the tone and the level of language is appropriate.

EXTENDING YOUR WRITING

You may want to expand this activity into a research project. Interview several people, both younger and older than you, and ask them the same questions about aging that you asked yourself in prewriting. Compare the results, paying particular attention to how the use of tenses varies with age.

for **CHAPTER 8: USING MODIFIERS CORRECTLY** | pages 212–28

Choices: Exploring Modifiers

The following activities challenge you to find a connection between modifiers and the world around you. Do the activity below that suits your personality best, and then share your discoveries with your class.

CREATIVE WRITING

Modern Art

Some modern artists have made an entire career out of experimenting with conventional frames of reference. These artists might turn objects inside out, or they might place the color for an object next to, rather than on, the object. In short, the qualities that modify or characterize an object can be misplaced or disconnected. Picasso was an expert at this technique. Translate one of Picasso's wonderfully strange paintings into words. How have the modifiers been separated from what they modify? Post a copy of the painting and your interpretation in the classroom where people can examine them.

COMPUTER PROGRAMMING

U. Sage Knows All

Now that you know how to avoid using misplaced modifiers, share your knowledge with younger students. Create a video game in which everyone's favorite dispenser of wisdom, U. Sage, leads children through a maze of choices about where to place modifiers in sentences. You do not need to program the game; simply prepare a diagram showing what the game would look like and how players would progress through levels and screens. Of course, you'll want to include some examples of choices that the user must make.

REVIEW

Was, Is, and Ever Shall Be

When a modifier follows a verb, how do you know if the modifier is an adjective or an adverb? Being able to recognize linking verbs will help you distinguish the adjectives from the adverbs. If you're not quite sure about linking verbs, take the time to review them now. On a sheet of paper, neatly write the definition of linking verbs. Then, make a table of linking verbs and add examples of sentences using these verbs. Make copies and hand them out to your classmates.

DISCUSSION

More or Less Equal

Absolute adjectives such as *unique, equal,* and *perfect* should not be used by degrees. After all, two things are either equal or they're not. What do you think of this rule? Lead a discussion about this rule. Begin by writing a number of absolute adjectives on the chalkboard. For each word, discuss conditions under which this word might sensibly be used with *more* or *less.* Which absolute adjectives do you feel should never be used in comparisons? Explain your reasoning to the class.

MUSIC

Bad Rap

If you like rap music and you know *bad* means "good," you've got a head start on this project. Read over the section about *bad* and *badly* and the other pairs of troublesome modifiers in your textbook. Then, transform those rather ordinary bits of advice into an extraordinary rap song that will explain, perhaps with humor, the rules about these modifiers.

VISUAL

Go with the Flow

Sometimes a picture makes everything clear. Make a flowchart detailing the steps in identifying a modifier as an adjective or an adverb. Begin by identifying the questions you ask yourself as you consider the possibilities. Then, add a few example sentences to your chart and illustrate the steps you use to identify modifiers. Prepare your chart on poster board, and present it to the class.

Adjective or Adverb?

8a. If a word in the predicate modifies the subject of the verb, use the adjective form. If it modifies the verb, use the adverb form.

| **ADJECTIVE** | That music is **quiet.** [*Quiet* follows the linking verb *is* and modifies the subject *music*.] |

| **ADVERB** | The band played **quietly.** [*Quietly* modifies the verb *played*.] |

While many adverbs end in *–ly*, others do not. Furthermore, some adjectives also end in *–ly*. Some words can be used as both adjectives and adverbs.

ADVERBS   I'll call you **later.**   Who finished **first**?

ADJECTIVES   The **unruly** children are annoying.   My **first** choice is Brahms.

EXERCISE A   In each of the following sentences, draw an arrow from the underlined adjective or adverb to the word it modifies.

Example 1. She speaks only Dutch.

1. In European fairy tales, a dragon is usually bad.

2. Chinese dragons, however, are said to bring good fortune.

3. During the last Chinese New Year, a dragon moved slowly down the street.

4. I felt bad because I missed seeing the runner carrying the pearl of fire.

5. However, we all clapped loudly as we watched the parade.

EXERCISE B   In each of the following sentences, label the underlined word *ADJ* for *adjective* or *ADV* for *adverb*. Then, draw an arrow from the underlined word to the word it modifies.

Example 1. Ballet is a theatrical form of dance that first developed during the Renaissance.

6. Forms of dance contain recognizable elements.

7. The elements enable knowledgeable people to identify the type of dance.

8. A ballet usually includes the elements of music, costume, and scenery.

9. Anna Pavlova (1881–1931) was a famous ballerina from Russia.

10. Pavlova toured widely during her career.

11. In the 1910s and 1920s, the ballets of Sergei Diaghilev (1872–1929) were popular.

12. The productions of Diaghilev reflected a skillful collaboration between choreographer, designer, and composer.

13. Professionals are not the only ones who practice ballet.

14. Members of the general public take classes for fun or exercise.

15. Children happily perform *The Nutcracker* at Christmas.

Phrases Used as Modifiers

Like one-word modifiers, phrases can also be used as adjectives and adverbs.

EXAMPLES A letter **for Laura** arrived. [The prepositional phrase *for Laura* acts as an adjective that modifies the noun *letter*.]

Frozen solid, the sandwiches were not edible. [The participial phrase *Frozen solid* acts as an adjective that modifies the noun *sandwiches*.]

His statement was too far-fetched **to believe entirely.** [The infinitive phrase *to believe entirely* acts as an adverb that modifies the adjective *far-fetched*.]

EXERCISE A In each of the following sentences, draw an arrow from the underlined phrase to the word it modifies.

Example 1. The hoarse voice did not sound like Rachel's voice.

1. Now is not the time to play games.

2. Professor De La Rosa is writing instructions on the chalkboard.

3. Napping soundly, I did not hear the doorbell ring.

4. The answer to your question is yes.

5. When the streets are slick, drive with caution.

6. Sprinkled with pepper, the mashed potatoes tasted much better.

7. The sea churned too roughly for the windsurfers.

8. The wedding invitation, written in calligraphy, was unusual and quite beautiful.

9. "This is the document to encrypt with the new code," said the military officer.

10. The fan, anchored to the ceiling, provided welcome relief from the heat.

EXERCISE B In each of the following sentences, label the underlined phrase *ADJ* for *adjective* or *ADV* for *adverb*. Then, draw an arrow to the word the phrase modifies.

Example 1. One of my heroes is Colin Powell.

11. Born in Harlem, Colin Powell is the son of Jamaican immigrants.

12. Powell's parents taught him the value of hard work and education.

13. After graduating from college, Powell was commissioned as a second lieutenant in the Army.

14. For heroic achievement in combat, he earned a Bronze Star Medal.

15. Suffering from his own wounds, he had led his battalion to safety.

USAGE

USAGE

Clauses Used as Modifiers

Like words and phrases, clauses can also be used as adjectives and adverbs.

EXAMPLES The person **whom you saw** is Maggie. [The adjective clause *whom you saw* modifies the noun *person*.]

I went outside **after I cleaned my room**. [The adverb clause *after I cleaned my room* modifies the verb *went*.]

EXERCISE A In each of the following sentences, draw an arrow from the underlined clause to the word it modifies. Then, label the clause by writing above it *ADJ* for *adjective* or *ADV* for *adverb*.

Examples 1. The landscape architect whom the hotel hired is Petra.

2. Whenever I have a tough day, I jog at the track after school.

1. Before he bought a video from the Web site, Alfred checked other sites for a better price.

2. The game show contestant who won the grand prize was the woman from Montana.

3. The first comb that you should use on the horse is the wire currycomb.

4. Regis nibbled on fruit slices while Scott sipped apple juice.

5. Dale studies mathematics and science carefully because he wants to be an engineer.

EXERCISE B In each of the following sentences, underline the clause that is used as a modifier. Then, draw an arrow from the clause to the word it modifies.

Example 1. The novel that we are reading in English class is *Animal Farm*.

6. After I read *Animal Farm,* I became interested in the life of the author George Orwell.

7. George Orwell is the pen name that Eric Arthur Blair used.

8. Orwell was born to English parents who were living in Bengal, India.

9. Before he became a novelist, Orwell served in the Indian Imperial Police in Burma.

10. The country that is now called Myanmar was known as Burma then.

11. Orwell began writing essays, stories, and novels after he left Burma.

12. The poor who lived in Europe were the subject of *Down and Out in Paris and London*.

13. Another Orwell novel, which I read last year, is *1984*.

14. When he wrote the essay "Shooting an Elephant," Orwell included autobiographical material.

15. Before he died in 1950, Orwell had become famous and prosperous from his writing.

Phrases and Clauses Used as Modifiers

Like one-word modifiers, phrases and clauses can also be used as adjectives and adverbs.

PHRASES   The cheese dip **for the vegetables** is in the refrigerator.
ADJ

The players gathered at the volleyball net **to choose teams.**
ADV

CLAUSES   My favorite color, **which is chartreuse,** is a shade of green.
ADJ

The police questioned the suspect **because his fingerprints were on the weapon.**
ADV

EXERCISE In each of the following sentences, draw an arrow from the underlined phrase or clause to the word it modifies. Then, label the phrase or clause by writing above it _ADJ_ for _adjective_ or _ADV_ for _adverb._

Example 1. After I read about the Children's Crusade, I wrote a story about Nicholas.
ADV

1. During the summer of 1212, thousands of European children launched a religious crusade.

2. The children who formed the group were led by a French shepherd boy, Stephen.

3. In a vision, Stephen had received a letter from Jesus to deliver to the French king.

4. Journeying with the letter to the king, Stephen was joined by thousands of other children.

5. Some of the group decided to conquer the Holy Land, which was held by Muslims.

6. According to their plan, they would take the Holy Land with love, not violence.

7. Around thirty thousand children reached the French seaport Marseille before disaster struck.

8. Merchants who had offered them free transport to the Holy Land sold them as slaves in North Africa.

9. Inspired by Stephen's crusade, a ten-year-old boy named Nicholas continued Stephen's work.

10. In 1218, Nicholas, a German, began preaching about the Children's Crusade of 1212.

11. The children whom he attracted as followers numbered around twenty thousand.

12. Their path to the Holy Land led through Italy, where they split into groups.

13. Many children died of starvation and disease.

14. Because they needed to cross the Mediterranean Sea, some children went to Genoa.

15. No ship's captain was agreeable enough to allow them passage.

16. Traveling to Rome, some of the children encountered the pope, Innocent III.

17. Innocent III, who felt compassion toward the children, released them from their crusade vows.

18. Betrayed by slave traders, many of the children were sold as slaves.

19. One mystery that remains is the fate of Nicholas, the leader.

20. After the crusade was over, no trace of him remained.

USAGE

Bad and *Badly*/*Good* and *Well*

Bad is an adjective. In most cases, *badly* is an adverb.

ADJECTIVE   The odor coming from my locker is **bad.** [*Bad* modifies the noun *odor.*]

ADVERB   The locker **badly** needs a cleaning. [*Badly* modifies the verb *needs.*]

Good is an adjective. It modifies nouns and pronouns but not verbs. *Well* may be used either as an adjective or as an adverb. As an adjective, *well* has two meanings: "in good health" and "satisfactory." As an adverb, *well* means "capably."

ADJECTIVE   The team's performance was **good.** [*Good* modifies the noun *performance.*]

ADVERB   Oksana played especially **well.** [*Well* modifies the verb *played.*]

EXERCISE A   In each of the following sentences, underline the modifier in parentheses that is correct according to the rules of standard, formal English.

Example 1. He has been coughing *(bad, badly)* all morning.

1. The planks on this side of the bridge are *(good, well)*, but the others are broken.

2. The piano was so out of tune that it sounded *(bad, badly)* even to me.

3. Katia draws so *(good, well)* that everyone is sure she will win the art contest.

4. I feel *(bad, badly)* when I don't make good grades in my classes.

5. "All is *(good, well)*," the guard reported.

6. I spoke *(bad, badly)* in my first public speeches, but I have since gotten better.

7. My sister scored very *(good, well)* on the PSAT.

8. After several days of rest, I felt *(good, well)* enough for a short walk outdoors.

9. Without sunscreen, Duncan's fair skin burns *(bad, badly)* in the sun.

10. The doctor was pleased to see her patient was finally *(good, well)*.

EXERCISE B   Most of the following sentences contain an error in the form of a modifier (*bad, badly, good,* or *well*). Underline each error, and write the correct form of the modifier above it. If a sentence is already correct, write *C* after it.

Example 1. I was amazed at how g̲o̲o̲d̲ Chuck danced. *(well)*

11. With so much salt, the meatloaf tasted badly.

12. You did quite good on that pop quiz.

13. The child wasn't well for several days after his trip overseas.

14. LaTanya speaks French good enough to get her ideas across.

15. The student in driver's education drove bad.

Slow and Slowly/Real and Really

Slow is usually an adjective. *Slowly* is always an adverb.

ADJECTIVE   They danced a **slow** waltz. [*Slow* modifies the noun *waltz*.]

ADVERB   They danced **slowly**. [*Slowly* modifies the verb *danced*.]

Real is an adjective meaning "actual" or "genuine." *Really* is an adverb meaning "actually" or "truly."

ADJECTIVE   The frosting is made with **real** butter. [*Real* modifies the noun *butter*.]

ADVERB   Some "butter" is **really** flavored margarine. [*Really* modifies the verb *is*.]

EXERCISE A   In each of the following sentences, underline the modifier in parentheses that is correct according to the rules of standard, formal English.

Example 1. The beginning driver drove more (*slow*, *slowly*) than the other drivers.

1. I am a (*slow*, *slowly*) learner, but I learn more than those who don't study.

2. This telephone rings (*real*, *really*) loudly; I hope it has a volume control.

3. Before lifting weights, Tom always stretches his muscles (*slow*, *slowly*).

4. I wondered if the stones in the necklace were (*real*, *really*) or fake.

5. I am (*real*, *really*) sorry about what I did.

6. The bright orange sun sank (*slow*, *slowly*) below the horizon.

7. My Californian cousin has become a (*real*, *really*) movie star.

8. I swept the metal detector (*slow*, *slowly*) above the sand.

9. Did Zorro ever (*real*, *really*) exist?

10. Walking (*slow*, *slowly*), the group of children chatted softly.

EXERCISE B   Complete each of the following sentences correctly by writing *slow, slowly, real,* or *really* on the line provided.

Example 1. The shadowy figure moved _____*slowly*_____ through the darkness.

11. The flatware on the dining table is _____ silver, not stainless steel.

12. Gabrielle Reece is a _____ good athlete.

13. The drip from the faucet is _____, but we should fix it anyway.

14. The skateboarder coasted _____ to a stop.

15. The _____ hero of the incident is Meghan, who used CPR on the victim.

Language and Sentence Skills Practice

USAGE

Eight Troublesome Modifiers

Bad is an adjective. In most cases, *badly* is an adverb. *Good* is an adjective. *Well* may be used either as an adjective or as an adverb. As an adjective, *well* has two meanings: "in good health" and "satisfactory." As an adverb, *well* means "capably."

ADJECTIVES   His injury is **bad,** but his doctor is **good.** He'll be **well** again soon.

ADVERBS   Although practice went **well,** the team lost **badly.**

Slow is usually an adjective. *Slowly* is always an adverb. *Real* is an adjective meaning "actual" or "genuine." *Really* is an adverb meaning "actually" or "truly."

ADJECTIVES   The **slow** traffic was caused by a **real** horse-drawn carriage.

ADVERBS   The truth **slowly** dawned on me, and then I laughed **really** loudly.

EXERCISE A   In each of the following sentences, underline the modifier in parentheses that is correct according to the rules of standard, formal English.

Example 1. Eddie will play if he feels (good, *well*) enough.

1. Your orange shirt looks (good, well) with those pants.

2. The bus driver drove (real, really) carefully in the rush-hour traffic.

3. This furniture polish smells (bad, badly).

4. I can ice-skate really (well, good).

5. Those boots don't look too (bad, badly) to me.

6. We felt (bad, badly) that you missed the class trip.

7. Nahele can't draw as (well, good) as his brother.

8. The line was moving so (slow, slowly) that I feared we'd miss our train.

9. Our dress rehearsal didn't go (well, good) at all.

10. For emphasis, Officer Katz spoke (slowly, slow).

EXERCISE B   Each of the following sentences contains an underlined adjective or adverb. If the modifier is incorrect, write the correct form of the modifier above it. If the modifier is correct, write *C* above it.

Example 1. I think Valentine's Day is a real *really* romantic holiday.

11. A relationship that is progressing slow may benefit from a romantic dinner.

12. Some people are real serious when they say "No chocolates!"

13. They are careful about eating good all of the time.

14. I, of course, never feel bad about receiving candy.

15. On Valentine's Day I make all my friends feel well by giving them tiny candy hearts with messages on them.

Regular Comparison

8b. Modifiers change form to show comparison.

The three degrees of comparison are *positive*, *comparative*, and *superlative*.

POSITIVE	fine	silly	slowly	accessible
COMPARATIVE	finer	sillier	more slowly	less accessible
SUPERLATIVE	finest	silliest	most slowly	least accessible

EXERCISE A   In each of the following sentences, underline the correct form of the modifier in parentheses.

Example 1. This breeze is the (briskerest, *briskest*) wind we've had all week.

1. Learning to parachute was the (excitingest, most exciting) part of the course.

2. He runs (fast, faster) than any other boy on the team.

3. Patricia is the (more graceful, graceful) of the two dancers.

4. My father chose the (most expensive, expensivest) of the three drills.

5. This African Goliath beetle is the (heavy, heaviest) we've seen.

6. This baby photo is the (most beautiful, beautifulest) one.

7. A clean kitchen may be the (most effective, effectivest) prevention of pests.

8. This poem is funny, but that one is (funny, funnier).

9. The parking lot at school seems (crowded, less crowded) this year than last year.

10. I think that spearmint is (mild, milder) than peppermint.

EXERCISE B   Above the parentheses in each sentence, write the correct form of the modifier described in parentheses.

Example 1. Learning Chinese was (increasing comparative of *difficult*) *more difficult* than learning French.

11. Of all the languages I've studied, Spanish was the (increasing superlative of *easy*) to learn.

12. Translating a passage from Spanish to English is (increasing comparative of *fun*) for me than solving math problems.

13. I read information about languages (increasing comparative of *frequently*) than others my age.

14. My father speaks Yiddish (increasing comparative of *fast*) than I do.

15. Yiddish speakers are (decreasing comparative of *common*) than they once were.

Language and Sentence Skills Practice

USAGE

Irregular Comparison

8b. Modifiers change form to show comparison.

The three degrees of comparison are *positive*, *comparative*, and *superlative*.

The comparative and superlative degrees of some modifiers are irregular in form.

POSITIVE	bad	well	little	far
COMPARATIVE	worse	better	less	farther *or* further
SUPERLATIVE	worst	best	least	farthest *or* furthest

Do not add *–er*, *–est*, *more*, or *most* to irregularly compared forms.

INCORRECT	more worse, worser	more better, betterest
CORRECT	worse	better

EXERCISE A Above the parentheses in each sentence, write the correct form of the modifier described in parentheses.

Example 1. Mayor Cook created (*many,* ^more^ comparative) jobs than the last mayor.

1. Cats have a (*good*, comparative) sense of balance than many other animals.

2. Of the five competitors, Gisella threw the shot put (*far*, superlative).

3. Far (*many*, comparative) people live on that island than I thought.

4. I hope you feel (*well*, comparative) tomorrow.

5. Ed contributed (*little*, comparative) than anyone else in class.

6. Salim is the (*good*, superlative) athlete in our school.

7. The less they slept, the (*bad*, comparative) they felt.

8. Of all the contestants, Rufino performed (*well*, superlative).

9. It was the (*bad*, superlative) winter the pioneers had experienced.

10. I like Tony (*much*, comparative) than I did earlier.

EXERCISE B Most of the following sentences have errors in the use of comparative and superlative degrees of comparison. Underline each error, and write the correct form of the modifier above it. If a sentence is already correct, write *C* after it.

Example 1. Sheila's temperature is higher than Tariq's; she is ^worse^ <u>iller</u> than he is.

11. The firefighter said this is the baddest fire she has ever seen.

12. Rhonda, although short, is gooder at basketball than many of us.

13. Of the three desserts offered, I like fruit salad mostest.

14. The patient declared, "This is the wellest I've felt in days!"

15. Our new apartment is farther from the center of town than the old one.

Regular and Irregular Comparison A

8b. Modifiers change form to show comparison.

The three degrees of comparison are *positive, comparative,* and *superlative.*

The comparative and superlative degrees of some modifiers are irregular in form.

POSITIVE	blue	funny	creative	calm	much
COMPARATIVE	bluer	funnier	more creative	less calm	more
SUPERLATIVE	bluest	funniest	most creative	least calm	most

EXERCISE Most of the following sentences contain an error in the use of a modifier. Underline each error and write the correct form above it. If a sentence is already correct, write *C* after it.

Example 1. My hunger was <u>more bad</u> *worse* than I had thought, so I ordered three sandwiches.

1. This storm was even badder than the last one.

2. During the 1960s, Medgar Evers was one of the most outspoken civil rights activists.

3. My speech was humorouser than any other speech in the class.

4. Sharla was the intelligenter of the two job applicants.

5. Do you think Pocahontas was courageouser than Sacagawea?

6. Juan, Ricardo's twin brother, was more old by three-and-a-half minutes.

7. After Carmen started lifting weights, she bragged that she was stronger than her brother.

8. People who live along this road complain that it is the most bad in the entire township.

9. Floyd and his son are both landscape designers, but Floyd is the more well known of the two.

10. After the band had practiced, their performance sounded better.

11. Both the strawberry and the vanilla yogurt tasted good, but the strawberry was more sweet.

12. Looking across the water at the sunset, you can see the magnificentest view you can imagine.

13. Angelina is the most young of the three friends.

14. A new house is going to be expensiver today than it would have been a few years ago.

15. Why didn't you answer distinctlier?

16. I thought the questions on that test were more hard than usual.

17. Of all the go-carts in the race, Bart's went the most far.

18. Of the three poems I showed to the editor, he thought this one was written the wellest.

19. Beth and Ronny finished their science experiment more fast than the other teams.

20. Vicky became ill yesterday, and today she is iller than before.

Language and Sentence Skills Practice

Regular and Irregular Comparison B

8b.   Modifiers change form to show comparison.

The three degrees of comparison are *positive*, *comparative*, and *superlative*.

The comparative and superlative degrees of some modifiers are irregular in form.

POSITIVE	soon	windy	fortunate	slowly	bad
COMPARATIVE	sooner	windier	more fortunate	less slowly	worse
SUPERLATIVE	soonest	windiest	most fortunate	least slowly	worst

EXERCISE A   Above the parentheses in each sentence, write the correct form of the modifier described in parentheses to complete the sentence.

Example 1. Nancy is the (increasing superlative of *forgetful*) person I know.
most forgetful

1. This is the (increasing superlative of *bad*) drought we've had in a long time.

2. Larry's story is (decreasing comparative of *believable*) than Heath's story.

3. Twenty dollars is the (increasing superlative of *much*) I can spend at the mall.

4. I was (increasing comparative of *tired*) after today's kickboxing class than I was after the previous class.

5. Rob thinks that Norman is the (decreasing superlative of *friendly*) person in art class.

6. The scorched potatoes tasted bad, but the dry fish tasted (increasing comparative of *bad*).

7. Garrett enjoyed the trip (increasing comparative of *little*) than the others did.

8. Of the ten children who became ill, Charlie is the (increasing superlative of *ill*).

9. At the recital David played (increasing comparative of *well*) than usual.

10. The election results are the (decreasing superlative of *surprising*) news in the report.

EXERCISE B   In the following paragraph, underline each error in the comparative and superlative forms of modifiers. Then, above the error, write the correct form of the modifier.

Example [1] What is the most good teenage musical group ever?
best

[11] In the 1980s some musical groups were more well known than others. [12] One of the unusualest popular groups was a band called Menudo. [13] The singing group itself was more well known than any of its members because the individual members kept changing. [14] When a singer reached the age of sixteen, he was replaced by a more young one. [15] Thus, the sound remained consistenter than the performers.

HOLT HANDBOOK | Fourth Course

Use of Comparative and Superlative Forms A

8c. Use the comparative degree when comparing two things. Use the superlative degree when comparing more than two.

COMPARATIVE I like washing dishes more than drying them. [two things]

SUPERLATIVE The task I like most is cooking dinner. [more than two things]

8d. Include the word *other* or *else* when comparing one member of a group with the rest of the group.

EXAMPLE Alice is a better math student than anyone **else** in her class.

8e. Avoid using double comparisons.

EXAMPLE Juana is **taller** (not *more taller*) than Erica.

EXERCISE A Above the modifier in parentheses in each sentence, write the correct form of the modifier to complete the sentence.

Example 1. Of all the entries, this essay is the *most sophisticated* (sophisticated).

1. Of the three skaters, Karen moved (*assuredly*).

2. That was the (*violent*) storm of the summer.

3. Luckily, these instructions are (*simple*) than those.

4. That is one of the (*scary*) films I've ever seen!

5. Of all the talks, the last was the (*interesting*).

6. Julio is the (*practical*) member of his family.

7. Sirens are probably the (*irritating*) of all noises.

8. That show was (*entertaining*) than last year's.

9. This January is the (*warm*) of any I can remember.

10. This crate is (*big*) than the one that holds our books.

EXERCISE B Most of the following sentences contain an error in the use of a modifier. Underline each error and write the correct form above it. If a sentence is already correct, write *C* after it.

Example 1. My manicured yard looks better than *any other yard* ~~any yard~~ on the street.

11. Elsie is funnier than any woman I know.

12. I browsed through a number of shirts and selected the one I liked more.

13. Philip has a better chance at winning the audition than anyone else.

14. Riding dirt bikes is most fun than riding a ten-speed bicycle.

15. This container of yogurt is the less fresh one on the shelf.

Language and Sentence Skills Practice

USAGE

Use of Comparative and Superlative Forms B

| **8f.** | Be sure your comparisons are clear. |

When making comparisons, indicate clearly what items are being compared. State both parts of a comparison completely if there is any chance of misunderstanding.

UNCLEAR   My biology paper was much better than history. [A paper is compared to a class.]

CLEAR   My biology paper was much better than my history paper.

UNCLEAR   I like seafood more than Harry. [Is Harry being compared to seafood?]

CLEAR   I like seafood more than Harry does.

EXERCISE   On the lines provided, revise the sentences below to make the comparisons clear.

Example 1. I visit Grandmother Olson more often than Aunt Sabrina.   *I visit Grandmother*
Olson more often than I visit Aunt Sabrina.

1. Alyssa's handwriting is less legible than José. _____

_____

2. Tana's argument for the change was better supported than Kim. _____

_____

3. These items from the drugstore are cheaper than the salon. _____

_____

4. While in India, Wynona photographed the Taj Mahal more often than Elzie. _____

_____

5. The football program at my new school appears to be better than my last school. ___

_____

6. I laughed at the humorous mistake as much as Glenda. _____

_____

7. Marty sent a larger bouquet of flowers to Candace than Raquel. _____

_____

8. The volume on the radio is higher than the TV. _____

_____

9. On Saturday, Dayna spent more on groceries than Judy. _____

_____

10. Jerome complimented his date as often as Terry. _____

_____

HOLT HANDBOOK | Fourth Course

Use of Comparative and Superlative Forms: Review

8c.	Use the comparative degree when comparing two things. Use the superlative degree when comparing more than two.
8d.	Include the word *other* or *else* when comparing one member of a group with the rest of the group.
8e.	Avoid using double comparisons.
8f.	Be sure your comparisons are clear.

EXERCISE In each of the following sentences, add or delete a word or words to correct an error in the use of a modifier. Draw a caret (∧) to show where words should be added, and write the words above the caret. Cross out words that should be deleted. If a sentence is already correct, write *C* after it.

Example 1. The price of a good haircut is higher than ∧ last year.
                                                    it was

1. I found the television's remote control before my brother.

2. Of all the football players who played in the rain, Todd is muddier.

3. This is the least thickest the ice on the lake has been all winter.

4. I like steamed rice, but I like fried rice best.

5. If you hurry, you'll get better seats than anyone.

6. The essay question on the English exam was harder than biology.

7. Although the idea is the silliest one I've heard, I like it anyway.

8. The buffet table held corn, carrots, and beans. I chose corn since I like it better.

9. The mother-daughter camping trip occurs before any activity of the year.

10. The skirts on this rack are smaller than that rack.

11. Frankie tossed the ball higher than Johnny.

12. Of the two dishes, the shrimp tempura is less healthier than the steamed shrimp.

13. Everyone agrees that Brent writes more exciting stories than anyone in the class.

14. I buy more clothes over the Internet than stores.

15. Which of the two biographies is more passionately written?

16. When I was in the fifth grade, I thought Dixie Porter was the most prettiest girl in the world.

17. Luis likes his career more than Irma.

18. Of the numerous items I placed in the consignment store, the carved chest is more valuable.

19. I prefer goldfish to any pet because they don't bark, scratch, or need to go outside.

20. The temperatures in Florida are milder than Maine.

Correcting Dangling Modifiers

8g. Avoid using dangling modifiers.

A modifying word, phrase, or clause that does not clearly and sensibly modify a word or word group in a sentence is a *dangling modifier*. To correct a dangling modifier, add or replace words to make the meaning clear and logical.

> **DANGLING** After winning the Pulitzer Prize for *Fences, The Piano Lesson* was written. [Who won the Pulitzer Prize?]
>
> **CLEAR** After winning the Pulitzer Prize for *Fences*, August Wilson wrote *The Piano Lesson*.

EXERCISE Revise the sentences below to correct the dangling modifiers. Write the revised sentences on the lines provided. If a sentence is already correct, write *C* on the line.

Example 1. To finish the report early, Carly's study time must not be interrupted.

To finish the report early, Carly must not interrupt her study time.

1. After turning on the radio, the baby woke up.

_____

2. Cooked very slowly, the casserole was delicious.

_____

3. Startled by the unexpected noise, the heron took flight.

_____

4. Looking in the closet, her camera was found.

_____

5. After eating yogurt, grapefruit juice doesn't taste very good.

_____

6. Aiming at the target, the arrow hit the tree.

_____

7. When trying to understand new words, a dictionary is useful.

_____

8. Playing too close to the house, a window was broken.

_____

9. To reach the highest branch, Masako needed a longer ladder.

_____

10. While washing the dishes, a china cup was broken.

_____

Correcting Misplaced Modifiers

| **8h.** | Avoid using misplaced modifiers. |

A word, phrase, or clause that seems to modify the wrong word or word group in a sentence is a *misplaced modifier*. Place modifying words, phrases, and clauses as near as possible to the words they modify.

MISPLACED   Perched in the cage, I admired the large, gray parrot. [Was I perched in the cage?]

CLEAR   I admired the large, gray parrot perched in the cage.

MISPLACED   The students were planning a field trip in the library. [Was the field trip going to be in the library?]

CLEAR   The students in the library were planning a field trip.

EXERCISE   If a sentence contains a misplaced modifier, underline the misplaced modifier and draw an arrow from the modifier to the place it should go. If the sentence is already correct, write *C* after it.

Example 1. We examined the donated books and only chose the best ones for our library.

1. I bought a ladder to fix the roof that was sturdy.

2. Martin watched a radiant sunset climbing a hill.

3. Wanda offered me the book swinging in the hammock.

4. The horse without a saddle galloped toward the stable.

5. Earl discovered many beetles examining the rosebushes.

6. A letter without a stamp arrived from Phoenix.

7. Lorraine swatted the flies near the sandwiches that were buzzing around.

8. Carlos found another fuse in the drawer that was no good.

9. Isabel bought a blue dress from the clothing store in the mall with black stripes.

10. Under my bed I found my revised history paper.

USAGE

USAGE

Dangling and Misplaced Modifiers A

| **8g.** | Avoid using dangling modifiers. |

To correct a dangling modifier, add or replace words to make the meaning clear and logical.

DANGLING After looking on every street in the neighborhood, the lost cat was found.

CLEAR After looking on every street in the neighborhood, Cynthia found the lost cat.

| **8h.** | Avoid using misplaced modifiers. |

Place modifying words, phrases, and clauses as near as possible to the words they modify.

MISPLACED Blaring from the stereo, I didn't recognize the strange music.

CLEAR I didn't recognize the strange music blaring from the stereo.

EXERCISE A Underline the misplaced modifier in each of the following sentences. Then, draw an arrow from the modifier to the place where it should go in the sentence.

Example 1. The sheriff approached the town riding a huge white stallion.

1. From our seats we could see the stage clearly in the balcony.

2. The guest speaker had dedicated his book to his dog who was an archaeologist.

3. I bought the red coat from the new shop with the enormous hood.

4. Shining brightly in the distance, the weary travelers were happy to see a restaurant sign.

5. The magazine is in the pile on the third shelf that you requested.

EXERCISE B Revise the following sentences to correct dangling modifiers. Write the revised sentences on the lines provided.

Example 1. Seeing the dolphins in the water, photographing them was my first thought.

Seeing the dolphins in the water, I immediately wanted to photograph them.

6. After raking the leaves, they were carried to the compost pile. _____

_____

7. Walking in the sunshine, it felt warm. _____

_____

8. Peering through the trees, the path ahead was evident. _____

_____

9. Relieved, all of the tests had passing grades. _____

_____

10. To save money, many coupons were clipped. _____

_____

USAGE

Dangling and Misplaced Modifiers B

8g.	Avoid using dangling modifiers.

> **DANGLING**   Before entering the contest, the rules must be understood.
> **CLEAR**   Before entering the contest, you must understand the rules.

8h.	Avoid using misplaced modifiers.

> **MISPLACED**   Barbara gave her guests a tour of her home for the weekend.
> **CLEAR**   Barbara gave her guests for the weekend a tour of her home.

EXERCISE   Revise the following sentences to correct dangling or misplaced modifiers. Write the revised sentences on the lines provided.

Example 1. Looking at the disaster, the cause was evident. _Looking at the disaster, I thought_
the cause was evident.

1. The winners marched off the platform carrying ribbons and trophies. _____

_____

2. The smoke alarm went off while cooking my dinner. _____

_____

3. A young woman knocked on the door wearing a suit and a hat. _____

_____

4. Several students remained after class and spoke to the teacher who had questions. _____

_____

5. Rosetta is performing shows for children in hospitals that are very entertaining. _____

_____

6. To finish my project in shop class, more varnish would be necessary. _____

_____

7. Mother found a package outside our house tied with ribbons. _____

_____

8. Feeling quite hungry, the librarian's only thought was her upcoming lunch break. _____

_____

9. Covered in cream cheese, my friends will love these bagels. _____

_____

10. Walking from door to door, fliers were hung on each doorknob. _____

_____

Language and Sentence Skills Practice

Review A: **Forms of Modifiers**

EXERCISE Most of the following sentences contain an incorrect form of a modifier. Draw a line through each incorrect modifier. Then, above it, write the correct form. If a sentence is already correct, write *C* after it.

Examples 1. The quarterback didn't feel ~~good,~~ *well* so he rested all weekend.

       2. If a player doesn't practice ~~faithful~~ *faithfully* enough, he or she won't be ready for the game.

1. Even when the team plays good, the coach is seldom pleased.

2. Why should a coach feel bad about a loss or a tie game?

3. The coach believes that a loss or tie reflects poor on his ability.

4. Schools and colleges want teams that are coached successful.

5. A successful coach's team, of course, seldom loses badly.

6. If the team plays good, the coach will be happy.

7. Sometimes the losing players feel real disappointed.

8. The coach offers the players valuable advice.

9. Teams could win easy if all the players did as the coach instructed.

10. Teams who don't practice as often as they should improve more slow.

11. Is it easy to think clear in a locker room?

12. If a coach speaks too sharp, players may stop listening.

13. If a lecture is real negative, some players might not respond well.

14. A coach and a team in conflict usually perform badly.

15. To generalize about sports is to speak inaccurate.

16. After a long game against challenging opponents, the players felt tired.

17. A whining child behaved bad during the entire game.

18. Despite the grounds crew's efforts to paint the yard lines even, the paint job looked bad.

19. If you work more carefully and draw each line slow, you will see better results.

20. Because he was hot and tired after playing for so long, Carlos wasn't real excited about

    the game.

Review B: **Comparison of Modifiers**

EXERCISE A In each of the following sentences, draw a line through the error in comparison. Then, above it, write the correct form. If the error is a missing word, draw a caret (∧) where the word should be inserted and then write the word above the caret.

Examples 1. Of the two of you, she is clearly ~~tallest.~~ *taller*

        2. Rhode Island is smaller than any ∧ state. *other*

1. Mallory is the worse clarinet player I've ever heard.

2. Nico sings more better than anyone else in his class.

3. English is the more difficult subject for me.

4. Of the two sports, tennis is probably most popular.

5. Whoever in the class answers most quickest will win the game.

6. That star shines more brightly than any star in its galaxy.

7. Of all the songs I've heard you play, that last one was better.

8. Your brother is the more handsome senior I know.

9. Miguel is the most sincerest young man I've ever met.

10. Your car idles least smoothly than mine.

EXERCISE B Most of the following sentences contain an error in comparison. If the error is an incorrect form of a modifier, draw a line through the error. Then, above it, write the correct form. If the error is a missing word, draw a caret (∧) where the word should be and then write the word above the caret. If a sentence is already correct, write *C* after it.

Example 1. Ours was the ~~most happiest~~ win of all. *happiest*

11. When you compare football and baseball, football is the roughest game of the two.

12. For the most part, the players on the football team are bigger than the baseball team.

13. A tackle may be bigger than anyone in his class.

14. No player is more friendlier than our team captain.

15. Our team manager talks with the players more than the coach.

16. What was the worse moment of the team manager's life?

17. Of the two possibilities, this one is the most logical.

18. When our equipment disappeared, the manager was more stunned than anyone.

19. When it reappeared, the manager was more relieved than the coach was.

20. Our coach is better than any coach in the city.

Review C: Dangling and Misplaced Modifiers

EXERCISE A Most of the following sentences contain a dangling modifier. On the lines provided, revise each sentence so that its meaning is clear and correct. If a sentence is already correct, write C.

Example 1. While on routine patrol, a motorist in distress attracted the officer's notice.

While on routine patrol, the officer noticed a motorist in distress.

1. Stapling the pages carefully, Tamika admired the report. _____

_____

2. Covered with sweat from the hot sun, the ocean looked inviting. _____

_____

3. To iron my delicate silk shirt, the setting on the iron must be the correct temperature. _____

_____

4. Before learning of the party, my weekend seemed boring. _____

_____

5. Typing the command into the computer, the file was saved on the hard drive. _____

_____

EXERCISE B Most of the following sentences contain a misplaced modifier. Circle the misplaced modifier. Then, draw an arrow to show where it should go in the sentence. If a sentence is already correct, write C after it.

Example 1. Everyone saw that the pass was dropped (but the referee).

6. Our coach thanked me for the safety that produced the winning points after the game.

7. Between the bench and the press box, we learned there was a telephone.

8. The team was taken on a tour of the campus visiting our school.

9. After the game we saw a skit about a family's adventures in a magical forest.

10. At the end of the skit, a boy was reunited with his family who had wandered off by himself.

11. Watching the skit closely, the actors received loud applause from the athletes.

12. A cheerleader is rarely seen talking to the football captain in a long dress.

13. She was thanking him for a corsage of roses that he had given her.

14. The sports reporters could hear our pep band playing in the press box.

15. The dog had interrupted a play that was chased off the field.

Review D: Correct Use of Modifiers

EXERCISE Most of the following sentences contain an incorrect form of a modifier, a misplaced modifier, or a dangling modifier. On the lines provided, revise each sentence that contains an error. If a sentence is already correct, write C.

Examples 1. The gift was more costlier than I had expected it to be.

The gift was more costly than I had expected it to be.

2. A blue girl's coat has been found.

A girl's blue coat has been found.

1. Seeing that no damage had been done, the cars drove away in opposite directions. _____

_____

2. The cold juice tasted real good to the thirsty runner. _____

_____

3. Which pet have you had longest, your rabbit or your cat? _____

_____

4. Walking careful over the broken cobblestones, the woman made her way down the lane. _____

_____

5. I feel certain that you will get a good grade if you study well. _____

_____

6. Working long hours, success came to him after many years. _____

_____

7. Although her choice of colors wasn't the best, she arranged the flowers good. _____

_____

8. By looking through a telescope, the far shore could be seen dimly. _____

_____

9. Of the three movies we watched last weekend, the third one was the most scariest. _____

_____

10. A well-trained police officer remains calmly in emergencies. _____

_____

Proofreading Application: E-mail

Good writers generally are good proofreaders. Readers tend to admire and trust writing that is error-free. Make sure that you correct all errors in grammar, usage, spelling, and punctuation in your writing. Your readers will have more confidence in your words if you have done your best to proofread carefully.

When you communicate by e-mail or by letter with the representative of a company about its product or service, you want your writing to be descriptive, clear, and precise. The correct use of modifiers will help you to achieve this goal.

PROOFREADING ACTIVITY

Find and correct the errors in the use of modifiers in the following e-mail. Use proofreading symbols to make your corrections.

Example Becoming irritated by the poor service, *I composed* an e-mail ~~was compose~~d.

TO: customerservice@APMOSA.com

SUBJECT: Hiking Boots

   Until recently, I was probably more satisfied than any customer

you have ever had. However, after the experience I am about to

relate, someone at your company is going to have to work real hard

to convince me to buy anything else from Action-Packed Mail Order

Sports Apparel.

   About four weeks ago, the hiking boots I had ordered from your

company arrived. Excited to try them on, my anticipation quick

turned to disappointment when I saw they were obviously four sizes

too small. I sent them back with an explanation of the mix-up.

However, the problem got worser, not better. Yesterday, I received a

pair that were the correct size, but I have never seen defectiver

boots in my life.

   Please relay my message to the more appropriate department. I will

be interested to see how bad you want to keep me as a customer. In

the meantime, I will be checking into your competitor, Outdoor

Literary Model: Essay

I have been studying the traits and dispositions of the "lower animals" (so-called) and contrasting them with the traits and dispositions of man. I find the result humiliating to me. For it obliges me to renounce my allegiance to the Darwinian theory of the Ascent of Man from the Lower Animals, since it now seems plain to me that that theory ought to be vacated in favor of a new and truer one, this new and truer one to be named the Descent of Man from the Higher Animals.

In proceeding toward this unpleasant conclusion, I have . . . subjected every postulate that presented itself to the crucial test of actual experiment. . . .

Before particularizing any of the experiments, I wish to state one or two things which seem to more properly belong in this place than further along. . . .

Man is the Reasoning Animal. Such is the claim. I think it is open to dispute. Indeed, my experiments have proven to me that he is the Unreasoning Animal. . . . His record is the fantastic record of a maniac. I consider that the strongest count against his intelligence is the fact that with that record back of him, he blandly sets himself up as the head animal of the lot; whereas by his own standards, he is the bottom one.

—from "The Lowest Animal" by Mark Twain

EXERCISE A   Write each underlined modifier. Beside it, write its degree of comparison (*positive*, *comparative*, or *superlative*).

lower; comparative

_____   _____

_____   _____

_____   _____

_____   _____

_____   _____

From "The Lowest Animal" from *Letters from the Earth* by Mark Twain, edited by Bernard De Voto. Copyright 1938, 1944, 1946, © 1959, 1962 by the Mark Twain Company. Reprinted by permission of **HarperCollins Publishers, Inc.**

Literary Model (continued)

EXERCISE B Write each underlined modifier again. This time, write the word it modifies beside it.

lower; animals

_____   _____

_____   _____

_____   _____

_____   _____

_____   _____

EXERCISE C You work at a pet store on weekends. You have been asked by the father of a five-year-old boy to talk to the child about which animals make good pets, which ones do not, and why. Use several comparative and superlative forms of adjectives and adverbs in your answer, and underline each one.

_____

_____

_____

_____

_____

_____

_____

_____

_____

_____

_____

_____

_____

EXERCISE D Why is it sometimes more effective to use comparative and superlative forms of modifiers instead of positive forms?

_____

_____

_____

_____

for **CHAPTER 8: USING MODIFIERS CORRECTLY** | pages 212–28

Writing Application: Comparison-Contrast Essay

Making comparisons is a part of human nature. "This football team has the *worst* record in the district." "Out of all the movies produced this year, that movie is *most deserving* of an award." "The amusement park in your city is *more crowded* than the one thirty miles away." As you speak and as you write, you undoubtedly use comparisons frequently. When the comparisons you make are clear and correctly formed, you will help your listener or reader more readily grasp your intent.

WRITING ACTIVITY

You can sometimes understand one fictional character better by comparing and contrasting him or her with another fictional character. Write a comparison-contrast essay about two characters from the same fictional work or from two different works. In your essay, include at least three comparative and three superlative forms of modifiers. Make sure that each comparison is clear and correctly formed.

PREWRITING   As you decide which two characters you will analyze, be sure that they have some basic similarities but are also different enough to make the essay interesting. You should arrange your thoughts about each character in a chart. The way you structure the chart will depend on how you want to organize your essay. If you choose to use the block method, you will first present everything you have to say about one character and then everything you have to say about the second character. If you prefer the point-by-point method, you will present one aspect or issue at a time about both characters.

WRITING   Write an introductory paragraph that captures your reader's attention and ends with a thesis statement. In the body of the essay, develop your ideas with specific details, facts, examples, and quotations. End your essay by summarizing the information and showing how it supports your thesis statement.

REVISING   Ask yourself whether you can improve your essay by using transitions to connect and clarify ideas. Ask a classmate to read your draft and to tell you in his or her own words what the similarities and differences between the two characters are. If your classmate seems confused about any of the content, make appropriate revisions. Be sure that you have included at least three comparative and three superlative forms of modifiers and that each one is clear and correctly formed.

PUBLISHING   As you proofread your draft, focus on one line at a time. Look for errors in spelling, grammar, usage, and punctuation. Add your character comparison to any other essays you have written about literature, and compile your essays in an anthology.

EXTENDING YOUR WRITING

You may wish to develop this activity further. Using the voice and point of view of one of the characters in your essay, write a description of the other character. Use creative writing techniques to make the description sound as if the character actually wrote it.

Language and Sentence Skills Practice

Choices: Exploring Usage

The following activities challenge you to find a connection between usage errors and the world around you. Do the activity below that suits your personality best, and then share your discoveries with your class.

BUILDING BACKGROUND KNOWLEDGE

In Your Own Words

The entries in your glossary cover only a few of the usage errors that you are likely to encounter. What errors would you like to add to this list? Keep a journal of errors that you encounter over the course of five days. In your journal, make notes of usage errors that you think should be included in a textbook. Then, write your own additions to the glossary. Publish the glossary and give it to your classmates to use as a reference.

MATHEMATICS

By the Numbers

If you are good at math, use your skill to help your classmates master the usage of *amount* and *number*. Research the differences. Design several word problems focusing on *amount* or *number*. Your math problems should use both words correctly at least twice. Prepare a short explanation of each problem. Correctly use *amount* and *number* at least twice each in your explanation. Pass out copies of your problems to the class, and deliver your explanation as you solve each problem at the board.

DISCUSSION

That Wasn't Half Bad

Research the word *bad*. What does the Oxford English Dictionary say about this word? When was this word first used? What are its roots and original meanings? Apparently, over the years *bad* has acquired meanings that are all its own— meanings that have nothing to do with *good*. Fill the class in on your research. Then, lead a discussion of the ways that *bad* is used today. May it be used as more than one part of speech? How many meanings does it have?

TECHNOLOGY

Signs of the Times

You are living in the Information Age. Information requires communication. Consequently, communication and methods of communication are expanding daily. Brainstorm a list of the technological devices that are changing your world. Begin with portable phones. Lead a discussion of how each device has changed modern communications and language usage. Make predictions about how future devices might further change language usage. Publish your predictions on the class Web site.

WRITING

Ms. President

Let your classmates hear how language can exclude a whole group of people from a vital activity. Write a news report about an international meeting of the presidents and prime ministers of several countries in which all of the political figures are female. In fact, all authority figures are female. Use the vocabulary and sentence structure that you might find in any newspaper. When you are done, read your news report to the class. Then, ask your classmates to write a few sentences about how they felt as you read your report. Pass out a copy of the news report to your classmates and discuss how the language of the report might be revised to be more inclusive.

LOGIC

Logically Speaking

If you like math or logic, use mathematical equations or logic to show how two negatives become a positive. Create a handout that explains several examples, and give it to your classmates. Prepare your equations or logical arguments before you begin your presentation.

for CHAPTER 9: GLOSSARY OF USAGE pages 236–40

Glossary of Usage A

Review the glossary entries on pages 236–40 of your textbook for information on the correct usage of the following terms:

a, an	*a lot*	*being as, being that*
accept, except	*and etc.*	*beside, besides*
affect, effect	*anyways, anywheres, everywheres,*	*between, among*
ain't	*nowheres, somewheres*	*borrow, lend, loan*
all right	*at*	*bring, take*
all the farther, all the faster	*a while, awhile*	*bust, busted*
allusion, illusion	*because*	

USAGE

EXERCISE For each of the following sentences, underline the correct word or word group in parentheses. Base your answer on formal, standard usage.

Example 1. When we backpack through the canyon, we will (*bring*, <u>*take*</u>) plenty of water.

1. In biology, we studied the (*affects, effects*) of air pollution.

2. Gordon promised to (*bring, take*) souvenirs back from his trip to New Orleans.

3. (*Beside, Besides*) the alternates, the coach said we needed two more players and a goalie.

4. This store will (*accept, except*) your check as long as you have identification.

5. When you go out to the garage, please (*bring, take*) this bag of trash.

6. We have been here for an hour, but we (*ain't, aren't*) catching any fish.

7. The reason I called you is (*because, that*) I have a question.

8. Will you (*lend, loan*) me your umbrella?

9. Without more wind in the sails, this is (*as fast as, all the faster*) the sailboat can go.

10. The menu offered fifteen entrees to choose (*between, among*).

11. Are you (*allright, all right*)?

12. After the storm, there was (*a lot, alot*) of mud in the yard.

13. The story made (*illusions, allusions*) to the Bible.

14. Big Rapids isn't (*anywhere, anywheres*) near Detroit.

15. Where is my (*hammer, hammer at*)?

16. I will be there in (*awhile, a while*).

17. (*Being that, Because*) she is the oldest, she gets to choose the video.

18. Don't (*bust, break*) the switch on the camera.

19. I like to read science fiction, fantasy, horror, (*etc., and etc.*)

20. The movie lasts (*a, an*) hour and a half.

Language and Sentence Skills Practice

Glossary of Usage B

Review the glossary entries on pages 242–43 of your textbook for information on the correct usage of the following terms:

can, may	*discover, invent*	*emigrate, immigrate*
could of	*don't, doesn't*	*fewer, less*

EXERCISE A Each of the sentences below has one underlined word or word group. If that word or word group contains a usage error or an informal or awkward usage, write the correct word or word group above it. If the sentence is already correct, write C.

Example 1. <u>Can</u> I get you something to drink? *(May)*

1. Garrett A. Morgan, despite facing severe racial prejudice, <u>discovered</u> the first traffic light.

2. Please buy <u>less</u> bottles of soft drinks and more fruit juice at the store.

3. I <u>could of</u> defended my actions, but I did not.

4. The sky is overcast; we <u>may</u> get some rain soon.

5. My grandparents sometimes <u>doesn't</u> understand me.

6. The Statue of Liberty reminds us of the many people who <u>emigrated</u> to the United States.

7. If I make a weekly schedule, I waste <u>fewer</u> time than if I don't make a schedule.

8. During World War II, many Jews were forced to <u>immigrate</u> from their countries.

9. Holly, who is very tall, <u>can</u> reach the top shelf.

10. I <u>invented</u> a new, quicker route home from school.

EXERCISE B In each of the following sentences, cross out all errors in usage. Then, above the error, write the standard English usage. If the sentence is already correct, write C.

Example 1. Many well-known models have been in the business ~~less~~ *fewer* years than Iman.

11. The famous model Iman immigrated from Somalia.

12. Her family was wealthy, but she saw many Somalians who had fewer money.

13. She could of stayed in her hometown of Mogadishu, but she did not.

14. Photographer Peter Beard invented Iman at the University of Nairobi.

15. You may have seen her on fashion runways or in a movie.

16. With her fine bone structure, Iman may definitely perform her modeling assignments well!

17. Many immigrants in Iman's position might of put their homeland behind them.

18. Iman, however, don't let the memory of Somalia fade away.

19. She invented the importance of homeland and keeps Somalia in her mind.

20. In this way, she can project a certain image to the people watching her.

Glossary of Usage C

Review the glossary entries on pages 243–44 of your textbook for information on the correct usage of the following terms:

had of	*he, she, it, they*	*hopefully*
had ought, hadn't ought	*hisself, theirself, theirselves*	*imply, infer*

EXERCISE A In each of the following sentences, underline the word or word group in parentheses that is correct according to standard, formal English usage.

Example 1. He collected all of the flags *(hisself, himself)*.

1. From your extensive collection of flags, I can *(imply, infer)* that you like flags.

2. If I *(had, had of)* known about your collection, I'd have brought my own flags.

3. You *(had ought, ought)* to get the Ohio state flag.

4. The *(Ohioans they, Ohioans)* have an unusually shaped state flag.

5. Ohioans know *(themselves, theirselves)* to be the only state whose flag is not a parallelogram.

6. *(Hopefully, I hope)* I'll find a picture of the flag in this reference book.

7. The top and bottom *(edges they, edges)* create a pennant shape.

8. The *(flag, flag it)* also has a triangular notch cut out of the right edge.

9. My description *(implies, infers)* a forked edge on the right side of the flag.

10. I *(hadn't ought, ought not)* forget to mention the flag's colors: red, white, and blue.

EXERCISE B In each of the following sentences, underline the error in standard, formal usage. Then, above the underlined word or words, write the standard English usage. If the sentence is already correct, write C.

iris
Example 1. The iris it is Tennessee's state flower.

11. The horticulture club are proud of theirself for creating the exhibit of state flowers.

12. Hopefully these pasqueflowers from South Dakota will grow in my state.

13. I can imply their appearance from the description in this article.

14. You hadn't ought to pick bluebonnets from the side of Texas highways.

15. Mr. Garza he told me that Maine's state flower is the pine cone.

16. I wish I had of gotten some native violets in Illinois.

17. I didn't mean to imply that Oklahoma's flower, the mistletoe, is unattractive.

18. My Georgian cousin she used Cherokee roses in the decorations for her graduation party.

19. My escort to the pageant in Florida chose the bouquet of orange blossoms hisself.

20. We had ought to photograph the yucca while we are in New Mexico.

Glossary of Usage D

Review the glossary entries on pages 246–47 of your textbook for information on the correct usage of the following terms:

kind of, sort of	*leave, let*	*learn, teach*
kind of a(n), sort of a(n)	*like, as, as if, as though*	*of*
kinds, sorts, types	*a number of, the number of*	*off, off of*

EXERCISE   In each of the following sentences, underline the word or word group in parentheses that is correct according to standard, formal English usage.

Example 1. (*A number of, The number of*) entrants in the chili cook-off is quite large.

1. What (*kind of a, kind of*) sandwich do you like best?

2. There was a beautiful view of the ocean (*outside, outside of*) the cabin window.

3. Please (*let, leave*) me borrow the notes you took in history class on Friday.

4. I am sure I will be able to (*teach, learn*) all of my lines over the weekend.

5. Zahara's answer was (*kind of, rather*) vague.

6. Have you ever tried wearing one of (*this types, these types*) of hats?

7. (*A number of, The number of*) stories in our storytelling festival are set in the distant future.

8. The police have found the bicycle that was stolen (*off, from*) you.

9. That loud crash outside sounded (*as though, like*) it were nearby.

10. On Saturday afternoon my sister will (*teach, learn*) me to drive a car.

11. Move the cat (*off, off of*) the couch, please.

12. He acts (*like, as though*) he owns the place.

13. These (*sort, sorts*) of activities are strenuous.

14. (*Leave, Let*) the children go to the movies.

15. This car looks (*like, as if*) it has been abandoned.

16. Is it possible to (*learn, teach*) yourself calculus?

17. The horses run free (*outside, outside of*) the corral.

18. This is the (*kind of, kind of a*) song that I really like.

19. (*The number of, A number of*) bird species on the island is remarkable.

20. This painting looks (*like, as if*) it were painted by a child.

Glossary of Usage E

Review the glossary entries on pages 249–51 of your textbook for information on the correct usage of the following terms:

some, somewhat	*try and, try to*	*where*
suppose to, supposed to	*use to, used to*	*who, which, that*
than, then	*way, ways*	*without, unless*
them	*what*	
this here, that there	*when, where*	

EXERCISE A In each of the following sentences, underline the word or word group in parentheses that is correct according to formal, standard English usage.

Example 1. We were prepared (*some, <u>somewhat</u>*) for the hurricane.

1. We will not be able to make tacos (*without, unless*) you buy some cheese.

2. The Great Pyramid of Cheops was larger (*then, than*) any other pyramid.

3. Hermit crabs are (*them, those*) crabs that make their homes in other animals' shells.

4. These are the pages (*that, what*) you must study by Wednesday.

5. Ms. Pong is the woman (*which, that*) painted that mural.

6. You are (*suppose to, supposed to*) carry the trash out to the curb.

7. I can hit (*that, that there*) fencepost with an arrow shot from my bow.

8. I heard (*where, that*) the mayor would not run for reelection.

9. Kareem will (*try and, try to*) score a touchdown in this play.

10. We had driven quite a (*way, ways*) out of town before we got a view of the lake.

EXERCISE B In each of the following sentences, cross out the error in formal, standard usage. Then, above it, write the standard English usage. If the sentence is already correct, write *C*.

Example 1. Onomatopoeia ~~is when~~ *means that* a word imitates the sound associated with its meaning.

11. This rhyming dictionary will help your poetry writing some.

12. I used to compose sonnets using a rhyming dictionary for help in word choice.

13. Blank verse is when the lines in a poem do not rhyme.

14. This here blank verse poem has five iambic feet per line.

15. Free verse is poetry where there is no regular rhyme scheme, meter, or stanza formation.

The Double Negative

Avoid using *double negatives* in your writing and speaking. A double negative is the use of two negative words when one is enough. Common negative words are *hardly, no, not (n't), nothing, none,* and *scarcely.*

DOUBLE NEGATIVE	I didn't hardly have time to eat.
STANDARD	I **hardly** had time to eat.
STANDARD	I **didn't have** time to eat.

EXERCISE A   Read each of the following sentences, and decide whether it contains a double negative. On the line provided write either *DN* for *double negative* or *S* for *standard.*

Examples   _DN_   **1.** Nancy hasn't missed no football games this year.

_____   _S_   **2.** Rufino hasn't missed any football games this year.

_____ **1.** Linebacker Chris Singleton and his twin didn't hardly look different.

_____ **2.** Until 1989, Kevin hadn't hardly been sick at all.

_____ **3.** That year, Kevin didn't scarcely feel well.

_____ **4.** It turned out that he didn't have nothing mild.

_____ **5.** Leukemia is a blood disease, and some people with it don't get no better.

_____ **6.** Since Kevin was an identical twin, he didn't have to worry about finding a bone-marrow donor.

_____ **7.** Chris didn't hesitate none when his brother needed him.

_____ **8.** He couldn't scarcely worry about football when his brother's life was at stake.

_____ **9.** Today, Kevin doesn't have any more leukemia symptoms.

_____ **10.** Now he says that he doesn't take life for granted no more.

EXERCISE B   Revise each of the following sentences to correct double negatives. First, cross out the words that need to be changed. Then, write the revision above them.

Example 1. The winners ~~can't~~ ^{can} hardly wait for the presentation of the awards.

11. Sharks don't have no bones in their bodies.

12. I could hear something crawling through the grass, but I couldn't see nothing.

13. Isabel hadn't scarcely enough gasoline in the car to get home.

14. I thought I had a red pencil, but I couldn't find none.

15. I couldn't hardly tell the difference between the twins until I had known them awhile.

Nonsexist Language

Avoid using gender-specific language. Instead, use *nonsexist language*. Nonsexist language is language that applies to people in general, both male and female.

GENDER-SPECIFIC | The councilman addressed our committee about homelessness.

NONSEXIST | The **council member** addressed our committee about homelessness.

EXERCISE A In each of the following sentences, underline the gender-specific term. Then, above the term, write a revision using nonsexist language.

ordinary person
Example 1. How can the common man help the poor and hungry?

1. In my neighborhood, the mailmen are collecting donations of canned food.

2. A deliveryman will take all the donations to a local soup kitchen.

3. Some of the businessmen in nearby shops and offices set out boxes for donations.

4. They help their fellow man by taking these donations to a shelter for the homeless.

5. Some people think that mankind has become cold and uncaring.

6. The workers and housewives who donate food and clothing know that some people do care.

7. I know a seamstress who gives free sewing lessons at a women's shelter.

8. Our local weatherman collects coats each winter for the Salvation Army.

9. My cousin, who is a male nurse, donates his Saturdays to an inner-city health clinic.

10. With enough manpower, we will make a significant difference in our community.

EXERCISE B In each of the following sentences, cross out the gender-specific terms and awkward expressions. Then, above the term or expression, write a revision using nonsexist language.

supervisor
Example 1. Paul volunteers as a ~~foreman~~ for Habitat for Humanity.

11. Each of our congressmen volunteered his or her time to shelters in his or her hometown.

12. Enrico, who is a fireman, donated and installed fire extinguishers in tenement houses.

13. Any policeman who volunteered his or her time was asked to give personal-safety clinics.

14. Some stewards and stewardesses hosted a meeting on jobs in the airline industry.

15. A seamstress donated children's sleepwear made of a man-made, flame-proof material.

USAGE

USAGE

Review A: **Common Usage Problems**

EXERCISE A In each of the following sentences, underline the word or word group in parentheses that is correct according to the rules of standard, formal usage.

Example 1. (<u>Let</u>, *Leave*) me show you how to operate that camera.

1. It's a long (*way, ways*) from here to Lisbon.

2. Elias Howe (*discovered, invented*) the sewing machine.

3. When I go to camp, I always (*bring, take*) my fishing gear.

4. The dry weather is likely to have a bad (*affect, effect*) on the crops.

5. He made (*fewer, less*) mistakes than I did.

6. We will report the theft to the (*policeman, police officer*) who is standing over there.

7. You should not have (*any, no*) trouble with this assignment.

8. I hope you will (*accept, except*) my apology.

9. From what you said, the audience (*implied, inferred*) things that you had not intended.

10. For many years (*emigration, immigration*) out of that country has been severely restricted.

EXERCISE B Revise the following sentences to correct problems in usage. First, underline the word or word group that needs to be changed. Then, write the revision above it. If a sentence is already correct, write *C* above it. Base your answer on standard, formal usage.

                    meteorologist's
Examples 1. A <u>weatherman's</u> education is extensive.
                              allusions
          2. The poem contains many <u>illusions</u> to classical mythology.

11. A hiking party they spotted a brush fire and reported it to the ranger station.

12. Mrs. Ho wouldn't leave us go to the auditorium for rehearsal until we had cleaned up

    the classroom.

13. Being as I needed money, I took a part-time job.

14. Both firemen were affected by the heat from the raging flames.

15. She knows so much about science that she ought to get good grades in a chemistry course.

16. I wish I could of gone on the trip.

17. The commissioners will try and have their reports ready before the city council meets next week.

18. Both of the people which were under suspicion had good alibis.

19. The missing suitcase could not be found nowhere.

20. We were surprised to see her driving one of them foreign cars.

                                               HOLT HANDBOOK | Fourth Course

Review B: **Common Usage Problems**

EXERCISE A In each of the following sentences, underline the word or word group in parentheses that is correct according to the rules of standard, formal usage.

Example 1. Do you know the name of the person who (*discovered, invented*) zippers?

1. I'd like to (*learn, teach*) myself how to type.

2. The contestants shook hands as the announcer proclaimed, "May the best (*person, man*) win!"

3. (*Among, Between*) the three people running for office, I am the best-qualified candidate.

4. When you are tired of working, please sit down (*beside, besides*) Jake.

5. Tori and Phina never tell us (*anything, nothing*) about their activities.

6. The author (*implied, inferred*) that she would write a sequel.

7. According to a recent census, there are (*fewer, less*) young people today than there were twenty years ago.

8. In science class we learned about the (*affect, effect*) of acid rain on crops.

9. Wendy hasn't met the new student (*either, neither*).

10. No one in the class (*accept, except*) Daniella speaks a foreign language fluently.

EXERCISE B Revise the following sentences to correct problems in usage. First, underline the word or word group that needs to be changed. Then, write the revision above it. If a sentence is already correct, write *C* above it. Base your answer on standard, formal usage.

Examples 1. Carlito answered an ad for deliverymen, and he may get the job. *delivery people*

        2. The prize money will be divided equally between the four winners. *among*

11. Your essay is longer then any that I have written.

12. What sort of a party are you planning?

13. Being that you are taller than I, would you please hang the picture for me?

14. When a pipe busted last week, our house was flooded.

15. I could of done better if I had prepared more thoroughly.

16. I didn't join you because I was kind of tired.

17. Nowhere do the rules say that you cannot vote for yourself.

18. She could hardly believe that she had won first prize.

19. Where did you leave the book at?

20. This book is more interesting then the last one I read.

Review C: **Common Usage Problems**

USAGE

EXERCISE In each of the following sets of expressions, one expression contains a usage problem. Write the letter of the expression on the line provided. Then, write a revision in standard, formal usage.

Example 1. [a] didn't say anything
    [b] fewer synthetic fibers
    [c] the newly hired male nurse
    c the newly hired nurse

1. [a] can hardly think
   [b] everything except that
   [c] I had ought to

   _____

2. [a] seemed like we should
   [b] everywhere we go
   [c] a little way farther

   _____

3. [a] we must have done
   [b] letting the dog out
   [c] this here house

   _____

4. [a] the teacher who coaches
   [b] try and find it
   [c] a broken plate

   _____

5. [a] the crew's foreman
   [b] between the two of us
   [c] fall off the fence

   _____

6. [a] that kind of answer
   [b] this sort of a book
   [c] jumped off the pier

   _____

7. [a] didn't tell me anything
   [b] acted like they were tired
   [c] looking brighter than ever

   _____

8. [a] He had never been there.
   [b] He could hardly see.
   [c] Leave him finish it.

   _____

9. [a] I should of stayed.
   [b] She might have left.
   [c] He had never been there.

   _____

10. [a] feeling somewhat better
    [b] an appeal to the common man
    [c] letting him go home

   _____

Proofreading Application: Letter

Good writers generally are good proofreaders. Learn to become a careful proofreader so that you can correct errors in grammar, usage, spelling, and punctuation. Readers will have more trust in what you are communicating if you do your best to make sure that your writing is free of errors.

We use different levels of formality when we communicate. Furthermore, language can be standard (grammatically correct in formal and informal situations) or nonstandard (appropriate only in the most casual speaking situations and in writing that attempts to recreate casual speech).

PROOFREADING ACTIVITY

The following is a letter composed by a committee of eleventh-grade students. It contains several errors in usage. Find the errors and correct them, using proofreading symbols to replace incorrect words.

Dear Parents:

Its only October, and your probably thinking that the Junior-Senior Prom seems quite a ways off. However, when you start to consider the fund-raising that has to first take place, the Prom is closer then you might think. The reason that we are writing this letter is because we want to ask for your help as early as possible.

For last year's fund-raising, parents and students they began to try and solicit donations from local businesses in January. You couldn't hardly blame them for thinking that January was early enough. However, despite a aggressive campaign, by the time of the prom less than half the dollars needed had been raised. Of course, they might of had more success if they had started there solicitation earlier.

Anyways, we have learned from their experience. Being as we are starting our solicitation drive about three months earlier this year, hopefully we can collect more money. The number of donations we get are crucial to this year's Junior-Senior Prom, and you're involvement

Literary Model: Dialogue

(A) Taking off the apron as if we had real company, Mama said to me, "Son, You go gather the eggs, hear?..."

"Yes'm." My feet dragged me toward the back hall.

"Let them aiggs wait, Mary Willis," Grandpa ordered. "I want Will Tweedy to hear what I come to say. He'll know soon enough anyways..."

My mother asked, nervous-like, "You want us to all go sit in the parlor, sir?"

He shook his head. "Naw, Mary Willis, it won't take long enough to set down for."... When he began his announcement, you could tell he had practiced it. "Now, daughters, you know I was true to yore mother. Miss Mattie Lou was a fine wife.... Beloved by all in this here town, and by me, as y'all know.... Thirty-six year we had, and they was good years. I want y'all to know I ain't never go'n forget her."

(B) "Her fam'ly could be common as Camp's folks... I don't see how Loma could of married into that sharecropper white trash.... "

(C) "You like this hat, Will Tweedy?"

I didn't have much opinion about hats, or much interest either. "Well'm," I mumbled, "I cain't hardly tell what it's go'n look like yet."

Miss Love laughed. A hearty laugh.... "You're a good diplomat, Will Tweedy."

— from *Cold Sassy Tree* by Olive Ann Burns

EXERCISE A Underline six examples of nonstandard English that appear in the above excerpts. Do not underline misspelled words or errors in subject-verb agreement.

EXERCISE B Why do you think the author had the characters use nonstandard English?

_____

_____

_____

_____

_____

_____

Literary Model (continued)

EXERCISE C Write a short dialogue between two characters. Have them discuss their separate experiences of a similar event. Include several examples of nonstandard English in the speech of the second character. Underline each example.

_____

_____

_____

_____

_____

_____

_____

EXERCISE D

1. How would your dialogue be different if neither character's speech included examples of nonstandard English?

_____

_____

_____

_____

_____

2. In which forms of writing do you think nonstandard English would never be appropriate? Explain your answer.

_____

_____

_____

_____

_____

_____

Language and Sentence Skills Practice

233

Writing Application: Editorial

In informal situations, such as conversations and everyday writing, at times you probably use informal or nonstandard English. However, in formal situations, such as speeches and compositions for school, you should adapt your speaking or writing so that all instances of informal and nonstandard English are avoided. By using formal, standard English, you are more likely to create a favorable impression on your listener or reader.

INFORMAL/NONSTANDARD	Anyways, I busted a awesome CD player last night. And the reason is because I just wasn't paying attention to what I was doing.
FORMAL/STANDARD	I firmly believe that an antiquated policy such as restricting the length of boys' hair should be laid to rest alongside corporal punishment.

WRITING ACTIVITY

Write a letter to the editor of a newspaper, stating your opinion about an issue and trying to persuade readers to think or act a certain way with regard to that issue. The letter may be intended for a school or local newspaper. In your speech, include at least six examples covered in the standard usage guidelines in this chapter.

PREWRITING Choose an issue that is important to you and the people who will read your letter. Since these people are your audience, carefully consider their characteristics. What will be their interests and concerns? How can you appeal to them? Make one list of items of convincing support for what you believe. Include reasons, facts, or opinions from knowledgeable sources. Make another list of emotional appeals. Use vivid word pictures and powerful quotations that will make your audience understand your position.

WRITING Use the two lists to guide writing your draft. Begin with something that will grab your readers' attention. You might use a thought-provoking question or an interesting anecdote. Next, write a statement of opinion in which you identify the issue and state what you believe about it. Then, discuss each supporting point. Conclude your speech by restating your opinion or giving a specific suggestion about what your readers can do about the issue.

REVISING Ask yourself whether your letter follows these guidelines for writing business letters:

- Use a polite, respectful, professional tone.
- Use formal, standard English.
- Explain the purpose of your letter quickly and clearly.
- Include all necessary information.

In addition, check that you have used the correct format for a business letter.

PUBLISHING Try proofreading your letter beginning with the bottom line and moving to the top. This will help you concentrate on locating errors in spelling, grammar, and punctuation rather than on the content. Since you want to make a good impression with this letter, check once more to be sure that it is free of usage problems and that you have used standard, formal English exclusively. Use the glossary entries in this chapter to correct any common usage errors. With your teacher's permission, post your letter on a bulletin board or Web site.

EXTENDING YOUR WRITING

Polish this letter further and send it to the editor of your school or community newspaper.

for **CHAPTER 10: CAPITALIZATION** | pages 266–85

Choices: Investigating Capitalization

The following activities challenge you to find a connection between capital letters and the world around you. Do the activity below that suits your personality best, and then share your discoveries with your class.

BUILDING BACKGROUND KNOWLEDGE

As I Always Say

Do you have a proverb or quotation that you find yourself remembering from time to time? What is it? Ask your classmates if they have one, too. Then, ask them to write down their sayings and give them to you. Collect all the sayings and create a scroll that lists them all. You might want to put the appropriate student's name by each quotation. If you do, be sure to ask everybody to give permission for you to use his or her name. Clear your scroll's contents with your teacher before you hang it in the classroom.

LISTING

Your Hometown

For each rule in this chapter, find a real-life example from your town. Then, on one page, write each rule, along with your hometown examples. Give your classmates copies for their English notebooks.

FOREIGN LANGUAGES

Pardon, uh . . .

Become a citizen of the world. Learn the common titles of respect used by Spanish, English, German, Italian, Chinese, Japanese, Cherokee, and any other language that interests you. Be sure to find out if these titles are capitalized. (Do Japanese and Chinese use capitalization? If so, what does it look like?) Share your list with your classmates.

WRITING

Travel Brochure

If you could take a trip to any place in the world, where would you go? While you were there, what are some of the sights you would see? Do a bit of research about your dream travel destination, then write a travel brochure that tells your classmates about it. Decorate your brochure however you wish, but make sure the text of your ad includes at least five proper nouns.

HISTORY

The Fields of Academe

You are in school, but how much do you know about schools? When and where was the first formal school? How did it operate? Find out about schools throughout history. Include an investigation of early Chinese schools. (You'll be amazed.) Make a list of the names of these schools, the dates of their operation, and the country in which they functioned. Where possible, note also who their famous graduates were. Make sure that your capitalization and other punctuation is correct. Then, post notes on the appropriate places on a time line.

EDUCATION

Your Turn

You know what it feels like to take a quiz, but what does it feel like to write one? Using the rules for capitalization that appear in your textbook, write a ten-item capitalization quiz for your classmates. Your quiz should include ten sentences, each of which has at least one capitalization error. After your teacher looks over your quiz, make copies for the class.

GAME

Categories

Make a list of ten categories. Each category is a common noun, such as *cities* or *brand names*, that has an infinite number of proper nouns. Divide your class into groups of five to ten, and have each group sit in a circle. Pick an item on your list, and have the person to your left name a proper noun in your category that begins with the letter *A*. The next person names a proper noun that starts with *B*, and so on. Keep going until somebody gets stumped, then choose a new category. Once everybody gets the hang of it, set a ten-second time limit.

Language and Sentence Skills Practice

235

First Words, *I* and *O*, Salutations and Closings

10a. Capitalize the first word in every sentence.

> **EXAMPLE** **T**he cellist received a standing ovation after his performance.

The first word of a quoted sentence should begin with a capital letter.

> **EXAMPLE** Brian asked, "**W**ill you meet us in the lobby?"

Traditionally, the first word in a line of poetry is capitalized.

10b. Capitalize the pronoun *I* and the interjection *O*.

> **EXAMPLE** As your servant, **I** bow before you, **O** beloved King.

10c. Capitalize the first word in both the salutation and the closing of a letter.

> **EXAMPLES** **D**ear Armen, **M**y dearest Teresa, **S**incerely yours, **Y**ours truly,

EXERCISE A Underline each word that should be capitalized in the following sentences.

Example 1. <u>the</u> usher whispered, "<u>may</u> <u>i</u> please see your ticket?"

1. the main character said to the tiny ant, "what can i do for you, o mighty master?"

2. we watched that movie, and oh, did we laugh!

3. in the attic i found a box of old family photographs.

4. our class discussed the meaning of the line "the midnight sun casts shadows o'er my dreams."

5. her letters to me usually begin with "my dear Kayla," and end with "love always, Grandma."

EXERCISE B Underline each word that should be capitalized in the following items.

Example 1. <u>when</u> spring arrives, <u>i</u> begin counting the days until summer vacation.

6. Plutarch once said, "the mind is not a vessel to be filled but a fire to be lighted."

7. "a fire to be lighted" suggests the mind's potential.

8. "my dearest Sandra," the handwritten letter began.

9. Grandmother closed the letter with a simple "love, Grandma."

10. i always sign my letters to friends by writing "yours truly, Lisa" in cursive letters.

11. Finn asked, "have you seen the new documentary about Cuba?"

12. Heather answered, "no, not yet, but it's on my list."

13. the first line i read in the poem was "hear us, o Zeus."

14. what i heard was—oh, it's not important.

15. Walt Whitman's tribute begins, "o Captain! My Captain!"

MECHANICS

Proper Nouns and Adjectives A

10d. Capitalize proper nouns and proper adjectives.

(1) Capitalize the names of persons and animals.

PERSONS	**A**lexander the **G**reat	**T**heodore **R**oosevelt, **Jr.**
ANIMALS	**F**lipper	**C**hamp	**W**innie the **P**ooh

(2) Capitalize initials in names and abbreviations that come before or after names.

EXAMPLES   **J.R.R.** Tolkien   **S**ra. Serrano   Tyrone Foster, **Ph.D.**

EXERCISE A Underline each letter that should be capitalized in the following items. If an item is already correct, write *C* on the line provided.

Example _____ **1.** <u>dr</u>. <u>m</u>ary <u>m</u>. <u>b</u>oyd's office

_____ **1.** reading a dickens classic

_____ **2.** mary mcleod bethune

_____ **3.** my favorite shakespearean sonnet

_____ **4.** m.f.k. fisher

_____ **5.** the legendary mountain people

_____ **6.** the works of james joyce

_____ **7.** fluffy's grooming habits

_____ **8.** texas patriot don erasmo seguin

_____ **9.** the respected rebecca thatcher, ph.d.

_____ **10.** learning about dr. martin luther king, jr.

EXERCISE B For each of the following items, circle any letter that is incorrectly capitalized.

Example 1. Ⓕormer Ⓟresidential Ⓒandidate H. Ross Perot

11. The Well-known H. G. Wells Novel

12. Lassie The Courageous Collie

13. My Family Doctor, Emily Shapiro, M.D.

14. The Battles Of William The Conqueror

15. Auction Of A Renoir Masterpiece

Language and Sentence Skills Practice

Proper Nouns and Adjectives B

10d. Capitalize proper nouns and proper adjectives.

(3) Capitalize geographical names.

COUNTRIES	Vietnam	Canada	Nigeria
TOWNS, CITIES	San Juan	St. Louis	Tel Aviv
STATES	Pennsylvania	South Dakota	Rhode Island
REGIONS	the Southwest	the Middle East	New England
ISLANDS	Oahu	Pontine Islands	Roanoke Island
MOUNTAINS	Monte Rosa	Pyrenees	Pindus Mountains
BODIES OF WATER	Philippine Sea	Atlantic Ocean	Shark Bay
PARKS, FORESTS	Brechtel Park	Black Forest	Sequoia National Park
ROADS, STREETS	Route 66	West Fifth Street	Blue Ridge Parkway

EXERCISE A   Underline each word that should be capitalized in the following items. If an item is already correct, write *C* on the line provided.

Example _____ **1.** east of the <u>mississippi river</u>

_____ **1.** helicopter ride over the island of maui

_____ **2.** hiking through saskatchewan province

_____ **3.** north of the township

_____ **4.** a desert in the middle east

_____ **5.** a cruise on the mediterranean sea

_____ **6.** the capital city of haiti

_____ **7.** touring the east coast

_____ **8.** a country in the southern hemisphere

_____ **9.** driving on interstate 10

_____ **10.** door county, wisconsin

EXERCISE B   For each of the following items, circle any letter that is incorrectly capitalized.

Example 1. ⓢcuba ⒹIving off the Yucatan Peninsula

11. The West

12. The City of Detroit

13. Lafayette Parish Bus Route

14. Nova Scotia Coastline

15. The Sunbelt

16. South of Houston

17. A Region of South Dakota

18. Expedition on Mount Everest

19. Ferry to Dauphin Island

20. Bay Of Naples

238

MECHANICS

Proper Nouns and Adjectives C

10d. Capitalize proper nouns and proper adjectives.

(4) Capitalize the names of organizations, teams, institutions, and government bodies.

ORGANIZATIONS	**G**irl **S**couts of **A**merica	**A**merican **K**ennel **C**lub
TEAMS	**L**akeview **H**igh **C**ougars	**S**an **A**ntonio **S**purs
INSTITUTIONS	**W**estside **C**linic	**B**rown **U**niversity
GOVERNMENT BODIES	**E**nvironmental **P**rotection **A**gency	**F**ederal **B**ureau of **I**nvestigation

(5) Capitalize the names of businesses and the brand names of business products.

BUSINESSES	**G**eneral **E**lectric	**S**udz-o-matic **L**aundries	
BUSINESS PRODUCTS	**C**ompaq **D**eskpro	**H**onda **O**dyssey	**T**imex watch

EXERCISE A   Underline each word that should be capitalized in the following items. If an item is already correct, write *C* on the line provided.

Example _____ **1.** apple <u>macintosh</u> computer

_____ **1.** driving a new toyota tacoma pickup

_____ **2.** st. jude children's research hospital patient

_____ **3.** cheering chicago bulls fans

_____ **4.** duke university admissions office

_____ **5.** north carolina state senate committee

_____ **6.** american medical association recommendations

_____ **7.** kelley's hardware store specials

_____ **8.** campaign for democratic reforms

_____ **9.** habitat for humanity volunteer

_____ **10.** a tour of the smithsonian institution

EXERCISE B   For each of the following items, circle any letter that is incorrectly capitalized. If an item is already correct, write *C* on the line provided.

Example _____ **1.** Ⓣicket for a Portland Trailblazers Ⓖame

_____**11.** Newcomb College Freshman

_____**12.** St. Louis Cardinals Cap

_____**13.** Executives of Dell Computer Corporation

_____**14.** Frost National Bank Checking Account

_____**15.** National Honor Society Member

_____**16.** Congress

_____**17.** Southwestern Bell Operator

_____**18.** United States Air Force Academy

_____**19.** Department of State

_____**20.** The League of Women Voters

Language and Sentence Skills Practice

239

Proper Nouns and Adjectives D

| **10d.** | Capitalize proper nouns and proper adjectives. |

(6) Capitalize the names of buildings and other structures.

| EXAMPLES | **P**aramount **T**heater | the **W**hite **H**ouse | **G**reat **P**yramid |
| | **G**rand **H**otel | **S**ears **T**ower | **G**olden **G**ate **B**ridge |

(7) Capitalize the names of monuments, memorials, and awards.

| EXAMPLES | **M**uir **W**oods **N**ational **M**onument | **V**ietnam **V**eterans **M**emorial |
| | **L**incoln **M**emorial | **C**ongressional **M**edal of **H**onor | **G**rammy **A**ward |

EXERCISE A Underline each word that should be capitalized in the following items. If an item is already correct, write *C* on the line provided.

Example _____ **1.** the <u>eiffel tower</u> observation deck

_____ **1.** a rialto theater production

_____ **2.** a tour of the taj mahal

_____ **3.** the pulitzer prize-winning novel

_____ **4.** the leaning tower of pisa

_____ **5.** field trip to mount rushmore national memorial

_____ **6.** photographing the brooklyn bridge

_____ **7.** craters of the moon national monument

_____ **8.** honored by the national society of film critics award

_____ **9.** a civil rights memorial

_____ **10.** the top of the empire state building

EXERCISE B For each of the following items, circle any letter that is incorrectly capitalized. If an item is already correct, write *C* on the line provided.

Example _____ **1.** ⓣhe ⓕamed Heisman Trophy ⓦinner

_____ **11.** Crossing the Natchez Trace Parkway Bridge

_____ **12.** Newspaper Article about Windsor Castle

_____ **13.** The Ceiling of the Sistine Chapel

_____ **14.** Crossing a Suspension Bridge

_____ **15.** Booker Prize for Literature

MECHANICS

Proper Nouns and Adjectives E

| **10d.** | Capitalize proper nouns and proper adjectives. |

(8) Capitalize the names of historical events and periods, special events, and holidays and other calendar items.

HISTORICAL EVENTS	the **S**panish-**A**merican **W**ar	the **D**ark **A**ges
AND PERIODS	the **B**attle of **A**rgonne	**P**ax **R**omana
SPECIAL EVENTS	**V**eterans **D**ay **P**arade	**W**orld **S**eries
HOLIDAYS AND OTHER	**C**olumbus **D**ay	**F**ebruary
CALENDAR ITEMS	**B**lack **H**istory **M**onth	**T**uesday

EXERCISE A Underline each word that should be capitalized in the following items. If an item is already correct, write *C* on the line provided.

Example _____ **1.** fighting in the <u>american</u> <u>revolution</u>

_____ **1.** learning about the middle ages

_____ **2.** super bowl

_____ **3.** easter celebration

_____ **4.** the last day of the month

_____ **5.** living through the great depression

_____ **6.** new york city marathon competitor

_____ **7.** sunday brunch

_____ **8.** spring flowers

_____ **9.** the period of the reformation

_____ **10.** special olympics volunteer

EXERCISE B For each of the following items, circle any letter that is incorrectly capitalized. If an item is already correct, write *C* on the line provided.

Example _____ **1.** Memorial Day ⓣrip to the ⓛake

_____ **11.** Annual Labor Day Sale

_____ **12.** April Fool's Day Surprise

_____ **13.** Choosing a Father's Day Present

_____ **14.** Washington State Fair

_____ **15.** Bastille Day

Proper Nouns and Adjectives F

10d. Capitalize proper nouns and proper adjectives.

(9) Capitalize the names of nationalities, races, and peoples.

EXAMPLES	Pueblo	Hungarian	Arabic	Cambodian
	Hispanic	African American	Cherokee	Mexican American

(10) Capitalize the names of religions and their followers, holy days and celebrations, sacred writings, and specific deities.

RELIGIONS AND FOLLOWERS	Taoism	Islam	Christian	Buddhist
HOLY DAYS AND CELEBRATIONS	Hanukkah	Good Friday	Ramadan	Easter
SACRED WRITINGS	the Bible	the Koran	Rig-Veda	Psalms

EXERCISE Underline each word that should be capitalized in the following items. If an item is already correct, write *C* on the line provided.

Example _____ **1.** devout <u>buddhist</u> monk

_____ **1.** studying the talmud each week

_____ **2.** confucian social principles

_____ **3.** american indian tradition

_____ **4.** a lovely passover feast

_____ **5.** a presbyterian minister

_____ **6.** memorizing verses from genesis

_____ **7.** a maple leaf on the canadian flag

_____ **8.** making a muslim pilgrimage

_____ **9.** sufi poetry honoring allah

_____ **10.** navajo lineage in my family

_____ **11.** an italian restaurant

_____ **12.** a copy of the bhagavad-gita

_____ **13.** a meeting with the lutherans

_____ **14.** the japanese ambassador

_____ **15.** a british newspaper

_____ **16.** Athena's temple

_____ **17.** the european team

_____ **18.** reading from the torah

_____ **19.** a grecian urn

_____ **20.** an image of vishnu

Proper Nouns and Adjectives G

10d. Capitalize proper nouns and proper adjectives.

(11) Capitalize the names of ships, trains, aircraft, and spacecraft.

| **EXAMPLES** | the *Mayflower* [ship] | *Air Force One* [aircraft] |
| | *Orient Express* [train] | *Voyager 2* [spacecraft] |

(12) Capitalize the names of planets, stars, constellations, and other heavenly bodies.

| **EXAMPLES** | **J**upiter [planet] | **C**entauri [star] | **A**quarius [constellation] |
| | **G**anymede [moon] | **M**ilky **W**ay [galaxy] | **V**irgo **C**luster [cluster of galaxies] |

EXERCISE A For each of the following items, circle any letter that is incorrectly capitalized. If an item is already correct, write *C* on the line provided.

Example _____ **1.** An Ocean Voyage on the *Monitor*

_____ **1.** piloting the *Spruce Goose*

_____ **2.** a Telescopic View of the Andromeda Galaxy

_____ **3.** Crossing Territory on the *Orient Express*

_____ **4.** a Tour of the Famous *Queen Mary*

_____ **5.** the Rings of Saturn

_____ **6.** Studying the Constellation of Ursa Major

_____ **7.** Photographs of the *Spirit of St. Louis*

_____ **8.** the Tragedy of the R.M.S. *Titanic*'s Sinking

_____ **9.** a Planned Spaceflight to Mars

_____ **10.** the Moon as the Earth's Only Natural Satellite

EXERCISE B In each of the following sentences, circle any letter that should be changed from lowercase to capital or from capital to lowercase.

Example 1. The Little Dipper is a part of the larger Constellation Ursa Minor.

11. Jason is researching the Civil War battle between the *monitor* and the *merrimack,* two iron-

plated Ships.

12. Which ship did columbus actually sail on, the *niña,* the *pinta,* or the *santa maría*?

13. Sometimes, Pluto is actually closer to the sun than neptune.

14. The band is practicing a song about a famous train called *the city of New Orleans.*

15. Is betelgeuse really six hundred times as large as the Sun?

MECHANICS

Proper Nouns and Adjectives H

10d. Capitalize proper nouns and proper adjectives.

10e. Do not capitalize the names of school subjects, except course names followed by a number and the names of language classes.

EXAMPLES	geography	algebra	history	Calculus II	Art 101
	Sociology 212	English	Spanish	French	Japanese

EXERCISE A Each of the following sentences contains at least one error in capitalization. Cross out each incorrect word, and write it correctly in the space above.

                       Cherokee   *Chief*

Example 1. Studying the ~~cherokee~~ in social studies class, we read about ~~chief~~ Wilma Mankiller.

1. Hae Sin could see the rings around saturn with the telescope she had built for physics class.

2. The spacecraft *magellan* was sent to gather information about venus.

3. On august 28, 1963, more than 200,000 people gathered near the washington monument and the lincoln memorial to hear Dr. Martin Luther King, jr., speak.

4. I learned in my history II class that Dr. King won the nobel peace prize in 1964.

5. The only language course that Theodore could fit into his schedule was german.

EXERCISE B Underline each word that should be capitalized in the following items. If an item is already correct, write *C* on the line provided.

Example _____ **1.** an american history class

_____ **6.** two juniors and a sophomore

_____ **7.** westminster abbey

_____ **8.** the d-day invasion

_____ **9.** gold medal flour

_____ **10.** early summer

_____ **11.** classes in sculpting stone

_____ **12.** spanish history

_____ **13.** the federal reserve bank

_____ **14.** on yom kippur

_____ **15.** the boat *ariadne*

MECHANICS

Proper Nouns and Adjectives: Review

10d.   Capitalize proper nouns and proper adjectives.

10e.   Do not capitalize the names of school subjects, except course names followed by a number and the names of language classes.

EXERCISE A   On the line provided, rewrite each of the following items, using the correct capitalization.

Example 1. the special olympics _____*the Special Olympics*_____

1. first national bank _____

2. navajo settlement _____

3. alice walker _____

4. a vietnamese grocery store _____

5. Gulf Of Mexico _____

6. the president's council on aging _____

7. academy award _____

8. moons of jupiter _____

9. gallaudet university _____

10. charlotte hornets _____

EXERCISE B   Each of the following sentences contains at least one error in capitalization. Cross out each incorrect word, and write it correctly in the space above.

Example 1.   Martin Harper, ~~jr.~~, will contribute an article about the history of the ~~american red cross~~.
Jr. *American Red Cross*

11. Students from my English class at Evans High school in warren township entered the contest.

12. The guest speaker for chemistry class today will be h. lorenzo webber, m.d.

13. Linda planned to leave cleveland, on the southern shore of lake erie, travel southwest, and cross the mississippi river at st. louis, missouri.

14. Our neighbor mr. Renfro sometimes takes care of our dog, bubba, when we travel out of town.

15. Mr. Itoh has planned excursions to yellowstone national park and the black hills region.

16. They held the fourth of july picnic at Potter Park.

17. Kaloma plans to attend the university of virginia in the Fall.

18. Several mummies from ancient Egypt are on display at the british museum.

19. The american automobile association printed a booklet on memorial day celebrations.

20. Every saturday morning, the bijou theater shows animated movies.

Language and Sentence Skills Practice

Titles A

10f. Capitalize titles.

(1) Capitalize a person's title when the title comes before the person's name.

EXAMPLES **D**r. An Wang   **S**uperintendent Ignacio   **G**eneral Levine

Generally, a title used alone or following a person's name is not capitalized.

EXAMPLE Ferdinand Morales, the city's new **m**ayor, will lead the parade.

A title used alone in direct address is generally capitalized.

EXAMPLE Will you promise, **M**ayor, to weigh the proposal carefully?

(2) Capitalize a word showing family relationship when the word is used before or in place of a person's name, unless the word follows a possessive noun or pronoun.

EXAMPLES **A**unt Leona   **G**randpa Goodall   Eliza's **g**randpa   my **u**ncle Carlos

---

EXERCISE Circle each letter that is incorrectly lowercased or capitalized in the following items. If an item is already correct, write *C* on the line provided.

Example _____ **1.** Did ⓟresident Carter veto the bill?

_____ **1.** I gave her and professor Cho a copy of my research paper.

_____ **2.** Mr. Hemphill recently met Carrie Benjamin, our local business leader of the year.

_____ **3.** Can you discuss your long-range military strategy, captain?

_____ **4.** The county elected a new district attorney today.

_____ **5.** We are honored to accommodate you, senator Hall.

_____ **6.** My sister and I gave grandmother Todd a lovely brooch for her birthday.

_____ **7.** It has taken principal Harvey and ms. Lee ten minutes to silence the students in the main auditorium.

_____ **8.** President-elect Brown must wait two weeks before assuming office on the council.

_____ **9.** Our classmates think aunt Betty makes the best chocolate chip cookies.

_____ **10.** The speaker of the house rose to greet the king of Denmark.

Titles B

| **10f.** | Capitalize titles. |

(3) Capitalize the first and last words and all other important words in titles and subtitles.

BOOKS	*The Joy Luck Club*	*To the Lighthouse*
CHAPTERS IN BOOKS	"The Early Years"	"A Place for Us"
PERIODICALS	*Car and Driver*	*Chicago Tribune*
PLAYS	*Arsenic and Old Lace*	*The Piano Lesson*
MOVIES	*It's a Wonderful Life*	*The Hunchback of Notre Dame*
TV PROGRAMS	*Meet the Press*	*King of the Hill*
SONGS	"La Bamba"	"Saturday in the Park"

EXERCISE A Circle each letter that is incorrectly lowercased or capitalized in the following items. If an item is already correct, write *C* on the line provided.

Example _____ **1.** My uncle's favorite television program is (t)hird (r)ock from the (s)un.

_____ **1.** I keep a small print of Botticelli's *la primavera* taped to my bedroom mirror.

_____ **2.** Would you like to rent a copy of *Casablanca* this Friday?

_____ **3.** Edgar, who would like to be an engineer, has a subscription to *popular science* magazine.

_____ **4.** Mr. Scott said there will be questions about the Treaty Of Versailles on the test.

_____ **5.** My brother and I never miss an episode of the fascinating *nova*.

_____ **6.** Last summer Roseleen saw a production of *the importance of being earnest*.

_____ **7.** Dad can't find today's copy of *The New York Times* anywhere in the front yard.

_____ **8.** The first chapter of *the grapes of wrath* is very nicely constructed.

_____ **9.** Peter reads both the *columbia journalism review* and the *san jose mercury news*.

_____ **10.** "As time goes by" is the title of my grandparents' special song.

EXERCISE B Complete the following sentences by writing appropriate titles on the line provided. Use correct capitalization.

Example 1. Last weekend, I read *"To Build a Fire"* _____.

11. My favorite movie is _____.

12. The best poem I have ever read is _____.

13. _____ was just played on the radio.

14. The library just subscribed to _____.

15. The next production of the drama club will be _____.

MECHANICS

Titles: Review

10f.	Capitalize titles.

(1) Capitalize a person's title when the title comes before the person's name.

EXAMPLES **S**en. Mikulski   **J**ustice Scalia   **M**ayor Chong

(2) Capitalize a word showing family relationship when the word is used before or in place of a person's name, unless the word follows a possessive noun or a pronoun.

EXAMPLES **U**ncle Hector   **G**randmother Brooks   your **g**randmother   my **a**unt Melba

(3) Capitalize the first and last words and all other important words in titles and subtitles.

EXAMPLES "**T**he **S**ahara: **W**ildlife of the **D**esert"   *Gone with the Wind*

EXERCISE A Each of the following sentences contains at least one error in capitalization. Circle each lowercased letter that should be a capital, and draw a diagonal line through each capital letter that should be lowercased.

Example 1. May we please confer in your chambers, (j)udge?

1. No one expected archbishop Desmond Tutu to attend the ceremony.

2. Dixie asked her Aunt Margaret if she had ever seen the movie *the miracle worker.*

3. Willis delivers papers for the *detroit free press.*

4. Countee Cullen wrote the poem "from the dark tower."

5. Suzanne, Terri, and dad all attended the school play, *Fiddler On The Roof.*

EXERCISE B On the lines provided, rewrite the following items, using capital and lowercase letters as needed. If an item is already correct, write C.

Example 1. *The Return Of The Native*   *The Return of the Native*

6. *the dallas morning news* _____

7. governor Davis _____

8. the television program *60 Minutes* _____

9. the bill of rights _____

10. The first chapter in the guidebook _____

11. the painting *the night watch* _____

12. the last chapter of *the catcher in the rye* _____

13. the poem "the Love song of J. alfred Prufrock" _____

14. the book *Year of Liberty: the Great Irish Rebellion of 1798* _____

15. field marshal Bernard Montgomery _____

Abbreviations

10g. Generally, abbreviations are capitalized if the words that they stand for are capitalized.

EXAMPLES   Janelle Turner, **M.Ed.**   Brent Chisholm, **Jr.**

Mt. Olympus   Tampa, **Fla.**

267 Spring **A**ve.   **A**pt. 101

Cisco Systems, **I**nc.   American **A**ssn. of Retired Persons

AP [Associated Press]   **AFC** [American Football Conference]

EXERCISE   Rewrite the following sentences, correcting errors in the use and capitalization of abbreviations.

Example 1. Linwood J. Hynes hails from Woodland, MI.

Linwood J. Hynes hails from Woodland, Michigan.

1. A ferry operates on Lake Michigan between Muskegon, MI, and Green Bay, WI.

_____

2. Doctor, do you have time to see ms. Wahl this afternoon?

_____

3. The bus to LA leaves every morning at 10:15.

_____

4. The man in the passing jeep was Gen. Eisenhower.

_____

5. We live on Grand st. in Jackson, Miss.

_____

6. The speed limit in this area is 25 MPH.

_____

7. The patient is now in the care of dr. Thomas Seguin, m.d.

_____

8. Dan's favorite program is shown on Pbs.

_____

9. My favorite president was A. Lincoln.

_____

10. Do you enjoy the music of Harry Connick, Junior?

_____

Language and Sentence Skills Practice

249

MECHANICS

Titles and Abbreviations: Review

| **10f.** | Capitalize titles. |

EXAMPLES   **P**resident Carter   **A**unt Consuela   **Gen.** Colin Powell

Cry, the **B**eloved **C**ountry [book]   "**T**he **L**esson of **W**alls" [poem]

| **10g.** | Generally, abbreviations are capitalized if the words that they stand for are capitalized. |

EXAMPLES   **Dr.** Chiago   Marty Solomon, **Sr.**   Atlanta, **Ga.**

Atlas **M**ts.   211 **S.** First **St.**   Herd Manufacturing **Co.**

EXERCISE   Rewrite the following sentences, correcting errors in the use of abbreviations and capitalization.

Example 1. Merrick Elliott, senior, is President of the company. *Merrick Elliott, Sr., is*
president of the company.

1. The Greek playwright Euripides wrote *Iphigenia At Aulis*. _____

_____

2. Have you ever been to reed city, MI? _____

_____

3. The star of *Indiana Jones and the temple of doom* is H. Ford. _____

_____

4. Soon we will be able to address my sister as Dr. Emily Jackson, Ph.D. _____

_____

5. Gov. Harrington attended a conference at Nasa headquarters. _____

_____

6. My Uncle's favorite poem is "Stopping By Woods On A Snowy Evening." _____

_____

7. Has mayor Levine agreed to speak at Washington H. S.'s graduation? _____

_____

8. Carefully add three Oz. of saline solution to the mixture. _____

_____

9. José went to visit aunt Maria in Waukesha, Wisc. _____

_____

10. How many artists have recorded "yesterday" by J. Lennon and P. McCartney? _____

_____

MECHANICS

Review A: **Using Capital Letters**

EXERCISE A In each of the following pairs of items, circle the letter of the item that is capitalized correctly.

Example 1. [a] a hotel in Culver City   **[b]** a Hotel in Culver City

 1. **[a]** a Japanese kimono   **[b]** a japanese kimono

 2. **[a]** in a French-canadian newspaper   **[b]** in a French-Canadian newspaper

 3. **[a]** sailing up the Amazon River   **[b]** sailing up the Amazon river

 4. **[a]** a movie at the Avalanche Theater   **[b]** a movie at the Avalanche theater

 5. **[a]** one hotel in Culver City   **[b]** one Hotel in Culver City

 6. **[a]** Jacques Cousteau's ship, the *calypso* **[b]** Jacques Cousteau's ship, the *Calypso*

 7. **[a]** Gertrude Castaneda, R.N.   **[b]** Gertrude Castaneda, r.n.

 8. **[a]** distance between Mars and Earth   **[b]** distance between Mars and earth

 9. **[a]** studying History and English   **[b]** studying history and English

10. **[a]** an article in *Ebony*   **[b]** an Article in *Ebony*

EXERCISE B Most of the following sentences contain at least one error in capitalization. Circle each lowercased letter that should be a capital, and draw a diagonal line through each capital letter that should be lowercased. If a sentence is already correct, write *C* on the line provided.

Example _____ **1.** Evan said that her little Brother had seen *toy story* at least ten times.

_____**11.** A Statue of general Washington stands in the town's main square.

_____**12.** please give me your advice, o my wisest of friends.

_____**13.** she said, "isn't that hotel located on the east side of Times Square?"

_____**14.** On tuesday Irene went hiking on Sentry mountain with her younger sister.

_____**15.** in his speech on St. Patrick's Day, Mayor Brown mentioned Irish-American friendship.

_____**16.** Is Raleigh the Capital of north Carolina?

_____**17.** Why, gerald, i didn't know your Great-Grandfather fought in the Spanish-American War.

_____**18.** We waited in line for hours, but, oh, the concert was worth the wait!

_____**19.** sometimes i help out at my parents' store, which is on Jefferson Avenue.

_____**20.** "the nation's park system includes Glacier National Park," ms. garza continued.

Language and Sentence Skills Practice

MECHANICS

Review B: Using Capital Letters

EXERCISE A In each of the following pairs of items, circle the letter of the item that is capitalized correctly.

Example 1. [a] Sony corp. ([b]) Sony Corp.

1. [a] drove to Maricopa county   [b] drove to Maricopa County

2. [a] mirrors from the Bronze Age   [b] mirrors from the Bronze age

3. [a] a Labor day celebration   [b] a Labor Day celebration

4. [a] traveled West on the highway   [b] traveled west on the highway

5. [a] the Boston College team   [b] the Boston college team

6. [a] my pet rabbit buttons   [b] my pet rabbit Buttons

7. [a] Suds for Buds Pet Grooming   [b] suds for buds Pet Grooming

8. [a] the Stanley Cup   [b] the Stanley cup

9. [a] the Revolutionary war   [b] the Revolutionary War

10. [a] courses in Art and Spanish   [b] courses in art and Spanish

EXERCISE B Most of the following sentences contain at least one error in capitalization. Circle each lowercased letter that should be a capital, and draw a diagonal line through each capital letter that should be lowercased. If a sentence is already correct, write C on the line provided.

Example _____ **1.** He made the check out to the u.s. dept. of the treasury.

_____ **11.** Our local Theater is auditioning cast members for *The sound of music.*

_____ **12.** My aunt, a chef, works for a local restaurant named Pandora's Box.

_____ **13.** Her cousin has applied for a job at Compudata, inc.

_____ **14.** yesterday i climbed Squaw peak and got a wonderful view of Phoenix, Arizona.

_____ **15.** My high school is at Fifth Avenue and Forty-third Street.

_____ **16.** Have you ever been to Albany, the Capital of New York?

_____ **17.** Carlos asked, "are you going to try out for the soccer team, hank?"

_____ **18.** Please ask your Aunt for a copy of her book, *Traveling with Pets.*

_____ **19.** Did you see the articles in *PC Magazine* about the new Dell Computers?

_____ **20.** In Washington, D.C., one Senator announced plans for a new domestic program.

Review C: **Using Capital Letters**

EXERCISE A Most of the following sentences contain at least one error in capitalization. Circle each lowercased letter that should be a capital, and draw a diagonal line through each capital letter that should be lowercased. If a sentence is already correct, write *C* on the line provided.

Example _____ **1.** After watching (primetime live,) we had a discussion about the election.

_____ **1.** Mount rushmore National Park has large sculptures of four U.S. Presidents.

_____ **2.** The Captain told the team members, "we have to win this game!"

_____ **3.** A new pet store called Creepy critters opened near my house last summer.

_____ **4.** My best friend's family is planning to move West to Utah in May.

_____ **5.** He asked, "Where is the university located, north or south of here?"

_____ **6.** A hurricane is moving Northward along the Atlantic coast.

_____ **7.** There is a chapter of the National Honor Society at our High School.

_____ **8.** Delta Airlines advertises Winter vacations in sunny Florida.

_____ **9.** Two Broadway theaters are presenting shakespearean plays.

_____ **10.** President Clinton addressed a group of reporters on the lawn of the White house.

EXERCISE B In the following paragraph, circle each lowercase letter that should be a capital.

Example **[1]** I have also studied (whitman's) poem "When (lilacs last) in the (dooryard) (bloom'd."

[11] in 1866, walt whitman published a book of poetry called *sequel to Drum-Taps.* **[12]** the most famous poem from that collection is the one about the assassination of abraham lincoln titled "o captain! my captain!" **[13]** in this poem, the speaker is mourning the death of Lincoln. **[14]** The line "exult, o shores, and ring, o bells" conveys the great depth of the speaker's grief. **[15]** The first time that i read this poem, oh, was i sad!

Proofreading Application: Directions

Good writers are generally good proofreaders. Readers tend to admire and trust writing that is error-free. Make sure that you correct all errors in grammar, usage, spelling, and punctuation in your writing. Your readers will have more confidence in your words if you have done your best to proofread carefully.

Careful writers capitalize words as an indication to their readers that they are referring to a title or name of something, starting a new sentence, or referring to a specific person, event, place, or thing.

PROOFREADING ACTIVITY

The following is a set of directions intended for a foreign exchange student at a high school. The directions contain several errors in the standard use of capitalization. Use proofreading symbols to correct letters that are incorrectly capitalized or lowercased.

Example riding a bike to a Museum in downtown Carlston city is a great
idea if you're careful.

Giancarlo,

   According to your phone message, you want to ride that beautiful Tommasini Bike of yours downtown. All I have to say is, "be careful!" In general, drivers in carlston city and drivers in vicenza don't share the same attitude toward cyclists. Having said that, here are the directions you asked for to get from the Library on Fifty-Fifth street to the Museum of native american art.

   Leaving the parking lot, turn right onto George Washington avenue, and stay on it for four blocks. (You'll be heading West with the River on your right.) Turn right at the Westin hotel onto Esperanza Boulevard. Six blocks later you'll see Gateway cinema on your left. (We saw *The Prince Of Egypt* there in april, remember?) The museum is behind the movie theater. Since you're so interested in navajo culture, don't miss the museum's display on their pottery.

   See you tomorrow in Algebra (and enjoy your bike ride)!

Literary Model: Capital Letters in Poetry

Mother to Son
by Langston Hughes

Well, son, I'll tell you:
Life for me ain't been no crystal
    stair.
It's had tacks in it,
And splinters,
And boards torn up,
And places with no carpet on
    the floor—
Bare.
But all the time
I'se been a-climbin' on,
And reachin' landin's,
And turnin' corners,
And sometimes goin' in the dark
Where there ain't been no light.
So boy, don't you turn back.
Don't you set down on the steps
'Cause you finds it's kinder hard.
Don't you fall now—
For I'se still goin', honey,
I'se still climbin',
And life for me ain't been no
    crystal stair.

from **A Voice**
by Pat Mora

Even the lights on the stage unrelenting
as the desert sun couldn't hide the other
students, their eyes also unrelenting,
students who spoke English every night

as they ate their meat, potatoes, gravy.
Not you. In your house that smelled like
rose powder, you spoke Spanish formal
as your father, the judge without a
    courtroom

in the country he floated to in the dark
on a flatbed truck. He walked slow
as a hot river down the narrow hall
of your house. You never dared to race
    past him

to say, "Please move," in the language
you learned effortlessly, as you learned
    to run,
the language forbidden at home, though
    your mother
said you learned it to fight with the
    neighbors
. . . .

EXERCISE A

1. What rule of capitalization in poetry does Langston Hughes follow but Pat Mora break?

_____

2. What do you think was Mora's method of deciding which words to capitalize in her poem?

_____

Literary Model (continued)

MECHANICS | Language in Context: Literary Model

EXERCISE B

1. How does Hughes's method of capitalizing affect your reading of his poem? Does it create a particular style?

_____

2. How does Mora's method of capitalizing affect your reading of her poem? Does it create a particular style?

_____

EXERCISE C   Write a poem that contains at least ten lines. Use capitalization either to create a distinct style or to cause a reader to respond to certain words or images.

_____

_____

_____

_____

_____

_____

_____

_____

_____

_____

_____

_____

_____

EXERCISE D

1. Explain the method of capitalizing that you used in your poem.

_____

2. Do you think it would be effective to break traditional rules of capitalization in other forms of writing—for example, in book reports, essays, or business letters? Explain your answer.

_____

_____

for **CHAPTER 10: CAPITALIZATION**   pages 266–87

Writing Application: Letter

Good writers do not capitalize words arbitrarily, but rather as an indication to their reader that they are referring to a title, starting a new sentence, or referring to a specific person, place, or thing.

Read the following sentences.

  Have you seen the fields lately?

  Have you seen the Fields lately?

Because the word *fields* is capitalized in the second sentence, the reader understands that two or more people with the last name *Fields* are being discussed.

WRITING ACTIVITY

It's twenty-five years in the future. The Department of Intergalactic Diplomacy has just assigned you a pen pal from Planet Xylon. Write a letter to your pen pal in which you introduce yourself and tell the Xylonian about your work; your community and its special places or events; and your favorite books, movies, and music. Since you'll be mentioning proper nouns, names, and titles, refer to the rules for capitalization as needed.

PREWRITING   Before you write the first word, close your eyes for a few moments to visualize yourself, your living situation, and society in general twenty-five years from now. Let your imagi- nation run free! Then, freewrite on these topics for several minutes. Don't worry about complete sentences, spelling, or punctuation. If the flow of your thoughts stops, copy the last word until something new appears in your mind.

WRITING   Incorporate the results of your freewriting into the letter to your intergalactic pen pal. Be sure to use words and phrases that are lively and vivid. Provide many details such as names and titles. In addition, include the standard features of a personal letter: date, salutation, body, closing, and signature.

REVISING   Ask a classmate to close his or her eyes in order to concentrate better as you read the letter. At the conclusion, ask your classmate whether the language you used was sufficiently vivid and lively to help him or her visualize your descriptions and details. In addition, ask your classmate how you might make the sentences read more smoothly. Revise your letter accordingly.

PUBLISHING   Exchange letters with another classmate. Check each other's work for errors, paying special attention to capitalization. Consult a dictionary if you're not sure whether a word should be capitalized. With your teacher's permission, publish your letter and post it in your classroom or on your class Web site.

EXTENDING YOUR WRITING

Perhaps you could collect your classmates' letters and, adding your own, create an anthology titled *Intergalactic Pen Pals: A Glimpse at the Future.* The anthology could be presented to a middle school or elementary school library.

Choices: Examining End Marks and Commas

The following activities challenge you to find a connection between end marks and commas and the world around you. Do the activity below that suits your personality best, and then share your discoveries with your class.

HISTORY

Once Upon a Time

Once upon a time, there were no commas. Find out who started using commas and why. How has their use changed over the years? Create an annotated time line detailing your discoveries, and make copies for all your classmates.

BUILDING BACKGROUND KNOWLEDGE

Oops!

Nobody's perfect. If you look, you'll be able to find comma errors just about everywhere. Find them. Then compose a collage of comma errors in headlines, ads, and magazines. When you hang your collage in the classroom, explain the errors to the class. If you can't find any errors, that's fine. Just find examples of good comma usage.

DEMONSTRATION

Invasion of the Comma People

Is all this talk about punctuation getting old? Well, liven things up! Get together with a group of friends and prepare a demonstration of comma errors and corrections. Make giant cards with phrases and clauses written on them. Add cards with subjects, verbs, and complements. Make a couple of cards for appositives, too. Then, assign at least two people to be the commas. These people could make comma costumes (use your imagination) or just dress in black on the day of the demonstration. Have everyone hold a card and stand in sentence order at the front of the classroom. Then, move the comma people around to show errors and corrections.

ETYMOLOGY

The Quest

From what root does the word *question* come? What is the original meaning of the word's root? What other words use this root? Come up with answers to these questions. Then, prepare a poster that displays the family tree of this root and the words that have sprung from it.

DICTION

Lions and Tigers and Bears, Oh, My!

Exclamations are the scene stealers of writing. They set the tone of all that follows. But why, oh, why do people only use five or six interjections? Give your classmates some other interjections to use in their writing. Compile a long list of alternative interjections. When were these expressions popular? What are their meanings? For what, if any, situations are they appropriate? You can shorten your work if you search an electronic dictionary for the label *interjection* or *exclamation*. The plays of William Shakespeare are also a good source. Be sure to pass out copies of your list to all your classmates.

WRITING

Perennial Questions

The world is a mysterious place. Every person on earth is full of questions—questions about nature, human behavior, time, societies, and about oneself. What do you wonder about? Now's the time to write these questions down. Come up with about twenty of them. When you're done, share your questions with a group of friends to see how many questions you have in common.

End Marks

11a. A statement (a declarative sentence) is followed by a period.

> **EXAMPLE** Charles Drew was a famous scientist and doctor.

11b. A direct question (an interrogative sentence) is followed by a question mark.

> **EXAMPLE** Will you be going to the basketball game tonight?

11c. An exclamation (an exclamatory sentence or a strong interjection) is followed by an exclamation point.

> **EXAMPLES** Wow! How beautiful the mariachi music was!

11d. A request or command (an imperative sentence) is followed by either a period or an exclamation point.

> **EXAMPLES** Please don't walk on the new grass.   Get your dog out of my garden!

EXERCISE A On the line provided, classify each sentence by writing *DEC* for *declarative*, *INT* for *interrogative*, *EXC* for *exclamatory*, or *IMP* for *imperative*. Then, add the appropriate end mark to the sentence.

Example *IMP* **1.** Turn that music down at once!

_____ **1.** Did you have a good time in Sacramento

_____ **2.** A good breakfast is essential to a well-balanced diet

_____ **3.** Look out for that runaway horse

_____ **4.** What a ridiculous idea that is

_____ **5.** Some berries would taste good on that cereal

EXERCISE B Insert appropriate end marks in the following sentences.

Example 1. Are you going to the movies this Friday?

6. Please put the hammer back where you found it

7. What an extraordinary movie that was

8. Will the plane arrive in Vienna on time

9. Many of John Wayne's best films were directed by John Ford

10. Lana didn't know why the new key wouldn't work

11. In England, the day after Christmas is known as Boxing Day

12. Be careful That's an expensive piece of pottery

13. Have you ever wondered why the sky turns green before a tornado

14. Oh What a lovely bouquet of flowers

15. Remy could scarcely believe what he was seeing

Language and Sentence Skills Practice

Abbreviations A

| **11e.** | Many abbreviations are followed by a period. |

Abbreviate given names only if the person is most commonly known by the abbreviated form of the name.

EXAMPLES   Booker **T.** Washington   Susan **B.** Anthony   **N.** Scott Momaday

You may abbreviate social titles whether used before the full name or before the last name alone.

EXAMPLES   **Ms.** Ana Ling   **Dr.** Ricardo Fuentes   **Mr.** Johnson

You may abbreviate civil and military titles used before full names or before initials and last names. Spell them out before the last names alone.

EXAMPLES   **Gov.** Frank O'Bannon   **Governor** O'Bannon

Abbreviate titles and academic degrees that follow proper names.

EXAMPLES   Franco Jamison, **Sr.**   Robert Chuen, **Ph.D.**

EXERCISE   On the lines provided, rewrite the following items, abbreviating words where permissible and inserting periods where necessary.

Example   _Gen. Richard N. Hawthorne, Jr._   **1.** General Richard N Hawthorne, Junior

_____   **1.** the Reverend Burton Erickson

_____   **2.** Representative John Conyers

_____   **3.** Senator Kay Bailey Hutchison

_____   **4.** General Colin L Powell

_____   **5.** Rodney Johnson, *Philosophiae Doctor*

_____   **6.** Doctor Martin Luther King, Junior

_____   **7.** John Kim, Medical Doctor

_____   **8.** Mister Stephen Pescecane

_____   **9.** the novelist J G Farrell

_____   **10.** Colonel Conrad Kilgore

MECHANICS

Abbreviations B

> **11e.** Many abbreviations are followed by a period.

Abbreviations for many agencies and organizations are written as acronyms, without periods.

EXAMPLES   **DEA,** Drug Enforcement Administration   **WRAF,** Women's Royal Air Force

In regular text, spell out names of states and other political units. Abbreviate such names in tables, notes, and bibliographies.

EXAMPLES   Uncle Hiroshi's trip included stops in Detroit, Michigan, and Dayton, Ohio. [regular text]

Detroit, Mich.   Dayton, Oh. [table, note, or bibliography]

EXERCISE A   For each of the following sentences, underline the words that are commonly written as acronyms and write the acronym on the line provided.

Example _____*GAO*_____ **1.** This report was written by the <u>General Accounting Office</u>.

_____ **1.** Both of my parents are graduates of Michigan State University.

_____ **2.** All stockbrokers are governed by the rules of the Securities and

Exchange Commission.

_____ **3.** Claudia plans to play in the Women's National Basketball Association.

_____ **4.** Much good around the world has been done by the United Nations.

_____ **5.** My uncle is an agent with the Federal Bureau of Investigation.

EXERCISE B   On the lines provided, rewrite the following sentences to correct errors in the use of abbreviations. If a sentence is already correct, write *C*.

Example 1. Have you ever been to Los Angeles, Calif.?

Have you ever been to Los Angeles, California? _____

6. My mother was born near Springfield, IL.

_____

7. We are moving to New York, NY, next month.

_____

8. The book was published in Missoula, Montana, in 1999.

_____

9. The poet T. S. Eliot was born in St. Louis, MO, but lived much of his life in London, Eng.

_____

10. Maggio, Rosalie. *The Dictionary of Bias-Free Usage: A Guide to Nondiscriminatory Language.*
Phoenix, AZ: Oryx Press, 1991. _____

Abbreviations C

11e.   Many abbreviations are followed by a period.

Abbreviate the two most frequently used era designations, *A.D.* and *B.C.*

> **EXAMPLES**   The kingdom of Kush developed around 2000 **B.C.** and was a major cultural center until about **A.D.** 350.

In regular text, spell out the names of months and days. You may abbreviate them in tables, notes, and bibliographies.

> **EXAMPLES**   My sister will be married on the second **Saturday** of **September.** [regular text]
>
> **Sat.**   **Sept.** [table, note, bibliography]

The abbreviations *A.M.* and *P.M.* both follow the numerals designating the time.

> **EXAMPLES**   We began painting at 9:00 **A.M.** and took our lunch break at 12:30 **P.M.**

In regular text, spell out the names of units of measurement. Such names may be abbreviated in tables and notes when they follow a numeral.

> **EXAMPLES**   How many **liters** of water should a 130-**pound** person drink per day? [regular text]
>
> 4 **l** water   130 **lbs** [tables, notes]

EXERCISE   In the following sentences, underline any errors in the use of abbreviations and write the correct form above the sentence.

Example 1. The hearing will begin promptly at 7:30 P.M. on *January* Jan. 15, 2001.

1. King John signed the Magna Carta in 1215 AD.

2. The class starts promptly at 8:15 AM, so try to be on time.

3. Work began on the Parthenon in BC 447.

4. The basement to the house needs to be dug 12 ft deep.

5. "Then, in the fourth century BC," said the narrator, "Alexander the Great was born."

6. There are traces of inhabitants at the site as early as 650 AD, archaeologists say.

7. How many ft are there in a mile?

8. Sunday services are held at 7:00 AM, 9:00 AM, and 6:00 PM.

9. The first invasions of the Anglo-Saxons may have occurred as early as the fifth century AD.

10. All entries in the contest must be submitted by Fri., Dec. 8, 2000, at one o'clock PM.

MECHANICS

Abbreviations Review

11e.	Many abbreviations are followed by a period.

EXERCISE On the lines provided, rewrite the following sentences, correcting errors in the use of abbreviations.

Example 1. Langston was treated by Dr. Elena Chavez, MD, in Chicago, IL.

Langston was treated by Dr. Elena Chavez (or, Elena Chavez, M.D.), in Chicago, Illinois.

1. In BC 384, the philosopher Aristotle was born.

_____

2. The keynote speaker for the conference will give her address at 9:00 AM on Oct. 28, 2001.

_____

3. Doesn't the water table start at a depth of 12 ft, 9 in?

_____

4. My grandmother lived for a long time at 1428 Rae Dell Ave., Austin, TX.

_____

5. Please forward all mail to Michiko Conroy, 1200 Michigan Ave, Ann Arbor, MI 48104.

_____

6. According to the dictionary, Chaucer may have been born in 1340 AD.

_____

7. Mr Walter R Estlund comes from Minneapolis, Minn.

_____

8. Now, add the following to the stew: 1 tsp. salt, 1 tbsp. basil, 6 oz. chicken broth.

_____

9. The television set's measurements are as follows: 26 in wide, 18 in deep, and 22 in tall.

_____

10. Martina Gonzalez, PhD, has recently been hired by O.S.H.A.

_____

MECHANICS

Language and Sentence Skills Practice

Commas with Items in a Series

| **11f.** | Use commas to separate items in a series. |

EXAMPLE The parents hid Easter eggs behind rocks, under picnic tables, and in the trees.

| **11g.** | Use commas to separate two or more adjectives preceding a noun. |

EXAMPLE Hector was an inquisitive, intelligent student.

EXERCISE Add commas where they are needed in the following sentences. If a sentence is already correct, write *C* before the item number.

Example 1. The book contains many photographs of our wild, beautiful national parks.

1. Kanoa's winning painting was of a scarlet rose a yellow tulip and a blue iris.

2. The main ingredient in Katya's salad dressing is delicious tangy blue cheese.

3. Dennis Talia and Giuseppe volunteered to rake the park.

4. The hurricane season brought hail high winds and thunderstorms to the coast.

5. I cooked and cleaned and went shopping for my elderly aunt.

6. She baked a loaf of bread she made soup and she cut up some fresh berries.

7. Randall's jogging route took him around the lake up a steep hill and across an empty field.

8. I believe that large old colorful rug was woven by my grandmother.

9. The thick black clouds gathering overhead threatened rain at any moment.

10. The fire began because of an electrical short circuit.

11. The ship left harbor on a cool clear evening.

12. Mars is sometimes known as the angry red planet.

13. We had to decide among the dog the cat and the marmoset.

14. He looked for his glasses on the kitchen counter on his desk and on the bedside table.

15. Some of my favorite Cajun foods include jambalaya red beans and rice and gumbo.

16. The damp gray mist crept over the moors as the moon rose.

17. The shortstop dashed forward snatched up the ball and hurled it toward first base.

18. The hiking trail wound up the hill through the thicket and alongside the waterfall.

19. The three books that make up *The Lord of the Rings* are *The Fellowship of the Ring The Two Towers* and *The Return of the King*.

20. I don't think that shirt looks good with the bright purple tie.

264

Commas with Independent Clauses

| **11h.** | Use a comma before *and, but, for, nor, or, so,* or *yet* when the conjunction joins independent clauses. |

> **EXAMPLES** Radha loves to play in chess tournaments**, and** she is an able player.
>
> Jeff finished his chemistry project first**, but** his results were not reliable.

Don't confuse a compound sentence with a simple sentence that has a compound verb.

COMPOUND SENTENCE Cal wrote a short story**, and** he sent it to a magazine editor.

SIMPLE SENTENCE Cal wrote a short story **and** sent it to a magazine editor.

EXERCISE Add commas where they are needed in the following sentences. If a sentence is already correct, write *C* before the item number.

Example 1. Don't talk to the lifeguard**,** or she will lose her concentration.

1. Guillermo ordered two books from a catalog but they haven't arrived yet.

2. Hank gave away the tickets for he had made other plans and couldn't go.

3. Dr. Ling saw her surgery patients and then left for the conference.

4. The play was received well by the audience but the critics disliked it.

5. He refused to build a new fence nor would he repair the old one.

6. The test was very difficult yet everyone in the class passed it.

7. There was a long line in front of the theater so we decided to go to a concert.

8. Are you going to the football game or do you want to play squash?

9. Jason followed all the directions carefully but could not get the plants to grow.

10. The lake was calm and the moon was a bright, yellow crescent.

11. We've tried all sorts of cat foods yet Sparky is never satisfied.

12. Gustavo lifted the lid of the box and looked inside.

13. Basia had not cleaned her room nor had she started tidying the garage.

14. Ross missed the most spectacular meteor of the night for he had his back turned at the time.

15. I don't really like scary movies but I'll come with you anyway.

16. Suzanne brought some CDs to the party and her sister Rosalynne brought some tapes.

17. Did you let the dog out this afternoon or did he get out on his own?

18. Margaret welcomed her guests and offered each of them a glass of punch.

19. My sister had not come home yet so I decided to start dinner by myself.

20. I cannot list the encyclopedia in my bibliography for I did not use it while writing my report.

Language and Sentence Skills Practice **265**

MECHANICS

Commas with Nonessential Clauses and Phrases

11i. Use commas to set off nonessential subordinate clauses and nonessential participial phrases.

A *nonessential* (or *nonrestrictive*) subordinate clause or participial phrase contains information that is not necessary to the basic meaning of the sentence.

    NONESSENTIAL CLAUSE   Gloria**, who lives next door,** is my best friend.

    NONESSENTIAL PHRASE   Myron**, sitting by the pond,** thought about his future.

An *essential* (or *restrictive*) subordinate clause or participial phrase is not set off by commas because it contains information that is necessary to the meaning of the sentence.

    ESSENTIAL CLAUSE   The playwright **whom I most admire** is Lillian Hellman.

    ESSENTIAL PHRASE   All people **working in that factory** assemble cars.

EXERCISE A On the line provided before each sentence, write *N* if the underlined clause or phrase is nonessential. Write *E* if it is essential. Then, add commas wherever they are needed.

Example ___*N*___ **1.** The roses, which look nice in that vase, were a gift from Al.

_____ **1.** She returned all the books that she had borrowed from the library.

_____ **2.** All students trying out for the track team should be excellent runners.

_____ **3.** Robert Frost who taught at Harvard University was a great poet.

_____ **4.** The man leading the parade is the mayor of our town.

_____ **5.** The Nineteenth Amendment to the U.S. Constitution which was adopted in 1920

        granted women the right to vote.

_____ **6.** Trucks carrying explosives were not allowed to pass through the tunnel.

_____ **7.** I believe you'll like the chicken enchiladas which are a specialty at this restaurant.

_____ **8.** Our kitchen recently remodeled is the most comfortable room of all.

_____ **9.** Sylvia studied the theater's show times listed on page 8 of the newspaper.

_____ **10.** Everyone who wants to have a successful garden must weed it regularly.

EXERCISE B Add commas to the following sentences where necessary. If a sentence is already correct, write *C* before the item number.

Example 1. Moira, thinking hard, finally remembered the answer to the question.

11. John who was named after his father decided to name his son something else.

12. Dermot remembering his training lifted the box with his knees and not with his back.

13. The students who finished the test before eleven o'clock were allowed to leave early.

14. The congresswoman first elected to the House of Representatives in 1998 served for six years.

15. Many books written by Stephen King have been made into movies.

HOLT HANDBOOK | Fourth Course

Commas with Introductory Elements

11j. Use a comma after certain introductory elements.

EXAMPLES **Yes,** I'd like to see that movie. [introductory word]

Okay, let's see it tonight. [mild exclamation]

Smoldering, the embers emitted a soft glow. [participle or participial phrase]

From all of the Mexican foods on the table, I took a small serving of each. [long or multiple prepositional phrases]

While the spectators cheered, Pasqual ran forty yards. [adverb clause]

EXERCISE Add commas where they are needed in the following sentences. If a sentence is already correct, write *C* before the item number.

Example 1. Riding on the bus, Tanay suddenly felt sleepy.

1. When I moved from Georgia to North Dakota I learned what *winter* means!

2. Well I want to read more about the candidates before I make my decision.

3. Walking through the museum we saw many interesting exhibits.

4. At the end of *The African Queen* Charlie and Rose get married.

5. Yes I would be happy to give you a ride to the airport.

6. While mowing the lawn Gigi found a small patch of forget-me-nots.

7. In the shop window we saw Eric Kraft's latest novel.

8. On a clear day in the early spring flocks of migrating birds swept by.

9. Why what a surprise to travel all the way to New York and meet a neighbor!

10. Whispering Lars told her the secret ingredient in his spaghetti sauce.

11. Laughing Jim put the magazine back on the table.

12. Well let me think about that for a moment.

13. Of all the short stories in the anthology my favorite is "A Rose for Emily" by William Faulkner.

14. While the audience was dazzled by the flash the magician disappeared.

15. When the scarecrow said good-bye to Dorothy Steve began to cry.

16. On the lawn we found the morning newspaper.

17. Sweating the runner finished the race at the hottest part of the day.

18. Okay let's start the game.

19. Out of all the cats in the shelter Jorge picked the orange tabby.

20. As her father looked on proudly Celia took the gold medal for gymnastics.

Language and Sentence Skills Practice

Commas with Interrupters

11k. Use commas to set off an expression that interrupts a sentence.

(1) Use commas to set off nonessential appositives and nonessential appositive phrases.

> **EXAMPLE**   Paul Newman**, the famous actor and director,** is a generous philanthropist.

(2) Use commas to set off words used in direct address.

> **EXAMPLE**   As I have said before**, Luisa,** you are a fine writer.

(3) Use commas to set off parenthetical expressions.

> **EXAMPLE**   I believe**, in fact,** that this city needs more recreational areas.

EXERCISE   Add commas where they are needed in the following sentences. If a sentence is already correct, write *C* before the item number.

Example 1. The first city on their itinerary was Harrisburg, the capital of Pennsylvania.

1. Senator Schwartz I believe is the best candidate for that office.

2. Elephants the largest mammals in Africa are now considered endangered.

3. Dorothea tell me about your scholarship to Stanford University.

4. Ana is the only student in our school in fact who has ever lived in China.

5. I'd like to understand Kris your feelings that led to your decision.

6. Are you familiar with the works of the photographer Julia Cameron?

7. Dr. Montero the only pediatrician on the staff has office hours today.

8. Only synthetic materials she says will be used in clothes of the future.

9. In *Casablanca* for example Humphrey Bogart delivers a startling performance.

10. I'd appreciate your prompt reply Mr. Montgomery.

11. If I've told you once Nicci I've told you a thousand times, don't slouch at the dinner table.

12. Do you know the car I mean the red convertible with the silver hubcaps?

13. Accepting the award will be Emily James the producer of the documentary.

14. This manuscript reads like the work of author Sandra Cisneros.

15. Meanwhile the train pulled into Waterloo Station.

16. M. R. James not Henry James wrote the ghost story "Casting the Runes."

17. Dr. Livingston I presume?

18. The actor Edward James Olmos will be our speaker this morning.

19. The elephant for instance is native to both Africa and India.

20. Have you ever seen *Paths of Glory* the anti-war film by Stanley Kubrick?

HOLT HANDBOOK | Fourth Course

for **CHAPTER 11: PUNCTUATION** | *pages 298–311*

Using Commas

11f. Use commas to separate items in a series.

11g. Use commas to separate two or more adjectives preceding a noun.

11h. Use a comma before *and, but, for, nor, or, so,* or *yet* when the conjunction joins independent clauses.

11i. Use commas to set off nonessential subordinate clauses and nonessential participial phrases.

11j. Use a comma after certain introductory elements.

11k. Use commas to set off an expression that interrupts a sentence.

EXERCISE Add commas where they are needed in the following sentences. If a sentence is already correct, write *C* before the item number.

Example 1. Lisa, may I offer you some juice or a glass of spring water?

1. Oh have you seen my dog Wolfie?

2. Tonya who read the book before I did enjoyed it enormously.

3. Seth wanted to play in the band but he couldn't make it to rehearsal on Tuesday.

4. Have you seen the movie, too?

5. Clarence by practicing all weekend was able to play the song on the guitar on Monday.

6. The reflection off the water threw bright quivering spots against the side of the boat.

7. *Reverie* our high school's literary magazine is accepting submissions.

8. The initial research was done by Raji, Candace, and Benson.

9. Gosh you've really grown since I saw you last.

10. Have you ever seen *2001: A Space Odyssey* the film by Stanley Kubrick?

11. The batter knocked the dirt off her cleats put on a helmet and took a couple of swings.

12. Which towel do you want, the red one the blue one or the green one?

13. Linda considered attending the seminar but decided to stay home and work instead.

14. The bright red car nosed carefully through the narrow crowded street.

15. The dark mysterious stranger loomed in the doorway.

16. Yes I think you could say I'm bored.

17. The actress who played Queen Elizabeth Judi Dench won an Academy Award.

18. You may help yourself to the buffet, or you may order from the menu.

19. My friend Barton McManus Jr. has a great recipe for curry.

20. Tom Hanks Sylvester Stallone and Gene Hackman have all done voices for animated films.

MECHANICS

Conventional Uses of Commas

11l. Use commas in certain conventional situations.

(1) Use commas to separate items in dates and addresses.

EXAMPLES   On Monday, January 3, 2001, my brother learned that he had been accepted at Wittenberg University in Springfield, Ohio.

(2) Use a comma after the salutation of a personal letter and after the closing of any letter.

EXAMPLES   Dear Margarita,   Dear Ms. Varghese,   Yours truly,   Sincerely,

(3) Use a comma to set off an abbreviation, such as *Jr., Sr.,* or *M.D.,* that follows a person's name.

EXAMPLE   Rita S. Sanchez, **M.D.,** is our family doctor.

EXERCISE A   Add commas where they are needed in the following items. If an item is already correct, write *C* before the item number.

Example 1. On June 8, 2002, I hope to visit my cousins in San Juan, Puerto Rico.

1. On November 15 1999 the mayoral race was won by Herbert E. Thomas Jr.

2. By Tuesday February 29 2000 you must have your car inspected.

3. You can reach Kyle Forsyth M.D. at 243 First Street Philadelphia Pennsylvania 19002.

4. Sincerely yours

   Charlene Watson DVM

5. My dentist, Susan Schwartz D.D.S., graduated from dental school in June 1999.

EXERCISE B   Insert commas where they are needed in the following personal letter.

Example I received my acceptance letter on March 15, 2000.

May 31 2000

Dear Mr. Jackson

On June 11 2000 I will finally graduate. I want to thank you for being such an inspiring, dedicated teacher. Your classes were always interesting, challenging, and enlightening. You always encouraged me to follow my dreams.

Thanks for writing such a terrific recommendation for me! Please plan on visiting me there next fall. My address will be 1255 Village Avenue Springfield Ohio 45501.

Sincerely

Rashard Brooks

Commas: Review

Review pages 298–314 of your textbook for rules on the use of commas.

EXERCISE In the following sentences, insert commas where necessary.

Example 1. Our art teacher, Ms. Sasajima, is one of the best painters I know.

1. The tour guide handed out tickets programs maps and brochures.

2. Sally knew that she would succeed if she studied hard read all the books and attended class.

3. Sparks was a wet cold miserable hungry dog by the time we got home.

4. They had fresh cold orange juice at breakfast.

5. Colin called the twins and I took care of all the other arrangements.

6. My sisters agreed with me but I had a hard time convincing Uncle Stu.

7. Laszlo Neumann who won the Nichols Prize last year will perform at the Arts Center.

8. Austria's capital is Vienna which is well-known for its architecture and gracious lifestyle.

9. Wow did you see that fly ball?

10. You will I trust pass on the message.

11. My new address is 45 Basil Road Stony Brook New York 11732.

12. On Monday January 15 1999 the Bigelows' new baby was born.

13. After lunch the Pasternaks' new neighbors the Botsteins came over for coffee.

14. Portman Callow Jr. will be our new state representative.

15. Sure I'll come if you want me to.

16. The main language of Finland is Finnish which is distantly related to Hungarian.

17. Lionel lives at 122 Main Street Kyle Texas 78664.

18. Didn't Thaddeus Flatow the famous modern composer write an opera called *Maria Theresia*?

19. Tim please answer the phone.

20. The graduation ceremony will of course be held in College Hall.

MECHANICS

Review A: **End Marks and Abbreviations**

EXERCISE A Add the appropriate end mark to each of the following sentences.

Example 1. Arturo helped the dog over the fence.

1. What's the name of the woman with the dachshund

2. Stop the car immediately

3. The helicopter descended as low as the treetops

4. Be careful not to let the cat out when you open the door

5. Look out The ladder is falling

6. Come to dinner at our house tomorrow night

7. Do you remember where you left the keys to the cabinet

8. Set the groceries on the counter

9. May I offer a suggestion

10. So, what do you think

EXERCISE B On the lines provided, rewrite the following sentences to correct any errors in the use of abbreviations. Also, abbreviate words where permissible and insert or delete periods where necessary.

Example 1. Trish L LeBlanc resides at 2800 Congress Ave., Austin, Texas, 78704.

Trish L. LeBlanc resides at 2800 Congress Avenue, Austin, TX 78704.

11. Rep. Tataglia of NY serves on the oversight committee for the National Aeronautics and Space Administration. _____

_____

12. Mister Tom S Petersen, Junior, hails from Wheeling, W. Va. _____

_____

13. Please send my mail to 1124 Mile Rd., Big Rapids, Mich. 49307. _____

_____

14. Doctor Wanda Jackson will attend the annual A.M.A. convention this year. _____

_____

15. The Roman Empire was established by the emperor Augustus in BC 27, and lasted until it was divided in the fourth century AD. _____

_____

MECHANICS

Review B: **Commas**

EXERCISE A Add commas where they are needed in the following sentences. If a sentence is already correct, write *C* before the item number.

Example **1.** Studying the stars and planets, the Incas used their observations to predict the seasons.

1. When the Spaniards arrived in South America they found that most of the western part of the continent was controlled by the Incas.

2. At the time of the Spanish conquest the Inca empire extended as far north as Ecuador and as far south as Chile and Argentina.

3. The remains of the capital city of the Incas can be seen today at Cuzco a city in southern Peru.

4. The Incas were excellent architects engineers and artisans.

5. Unlike the Aztecs and the Mayas however the Incas never developed a system of writing.

6. Their historical traditions were preserved in spoken form not in written form.

7. They used knotted strings to keep track of official statistics and accounts.

8. These knotted strings which were called *quipu* served as an aid to the memory.

9. The Incas had no currency system but they developed an ingenious method of collecting taxes.

10. All taxes were collected in the form of labor: farmwork on government lands service in the military forces or work on public construction projects.

EXERCISE B Add commas where they are needed in the following sentences. If a sentence is already correct, write *C* before the item number.

Example **1.** The architect, not the construction company, is responsible for the design.

11. The *Readers' Guide* is an index to magazine articles stories and poems.

12. Kelly and Jerome who are taking an advanced computer course produced a graphic display.

13. My uncle lives in Montgomery the capital of Alabama.

14. When you fly cross-country you can sometimes pass the time by watching a movie.

15. The players sitting on the bench hoped for a chance to enter the game.

16. Hoping for good weather my parents planned a family picnic.

17. Did you know Mr. Franklin that Thomas has moved to Buffalo New York?

18. I do not have the report ready today but I hope to finish it by Friday.

19. Many people were involved in creating costumes designing sets and composing music.

20. Well I didn't know that you expected to be invited.

MECHANICS

Review C: **End Marks and Commas**

EXERCISE   Add commas, periods, question marks, and exclamation points where they are needed in the following sentences.

Example 1. They hiked in the Blue Ridge Mountains, which are famous for their beautiful views.

1. Smiling and bowing the dancer took another curtain call.

2. Didn't you answer the telephone, Tiffany

3. We moved to Colorado on September 30 1999.

4. I'm sorry Rae, but I didn't hear what you said

5. Oh you don't have to tell me if you don't want to.

6. The letter was addressed to Chane E. Johnson M.D.

7. In our school classes regularly begin at 8:15 A.M.

8. Last summer I did nothing for two months but swim sail and fish

9. My how cold it is

10. Her father has gone to Denver, Colorado on a business trip.

11. The play was written by J. D. Tallchief a junior.

12. My sister was born on January 25 1985 and I was born on May 22 1987.

13. Don't you know where the bookstore is, Elvin

14. Katrina, don't sneak up on me like that

15. Before the game was over most of the players were covered with mud.

16. Margaret Mead Ph.D., was a famous anthropologist.

17. We must be late for the lights in the theater are dim

18. On our team players vote to choose the captain.

19. After our exciting raft trip down the rapids of the Colorado we had many stories to share

20. Smiling nervously the children took their positions on stage

21. Herbert E Fiorello Jr has an office on Sunset Boulevard.

22. Are you sure that the store is located on Tetra Avenue

23. I'll meet you on the corner of Fourteenth Street at 8:30 AM

24. Didn't Dr An Wang establish Wang Laboratories, Inc, in 1951

25. We saw Harry Connick, Jr, perform at the benefit concert

Proofreading Application: Script

Good writers are generally good proofreaders. Readers tend to admire and trust writing that is error-free. Make sure that you correct all errors in grammar, usage, spelling, and punctuation in your writing. Your readers will have more confidence in your words if you have done your best to proofread carefully.

With commas and end marks, writers can communicate where their readers should pause and with which type of expression they should read sentences. Commas can also help show the relationships among words and ideas. People reading a film or video script must pay special attention to commas and end marks as cues or indicators of the type of tone and pitch they should use as they deliver their lines.

PROOFREADING ACTIVITY

The following excerpt from a video script intended for an adolescent audience contains errors in the use of end marks and commas. Use proofreading symbols to indicate missing commas and incorrect end marks.

Example MALE: Roxanne, who is that girl on crutches ∧?

[In the cafeteria.]

FEMALE: Wow. That's Elissa Steinman on crutches. What happened to her.

MALE: Sssh Roxanne. She'll hear you. Her doctor found a stress frac-ture yesterday. She won't be able to do any gymnastics for four weeks.

FEMALE: That's horrible. Do you know how much gymnastics means to her.

MALE: Didn't we just finish studying bones in science class.

FEMALE: Right We learned that even young people can have bone-relat-ed problems. If you don't get enough calcium your body starts steal-ing it from your bones. When that happens your bones get porous fragile and weak. Then you can more easily get a stress fracture. I wonder if that was Elissa's case.

MALE: But Roxanne I'm an athlete and everyone says I'm underweight. I don't want to end up like Elissa. So what should I do.

Language and Sentence Skills Practice

275

Literary Model: Short Story

> It hurt to be pinned in twelve seconds in a nonleague wrestling match, especially at the end of the 1960s when, except for a few dads and moms and the three regulars with faces like punched-in paper bags, the bleachers were empty of spectators. It hurt to stand under the shower looking at fingerprints still pressed in my arm where my opponent, whose name was Bloodworth, gripped, yanked, and with a grin on his face threw me on my back. The guy next to me had fingerprints around his wrist and arm. Another guy was red around his chest. His eyes were also red. We lost by plenty that night, but coach wasn't too mad.
>
> —from "The Wrestlers" by Gary Soto

EXERCISE A   As you read the excerpt above, you may not have thought much about commas. Even so, commas make a big difference in Gary Soto's words. To see what a difference commas can make, read the sentence below. It is a copy of the first sentence of the excerpt, only this time it has been printed with no commas.

> It hurt to be pinned in twelve seconds in a nonleague wrestling match especially at the end of the 1960s when except for a few dads and moms and the three regulars with faces like punched-in paper bags the bleachers were empty of spectators.

Which version was easier to read—the version with commas or without? Why?

_____

_____

_____

_____

From "The Wrestlers" from *A Summer Life* by Gary Soto. Copyright © 1990 by **University Press of New England.** Reprinted by permission of the publisher. Electronic format by permission of **Gary Soto.**

Literary Model (continued)

EXERCISE B Write *a*, *b*, or *c* on each line below to show which comma rule is demonstrated in the bold-faced part of that item. You will write each letter only once.

(a) Use commas to separate items in a series.
(b) Use commas to set off an expression that interrupts a sentence.
(c) Use a comma before *and, but, for, nor, so,* or *yet* when the conjunction joins independent clauses.

_____ **1.** It hurt to be pinned in twelve seconds in a nonleague wrestling match, especially at the end of the 1960s when, **except for a few dads and moms and the three regulars with faces like punched-in paper bags,** the bleachers were empty of spectators.

_____ **2.** It hurt to stand under the shower looking at fingerprints still pressed in my arm where my opponent, whose name was Bloodworth, **gripped, yanked, and with a grin on his face threw me on my back.**

_____ **3. We lost by plenty that night, but coach wasn't too mad.**

EXERCISE C As you have seen, commas can be used in many ways to make writing easier to understand. Write a paragraph as if you were telling a story in a letter to a friend. In your paragraph, use commas in at least three different ways.

_____

_____

_____

_____

_____

_____

_____

_____

EXERCISE D Now, read over the paragraph. Which comma rule that you used seems the most important to you? How did this rule help make your writing easier to understand?

_____

_____

_____

Writing Application: Magazine Advertisement

Writers generally can't insert cues in their text such as "to be read as an exclamation" or "this is said in a questioning tone." Instead, they use punctuation marks to indicate nonverbal cues. For example, read the following three sentences aloud, using the tone and pitch indicated by each end mark.

EXAMPLES   You have to go.   You have to go?   You have to go!

Punctuation marks often affect meaning. Read the following sentence aloud. Is Rochelle being given the information or will she be studying Spanish?

EXAMPLE   Rochelle, Curtis and Maryann are going to study Spanish next summer in Honduras.

Although punctuation marks by themselves will not always clarify a confusing sentence, they're certainly useful. They can enhance your writing and help you to express yourself more clearly.

WRITING ACTIVITY

Nonverbal cues such as tone and pitch are used in spoken advertisements to make them more effective and appealing. However, in printed advertisements, effectiveness and appeal rely in part on the words (called the *copy*) and the punctuation. You're going to create a magazine advertisement for a product. In the copy, include each kind of end mark at least once, as well as one example of each of the following: a comma separating items in a series, a comma setting off words used in direct address, and a comma setting off an introductory adverb clause.

PREWRITING   List some possible products for your advertisement and choose one you think you can effectively promote. First, decide who your audience will be. Next, create a chart with the following advertising techniques as column heads: loaded words, snob appeal, testimonials. In each column, jot down ideas you could use in the advertisement. Then, make a rough sketch of the layout, including the images. This will give you an idea of how much copy you will need to write.

WRITING   Write a short and direct headline that will immediately attract the reader's attention. Using the ideas in your chart, write the copy. You may decide not to use all three techniques, especially since a limited amount of text can appear in the advertisement.

REVISING   Have at least two classmates critique your advertisement. Ask them whether it is persuasive and how it could be improved. Could you make the text more succinct? Could you use modifiers that are more descriptive, precise, or vivid? Could you make the advertisement more effective by changing the layout? Check that you have included the end marks and uses of commas specified above.

PUBLISHING   Proofread your advertisement carefully, paying special attention to the use of commas and end marks. Any error in such a small amount of text is sure to jump out at readers and detract from your message. Perhaps you and your classmates could post your advertisements on a class or hall bulletin board.

EXTENDING YOUR WRITING

Translate your print advertisement into a video script, and videotape it. Make sure that any dialogue is properly punctuated to help your actors read your words as smoothly and as naturally as possible. A competition could be held in which students vote on the most effective advertisement.

Choices: Exploring Punctuation

The following activities challenge you to find a connection between punctuation and the world around you. Do the activity below that suits your personality best, and then share your discoveries with your class.

MATHEMATICS

Proper Proportions

Mathematicians use colons to express ratios. Prepare a short presentation on ratios. Include the etymology of the word *ratio*, several examples of ratios, and conversions of ratios into percentages. Also, include examples of the most common uses of ratios, such as in scale models. Be sure to highlight the colons in your written examples.

WRITING

Linguistic Acrobatics

Look up the word *punctuate* in a good dictionary. Then, write a sentence for each meaning of the word. With your teacher's permission, present your sentences to the class, explaining the different meaning of each use of the word *punctuate*.

INVENTION

On Your Marks

Have you ever thought that the English language needed more forms of punctuation, that what we use just doesn't meet all of our needs? Make up a new use for a mark of punctuation or create a new punctuation mark—one that expresses what *you* want. Make up a few rules to go along with your new mark while you're at it. Then, present your ideas to the class.

MUSIC

Words and Music

Words and mathematical formulas are not the only systems of written communication that are punctuated. Musical scores are also punctuated. If you can read sheet music, compare musical scores with English punctuation. What features do they have in common? Prepare visual examples to show to your classmates. If possible, play the passages that you are using as examples.

GRAPHICS

Stand Alone Unit

Before you start peppering your writing with semicolons and colons, prepare a study poster to help you and your classmates completely understand the difference between a subordinate clause and an independent clause. Include a clear definition of each type of clause. Then, thumb through magazines or newspapers to find several examples of independent and subordinate clauses. Highlight the clauses in each example you find, and cut out the sentences. Next, paste them on your poster beneath the appropriate definition. With your teacher's permission, hang the poster in the classroom, and refer to it as you study colons and semicolons.

CREATIVE WRITING

A Checkered Past

Make up your own story about how semicolons came to be. To get ideas for your creation story, look up the word semicolon in a good dictionary. Also, consider the following questions: What is the semicolon's relationship to the comma and the colon? Which mark came first, the semicolon or the colon? Why?

DISCUSSION

The Colon: A Mark of Excellence

You have learned that a colon is used between a title and a subtitle, right? Well, put that knowledge into practice. Are you crazy about books? Music? Art? Whatever your interest, research and compile a list of at least twenty titles of books, music, or works of art that have a subtitle. Type up your list, and share it with your classmates. Then, ask yourself and your classmates this question: What function does a subtitle serve? Lead a discussion on why subtitles are so commonly used.

Semicolons A

| **12a.** | Use a semicolon between independent clauses that are closely related in thought and that are not joined by *and, but, for, nor, or, so,* or *yet.* |

EXAMPLE   The big game is tomorrow; I'm mentally prepared.

| **12b.** | Use a semicolon between independent clauses joined by a conjunctive adverb or a transitional expression. |

EXAMPLE   The garden was my idea; therefore, I should be in charge of it.

EXERCISE   Insert semicolons where they are needed.

Example 1. Nod your head if you agree; I can't tell by your facial expression alone.

1. David prefers classical music I prefer blues.

2. Miguel wants to go on vacation this summer therefore, he is working after school to save money.

3. The rain started late last night it is expected to stop sometime this afternoon.

4. Gladys brought four apples to the barn however, her horse ate only three of them.

5. Li voted against the tax increase she expressed her opinions at the town meeting.

6. The sailboat race began on time unfortunately, the judges were late.

7. No one in the audience noticed the loud crash it sounded like part of the movie.

8. The women wanted to play softball the men decided to sit in the shade.

9. Liang is a moody person he is often, for example, quiet and withdrawn.

10. The orchestra stopped playing the dancers sat down.

11. Mrs. McDuff had longed for peace and quiet she only got it when the neighbors moved.

12. Papa is eager to retire his last day at work is next Friday.

13. The kids wanted to watch a video the adults preferred to go outside.

14. Martha was always punctual the rest of the class usually came in late.

15. Joel is not here today therefore, we will have to postpone his birthday celebration.

16. Our terrier enjoys hiding things those things sometimes include our shoes and socks.

17. Pierre did his best on the exam his reward was the highest grade in the class.

18. The train rounded the curve at high speed the deer just barely got out of the way in time.

19. General Dupont remembers the day war was declared he says he was in his parents' kitchen.

20. Sergio Montale, the famous tenor, is singing tonight all seats have been sold out for weeks.

MECHANICS

Semicolons B

12c. You may need to use a semicolon (rather than a comma) before a coordinating conjunction to join independent clauses that contain commas.

EXAMPLE   On Tuesday, March 11, we'll be in Atlanta; and the day after that, barring any glitches, we'll be in Chicago.

12d. Use a semicolon between items in a series if the items contain commas.

EXAMPLE   My grandmother is going on an AARP tour to Prague, Czech Republic; Vienna, Austria; and Stockholm, Sweden.

EXERCISE   In the following sentences, put a caret (∧) over any comma that should be a semicolon, and write a semicolon above the caret.

Example 1. Kim had pen pals in Tokyo, Japan, Paris, France, and Toledo, Spain.

1. The tour will include stops in St. Petersburg, Russia, Kiev, Ukraine, Bucharest, Romania, Athens, Greece, and Cairo, Egypt.

2. In a surge of productivity, Jim watered the lawn, took out the trash, and swept the driveway, and his sister, Jenny, washed the car and the dog.

3. Ruth has relatives living in Jerusalem, Israel, London, England, and Rome, Italy.

4. The committee invited speeches from Maya Angelou, a poet, Amy Tan, a novelist, and Neil Simon, a playwright.

5. You may sign up for the seminar on Wednesday, January 29, Friday, February 7, Monday, February 10, or Friday, February 14.

6. The only people who came to the meeting were Jim, a writer, Mike, a car mechanic, Olivia, a dancer, and José, a computer programmer.

7. Last Friday, at the very last minute, we handed in our papers, and according to the schedule, we should get our grades next month.

8. Our class is currently studying *A Tale of Two Cities*, the Dickens novel, *The Fire Next Time*, James Baldwin's masterpiece, and *The Chosen*, Chaim Potok's story about two Brooklyn boys.

9. Wednesday I'll be at home working on my project, if I have the time, but on Thursday, if all goes according to plan, I'll be on my way overseas.

10. The band members plan to raise funds by holding a car wash on Friday, November 16, from 6:00 to 9:00 P.M., Saturday, November 17, from 10:00 A.M. to 5:30 P.M., and Sunday, November 18, from 2:00 to 6:00 P.M.

Semicolons C

12a.	Use a semicolon between independent clauses that are closely related in thought and that are not joined by *and, but, for, nor, or, so,* or *yet.*
12b.	Use a semicolon between independent clauses joined by a conjunctive adverb or a transitional expression.
12c.	You may need to use a semicolon (rather than a comma) before a coordinating conjunction to join independent clauses that contain commas.
12d.	Use a semicolon between items in a series if the items contain commas.

EXERCISE In the following sentences, insert semicolons where they are needed. Put a caret (∧) over any comma that should be a semicolon, and write a semicolon above the caret.

Example 1. If the meeting finishes in time, we should be out by 6:30 ; if it runs over, we'll give

you a call.

1. The sun is beginning to set soon the sky will be dark.

2. Performances will take place several times this month with matinees on Saturday, August 12,

Sunday, August 13, and Saturday, August 26.

3. Tom, our raucous young neighbor, started playing the drums every night after dinner, soon

the noise was so bad we had to complain to his parents.

4. Going to the lake was my idea therefore, I should make the reservations.

5. We always wash our car on the weekend judging by its appearance, they wash theirs, too.

6. Give Jane a call if you want a ride to the meeting I won't be able to make it.

7. Grandfather has lived in Cork, Ireland, Boston, Massachusetts, Providence, Rhode Island, and

Kenosha, Wisconsin.

8. Ted, my cousin, and Sally, his friend, are coming over to dinner, so Ernie, my older brother,

and I are doing the cooking.

9. Most trees, such as the elm, the sycamore, the oak and the birch, lose their leaves in the winter,

there are some, however, such as the pine, that retain their leaves in all seasons.

10. On Monday, March 10, the band is scheduled to arrive, and two days later, if all goes well,

they'll be performing at the White House.

Colons A

12e.	Use a colon to mean "note what follows."

(1) Use a colon before a list of items, especially after expressions such as *the following* and *as follows*.

> **EXAMPLE**   The duties of this job are as follows**:** help unload the delivery trucks, sweep the aisles, and stack items on the shelves.

(2) Use a colon before a long, formal statement or quotation.

> **EXAMPLE**   Then he addressed the crowd**:** "Many of you here have become discouraged. You feel that no one cares that this power plant is polluting your water and your air. Don't give up, though. Together we *are* making progress, and together we will shut this thing down!"

12f.	Use a colon before a statement that explains or clarifies a preceding statement.

> **EXAMPLE**   Sami left before the rest of us**:** She had to be there early to help with the costumes.

EXERCISE   Some of the following sentences are missing colons. Insert colons where necessary. Also, triple underline any letter that should be capitalized but is not. If a sentence is correct as it is, write *C* at the end of the sentence.

> **Example 1.** For lunch, Henry ate a double-decker sandwich, a big salad, and an orange**:** he was
>
>   very hungry.

1. We will read works by the following poets Emerson, Poe, Dickinson, and Frost.

2. Hershel looked for his calculator in the kitchen drawers, his closet, and his bookbag.

3. Sara arrived at the party late she had trouble getting her car to start.

4. At the end of her lecture, Mrs. Bell had this to say "as you have learned, the Romanticism of the nineteenth century was much more than an emphasis on romantic love. It was, in a way, an intellectual movement—a movement that gives us insight into the way authors of the nineteenth century viewed humanity."

5. My goals are as follows to go to college, to study medicine, and to become a surgeon.

6. For her birthday, Sofia received these gifts a sweater, two books, gloves, and roses.

7. The Tsongs donated several items for the raffle a lamp, two chairs, and some books.

8. Helen stayed home yesterday she wasn't feeling well.

9. Patrick Henry offered these words on freedom "give me liberty or give me death."

10. Angela ordered three magazines *Time, Essence,* and *The New Yorker.*

MECHANICS

Colons B

12g. Use a colon in certain conventional situations.

(1) Use a colon between the hour and the minute.

EXAMPLES   4:30 P.M. today   7:55 A.M.

(2) Use a colon between chapter and verse in Biblical references.

EXAMPLES   John 3:16   Colossians 3:2

(3) Use a colon between a title and a subtitle.

EXAMPLES   *Star Wars: Return of the Jedi*   *Ishi: Last of His Tribe*

(4) Use a colon after the salutation of a business letter.

EXAMPLES   To Whom It May Concern: Dear Ms. Fielding:

EXERCISE   In the following sentences, insert colons where necessary. If a sentence is correct as it is, write *C* at the end of the sentence.

Example 1. Misha is leaving at 5:15 P.M. this afternoon.

1. Mom frequently quotes from the Bible; her favorite quotation is from Exodus 1 6–15.

2. Every morning at 7 00 A.M., the alarm clock goes off and the dog starts barking.

3. There are numerous museums and art galleries in Chicago, the nation's third-largest city.

4. Mira is reading *Gandhi A Life,* a biography of the Mahatma.

5. Dear Mr. Adams

Please acknowledge receipt of the enclosed shipment.

Sincerely,

Jeff Holt

6. Under the couch I found the old copy of *Yodeling A Beginner's Primer* that I thought I had lost.

7. Isn't II Samuel 6 14 the passage in the Bible in which David dances before the Lord?

8. Dr. Sharif wrote a fascinating little book called *Tesellation The Art of Illusion.*

9. Tamara looked for Scamp in the hallway, under the stairs, and in the attic.

10. Between 3 30 and 5 00 every afternoon, the noise in the street is unbelievable.

Colons C

12e. Use a colon to mean "note what follows."

EXAMPLE You need to shop for several items**:** brown shoelaces, a quart of milk, five or six carrots, and a tube of toothpaste.

12f. Use a colon before a statement that explains or clarifies a preceding statement.

EXAMPLE Suddenly, Margo screamed**:** There were fire ants all over her feet.

12g. Use a colon in certain conventional situations.

EXAMPLES 8**:**30 P.M. Matthew 2**:**13 Dear Sir**:**

EXERCISE Add colons where necessary in each of the following sentences. Also, triple underline any letter that should be capitalized but is not.

Example 1. Please bring the following items to the picnic tomorrow**:** a volleyball, a volleyball net, and a cooler.

1. Dear Dr. Heather Williams

2. My sermon today comes from Psalm 91 4–5.

3. Tonya will do her book report on *Asian American Dreams The Emergence of an American People*.

4. My father is reading *Galileo's Daughter A Historical Memoir of Science, Faith, and Love*.

5. Ricardo, set your alarm for 5 15 A.M. we have to pick up your grandfather at 7 00 A.M.

6. The following are my favorite fantasy writers Ursula K. Le Guin, Robert Holdstock, John Crowley, and J.R.R. Tolkien.

7. Jimmy had this to say about the new schedule adopted at last night's school board meeting "I'm glad the school board approved the new schedule. I think it will be a benefit to students and teachers alike."

8. After opening the elaborately wrapped present, Jane became confused the box that someone had taken great pains to wrap was empty.

9. Over the summer vacation, Lee visited four states Utah, Colorado, New Mexico, and Arizona.

10. No one expresses despair better than Shakespeare's doomed king Macbeth "Tomorrow and tomorrow and tomorrow / Creeps in this petty pace from day to day, / To the last syllable of recorded time."

Review A: Semicolons and Colons

EXERCISE A In the following sentences, place semicolons and colons where they are needed. If a sentence contains an incorrect comma, draw a caret (∧) over the comma, and write the correct punctuation above the caret.

Example 1. The view from the pass includes the following landmarks:͡ Lake Geneva, except for

the extreme eastern part;͡ Geneva itself, including suburbs and outlying districts;͡ and

the entire chain of the Savoy Alps.

1. My father drinks black coffee, my mother prefers tea.

2. Dear Mrs. R. Volpe

3. All applicants for the job must furnish the following items of information, date of birth, grade

in school, and names of two personal references.

4. We had all been warned about the test, nonetheless, few of us were prepared for it.

5. We should take Jerry out to lunch, he really came through for us on that project.

6. These three girls have been nominated for vice-president of the class Siobhan Reilly, Olive

Caccione, and Sarah Golder.

7. It had rained all morning, at 1 00 P.M., however, the sun appeared.

8. I thought you had read the book, otherwise, I wouldn't have asked you about it.

9. The candidate finished her speech with a final comment "If I am elected, I will do everything

in my power to fulfill the promises I have made."

10. Richard bought a new CD titled *Julian Bream The Ultimate Guitar Collection*.

EXERCISE B In the following sentences, place semicolons and colons where they are needed. If a sentence contains an incorrect comma, draw a caret (∧) over the comma, and write the correct punctuation above the caret.

Example 1. Carol bought balloons, plates, and napkins;͡ and Joel bought party hats and snacks.

11. John 3 16 is probably the most famous scripture in the Bible.

12. Jane went to the play with Cora, Peter, and David, and Alex, Jane's brother, went with Gary.

13. Felix didn't get to sleep until 2 30 A.M., he had to finish an important project.

14. Karen has traveled to many places Barcelona, Spain, London, England, and Sydney, Australia.

15. The new reporters on the staff of the school newspaper are Joaquín Sunders, a sophomore, and

Leslie Crim, a junior, and Virgil Bates, a member of the senior class, is the new managing editor.

MECHANICS

Review B: **Semicolons and Colons**

EXERCISE A   Correct the punctuation in the following sentences by placing semicolons and colons where they are needed. If a sentence contains an incorrect comma, draw a caret (∧) over the comma, and write the correct punctuation above the caret.

Example 1. I can stay until 3:00 P.M., at 4:00 P.M. I am expected at home.

1. Here are my New Year's resolutions to read more, to exercise more, and to eat fewer snacks.

2. Dear Mrs. Kay

3. At 5 45 P.M., Jocelyn and Theresa arrived at the auditorium. Jocelyn put up streamers, posters, and banners, and Theresa set up the sound equipment, chairs, and podium.

4. Barry wants to title his autobiography *Barry Retrospective of a Great Man*.

5. The applicant was very nervous during the interview, nonetheless, she got the job.

6. Before making a hiring decision, the personnel director considered the following qualifications, work experience, educational background, and personality.

7. The book was a conduit for her bad feelings, it gave her a more positive outlook.

8. The three students who are vying for first place in the talent show are Marla Jones, a singer, Jerry Green, a pianist, and Leslie Ricardo, a dancer.

9. I am an excellent swimmer, my brother, on the other hand, prefers skating.

10. Three students received A's on the test Johnnie B. Baker, Toni Mancuso, and Rory Milano.

EXERCISE B   Correct the punctuation in the following sentences by placing semicolons and colons where they are needed. If a sentence contains an incorrect comma, draw a caret (∧) over the comma, and write the correct punctuation above the caret.

Example 1. A. Thomas is a very unusual author, she wrote her first book at the age of thirteen.

11. Gary deserves to win his science project is clearly the best in the room.

12. Henry prefers Italian food, Lisa prefers Chinese food.

13. "Whither thou goest, I will go," as it says in Ruth 1 16.

14. The last words of the dying pirate were mysterious "From the base of the torso tree, take long steps three. From that spot toward the shore, walk apace twenty more. There, if you stand at sunset's wane, you will see the shadow that leads to spoils and gain."

15. I decided to decorate my room with some stuff I found in the attic a movie poster, which once belonged to my brother, an old New York Yankees pennant, the first pennant I bought with my own money, and a model of the original starship *Enterprise*.

Language and Sentence Skills Practice

Review C: Semicolons and Colons

EXERCISE A   Correct the punctuation in the following sentences by placing semicolons and colons where they are needed. If a sentence contains an incorrect comma, draw a caret (∧) over the comma, and write the correct punctuation above the caret.

Example 1. The Bible reading began with John 14.∶27 and ended with Psalms 39.∶1–6.

1. Mr. Jackson's plane arrived twenty minutes late because of the dense fog, consequently, he missed the flight to Denver.

2. The Arthurs are not home, they've left for work.

3. Amy wanted to visit Tucson, San Diego, and Austin, but Helen wanted to visit Seattle, Las Vegas, and Phoenix.

4. The meeting is scheduled for 3 30 this afternoon please don't be late.

5. The following committees will report budget, membership, awards, and programs.

EXERCISE B   Insert semicolons and colons where necessary in the following letter.

Example [1] Are you familiar with *Sharing the Universe* ∶ *Perspectives on Extraterrestrial Life*?

[6] Dear Sir or Madam

   [7] I am preparing a report on SETI, or the Search for Extraterrestrial Intelligence, and I would like to be as well prepared as possible. I have already read *We Are Not Alone The Continuing Search for Extraterrestrial Intelligence* by Walter Sullivan. **[8]** My science teacher has recommended that I get your opinion on SETI. She has also suggested that I read books by the following authors Carl Sagan, Frank Drake, and Jean Heidmann.

   [9] I know that not all scientists are optimistic about the chances for extraterrestrial life the book *Rare Earth Why Complex Life Is Uncommon in the Universe* makes the case that earth is the only place in the universe where animal life lives. **[10]** I am eager to learn about your views on SETI. Thank you for your time I hope to hear from you soon!

Yours sincerely,

Arundhati Chandrasekhar

HOLT HANDBOOK | Fourth Course

Proofreading for Semicolons and Colons

Good writers are generally good proofreaders. Readers tend to admire and trust writing that is error-free. Make sure that you correct all errors in grammar, usage, spelling, and punctuation in your writing. Your readers will have more confidence in your words if you have done your best to proofread carefully.

Semicolons and colons give signals to your readers about the relationships between ideas. Both can help you make long, complex sentences more comprehensible. When writing instructions, be sure to proofread carefully to ensure the correct use of semicolons and colons.

PROOFREADING ACTIVITY

The following set of instructions contains several errors in the use of semicolons and colons. Use proofreading symbols to make your corrections.

Chelsea's Chocolate Cookie Cheesecake; A Fast and Easy Recipe

Would you like to make a dessert that's light on the calories; as well as the preparation time? This recipe requires only a few ingredients and about fifteen minutes however; the result is a delicious and impressive *pièce de résistance*.

You will need the following ingredients 2 eggs, $\frac{1}{2}$ cup of sugar, 2 eight-ounce packages of low-fat cream cheese, and 1 teaspoon of vanilla. You will also need: a commercially prepared pie crust made of chocolate cookies, indeed, the crust is what makes the dessert so special.

Prepare the filling as follows; mix the cream cheese, vanilla, and sugar with an electric mixer, then, mix in the eggs until everything is well blended. Pour the filling into the pie crust, bake it for 40 minutes in an oven preheated to 400 degrees. After baking the cheesecake, put it in the refrigerator for at least 3 hours, the cheesecake needs plenty of time to cool. Then—*voilà*—the cheesecake is ready to serve!

Literary Model: Narrative

> One step brought us into the family sitting-room, without any introductory lobby or passage: they call it here "the house" pre-eminently. It includes kitchen and parlour, generally; but I believe at Wuthering Heights the kitchen is forced to retreat altogether into another quarter: at least I distinguished a chatter of tongues and a clatter of culinary utensils deep within; and I observed no signs of roasting, boiling, or baking about the huge fire-place; nor any glitter of copper saucepans and tin cullenders on the walls.... The floor was of smooth, white stone; the chairs, high-backed, primitive structures, painted green: one or two heavy black ones lurking in the shade....

—from *Wuthering Heights* by Emily Brontë

EXERCISE A

1. On the lines below, copy the excerpt, replacing the semicolons and colons with periods.

_____

_____

_____

_____

_____

_____

_____

_____

2. How does the substitution of periods affect the readability and the comprehensibility of the excerpt? Support your response by discussing specific sentences from the excerpt.

_____

_____

_____

_____

_____

_____

for **CHAPTER 12: PUNCTUATION**   *pages 322–28*

Literary Model (continued)

EXERCISE B

1. Why do you think Brontë used many semicolons and colons instead of periods in this excerpt?

_____

_____

_____

2. Describe the style of writing that results from her repeated use of semicolons and colons.

_____

_____

_____

EXERCISE C   Write a paragraph describing a section of a house—either your own, one you have been in, or one you can imagine. Use at least two semicolons and two colons to increase readability or to clarify the relationship between ideas.

_____

_____

_____

_____

_____

_____

_____

_____

EXERCISE D

1. Why did you decide to use semicolons and colons in some sentences and periods in others? Explain.

_____

_____

_____

2. Choose one sentence containing a semicolon or colon and describe why the use of the semicolon or colon is necessary.

_____

_____

_____

for **CHAPTER 12: PUNCTUATION**   **pages 322–28**

Writing Application: Journal Entry

Punctuation marks and road signs have at least two things in common. They both have the function of providing useful information. Both of the two general categories are composed of specific types that each indicate something different. For example, a red octagonal sign tells you to stop, and a yellow triangular sign tells you to yield. A colon usually indicates that a list or an explanation is to follow, and a semicolon usually indicates that another independent clause is to follow. Punctuation marks, including semicolons and colons, can help you separate your ideas and show the relationship between them.

WRITING ACTIVITY

The essay you submitted in a writing competition placed first. The prize was a six-day trip to the city of your choice. The only hitch was that you had to keep a journal detailing how you spent each day, including times and places, in prose form. You have to deliver the journal to the contest organizers. You will need to use your imagination to compose the completed journal, which will contain six entries. In your journal, include at least two uses of colons and three uses of semicolons.

PREWRITING   Decide which city will be the destination for your prize trip. Brainstorm specific places and experiences. Be sure to include sensory details to give readers a clear picture of your trip; in addition to descriptions of visual images, incorporate descriptions that address hearing, smelling, tasting, and perhaps touching.

WRITING   Use the results of your brainstorming to guide your draft. Write so that your readers can easily imagine themselves in the very situations and scenes that you describe. Be sure to use semicolons and colons to increase readability and to clarify the relationship between ideas.

REVISING   Have a classmate read your draft. Ask him or her how you could revise the journal to make it clearer and more descriptive. Look carefully at the draft yourself with the idea of deleting or revising weak words, clichés, and awkward-sounding or wordy sentences. Check that you have included at least two uses of colons and three uses of semicolons. Continue revising this creative piece until you judge it to be completely polished.

PUBLISHING   Proofread your journal entries for errors in grammar, usage, spelling, and punctuation. Create a writing anthology that includes examples of your best work. Then, add your journal to the anthology.

EXTENDING YOUR WRITING

You may wish to use this writing as the basis for another project. You could develop the journal into a factual short story in which you describe real people and events you experienced while on vacation. You could also use the journal as the basis of a fictional short story in which you create quirky, fictitious characters and hilarious situations.

Choices: Exploring Punctuation Marks

The following activities challenge you to find a connection between punctuation marks and the world around you. Do the activity below that suits your personality best, and then share your discoveries with your class.

ETHICS

Fair Play

One reason that ellipses are used sparingly is that they can be misused. A careless use of ellipses can twist a speaker's words. Show your classmates how ellipses can be used unethically. Prepare five pairs of examples: Each pair should include a direct quotation and an abbreviated version of the quotation that contains unethically placed ellipses. Show the unethical passage to the class, and read it aloud. Ask the class to summarize the author's statement. Then read the full, unedited version. Ask your classmates to compare the two versions.

DRAMA

Hollywood Types

If you and your friends have been waiting for the right moment to grab the spotlight, this is it! You can write your own story with dialogue and perform it for the class. You could even videotape the story if you like. You'll need several people. One will be a narrator, and at least two more will act out the dialogue. The first step is to decide on the focus of your story. Next, you'll need to write your story in prose, using quotation marks for the speakers' exact words. Once you've got a final draft, begin rehearsals.

MUSIC

The Rite of Spring

Acquaint your classmates with some of the great symphonies and operas. Prepare a list of your favorites, using italics and capital letters where appropriate. (If you're a connoisseur, you may want to use stars to rank the pieces.) Then, choose your favorite piece and write a review of it or historical account about it. Share your musical knowledge with the class by posting your list of favorite works, along with the description you wrote about your favorite piece. If possible, play recordings for the class.

HISTORY

Spirit of St. Louis

Whenever you see the names of famous planes, you probably find the name of a plane piloted by Charles Lindbergh. His was the craft that first flew from North America to Europe. Hailed as a hero, Lindbergh gained unimaginable fame because he showed the world what could happen with an abundance of imagination and determination. Other aircraft have also played their roles in history. What are their names? What are their stories? Find out. Write five short descriptions of these planes and their pilots' achievements. Add illustrations if you wish. Be sure to capitalize and italicize the name of each plane.

HISTORY

Bubba and BJ

Lots of famous people are known by nicknames. As you've probably noticed, nicknames are often written in quotation marks. Compile a list of nicknames of current celebrities and famous historical figures. Just for fun, create a matching test. Write each nickname in quotation marks in the first column, and write each real name in the second column. Hand out copies to your classmates.

WRITING

Chirp, Shout, or Mumble

Write a creative story that involves two or three characters having a conversation. As you write, try to use *said* only once; using synonyms will liven up your writing. If you need inspiration, think back to interesting dialogues in your favorite novel or short story. Ask to post your story in the classroom. Before you do, though, correct any punctuation errors.

Language and Sentence Skills Practice

293

Italics and Titles

Italics are printed letters that lean to the right. *This sentence is printed in italics.* When you are writing or typing, indicate italics by underlining.

    UNDERLINING   I enjoyed the book <u>The Heart Is a Lonely Hunter</u>.

        ITALICS   I enjoyed the book *The Heart Is a Lonely Hunter*.

13a.   Use italics (underlining) for titles and subtitles of books, plays, long poems, periodicals, works of art, movies, TV series, and long musical works and recordings.

EXERCISE A   Underline all words that should appear in italics in the following sentences.

Example 1. Mar'a refers to Van Gogh's <u>Sunflowers</u> in the twelfth section of her long poem

                  <u>Daughters of the Earth</u>.

1. Eric's favorite painting is N.C. Wyeth's Robin Hood and His Mother on Their Way to Nottingham Fair.

2. Have you ever read Mark Twain's The Adventures of Tom Sawyer?

3. George Orwell's novels include Animal Farm and 1984.

4. The school drama group will stage The Tragedy of Julius Caesar next week.

5. James Russell Lowell edited a magazine called the North American Review.

6. Of all of Billy Joel's albums, I think that The Stranger is his best.

7. My grandfather rarely misses an episode of Sixty Minutes.

8. I can't decide which is the better film, Lawrence of Arabia or The Third Man.

9. Have you listened Ravel's long musical composition called Bolero?

10. Donatello's Julius Caesar can be found in the Louvre, in Paris.

EXERCISE B   Underline the titles that should appear in italics in the following paragraph.

Example   **[1]** Last night I watched an episode of <u>Great American Writers</u> that focused on Leslie Marmon Silko.

    [11] Did you know that Silko's Ceremony was the first full-length work of fiction ever published by a Native American woman? **[12]** Mia and I think the book is fantastic, but we also like Laguna Woman: Poems as well as Storyteller, two other books by Silko. **[13]** The librarian recommended to us Almanac of the Dead, but we haven't read it yet. **[14]** Mia is writing a documentary film about the fiction of Leslie Marmon Silko. **[15]** She wants to call the film The Storyteller's Voice.

Italics: Names, Letters, Symbols, and Foreign Words

13b. Use italics (underlining) for the names of ships, trains, aircraft, and spacecraft.

   EXAMPLES *Spirit of St. Louis*

   Carpathia

13c. Use italics (underlining) for words, letters, symbols, and numerals referred to as such and for foreign words that have not been adopted into English.

   EXAMPLES the number *8*

   bonjour

EXERCISE A Underline all words, letters, numerals, and symbols that should appear in italics in the following sentences.

Example 1. There's no t in the word pizza, but it sounds as if there is.

1. The Queen Elizabeth, once a transatlantic ship, is now docked in California.

2. Sally K. Ride, the first American woman in space, flew aboard Challenger on the seventh shuttle mission.

3. Try the pollo asado with a little of this sauce.

4. I know the writer of the article is enthusiastic, but she has used too many !'s.

5. Pierre writes his 7's with a line through the middle.

6. Do the words dale and vale mean the same thing?

7. The book Twenty Thousand Leagues Under the Sea is set on a submarine called Nautilus.

8. The Italian word trattoria is a term used for an inexpensive restaurant.

9. In Spanish, the letter h is always silent.

10. To praise a Chinese cook, use the expression ding hao, which means "excellent."

EXERCISE B Underline the words or letters that should appear in italics in the following paragraph.

Example **[1]** Brad could not decide whether to give his train a name from another language, such as the Latin fero.

[11] Brad asked about his friend Derrick's model train named the Spirit of Des Moines.

[12] Derrick explained that he was inspired by the name of Charles Lindbergh's plane, the Spirit of St. Louis. **[13]** "What do you think of the Ghost of Christmas Past as the name for my model train?" Brad asked. Derrick said he didn't think it was the same kind of spirit. **[14]** The word spirit has more than one meaning. **[15]** "If you do name it that, however," Derrick said, "paint the letters in alternating green and red, and make the G, C, and P in the name look creepy."

Language and Sentence Skills Practice

Italics Review

Review pages 337–339 of your textbook for rules on the use of italics.

EXERCISE A   Underline all words, letters, numerals, and symbols that should appear in italics in the following sentences.

Example 1. Did you read the article on Shakespeare's <u>As You Like It</u> in <u>The Atlantic Monthly</u>?

1. Anne Tyler's novel Breathing Lessons won a Pulitzer Prize.

2. Nicole's mother reads The Wall Street Journal each morning during breakfast.

3. Jorge and Melinda attended a performance of Mozart's Don Giovanni.

4. Do you ever confuse handwritten 4's with 9's?

5. Semper fidelis is the motto of the U.S. Marine Corps.

6. I watched a TV show called On the Ocean Floor about the search to find the wreck of the Titanic.

7. The t in the word beret is silent.

8. Someone told Martha the & symbol was called an ampersand.

9. There should be a show on TV called No Commercials.

10. Tim dreams of taking a ride on the space shuttle Endeavour.

EXERCISE B   Underline all words, letters, numerals, and symbols that should appear in italics in the following sentences.

Example 1. Why did Malcolm X choose the letter <u>X</u> for his name?

11. Langston Hughes' autobiography is called The Big Sea.

12. Gerald likes to do the crossword puzzle in The New York Times.

13. The French merci and the Spanish gracias both mean "thank you."

14. The new children's train at the park is called the Sutton Sidewinder.

15. Edgar Lee Masters wrote Spoon River Anthology, a favorite of mine.

16. Do you write capital Q's with little curlicue tails?

17. The # symbol on the telephone is the pound sign.

18. Can you believe she has never seen the movie Star Wars?

19. If the president flies in Air Force One, what does the vice president fly in?

20. Mrs. Chang reminded us there is only one l in the word traveled.

Quotation Marks in Direct Quotations

13d. Use quotation marks to enclose a *direct quotation*—a person's exact words.

> **EXAMPLES**   "Now is the time," Ms. Shapiro reminded us, "to practice your skills."
>
> "The play is about to begin," the usher said. "Please take your seats."
>
> "The azaleas are beginning to bloom," said Glinka, "and they're especially beautiful this year."
>
> Marcia planted what she called "the happy flowers": tulips, sunflowers, and daisies.
>
> Who said, "This is my favorite flower"?

EXERCISE A   Add quotation marks as needed to the following sentences.

Example 1. Who said, "These assignments need to be completed by Friday"?

1. Let's visit the children's museum, suggested Marcela, and we'll be able to see the new robots they've added.

2. Jerome said, I think I may have solved the mystery; we waited for him to continue.

3. Don't most children know the song that begins, Mary had a little lamb?

4. Is anyone in here? asked the visitor. Would someone please answer?

5. If you could buy a mountain, asked Andrés, which mountain would you buy?

EXERCISE B   On the lines provided, rewrite these sentences to correct all errors in punctuation and capitalization.

Example 1. Bill asked, where did I put my coat? _Bill asked, "Where did I put my coat?"_

6. I am the king of the world! the child shouted. _____

_____

7. Jennifer referred to three of her pets as "the friendliest and easiest to handle:" the striped kitten, the old Bassett Hound, and the parrot. _____

_____

8. Joel said, in my hometown, we used to walk along the Mississippi River levee. _____

_____

9. Rabbits, added Gwendolyn, can make excellent pets for responsible pet owners. _____

_____

10. Theodore remarked This is my favorite poem; we had heard Theodore say that about several different poems, however. _____

_____

Quotation Marks in Dialogue and Passages A

13e.	When you write dialogue (a conversation), begin a new paragraph every time the speaker changes, and enclose each speaker's words in quotation marks.
13f.	When a quoted passage consists of more than one paragraph, put quotation marks at the beginning of each paragraph and at the end of the entire passage. Do not put quotation marks after any paragraph but the last.

EXERCISE   Add quotation marks as needed to each of the following dialogues. Additionally, insert the paragraph mark (¶) before any word that should begin a new paragraph.

Example 1. "How are we doing today?" the nurse asked. ¶ "I feel fine," said the patient.

1. What are we going to be studying today? asked Raymond. We will be studying three sonnets written in three different periods of history, answered the teacher.

2. The treasurer of the club said, Here's the report. We're not doing as badly as we thought, said the club president.

3. Which part should I read? asked the actor. Read only the first and third paragraphs, answered the director, and omit the rest of the page.

4. I read about Winston Churchill today, said Jacqueline. Did you find it interesting? asked Connie. Oh, yes, answered Jacqueline, I'm going to be writing my history report about him.

5. People in history class say clever things, Rita complained. I could never be that witty. Yasmin agreed. I have trouble staying awake, she said. It's my first class after lunch.

6. Are you coming with us to see the French film? asked Pierre. Yes, I think I will, answered Clara. It will be a good opportunity to practice my listening skills in French.

7. The cats will need fresh food and water twice a day while I'm gone, said Miki. You don't have to worry, answered Tsiyoshi. They're in good hands with me.

8. I need to schedule an appointment for Wednesday, said the anxious caller. What time would you like to come in? asked the receptionist. Please schedule me for the first opening in the morning, answered the patient.

9. Who wants to go to the zoo with me today? asked Mrs. Carter. I do, said Juan. I can't go today, said Rudolfo. I have to stay home and study.

10. Shekoufeh asked, Do you know what my name means in Persian? No, answered Amy. What does it mean? It's a type of flower, explained Shekoufeh.

MECHANICS

Quotation Marks in Dialogue and Passages B

13e. When you write dialogue (a conversation), begin a new paragraph every time the speaker changes, and enclose each speaker's words in quotation marks.

13f. When a quoted passage consists of more than one paragraph, put quotation marks at the beginning of each paragraph and at the end of the entire passage. Do not put quotation marks after any paragraph but the last.

EXERCISE   Add quotation marks as needed to each of the following dialogues. Additionally, insert the mark (¶) before any word that should begin a new paragraph.

Example 1. "I think Dr. King wrote the best speech ever written," explained Nell. ¶Josie disagreed, saying, "Lincoln wrote the most moving speech."

1. Did you read the short story for English class? asked Melvin. Yes, I read it last night, answered María, and I really enjoyed it.

2. Are you going on the class field trip? asked Sheila. I've never visited the natural science musem before, answered Marc, so I signed up for the longer field trip on Friday. Then I'll be riding the bus with you, answered Sheila. I signed up for the longer visit, also.

3. I can't wait to see you and Uncle Tomás, said Esperanza. It won't be much longer, answered Pam. Your uncle and I will be on the next flight to Atlanta.

4. My parents just bought a new car, said Douglas. What kind of car did they buy? asked Sarah. I don't know what make it is, answered Douglas, but it is a hideous bright green color.

5. Does your dog do any tricks? asked Roberto. Sure, replied Camila. He can beg, roll over, and eat! Eating is not a trick! answered Roberto. That's what you think, added Camila.

6. When I was six, I could do cartwheels and flips, said Sergei. Can you still do any acrobatics? asked Natasha. Only in the water, answered Sergei.

7. What did the coach ask us to do first? asked the swimmer in the second lane. We are supposed to warm up for fifteen minutes with dolphin kicks, answered another swimmer.

8. Which book did you choose to read? asked Terry. I read a biography of composer Igor Stravinski, answered Kimberly.

9. Are you going to the park with us? asked Jane. What time are you leaving? asked Karl. As soon as you're ready, answered Jane. Let's go right now, announced Karl.

10. History class was interesting today, said Noriyuki. It was like hearing a bunch of short stories, answered Carlos. Some of those short stories seemed like tall tales to me! said Noriyuki.

Quotation Marks and Titles

13g. Use quotation marks to enclose titles (including subtitles) of short works such as short stories, poems, essays, articles, songs, episodes of TV series, and chapters and other parts of books and periodicals.

SHORT STORY	"The Bass, the River, and Sheila Mant"
POEM	"I Wandered Lonely as a Cloud"
SONG	"Happy Birthday to You"

MECHANICS

EXERCISE A Insert quotation marks where they are needed in the following sentences.

Example 1. Is Kendra's favorite poem "The Moon Was But a Chin of Gold"?

1. The TV show's Hooray for Hollywood episode contains some of the cast's best moments.

2. Mrs. Tennant told the class that the essay How I Spent My Summer Vacation on her desk had

   no name on it.

3. Tyler and Guillaume studied the imagery in the poem Ex-Basketball Player.

4. Do you recall reading an article called Cooking with Bananas?

5. Ray thought the setting of Stopping by Woods on a Snowy Evening was very beautiful.

6. Chapter 4 of the book is Koala Bears and Other Hazards, not Life Down Under.

7. Devika gets very teary-eyed singing Auld Lang Syne.

8. Tony is writing an article for the school newspaper. School in Space? is the title.

9. The book contains three sections: Home, Abroad, and Return.

10. Tara can recite the lines of Heart! We will forget him! from memory.

EXERCISE B Insert quotation marks to enclose correctly the titles found in the following paragraph.

Example   **[1]** Miguel is working on a series of short films he calls " Edgar Allan Poe and

            Greenland High School. "

   [11] Miguel got the idea from reading The Pit and the Pendulum, which reminded him of study

hall. **[12]** He used ideas from the story for his first episode, which he called The Pencil and the

Ticking Clock. **[13]** The second was called Gym, based on The Masque of the Red Death. **[14]** The

Lock on My Locker Is Broken was inspired in part by Poe's The Gold Bug. **[15]** The final episode

of Miguel's film was called The Fall of Greenland Greenhouse, based on Poe's The Fall of the

House of Usher.

Single Quotation Marks, Slang, and Technical Terms

13h.   Use single quotation marks to enclose a quotation or a title within a quotation.

> **EXAMPLES**   Sami said, "The coach asked, 'Why were you late for practice?' and then he made me run four laps."
>
> Brad Michaels said to the audience at his Russian concert, "I'd like to end the evening with the song 'Back in the U.S.S.R.,' by the Beatles."

13i.   Use quotation marks to enclose slang words, technical terms, and unusual uses of words.

> **EXAMPLES**   Allen Ginsberg was a prominent poet of the "beat" generation.
>
> "Stengelese" was a type of double talk named after baseball manager Casey Stengel.

EXERCISE A   Add quotation marks to these sentences, using double and single quotation marks as needed.

Example 1. Mr. Turner asked, "Did you read the poem 'We Real Cool'?"

1. I'm not sure, she said, who first said Remember the Alamo!

2. Marion said, Then he said, Stay away from that tree.

3. I read in the newspaper, Todd said, that many teens enjoy mountain biking.

4. Wasn't it Sandra, she asked, who said, I'll remember to pick up the dessert?

5. Akela said, My favorite poem to read aloud is The Hollow Men.

6. The coach yelled, Who said Time out?

7. Irving Berlin wrote the song God Bless America, Suki informed the class.

8. It was Timothy, Dan explained, who came up with our team's slogan We shall meet our obstacles with confidence.

9. No one knows who first used the expression G. I. Joe, Dr. Shaw said.

10. According to Mrs. Simmons, Jim mentioned, Everything comes to an end eventually.

EXERCISE B   Select five current slang expressions or technical terms. On the line provided, use each expression in a complete sentence. Make sure that you punctuate the sentences correctly and use language appropriate for the classroom.

Example 1. _Marcus said the car looked "phat," not fat._

11. _____

12. _____

13. _____

14. _____

15. _____

Ellipsis Points

13j. Use ellipsis points (. . .) to mark omissions from quoted material.

(1) When you omit words from the middle of a sentence, use three spaced ellipsis points.

(2) When you omit words from the beginning of a sentence within a quoted passage, keep the previous sentence's end punctuation and follow it with the points of ellipsis.

(3) When you omit words at the end of the sentence within a quoted passage, keep the sentence's end punctuation and follow it with the points of ellipsis.

(4) When you omit one or more complete sentences from within a quoted passage, keep the previous sentence's end punctuation and follow it with the points of ellipsis.

13k. Use three ellipsis points (. . .) to indicate a pause in written dialogue.

EXERCISE   Omit the underscored parts of the following sentences and write the resulting sentences on the lines given. Use ellipsis points to punctuate each omission correctly.

Example 1. "It is time for a change, my fellow citizens, and we must act now."   *"It is time for a change. . . . [W]e must act now."*

1. "In my classmate's essay on salad 'The Grass We Eat,' Brent discusses the variety of edible leaves that people consume all over the world." _____

_____

2. Marianne wrote in her essay, "I believe children are the key to our future. They will continue their ancestors' quest for happiness and truth. Therefore, we should try to nurture them."

_____

_____

3. "Elizabeth has worked as a secretary and reporter for the local magazine. She has also appeared regularly on radio shows." _____

_____

4. "Roberto has written articles for various newspapers. They have been syndicated in many newspapers. He has also written essays published in scholarly journals." _____

_____

5. "Tom is a very funny person. Carlota thinks that it is no mistake that he received the award for best new comedian." _____

_____

MECHANICS

Quotation Marks Review A

Review pages 341–346 of your textbook for punctuation rules for writing quotations, dialogues, and titles.

EXERCISE Add quotation marks where they are necessary in each of the following sentences.

Example 1. The author titled Chapter 3 "Where Do We Go from Here?"

1. I admire Nikki Giovanni's poem, Poem for a Lady Whose Voice I Like.

2. Stevie Wonder wrote the song You Are the Sunshine of My Life.

3. Where are you going? asked my mother. It's getting late.

4. This quotation is from my English class essay entitled Understanding Me.

5. Margaret said, They paved the old dirt road and put up a parking lot in the old wheat field.

6. I'll try, exclaimed Alex, but I don't know if I'll be able to convince him.

7. My sister's poem for class, said Bill, is about birds and is called The Flight of the Free.

8. Where are you going? asked Stacey. Don't you realize we could be late for the concert?

9. I think Mary said Walk two blocks and then turn right, said Mark with a quizzical look.

10. The horse that won the race was known to be a mudder.

11. Jailhouse Rock is one of my all-time favorite songs, Aunt Missy told us.

12. Has anybody seen my new green jacket? quizzed Jack. I can't find it anywhere!

13. The first poem in Michael's collection is called The Mystery.

14. As soon as Jed turned the corner, he heard a man shout, Look! That bird just stole my sandwich!

15. Every time she walks by the polling center, Demetria notices the sign for Kelly The Kid Turner, who is running for county commissioner.

16. Of all the short stories written in our summer writing class, my favorite was the one called Julie Sue's Famous Fifteen Minutes.

17. Suzanne said, Have you got a parrot?

18. Can you believe this? remarked Keshon. Last night I had a dream that I was a cartoon.

19. Mr. Norton said, Class, please turn to page 167 and read the essay titled Strengthening Your Writing.

20. When I asked Mom for permission, said Georgina, she told me Okay, but only as long as you clean your room first.

Quotation Marks Review B

Review pages 341–346 of your textbook for punctuation rules for writing quotations, dialogues, and titles.

EXERCISE   On the lines provided, rewrite these sentences, correcting all punctuation errors and adding single and double quotation marks as needed. If a sentence is already correct, write C on the line.

Example 1. Tasha listed these sports as way cool: golf, skateboarding, karate, and fly fishing.

Tasha listed these sports as "way cool": golf, skateboarding, karate, and fly fishing.

1. The advertising slogan, "Try It and Buy It," is puzzling to me, Kim said. _____

_____

2. Hunter said, "Jane's saying, 'Speak softly to avoid attracting attention,' is wise advice." ____

_____

3. My favorite Beatles' song is Let It Be, Carlo said. _____

_____

4. Andrea said, The sign on my cousin's bedroom door reads Enter at Your Own Risk. _____

_____

5. The fish is swimming in circles, said Marco. I wonder why it's doing that. _____

_____

6. "According to the sign-up sheet, announced Miss Green, Annie will read her poem, called

Morning Glories, right now." _____

_____

7. I don't mind being called "Lefty," retorted Uncle Miguel, there's nothing wrong with being

left-handed. _____

_____

8. Yesterday Dad told us that "one of his favorite songs is "Desperado."" _____

_____

9. In a quiet whisper, Millicent asked, "Did you hear what she just said"? _____

_____

10. The guide told the tourists, 'Remember three things:' stay together on the trail, listen to my

instructions, and have fun! _____

_____

MECHANICS

Review A: **Italics and Quotation Marks**

EXERCISE A In the following sentences, supply italics (underlining) or quotation marks wherever needed.

Example 1. Lowell's poem "Patterns" can be found in <u>The Home Book of Verse.</u>

1. Tomorrow's history assignment is reading Chapter 9, The Middle Ages in England.

2. Two of her favorite old-time movies are Foreign Correspondent and The Maltese Falcon.

3. In Silent Snow, Secret Snow, a short story by Conrad Aiken, a boy thinks he hears snow falling, but there is none.

4. Joseph and His Brothers, a novel by Thomas Mann, is based on a Biblical legend, Arthur said.

5. My favorite aunt subscribes to The Wall Street Journal, a newspaper devoted to business and financial news.

EXERCISE B Add, delete, or replace quotation marks and other marks of punctuation as needed in the following sentences.

Example 1. Barbara exclaimed happily, " What a surprise! "

6. Did the sign say Slow or Stop?

7. Our favorite proverb is this one: Wisdom is the principal thing; therefore get wisdom.

8. Actually, no camera is truly automatic, she explained.

9. Mr. Pakunas asked, How and why does osmosis take place?

10. When you answer me, the officer barked explosively, call me Sir.

11. The following students from our school have entered a contest called Talented Teens: Ned Baum, Lucia Gaines, and Estelle Peterson.

12. Have you read Eudora Welty's story A Worn Path?, he asked.

13. Wasn't it Shakespeare who wrote, Ill blows the wind that profits nobody.

14. A delighted child screamed, It's snowing!

15. No, I have no definite plans for Saturday said Betty.

Language and Sentence Skills Practice

MECHANICS

Review B: **Italics, Quotation Marks, and Ellipsis Points**

EXERCISE A   On the line provided, write two titles or names that belong in each category. Underline all words that should appear in italics, and add quotation marks where needed.

Example 1. musical works   *Beethoven's Ode to Joy, Stravinsky's Rite of Spring*

1. ships or airplanes _____

2. songs _____

3. albums _____

4. poems _____

5. periodicals _____

EXERCISE B   Omit the underscored parts of the following sentences, and write the resulting sentences on the lines given. Use ellipsis points to punctuate each omission correctly.

Example 1. The fire engine sped past. Sam covered his ears, and those on the sidewalk stood still.

The fire engine sped past. . . . [T]hose on the sidewalk stood still.

6. Courtney has an uncle in Madrid, some friends in Rome, and a great-aunt in Istanbul.

_____

_____

7. The tower jutted from the old walls at an angle not exactly perpendicular to the ground.

_____

_____

8. Warren is a big fan of Romantic poets, but he does not enjoy reading Wordsworth. How can he like the Romantics and not enjoy Wordsworth? Warren says Blake is more interesting.

_____

_____

9. Theodore's favorite tree is the pecan, which he likes even more than the oak. There is a small grove of pecan trees behind his house, near the creek. _____

_____

10. Julie is the highest scorer on the volleyball team. She decided to go to college when she was awarded a scholarship. _____

_____

MECHANICS

Review C: Italics, Quotation Marks, and Ellipsis Points

EXERCISE A In each of the following sentences, supply italics (underlining) or quotation marks wherever they are needed.

Example 1. <u>My Several Worlds</u> is one of two autobiographies by Pearl Buck.

1. One of my favorite poems by Langston Hughes is Dreams, which is included in his collection The Dream Keeper and Other Poems.

2. Through the Tunnel, a short story by Doris Lessing, deals with the transition from childhood to adulthood.

3. I particularly enjoy reading the food section in the Wednesday edition of the Washington Post.

4. I hope to see the movie Star Wars when it is shown on television.

5. I have begun reading Chapter 13, The Story of Maize, in C.W. Ceram's book The First American.

EXERCISE B Add quotation marks where they are needed in the following sentences.

Example 1. "Do you know how to get to San Miguel de Allende?" he asked.

6. Theo exclaimed, I can't believe I ate the whole thing!

7. It's unfortunate that you did, said the doctor.

8. The coach asked, Who is on first?

9. Never fear! Jacques said with a smile.

10. The moral of one of Aesop's tales is Beware of grasping at shadows; you just may lose the substance.

11. Actually, I'll be free this afternoon, she commented.

12. Jamie said, The common saying familiarity breeds contempt may be true, but I prefer the saying absence makes the heart grow fonder.

13. Why, oh, why, cried Eric, do we always wait until the last minute!

14. The driver asked, Whatever happened to the sign Falling Rocks?

15. The child declared, I'd like to come with you to the park.

MECHANICS

Proofreading Application: Letter

Good writers generally are good proofreaders. Readers tend to admire and trust writing that is error-free. Make sure that you correct all errors in grammar, usage, spelling, and punctuation in your writing. Your readers will have more confidence in your words if you have done your best to proofread carefully.

Have you ever thought about what road signs and punctuation marks have in common? They are both visual cues that provide specific information. When you write a letter to be printed in a publication, you communicate more effectively when you use correct punctuation marks.

PROOFREADING ACTIVITY

The following is a letter to the editor of a high school newspaper. It contains errors in the use of italics, quotation marks, ellipsis points, and paragraph breaks. Use proofreading symbols to make your corrections.

Dear Editor:

I would like to express my opinion about the upcoming vote regarding mandatory school uniforms at LBJ High.

The strongest protest against wearing uniforms centers on a freedom being taken away from students. They don't let us leave campus for lunch anymore, the sophomore class president told me. "And now they want to dictate what we can wear." This same individual happens to be a member of the group I call Fashion Patrol. These students' preoccupation with haute couture (that's "high fashion for those who don't speak French) prevents them from seeing the positive effects of students dressing equally.

There are positive effects. An article in the May 2001 Ridgeview High newspaper, The Ridgeview Clarion, states, Despite all the doubts students first had . . the general consensus at Ridgeview is that people are interacting in a less superficial way." Cory Fernandez, Fairmont's star soccer player, cited other benefits: "Think of all the money we'll save by not having to buy so many clothes. It means more CD's, more computer games." Cory went on to say, "Besides, don't students want to save themselves the hassle of choosing what to wear five days a week?

In my opinion, the benefits of school uniforms outweigh the harms. I hope the school board agrees.

for **CHAPTER 13: PUNCTUATION**   pages 341–46

Literary Model: Narrative

The room next to me is empty till one morning a girl's voice says, Yoo hoo, who's there?
I'm not sure if she's talking to me or someone in the room beyond.
Yoo hoo, boy with the typhoid, are you awake?
I am.
Are you better?
I am.
Well, why are you here?
I don't know. I'm still in the bed. They stick needles in me and give me medicine.
What do you look like?
I wonder, What kind of a question is that? I don't know what to tell her.
Yoo hoo, are you there, typhoid boy?
I am.
What's your name?
Frank.
That's a good name. My name is Patricia Madigan. How old are you?
Ten.
Oh. She sounds disappointed.
But I'll be eleven in August, next month.

—from "Typhoid Fever," excerpted from *Angela's Ashes* by Frank McCourt

EXERCISE A   Even though the author did not use quotation marks, the above excerpt contains many direct quotations. Underline each direct quotation in the excerpt.

EXERCISE B

1. Why do you think the author chose not to use quotation marks to indicate direct quotations?

_____

_____

2. How did you react to the author's style with regard to punctuating direct quotations?

_____

_____

_____

From "Typhoid Fever" from *Angela's Ashes: A Memoir* by Frank McCourt. Copyright © 1996 by Frank McCourt. Reprinted by permission of **Scribner, a division of Simon & Schuster.**

for **CHAPTER 13: PUNCTUATION**   pages 341–46

Literary Model (continued)

EXERCISE C Using McCourt's story as a model, write a brief narrative about an interaction between two people who are meeting each other for the first time. The point of view does not have to be first-person. Include direct quotations, but do not punctuate them with quotation marks.

_____

_____

_____

_____

_____

_____

_____

_____

_____

_____

_____

_____

_____

_____

_____

EXERCISE D Do you think the lack of quotation marks in your narrative is enhancing or distracting? Explain your answer.

_____

_____

_____

_____

_____

_____

_____

_____

_____

_____

_____

_____

Writing Application: Vignette

Using direct rather than indirect quotations can enliven a piece of writing, especially one of fiction. Consider the different effects produced by the following sentences.

EXAMPLES Sobbing, Marta said that she'd experienced something horrific.

Marta said between sobs, "It was horrible—the most terrifying thing I've ever experienced!"

When you use direct quotations, pay close attention to capitalization and punctuation. A direct quotation that is incorrectly capitalized or punctuated may be confusing to your readers.

WRITING ACTIVITY

Write a vignette, or brief story, that consists primarily of a dialogue between two people. Include at least two quoted sentences that are divided by an interrupting expression (called a dialogue tag) and at least one quotation or title within a quotation.

PREWRITING To find an idea for your vignette, you may want to ask yourself "What if?" questions. Alternatively, you can consider interesting people, events, places, personal experiences, or dreams as story material. Once you have chosen an idea, jot down thoughts about your intended audience and the tone you will use (humorous? suspenseful? ironic?). Next, create a story map that includes the following story elements: characters, setting, plot, and point of view. Decide whether you will write in first-person, third-person limited, or third-person omniscient point of view. Determine what the conflict will be. Then, chronologically list the events of the plot.

WRITING Use your notes and your story map to write a draft of your vignette. Write dialogue that is realistic, yet makes the characters interesting. Include events that create suspense as they build on each other until the conflict is resolved. Use sensory details that help establish a mood.

REVISING Read your vignette to two or more classmates, having them concentrate on the effectiveness of the conflict and the clarity of the plot. Revise your draft, incorporating your classmates' feedback. Be sure that you have included at least two quoted sentences that are divided by a dialogue tag and at least one quotation or title within a quotation.

PUBLISHING Proofread your dialogue for errors in spelling, grammar, and punctuation. Remember the following rules as you proofread the quoted material:
- Begin a new paragraph each time the speaker changes.
- Use quotation marks around each speaker's words.
- Separate dialogue tags from the rest of the sentence with a comma, question mark, or exclamation point. Begin a new sentence with a capital letter.
- Don't capitalize the second part of a sentence that is separated by the dialogue tag.

Finally, stage a dramatic reading of your dialogue in front of your class.

EXTENDING YOUR WRITING

You may want to develop your dialogue into a short stage play or screenplay. Flesh out your characters. Then, compose dialogue between your characters that allows them to come alive. Finally, perform or videotape your completed dialogue.

Choices: Exploring Punctuation

The following activities challenge you to find a connection between punctuation and the world around you. Do the activity below that suits your personality best, and then share your discoveries with your class.

The Case for Other Cases

Interview several foreign language speakers and ask them about the use of possessives in their languages. How do their languages handle possessives? Do they have possessive cases? If so, do they have apostrophes? If a language does not have apostrophes, how does it indicate possession? Create a chart that shows how at least three different languages indicate possession.

In Old Mexico

In English-speaking countries, last names are sometimes hyphenated to show either a woman's maiden name and her married name or to show the family names of two lines of descent. How are surnames handled in Mexico? Find out and tell your classmates by giving a brief presentation.

1492

Do you know what happened in 1492? Of course you do. It's one of the dates that every American should know. Create a list of what you consider to be the most important dates in American history. Ten or twenty should be enough. Then, write sentences describing each event, and put the appropriate date in parentheses. Cut out your sentences, and paste them in the appropriate places on a time line.

$a(b+c)$

How are parentheses used in mathematics, especially in algebra? Find some good examples, and explain them to the class. Make connections between your examples and terms that the class already knows, such as subject, predicate, complement, and clause. You may wish to translate equations into words.

P-38's and F-15's

In everyday life, hyphens are used in ways other than dividing or combining words. Find other uses for hyphens. How does the military use them? How do businesses use them? Make a poster that illustrates the many uses of hyphens. Hyphens are handy little things, aren't they?

Dig Deep

The word *apostrophe* has an interesting root. Look up the meaning of this root. While you've got the dictionary open, look around and find a meaning of *apostrophe* that doesn't involve punctuation. Finally, do a bit of research and see if you can find out when apostrophes were first used as marks of punctuation. When you've dug up as much information as you can about apostrophes, summarize the information that you have found in the form of a brief report. Make copies and pass them out to your classmates.

Time's a Wastin'

Writers sometimes use apostrophes in dialogue to re-create the sound of regional dialects. The apostrophes indicate missing letters, as they do in contractions such as *don't*. Find some examples of this use of apostrophes in literary works and share them with your class. Then, lead the class in a discussion of this technique. What is its effect? Does it successfully re-create the intended dialect? Does it make the dialogue seem more or less realistic? Does it add regional flavor to the work? Is it demeaning to the group whose dialect is being imitated?

Apostrophes A

The possessive case of a noun or pronoun shows ownership or possession.

14a. To form the possessive of most singular nouns, add an apostrophe and an *s*.

When forming the possessive of a singular noun ending in an *s* or a *z* sound, add only an apostrophe if the noun has more than one syllable and the addition of *s* would make the noun awkward to pronounce.

   EXAMPLES   Maria's cat   the animal's food   Mr. Waters' yard

14b. To form the possessive case of a plural noun ending in *s*, add only the apostrophe.

The few plural nouns that do not end in *s* form the possessive case by adding an apostrophe and an *s*.

   EXAMPLES   the ponies' saddles   the mice's nests   the deer's natural predators

EXERCISE A Rewrite the following phrases, using the possessive case.

   Example 1. the den of wolves   _the wolves' den_____

1. men of Columbia   _____

2. games for children   _____

3. books by Alcott   _____

4. the legs of the table   _____

5. plays by Euripedes   _____

6. the house of Ms. Andrews _____

7. the cabs of those drivers _____

8. the views of a citizen   _____

9. lunch for Lois   _____

10. the skis that Alvin owns _____

EXERCISE B Some of the possessive case nouns in these phrases are correct, and others are not. On the lines provided, revise those that are incorrect. If a phrase is correct, write *C* on the line.

   Example 1. women's office   _____C_____

11. James's kite   _____

12. my two coach's pep talk _____

13. the mens' team   _____

14. four geeses' eggs   _____

15. the children's bicycles _____

Apostrophes B

14c.	Do not use an apostrophe with possessive personal pronouns or with the possessive pronoun *whose*.

14d.	To form the possessive of an indefinite pronoun, add an apostrophe and an *s*.

EXAMPLES	That is **my** coat.	That coat is **mine.**
	That is **someone's** hat.	**Everybody's** ideas have been heard.

EXERCISE A   Rewrite the following sentences by changing the possessive pronoun in each from a complement or object of a preposition to an adjective placed before the noun.

Example 1. This is a pencil of hers.   *This is her pencil.*

1. Is this encyclopedia yours? _____

2. He bought a puppy of theirs. _____

3. That dachshund is a dog of someone. _____

4. This bookcase is ours. _____

5. The environment is the concern of everyone. _____

EXERCISE B   Some of the possessive case pronouns in the following sentences are correct, and others are not. On the lines provided, revise those that are incorrect. If a sentence is correct, write *C* on the line.

Example 1. Dave picked up the jacket from the seat, but when he got home he found the jacket was someone elses.

> *Dave picked up the jacket from the seat, but when he got home he found the jacket was*
>
> *someone else's.*

6. Jonah and Billie spent the day at the mechanic's, which was not eithers' idea of fun.

_____

7. One dog at the show wore a little suit; it's owner wore a matching dress.

_____

8. His is the fastest radio-controlled airplane I have ever seen.

_____

9. Renaldo was looking for a pencil to borrow, so I loaned him your's.

_____

10. Patrice and Jeremy have been each others' best friend since they were born.

_____

Apostrophes C

14e. Form the possessive of only the last word in a compound noun, such as the name of an organization or a business, and in a word group showing joint possession.

EXAMPLES   my mother-in-law's cat   Rafael and Tom's report

14f. Form the possessive of each noun in a word group that expresses individual possession of similar items.

EXAMPLE   Mary's and Daniel's reports are on the desk.

EXERCISE A   On the lines provided, write the possessive forms of the following items.

Example 1. the store of Frank and Herman   *Frank and Herman's store*

1. the camera Kate and Ali share   _____

2. the dog of the Juarez family   _____

3. a painting by his sister-in-law   _____

4. the books belonging to the law firm of Goldsmith, Moss, and Schwartz   _____

_____

5. the works of Twain and the works of Hawthorne   _____

EXERCISE B   Some of the possessives in the following sentences are correct, and others are not. On the lines provided, revise those that are incorrect. If a sentence is correct, write *C* on the line.

Example 1. Clarissa and Tad's scores on the test were both very high.

   Clarissa's and Tad's scores on the test were both very high.

6. Molly and his science fair project involved a few controlled explosions.

_____

7. I admire both Sheena and Vaughn's determination in finishing the race.

_____

8. Tobias and Catherine's Spanish class went on a field trip yesterday.

_____

9. Gia and Bert's batches of cookies taste exactly the same.

_____

10. After the dance, they plan to go to Harrison's and Sullivan's Cafe.

_____

Language and Sentence Skills Practice

MECHANICS

Apostrophes Review A

14a.	To form the possessive of most singular nouns, add an apostrophe and an *s*.
14b.	To form the possessive case of a plural noun ending in *s*, add only the apostrophe.
14c.	Do not use an apostrophe with possessive personal pronouns or with the possessive pronoun *whose*.
14d.	To form the possessive of an indefinite pronoun, add an apostrophe and an *s*.
14e.	Form the possessive of only the last word in a compound noun, such as the name of an organization or a business, and in a word group showing joint possession.
14f.	Form the possessive of each noun in a word group that expresses individual possession of similar items.

EXERCISE Some of the following possessives are correct, and others are not. On the lines provided, revise those that are incorrect. If a possessive is already correct, write *C* on the line.

Example 1. Jane and Ellen's bicycles *Jane's and Ellen's bicycles*

1. Harolds and her parakeet _____

2. that telescope of your's _____

3. James' garden _____

4. the mice's litters _____

5. the FBIs investigation _____

6. it's bottom drawer _____

7. Garcia and Rodriguez's Restaurant _____

8. the football of his's _____

9. the monkey's tails _____

10. someone elses nameplate _____

Apostrophes D

14g. Use an apostrophe to show where letters, words, or numerals have been omitted in a contraction.

Do not confuse contractions with possessive pronouns.

EXAMPLES I'm sure it's his book.   Let's guess whom he'll vote for.

Who's graduating in '05?   **Whose** car is parked here?

Generally, the adverb *not* can be shortened to *n't* and added to a verb without any change in the spelling of the verb. However, *cannot* becomes *can't* and *will not* becomes *won't*.

EXAMPLES I **did not** go to the meeting.   I **didn't** go to the meeting.

I **will not** go to the meeting.   I **won't** go to the meeting.

EXERCISE A On the lines provided, change these items into contractions.

Example 1. cannot _____ *can't* _____

1. will not _____

2. we are _____

3. she is _____

4. were not _____

5. he has _____

6. it is _____

7. you are _____

8. he would _____

9. we had _____

10. should have _____

EXERCISE B The following paragraph contains ten errors in the usage of contractions and possessive pronouns. Cross out any errors and write the corrections above them.

Example ~~Its~~ *It's* been a long time since I've been to a museum.

Theirs a great exhibit at the Philadelphia Maritime Museum. Im sure your going to enjoy it because of it's superior quality and because of you're interest in crew races. The exhibit features Thomas Eakins, who's painting's are incredibly lifelike. Some of his works are of crews rowing in Philadelphia. To make his paintings of the crews accurate, Eakins first took they're pictures. Then he made elaborate sketches, figuring out the exact perspective. Their all their in the exhibit—the photographs, sketches, and finished paintings.

Apostrophes E

| **14h.** | Use an apostrophe and an *s* to form the plurals of numerals, symbols, all lowercase letters, some uppercase letters, and some words referred to as words. |

EXAMPLES In his report on ballet, Jim's handwritten *tutu*'s all had *u*'s that looked like *o*'s.

EXERCISE A On the lines provided, write the plurals of the following items, using apostrophes.

Example 1. *p* and *q* _____ *p's and q's* _____

1. ABC _____

2. *I* and *O* _____

3. *Oh* and *Ah* _____

4. *t* _____

5. *so* _____

6. *Jr.* _____

7. *if, and,* or *but* _____

8. 1950 _____

9. all of the 7 _____

10. *X* and *O* _____

EXERCISE B On the lines provided, write the plurals of these items, using apostrophes.

Example 1. *U* and *A* _____ _____

11. *please* and *thank you* _____

12. 3 _____

13. @ _____

14. ! _____

15. 4 and 5 _____

16. *P. S.* _____

17. 85 _____

18. *yes* and *no* _____

19. *oh* _____

20. * _____

Apostrophes Review B

14a.	To form the possessive of most singular nouns, add an apostrophe and an *s*.
14b.	To form the possessive case of a plural noun ending in *s*, add only the apostrophe.
14c.	Do not use an apostrophe with possessive personal pronouns or with the possessive pronoun *whose*.
14d.	To form the possessive of an indefinite pronoun, add an apostrophe and an *s*.
14e.	Form the possessive of only the last word in a compound noun, such as the name of an organization or a business, and in a word group showing joint possession.
14f.	Form the possessive of each noun in a word group that expresses individual possession of similar items.
14g.	Use an apostrophe to show where letters, words, or numerals have been omitted in a contraction.
14h.	Use an apostrophe and an *s* to form the plurals of numerals, symbols, all lowercase letters, some uppercase letters, and some words referred to as words.

EXERCISE Some of the following possessives are correct, and others are not. On the lines provided, revise those that are incorrect. If a possessive is correct, write *C* on the line.

Example 1. Carlos' notebook   *Carlos's notebook*

1. the one UFOs behavior   _____

2. the bus' drivers hat   _____

3. someone elses'   _____

4. Keyshon's and her chess game   _____

5. the kite and its tail   _____

6. Mr. Jones' address   _____

7. four 7s   _____

8. too many *therefore*s   _____

9. a womens' shop   _____

10. my sister's-in-law's job   _____

Apostrophes Review C

14a.	To form the possessive of most singular nouns, add an apostrophe and an *s*.
14b.	To form the possessive case of a plural noun ending in *s*, add only the apostrophe.
14c.	Do not use an apostrophe with possessive personal pronouns or with the possessive pronoun *whose*.
14d.	To form the possessive of an indefinite pronoun, add an apostrophe and an *s*.
14e.	Form the possessive of only the last word in a compound noun, such as the name of an organization or a business, and in a word group showing joint possession.
14f.	Form the possessive of each noun in a word group that expresses individual possession of similar items.
14g.	Use an apostrophe to show where letters, words, or numerals have been omitted in a contraction.
14h.	Use an apostrophe and an *s* to form the plurals of numerals, symbols, all lowercase letters, some uppercase letters, and some words referred to as words.

EXERCISE Most of the following sentences contain errors in apostrophe usage. Cross out the error and write the word correctly above it. If a sentence is correct as it stands, write *C* after the sentence.

Example 1. The student ~~councils~~ *council's* decision was applauded for ~~it's~~ *its* wisdom.

1. After a weeks absence the student had a lot of schoolwork to do.

2. Always remember to dot your *i*s.

3. Students papers are on file in the main office.

4. The Washingtons house was flooded last week.

5. Bad weather forced the Lees to cancel the childrens party.

6. In a democracy everyones vote counts.

7. That book is one of theirs.

8. The geese hissed at Fiona and my bicycles.

9. The judges were impressed by the dancers skill and by her poise.

10. None of the clerks could find the mens shirts.

Hyphens A

14i. Use a hyphen to divide a word at the end of a line.

(1) Do not divide a one-syllable word.

(2) Divide a word only between syllables.

> **EXAMPLE** Emily Dickinson lived a life of soli-
> tude.

(3) Divide an already hyphenated word only at the hyphen.

Incorrect	**Correct**
I feel quite self-con- fident.	I feel quite self- confident.

(4) Do not divide a word so that one letter stands alone.

Incorrect	**Correct**
My poem is a- bout China.	My poem is about China.

EXERCISE A For each word below, write *Correct* if the hyphen or hyphens mark places where the word may be divided. Write *Incorrect* if the word may not be divided at each of the marked points.

Example 1. ru-nning ___*Incorrect*___

1. ter-rible _____

2. self-a-ware _____

3. ta-ngle _____

4. extraordinar-y _____

5. pla-te _____

EXERCISE B On the lines provided, write these words with hyphens, showing possible places in which to break them if they were to appear at the end of a line. If you are unsure where to break a word, look it up in a dictionary. If a word should not be divided at the end of a line, write *No Hyphen*.

Example 1. simple ___*sim—ple*___

6. cannot _____ **11.** syllable _____

7. undo _____ **12.** self-awareness _____

8. return _____ **13.** chilling _____

9. strength _____ **14.** around _____

10. technique _____ **15.** anatomy _____

MECHANICS

Hyphens B

Some compound words are written as one word; some are hyphenated; and some are written as two or more words.

EXAMPLES   **steamboat**   **steam-driven**   **steam engine**

14j.	Use a hyphen with compound numbers from *twenty-one* to *ninety-nine* and with fractions used as modifiers.
14k.	Use a hyphen with the prefixes *all-, ex-, great-,* and *self-;* with the suffixes *-elect* and *-free;* and with all prefixes before a proper noun or proper adjective.
14l.	Hyphenate a compound adjective when it precedes the noun it modifies.

Do not use a hyphen if one of the modifiers is an adverb ending in *–ly.*

EXERCISE A   Insert hyphens where necessary in the following phrases. If the phrase is already correct, write *C* on the line provided.

Example _____ **1.** a well‑trained dog

_____ **1.** twenty four delegates   _____ **6.** the president elect of France

_____ **2.** an ex football player   _____ **7.** a really great opportunity

_____ **3.** a self conscious dancer   _____ **8.** one fourth tablespoon of oil

_____ **4.** a vacation in mid July   _____ **9.** a pro Russian trade agreement

_____ **5.** one third cup of milk   _____ **10.** a suit that was custom fitted

EXERCISE B   On the lines provided, rewrite these phrases, correcting any errors in the placement of hyphens. If a sentence is already correct, write *C* on the line.

Example 1. her ex husband   _____ *her ex‑husband* _____

11. a self-appointed expert _____

12. an intentionally-dropped ball _____

13. thirty two students _____

14. a man who is self-important _____

15. a pre Columbian vase _____

16. a one-third return on an investment _____

17. one-fourth of the time _____

18. her great uncle _____

19. the best-all-around player _____

20. a play that is well-written _____

322

Hyphens C

Some compound words are written as one word; some are hyphenated; and some are written as two or more words.

EXAMPLES   **redhead**   **red-hot**   **red tape**

14j.	Use a hyphen with compound numbers from *twenty-one* to *ninety-nine* and with fractions used as modifiers.
14k.	Use a hyphen with the prefixes *all-, ex-, great-,* and *self-;* with the suffixes *-elect* and *-free;* and with all prefixes before a proper noun or proper adjective.
14l.	Hyphenate a compound adjective when it precedes the noun it modifies.

Do not use a hyphen if one of the modifiers is an adverb ending in *–ly.*

EXERCISE A   Insert hyphens where necessary in the following phrases. If the phrase is already correct, write *C* on the line provided.

Example _____ **1.** a well ─played game

_____ **1.** a self absorbed actor   _____ **6.** a convention in mid February

_____ **2.** an ex scientist   _____ **7.** a really fine shot

_____ **3.** two thirds teaspoon of salt _____ **8.** the secretary elect of the council

_____ **4.** eighty eight keys   _____ **9.** a post Cold War treaty

_____ **5.** three quarters cup of flour _____ **10.** a dictionary that is up to date

EXERCISE B   On the lines provided, rewrite these phrases, correcting any errors in the placement of hyphens. If a sentence is already correct, write *C* on the line.

Example 1. an aide de camp   *an aide─de─camp*

11. one-third of the students   _____

12. a three-quarter turn   _____

13. a well known song   _____

14. the first-back-yard basketball court   _____

15. a pre Victorian poet   _____

16. a recently-added class   _____

17. twenty two blackbirds   _____

18. a self-styled critic   _____

19. his ex father in law   _____

20. an oven that is self-cleaning   _____

Dashes

14m. Use a dash to indicate the beginning and the end of an abrupt break in thought or speech or to indicate an unfinished thought.

> **EXAMPLES**   Wild deer—look! there's one over there—often come to this field.
>
>   "Where—where have you been?" he stammered.
>
>   "I believe that—" she began but then stopped shyly.

14n. Use a dash to mean *namely, that is,* or *in other words,* or to otherwise introduce an explanation. Also, use a dash after the explanation if the sentence continues.

> **EXAMPLE**   My dad's store—a clothing store in Melrose—sells those shoes.

EXERCISE   In each of the following sentences, insert dashes where necessary.

Example 1. Matt, or Matthew‸he goes by either name‸is a hard worker.

1. In any inclement weather snow, sleet, hail, or heavy rain we like to take the vehicle with four-wheel drive.

2. The score was absurdly low a total of only forty points for a varsity game.

3. Teya has four other pets a dog, two ferrets, and a Shetland pony.

4. "Could I please speak to" George began, but he had already been put on hold.

5. The goal of the game checkmating the opponent's king often gets more difficult the fewer pieces you have left.

6. Yvonne's uncle moved to Switzerland to realize his lifelong dream becoming a world-class yodeler.

7. Your application you should have been told this earlier was supposed to have been mailed no later than last week.

8. "What" Pedro started to say but stopped himself. "Elian, is that really you?"

9. The clutter in our neighbor's backyard two cars, three sheds, a swingset, and a life-size metal sculpture of a mastodon had already attracted quite a bit of attention.

10. What I need I'm sorry; I should have said it more clearly is a small stone, not a small stoat.

MECHANICS

Parentheses

14o. Use parentheses to enclose informative or explanatory material of minor importance.

EXAMPLES	Monarch Street (just two blocks from here) is a major thoroughfare.
	Wash the floor with hot water. (Don't forget to add soap!)
	Bastille Day (it's the fourteenth of July) is celebrated by the Sallé family.

EXERCISE Rewrite each of the following sentences on the lines provided, adding parentheses where necessary.

Example 1. This painting a watercolor is of my grandmother's house.

This painting (a watercolor) is of my grandmother's house.

1. She began painting six years ago that was 1997 and hasn't stopped since.

_____

2. My grandmother lives in Tucson it's in southern Arizona and likes it there.

_____

3. Have you ever seen a saguaro a kind of cactus?

_____

4. There are lots of cactuses in southern Arizona. Is the plural of *cactus cacti*?

_____

5. My favorite time of the day is sunset I'm never awake for sunrise.

_____

6. When the sun sets about six o'clock this time of year over the desert, the sky lights up.

_____

7. My sister Carla she is only ten has started painting as well.

_____

8. I don't do anything artistic myself; I'm more of an athlete. I can't sit still for very long.

_____

9. While my grandmother and sister paint, I go hiking. Hiking the mountains and canyons in Arizona is incredible!

_____

10. I tell them that when I become a world-famous mountain climber which should happen when I'm about twenty-five I'll let them paint my portrait.

_____

Brackets

14p.	Use brackets to enclose an explanation or added information within quoted or parenthetical material.

> **EXAMPLES** Coach Chan reported that the team was "one hundred percent, absolutely, positively ready for [the rematch against arch-rival Central High School] next week."

EXERCISE Read the following brief passage. Then, revise each of the numbered sentences that follow by adding brackets as they are needed to enclose additions to quoted material.

Example 1. Principal Lawrence claims that "Johnson [athletic teams] can hold [their] own with anyone in the district."

Central High School and Johnson High School have a rivalry that "goes back decades, to when I attended class here," Principal Debra Lawrence says. "At the start, it was Central who beat us at every sport. Now, we here at Johnson can hold our own with anyone in the district."

Coach Chan agrees. "When I first got here, all anyone would ever talk about was the Central game. So far, we've won six and lost four, which isn't too bad, considering our opposition."

As one student expressed the rivalry, "Off the field, we're best friends, but when we're playing each other, there's nobody we want to beat more than Central."

1. One student reports that "there's nobody we Johnson High teams want to beat more than Central."

2. Principal Debra Lawrence says that the rivalry "goes back decades, to when she attended class here at Johnson."

3. Coach Chan attests that when he "first got here to Johnson High School, all anyone would ever talk about was the Central game."

4. Do you agree with Coach Chan that Johnson's record of six wins and four losses against Central High School "isn't too bad, considering our Johnson's opposition"?

5. Principal Lawrence wasn't exaggerating when she said, "At the start, it was Central who beat us Johnson High School at every sport."

Hyphens, Parentheses, Dashes, Brackets

| **14i.** | Use a hyphen to divide a word at the end of a line. |

| **14m.** | Use a dash to indicate the beginning and the end of an abrupt break in thought or speech or to indicate an unfinished thought. |

| **14n.** | Use a dash to mean *namely, that is,* or *in other words,* or to otherwise introduce an explanation. Also, use a dash after the explanation if the sentence continues. |

| **14o.** | Use parentheses to enclose informative or explanatory material of minor importance. |

| **14p.** | Use brackets to enclose an explanation or added information within quoted or parenthetical material. |

EXERCISE A On the lines provided, write these words with hyphens, showing possible places in which to break them if they were to appear at the end of a line. If you are unsure where to break a word, look it up in a dictionary. If a word should not be divided at the end of a line, write *No Hyphen*.

Example 1. breadth _____*No Hyphen*_____

1. proofread _____
2. width _____
3. semiconscious _____
4. course _____
5. opaque _____

6. free-floating _____
7. gloomy _____
8. abstract _____
9. lovely _____
10. self-sustaining _____

EXERCISE B On the line before each sentence, write *D* if the underlined words should be set off by dashes. Write *P* if they should be set off by parentheses. Write *B* if they should be set off by brackets.

Example ___*B*___ **1.** Cynthia wrote in her essay that she has "loved studying photography for many years and that taking pictures has long been a passion of <u>hers</u>."

_____ **11.** Margaret Bourke-White <u>I love her photographs!</u> led a fascinating life.

_____ **12.** Margaret <u>also called Peggy</u> traveled all over the world.

_____ **13.** Along the way she obtained two strange pets <u>alligators!</u>

_____ **14.** Her war photos <u>especially those showing prisoners of war</u> make me shudder.

_____ **15.** My best friend, Cynthia, wrote, "Margaret Bourke-White's picture <u>of Stalin</u> is an especially masterful shot, showing as it does his boldness."

Language and Sentence Skills Practice

Review A: **Punctuation**

EXERCISE   Most of the following sentences contain one or more errors in apostrophe usage. On the line provided, rewrite the sentence correctly.

Example 1. His sister's-in-law book had lost it's spine.   *His sister-in-law's book had lost its spine.*

1. The firefighters boots were at the foot of their beds. _____

_____

2. Jana wrote her *7s* with a crossbar, as the French write theirs. _____

_____

3. After three days of traveling, both Millers and Allans teams reached the mountains. _____

_____

4. The director listened attentively to everyones ideas. _____

_____

5. The editor-in-chiefs suggestions were good ones. _____

_____

6. Sally and James' reports each had two grades: one for content and one for form. _____

_____

7. Carlos's and Bobby's plan helped in the search for the childrens dog. _____

_____

8. Both the Wilsons and the Thomases picnics were held in the Thomases backyard. _____

_____

9. Your letters are hard to read because you never cross your *ts*. _____

_____

10. Most of the FBIs agents doubted the womans word. _____

_____

MECHANICS

Review B: Punctuation

EXERCISE A Following are five sets of expressions. One of the expressions in each set contains an error in the use of hyphens or apostrophes. Rewrite the expression in its correct form on the line provided.

Example 1. [a] the child who's here [b] Ciara's and Ramona's sister [c] a well-informed person

Ciara and Ramona's sister

1. [a] Jonah's and Sam's feelings [b] each other's views [c] a blue gray shirt

_____

2. [a] if you're ready [b] NASAs plans [c] his *p*'s and *q*'s

_____

3. [a] a poorly organized paper [b] his self sufficiency [c] two hours later

_____

4. [a] a well done steak [b] five minutes of waiting [c] Tomas's lost pen

_____

5. [a] the president-elect [b] any person's promise [c] forty four teammates

_____

EXERCISE B On the lines provided, rewrite the following sentences. Punctuate the sentences by inserting dashes, parentheses, or brackets where they are needed. Hint: Do not add commas or semicolons.

Example 1. I don't understand why the car needs to be overhauled it's practically brand-new.

I don't understand why the car needs to be overhauled—it's practically brand-new.

6. The Steiners I don't believe you've met them are neighbors of ours. _____

_____

7. We do odd jobs to earn money washing windows, mowing lawns, cleaning basements. _____

_____

8. The index includes more data on this experiment. See page 783 Graph 3. _____

_____

9. Everyone knows the first words "Four score and seven years ago . . . " of the Gettysburg

Address. _____

_____

10. Alec Guinness 1914–2000 was a star of theater and film. _____

MECHANICS

Review C: **Punctuation**

EXERCISE A   Following are five sets of expressions. One of the expressions in each set contains an error in the use of hyphens or apostrophes. Rewrite the expression in its correct form on the line provided.

Example 1. [a] the storm of 88 _____ *the storm of '88*
         [b] Find the X's
         [c] flipped its lid

1. **[a]** an hour's time _____
   [b] your brother's-in law's name
   [c] nobody's car

2. **[a]** Thirty third Street _____
   [b] a few days' journey
   [c] everyone's presents

3. **[a]** twelve o clock _____
   [b] my ex-counselor
   [c] one third of the class

4. **[a]** your self esteem _____
   [b] five days before
   [c] a carelessly drawn sketch

5. **[a]** Jonah's and Sam's pet _____
   [b] every person's beliefs
   [c] an after-lunch appointment

EXERCISE B   Punctuate each of the sentences by inserting dashes, parentheses, or brackets where they are needed. Hint: Do not add commas or semicolons in these sentences.

Example 1. I can't figure out what happened to my pen — it was on my desk a minute ago!

6. Did you realize that my aunt my mother's sister is married to your uncle Emil?

7. The zookeeper's announcement "A cat has escaped!" did not alarm us.

8. My sister she's a copywriter for an advertising company writes poetry in her spare time.

9. We dined at the home of Mrs. Algoma Whitefeather the former Algoma Tucker.

10. Mayor Jenkins stated, "The problem the current crime wave is under control."

MECHANICS

for **CHAPTER 14: PUNCTUATION**   *pages 356–70*

Proofreading Application: Research Paper

Good writers are generally good proofreaders. Readers tend to admire and trust writing that is error-free. Make sure that you correct all errors in grammar, usage, spelling, and punctuation in your writing. Your readers will have more confidence in your words if you have done your best to proofread carefully.

When you write a research paper, the words you use are the principal part of your communication with readers. However, a secondary component of that communication is punctuation. Punctuation marks help you to establish relationships among the words and ideas you employ. Consider these punctuation marks as tools at your disposal in your construction of a precisely and clearly written research paper.

PROOFREADING ACTIVITY

The following is an excerpt from a research paper. It contains several errors in the use of apostrophes, hyphens, dashes, parentheses, and brackets. Use proofreading symbols to add apostrophes, hyphens, dashes, parentheses, and brackets.

Desiderius Erasmus 1466?–1536 was an eminent Dutch scholar and writer despite his humble beginnings: He was born out of wedlock to a priest and a physicians daughter. Perhaps his humble beginnings helped him to be the downtoearth man he was. He became a priest in 1492 the year Columbus first landed in the Americas and studied at the University of Paris. He found that being a priest did not agree with him, and eventually he received the Popes permission to live as a secular scholar that is, a worldly as opposed to a religious man of study. During his lifetime, he wrote an enormous number of letters more than 1,500 of them still exist! and befriended some of the most famous English scholars of the era. (These include statesman and writer Sir Thomas More 1478–1535 and John Colet 1467?–1519, founder of Saint Paul's School.) These scholars writings and efforts helped to establish humanism the intellectual movement that arose from the study of classical literature and led to the Renaissance in

Language and Sentence Skills Practice

Literary Model: Short Story

> I was sick—sick unto death with that long agony; and when they at length unbound me, and I was permitted to sit, I felt that my senses were leaving me. The sentence—the dread sentence of death—was the last of distinct accentuation which reached my ears. After that, the sound of the Inquisitorial voices seemed merged in one dreamy, indeterminate hum. It conveyed to my soul the idea of *revolution*—perhaps from its association in fancy with the burr of a mill wheel. This only for a brief period, for presently I heard no more. Yet for a while, I saw—but with how terrible an exaggeration! I saw the lips of the black-robed judges. They appeared to me white—whiter than the sheet upon which I trace these words—and thin even to grotesqueness; thin with the intensity of their expression of firmness—of immovable resolution—of stern contempt of human torture. I saw that the decrees of what to me was Fate were still issuing from those lips.
>
> —from "The Pit and the Pendulum" by Edgar Allan Poe

EXERCISE A

1. Circle each of the dashes that Edgar Allan Poe uses in the passage above, which opens the short story "The Pit and the Pendulum."

2. What punctuation marks could Poe have used in place of the dashes?

_____

EXERCISE B

1. Why do you think Poe uses dashes in this passage instead of other punctuation marks?

_____

_____

_____

2. How do the dashes affect the way you read this passage? (Hint: Try reading the passage aloud with the dashes. Then, try reading the passage as you would if the dashes were replaced with other punctuation marks, such as commas.)

_____

_____

_____

for **CHAPTER 14: PUNCTUATION** page 368

Literary Model (continued)

EXERCISE C Write a paragraph narrated by a character who is undergoing a terrible ordeal. Use punctuation, including dashes, to help establish voice—for instance, to indicate the strain upon the narrator as he or she tries to express his or her feelings.

_____

_____

_____

_____

_____

_____

_____

_____

_____

_____

_____

_____

EXERCISE D How does your use of punctuation contribute to the voice of the narrator? Be sure to include some specific details from your passage in your answer.

_____

_____

_____

_____

_____

_____

_____

Language and Sentence Skills Practice

MECHANICS | Language in Context: Writing Application

Writing Application: Definition

Each type of punctuation mark has specific functions that help you reach the goal of making your writing as clear as possible. Some of them help your reader understand the relationships among words or ideas that you are trying to get across in your writing. For example, the parentheses and brackets used in the following sentences indicate that what is within them is of lesser importance.

EXAMPLES   *The Magic Flute* was composed by Wolfgang Amadeus Mozart (1756–1791).

The professor announced, "Read Chapter 14 [of *Studies in Macroeconomics*] in its entirety for our next meeting."

Other punctuation marks provide specific information. For instance, apostrophes indicate possession (**Anya's** backpack) or omitted letters (**it's**). Hyphens are used to form some compound words (**self-reliance**) and to divide a word at the end of a line.

WRITING ACTIVITY

Choose a subject that interests you, and write an extended definition. Similar to a dictionary definition, your extended definition will name the general class or category to which the subject belongs and then name the characteristics that distinguish that particular subject from all the others in its general class. In your extended definition, use at least three of the five elements of punctuation (apostrophes, hyphens, dashes, parentheses, and brackets) discussed in this chapter.

PREWRITING   Choose a subject you would like to know more about. Make sure that it is complex enough that you can write at least one or two paragraphs about it. Freewrite for several minutes about the subject. Then, turn to reference sources to find examples, descriptive details, facts, and quotations about the subject.

WRITING   Begin your draft with a one-sentence definition that sounds like a dictionary definition but that you have crafted yourself. Then, use the results of your freewriting and your notes to extend the definition. Include descriptive details and/or quotations from an author.

REVISING   Set your draft aside for a while before you begin your final round of revision. When you read the extended definition again, ask yourself whether you could improve it by adding transitional words or phrases, taking out instances of wordiness, or replacing weak words with more precise and interesting ones. Be sure that you have used at least three of the five elements of punctuation mentioned above.

PUBLISHING   Proofread your extended definition for errors in spelling, grammar, and punctuation. In particular, ask yourself whether every sentence is a complete sentence, whether the tense and form of each verb is correct, and whether the report is free of errors in subject-verb and pronoun-antecedent agreement. Collect your classmates' extended definitions. Create an anthology titled *Defining the World Around Us*.

EXTENDING YOUR WRITING

You may wish to extend this activity by using it as the basis of a research report. Broaden the subject of your definition to include other related subjects, and write extended definitions on those. Explain how all the subjects are related, and if your extended definitions helped you discover any patterns, be sure to explain those as well.

for **CHAPTER 15: SPELLING**   pages 377–400

Choices: Exploring Spelling

The following activities challenge you to find a connection between spelling and the world around you. Do the activity below that suits your personality best, and then share your discoveries with the class.

VOCABULARY

Countdown

Since you're studying words, you may want to find out how many words are in the English language. It might interest you to know that scholars think that everyone has several separate vocabularies. There is a speaking vocabulary of words you use only in conversation. Then, there are words that you recognize when you read them but never speak—those belong to your reading vocabulary. Then there is a third group of words that you use when writing. How many words do you think the average person has in each group? Ask your librarian for guidance on how to research the answer. Then, post a chart giving the information.

COMPUTER PROGRAMS

Go Electronic

There are a number of computer games that can help you learn to spell better. For this project, find out what games are available. Do a bit of research. Look for advertisements and reviews of these programs. What do these programs offer a user? What age groups do they target? Don't be put off by programs for a younger age group because many have levels of varying difficulty. Report on these programs to the class.

ART

O or A?

Look closely at the entries in the words-often-confused list. In some of the pairs, one letter makes all the difference. Spot three of these pairs. Then, create pairs of illustrations. For each pair, draw an illustration that incorporates the letter that is often confused. For instance, for the words *capital/capitol*, you could illustrate *capitol* with a bird's-eye view of the building with a heavy circle around the dome. Each of your drawings should have a letter incorporated into it. Post your illustrations in the classroom.

HISTORY

Private Investigator

Who was or is Noah Webster, and what does he have to do with spelling? Find out, and make appropriate notes on a timeline. Then, give a short speech to your class or write a few pages explaining his relationship to spelling.

LEXICOGRAPHY

Schwa?

Have you ever noticed those little marks and weird letters that some dictionaries use to show pronunciation? It's hard to talk about these marks if you don't know what to call them. Find out the names of these strange marks and letters. Also, find out what function the upside-down *e* serves. Then, write up a memo that includes all of the marks and examples using them, and make copies for your classmates to keep in their English notebooks.

GAME

Snakes and Ladders

If you misspell more words than you spell correctly, here's a project for you. Create a board game in which the only way to reach the end is to correctly spell misspelled words. Every time you land on a misspelled word and spell it correctly, you advance three spaces. If you spell it incorrectly, you go back three spaces. Most of the words will be misspelled, but a few tough ones will already be correct, just to keep it interesting. Use some graph paper to compose your game. Write the correct words first, then anything goes! When you've written all the words in, you can link them with a trail and draw illustrations around them.

Language and Sentence Skills Practice

Good Spelling Habits

15a. To learn the spelling of a word, pronounce it, study it, and write it.

(1) Pronounce words carefully.
(2) Spell by syllables.

> **EXAMPLES**   prob * **a** * bly [not *probly*]
>
> in * vi * ta * tion [four syllables]

(3) Use a dictionary.
(4) Proofread for careless spelling errors.
(5) Keep a spelling notebook to list and review difficult words.

EXERCISE A . Proofread the following sentences, underlining misspelled words. If you are unsure about the spelling of any word, use a dictionary. Above the misspelled word, write the word correctly.

> *favorite*
> **Example 1.** One of my <u>favrite</u> movie stars is Harrison Ford.

1. George Lucas produced his first film when he was a collage student.

2. The film, entitled *THX 1138:4EB*, won first prize at the National Student Film Festival in 1967.

3. Upon gradiation from the University of Southern California, Lucas made *American Graffiti*.

4. Featured in a miner role in that film was newcomer Harrison Ford.

5. *American Graffiti* was such a popular movie that Lucas was able to pursuade a major

   Hollywood studio to support "a little space movie."

6. That "little movie" evolved into *Star Wars*, which was an overnight sucess.

7. Lucas then hired Lawrence Kasdan to complete a script for the sequel, *The Empire Strikes Back*.

8. Kasdan also wrote the third film of the *Star Wars* trillogy, *The Return of the Jedi*.

9. The *Star Wars* vehicles made a star out of acter Harrison Ford.

10. Kasdan's next project, *Raiders of the Lost Ark*, brought Ford the roll of a lifetime—Indiana Jones.

EXERCISE B   In each of the following groups of words, one word is misspelled. Underline the misspelled word. Then, write the word correctly on the line provided.

Example 1. financial, <u>sophmore</u>, situated, civilization _____ *sophomore* _____

11. liability, perspiration, souvinir, benefited _____

12. suger, lightning, coming, grammar _____

13. priority, answer, athelete, calendar _____

14. conscience, February, villain, maintainance _____

15. straight, seperate, dissimilar, Tuesday _____

ie and *ei*

15b. Write *ie* when the sound is long *e*, except after *c*.

EXAMPLES	bel**ie**ve	rel**ie**ve	n**ie**ce	dec**ei**ve	perc**ei**ve
EXCEPTIONS	**ei**ther	l**ei**sure	n**ei**ther	s**ei**ze	w**ei**rd

15c. Write *ei* when the sound is not long *e*.

EXAMPLES	fr**ei**ght	h**ei**ght	n**ei**ghbor	forf**ei**t
EXCEPTIONS	fr**ie**nd	misch**ie**f	d**ie**

EXERCISE A   In the following sentences, underline any misspelled words. Above each misspelled word, write the word correctly. If a sentence is already correct, write *C* after it.

Example 1. How much does the parcel w~~ie~~gh? *(weigh)*

1. I believe that the reign of King Juan Carlos of Spain began in 1975.

2. Stripping all the biege paint off the old table was quite an achievement.

3. Bert pulled in the horse's reins and brought the sliegh to a stop.

4. The employee's deceit was discovered, and he was fired.

5. The automobile manufacturers concede that deisel engines are more efficient.

6. One of Brazil's chief exports to foriegn countries is cocoa.

7. A theif has succeeded in seizing the diamonds.

8. The tool shed contained niether shovels nor rakes.

9. Because he is a weight lifter, Hugo eats plenty of protien daily.

10. The preist received his visitors in the garden at the back of the cathedral.

EXERCISE B   In each of the following sentences, underline the word in parentheses that is spelled correctly.

Example 1. The sculpture was draped with a *(viel, veil)* until the formal presentation.

11. The sculptor is a *(freind, friend)* of mine.

12. Kareem's completion of the statue was a great *(acheivement, achievement)*.

13. He has already *(received, recieved)* praise for some of his other sculptures.

14. Kareem devotes most of his *(leisure, liesure)* time to sculpting.

15. He creates statues using *(either, iether)* stone or clay.

MECHANICS

Language and Sentence Skills Practice

–cede, –ceed, and –sede

15d.   The only English word ending in **–sede** is *supersede*. The only words ending in **–ceed** are *exceed*, *proceed*, and *succeed*. Most other words with this sound end in **–cede**.

EXAMPLES   con**cede**, pre**cede**, re**cede**, ac**cede**

EXERCISE A   In each of the following sentences, underline the word in parentheses that is spelled correctly.

Example 1. After lunch, we will (*procede*, <u>proceed</u>) to install the software.

1. Bugs in the software have caused sales to (*receed*, *recede*).

2. Questions and complaints about the product (*preceded*, *preseded*) returns for refunds.

3. The software company (*conseded*, *conceded*) that an updated version is necessary.

4. Soon a new version of the program will (*superceed*, *supersede*) the current version.

5. The software company will soon (*procede*, *proceed*) to launch its advertising campaign.

6. A software company must (*acceed*, *accede*) to its customers' demands.

7. The company is confident that the new version will (*succeed*, *sucede*).

8. Expectations, however, often (*exsede*, *exceed*) reality.

9. A systems administrator must often (*intercede*, *intersede*) with software manufacturers.

10. Many software engineers work to make a software program (*succeed*, *succede*).

EXERCISE B   Underline the error in each of the following sentences. Then, above the error, write the word correctly. If a sentence is already correct, write *C* after it.

Example 1. Due to a dry spell, the water level has <u>receeded</u>. *(receded)*

11. The sound of loud laughter preseded Paul into the room.

12. The rookie player proceded to become a star outfielder.

13. Before the tides resede, we'll unload the freight from the ship at the pier.

14. The lawyer promised to intersede with the police for her client.

15. Marta is focused and dedicated; she will surely succeed at her goals.

16. Do you think the others will accede to our plan?

17. During the argument, Matt refused to conceed a single point.

18. We expect the river to recede after the rain stops.

19. The substitute teacher's plans superceded those of Mr. Beasley.

20. It is wise not to excede the speed limit.

HOLT HANDBOOK | Fourth Course

Adding Prefixes

15e. When adding a prefix, do not change the spelling of the original word.

> **EXAMPLES** pre + view = **pre**view   mis + state = **mis**state

EXERCISE On the lines provided, write each of the following words, adding the prefixes given.

Example 1. mis + use = _____*misuse*_____

1. re + decorate = _____

2. un + necessary = _____

3. re + election = _____

4. dis + service = _____

5. im + possible = _____

6. mis + matched = _____

7. pre + view = _____

8. de + regulate = _____

9. il + legible = _____

10. dis + embark = _____

11. un + pack = _____

12. im + prove = _____

13. de + rail = _____

14. un + do = _____

15. pre + fabricate = _____

16. re + evaluate = _____

17. de + construct = _____

18. mis + judged = _____

19. il + logical = _____

20. re + energize = _____

Language and Sentence Skills Practice

Suffixes –*ly* and –*ness*

15f. When adding the suffix –**ly** or –**ness,** do not change the spelling of the original word.

> **EXAMPLES**   soft + ly = **soft**ly   huge + ness = **huge**ness

Words ending in *y* usually change the *y* to *i* before –*ly* and –*ness*.

> **EXAMPLES**   busy + ly = busily   empty + ness = emptiness
> **EXCEPTIONS**   duly   slyly   truly   wholly   dryness

EXERCISE A   On the lines provided, write each of the following words, adding the suffixes given.

Example 1. large + ly = _____*largely*_____

1. severe + ly = _____

2. tidy + ly = _____

3. fresh + ness = _____

4. social + ly = _____

5. careless + ness = _____

6. barren + ness = _____

7. brave + ly = _____

8. curly + ness = _____

9. total + ly = _____

10. funny + ness = _____

EXERCISE B   Most of the following sentences contain an error in the spelling of a word ending in –*ly* or –*ness*. Underline the error. Then, above the error, write the word correctly. If a sentence is already correct, write *C* after it.

Example 1. Jill <u>loyaly</u> defended her friend's reputation.
loyally

11. Test the cake for doneness by inserting a toothpick in the center.

12. The young officer courageousely performed his duties.

13. Thea rowed her boat rapiddly across the lake.

14. Darnell's cheerfullness lifted my spirits.

15. The letter was signed, "Yours truely, A Secret Admirer."

16. The runners drank water thirstily.

17. The sweetness of the lemonade was created with an artificial sweetener.

18. These flower arrangements are really lovly!

19. The saltyness of the potato soup caused Ron not to eat it.

20. Lisa's inventivness is legendary.

Silent *e*

| **15g.** | Drop the final silent *e* before adding a suffix beginning with a vowel. |

> **EXAMPLES**   tune + ing = **tun**ing   pure + ity = **pur**ity

Exception: Keep the final silent *e* (1) in words ending in *ce* or *ge* before a suffix beginning with *a* or *o*, (2) in *dye* and in *singe* before *–ing*, and (3) in *mile* before *–age*.

> **EXAMPLES**   courage + ous = **courage**ous   dye + ing = **dye**ing   mile + age = **mile**age

| **15h.** | Keep the final silent *e* before adding a suffix beginning with a consonant. |

> **EXAMPLES**   grace + ful = **grace**ful   same + ness = **same**ness
>
> **EXCEPTIONS**   **nin**th   **aw**ful   **argu**ment

EXERCISE A   On the line provided, combine each word with the suffix, as directed.

Example 1. rate + ing = _____*rating*_____

1. scare + ing = _____

2. desire + able = _____

3. separate + ed = _____

4. fine + est = _____

5. retire + ing = _____

6. pronounce + able = _____

7. defense + less = _____

8. confine + ment = _____

9. opportune + ity = _____

10. continue + ous = _____

EXERCISE B   In each of the following groups of words, one word is misspelled. Underline the misspelled word. Then, on the line provided, write the word correctly.

Example 1. traceable, prepareing, outrageous   _____*preparing*_____

11. nineth, hopeful, hoping _____

12. advertisement, arguement, scary _____

13. mileage, rareity, coping _____

14. frustrated, laminated, eraseable _____

15. writeing, dancing, making _____

16. discouragment, taped, safest _____

17. movable, believeable, undertaker _____

18. laced, shaking, eliteist _____

19. ensnareing, movement, awful _____

20. baking, intimidateing, biting _____

Language and Sentence Skills Practice

MECHANICS

Words Ending in *y*

15i. For words ending in **y** preceded by a consonant, change the *y* to *i* before adding any suffix that does not begin with *i*.

   EXAMPLES   angry + ly = **angri**ly   happy + ness = **happi**ness   bury + ing = **bury**ing

15j. For words ending in **y** preceded by a vowel, keep the *y* when adding a suffix.

   EXAMPLES   survey + ing = **survey**ing   delay + ed = **delay**ed
   EXCEPTIONS   lay—**lai**d   pay—**pai**d   say—**sai**d   day—**dai**ly

EXERCISE In each of the following sentences, underline the word in parentheses that is spelled correctly.

Example 1. The day was filled with fun and (*merryment, merriment*).

1. Some of the teenagers (*played, plaied*) a game of touch football.

2. Ron and Frannie helped by (*carring, carrying*) bags of food to the picnic tables.

3. Martin made it his (*business, busyness*) to offer everyone a bottle of water.

4. Felix (*layed, laid*) red-and-white checkered cloths across the tables.

5. Fortunately, the mild spring weather was conducive to an (*enjoyable, enjoiable*) day outdoors.

6. Bart had (*relaid, relayed*) the message that everyone should bring sports equipment.

7. Carlos saw Jeremy (*trying, triing*) to carry a heavy plastic trash bin.

8. When Carlos peeked inside the bin, he (*spyed, spied*) dozens of water balloons.

9. Several playful dogs were (*scurring, scurrying*) among the people playing softball.

10. Doug assigned himself the (*enviable, envyable*) task of sampling desserts for the baking contest.

11. In the center of a large field, a group of friends was (*flying, fliing*) a long-tailed kite.

12. Kris (*easily, easyly*) recruited enough people for a sand volleyball game.

13. A few latecomers (*hurryed, hurried*) across the parking lot to join the crowd.

14. Someone suggested (*hungrily, hungryly*), "Let's eat!"

15. "Yes," agreed someone else. "We've (*delaid, delayed*) lunch long enough!"

16. "This banana bread has a few nuts in it," stated Marsha, "but the walnut bread is much (*nuttyer, nuttier*)."

17. Kris (*sayed, said*), "I'll have slices of both."

18. Doug asked, "How much curry is in the (*curried, curryed*) chicken?"

19. Waving her hands in front of her face, Marsha complained, "These (*flys, flies*) are everywhere!"

20. "Yes," agreed Felix, "they and the ants are (*annoying, annoyeing*)."

Doubling Final Consonants

15k.	Double the final consonant before adding a suffix that begins with a vowel if the word (1) has only one syllable or has the accent on the final syllable and (2) ends in a single consonant preceded by a single vowel.

EXAMPLES   spin + er = spi**nner**   run + ing = ru**nning**   prefer + ing = prefe**rring**

For words ending in *w* or *x*, do not double the final consonant.

EXAMPLES   few**er**   **fax**es   **throw**ing

EXERCISE A   On the line provided, combine each word with the suffix, as directed.

Examples 1. trap + ed = _____*trapped*_____

2. report + er = _____*reporter*_____

1. occur + ed = _____   **6.** happen + ed = _____

2. commit + ing = _____   **7.** perplex + ed = _____

3. shop + er = _____   **8.** snow + ing = _____

4. act + or = _____   **9.** chant + ing = _____

5. refer + al = _____   **10.** begin + er = _____

EXERCISE B   In each of the following groups of words, one word is misspelled. Underline the misspelled word. Then, on the line provided, write the word correctly.

Example 1. boxed, snaped, chatted _____*snapped*_____

11. fixxed, patted, imported _____

12. entrapped, readding, referred _____

13. jumped, guffawwing, runner _____

14. transmittable, cropped, unforgetable _____

15. packking, bowed, dropped _____

16. stabbed, trimed, cooped _____

17. taning, redder, foggier _____

18. rigging, stirring, snobish _____

19. alarmist, hiting, sadder _____

20. pretending, acquitted, treadding _____

MECHANICS

Prefixes and Suffixes Review

15e. When adding a prefix, do not change the spelling of the original word.

15f. When adding the suffix −**ly** or −**ness,** do not change the spelling of the original word.

15g. Drop the final silent *e* before adding a suffix beginning with a vowel.

15h. Keep the final silent *e* before a suffix beginning with a consonant.

15i. For words ending in **y** preceded by a consonant, change the *y* to *i* before adding any suffix that does not begin with *i.*

15j. For words ending in **y** preceded by a vowel, keep the *y* when adding a suffix.

15k. Double the final consonant before a suffix that begins with a vowel if the word (1) has only one syllable or has the accent on the final syllable and (2) ends in a single consonant preceded by a single vowel.

EXAMPLES   mis**spell, nice**ly, **din**ing, **use**ful, **liveli**ness, **enjoy**able, drop**ped**

EXERCISE   On the line provided, combine each word with the prefix or suffix, as directed.

Examples 1. ir + reversible = _____*irreversible*_____

2. spicy + ness = _____*spiciness*_____

1. dis + content = _____

2. un + natural = _____

3. im + mobile = _____

4. total + ly = _____

5. sedate + ly = _____

6. foreign + ness = _____

7. careless + ness = _____

8. dare + ing = _____

9. nice + est = _____

10. courage + ous = _____

11. deny + ed = _____

12. reply + ing = _____

13. hasty + ness = _____

14. convey + able = _____

15. deploy + ment = _____

16. annoy + ing = _____

17. bag + ed = _____

18. regret + able = _____

19. stun + ing = _____

20. plate + ful = _____

21. arrange + ment = _____

22. resolute + ly = _____

23. deny + able = _____

24. merry + ment = _____

25. alarm + ist = _____

MECHANICS

Forming Plurals of Nouns A

15l. The singular form of a noun names one person, place, thing, or idea. The plural form names more than one. Remembering the following rules will help you spell the plural forms of nouns.

(1) For most nouns, add *s*.
(2) For nouns ending in *s, x, z, ch,* or *sh,* add *es*.

   EXAMPLES   report—report**s**   class—class**es**   bench—bench**es**

(3) For nouns ending in **y** preceded by a vowel, add *s*.
(4) For nouns ending in **y** preceded by a consonant, change the *y* to *i* and add *es*.

   EXAMPLES   monkey—monkey**s**   poppy—popp**ies**

EXERCISE A   On the line following each singular noun, write its plural form.

Example 1. brush _____*brushes*_____

1. key _____
2. banana _____
3. pox _____
4. country _____
5. bunch _____
6. athlete _____
7. kiss _____
8. play _____
9. jinx _____
10. cry _____

11. crutch _____
12. bush _____
13. incinerator _____
14. crate _____
15. toy _____
16. fox _____
17. bunny _____
18. push _____
19. waltz _____
20. prefix _____

EXERCISE B   Each of the following sentences contains one plural noun that is spelled incorrectly. Underline the misspelled plural noun. Then, above it, write the correct form of the plural.

Example 1. For the costume party, we decided to go as Pilgrims and turkies. *(turkeys)*

21. We went to the costume shop to see what kinds of costumes they had hanging on the rackes.

22. Several boxxes held face paints and temporary-color hair sprays.

23. Accessorys such as wigs, hats, purses, fans, and eyeglasses were also displayed.

24. Shallow trayes beneath the glass counter displayed rings, necklaces, and fake fingernails.

25. After looking at an assortment of fake noses, masks, fake wounds, and eye patchs, I changed my mind and decided to go as a pirate.

MECHANICS

Forming Plurals of Nouns B

15l. The singular form of a noun names one person, place, thing, or idea. The plural form names more than one. Remembering the following rules will help you spell the plural forms of nouns.

(5) For some nouns ending in *f* or *fe,* add *s.* For others, change the *f* or *fe* to *v* and add *es.*

EXAMPLES   belief—belief**s**   thief—thie**ves**   leaf—lea**ves**

(6) For nouns ending in *o* preceded by a vowel, add *s.*

(7) For most nouns ending in *o* preceded by a consonant, add *es.* For some nouns ending in *o* preceded by a consonant (especially those referring to music) and for proper nouns, add *s.*

EXAMPLES   radio—radio**s**   potato—potato**es**   piano—piano**s**   Filipino—Filipino**s**

EXERCISE A   In each of the following sentences, underline the correct spelling of the word in parentheses to complete the sentence.

Example 1. Looking at the falling *(leafs, leaves)*, Rick knew he soon would be busy.

1. Rick repairs *(roofs, rooves)* and does other similar jobs.

2. Rick, Nigel, and their *(wifes, wives)* own Handy House and Lawn Services.

3. They live and work by the *(mottos, mottoses)* you see written here.

4. Hilary is a specialist at laying tiles for *(patioes, patios)*.

5. Rosa figures *(ratios, ratioes)* and analyzes figures as she manages the accounts.

6. Each day, she works with *(sheafs, sheaves)* of paper: invoices, purchase orders, work orders, and schedules.

7. Hilary recently designed a backyard garden for *(tomatos, tomatoes)* and other vegetables.

8. Nigel built new fences for a rancher who was having trouble with *(wolves, wolfs)*.

9. Rick, Nigel, Hilary, and Rosa all enjoy what they're doing with their *(lives, lifes)*.

10. They all share the same *(believes, beliefs):* find a job you enjoy, and enjoy your work every day.

EXERCISE B   In each of the following groups of plural nouns, one plural noun is misspelled. Underline the misspelled word. Then, on the line provided, write the word correctly.

Example 1. radios, sopranos, rodeoes _____*rodeos*_____

11. tempos, reefs, knifes _____

12. themselfs, cliffs, torpedoes _____

13. chefs, studioes, pianos _____

14. igloos, shelfs, tariffs _____

15. altos, mosquitoes, Eskimoes _____

Forming Plurals of Nouns C

| **15l.** | The singular form of a noun names one person, place, thing, or idea. The plural form names more than one. Remembering the following rules will help you spell the plural forms of nouns. |

(8) The plurals of a few nouns are formed irregularly.

(9) For a few nouns, the singular and the plural forms are the same.

EXAMPLES man—m**en**   ox—ox**en**   child—child**ren**

pants—pants   Japanese—Japanese   deer—deer

EXERCISE A In the following sentences, underline the correct spelling of the word in parentheses.

Example 1. The pet store has at least a dozen white (*mice, mouses*).

1. I bought a new kind of toothpaste that whitens (*teeth, tooths*).

2. The chef selected several large (*salmons, salmon*) and several lobsters.

3. The dirt path was packed hard from the tramp of many (*feet, foots*).

4. I read my little sister a bedtime story about two (*gooses, geese*) who lived in the city.

5. The group of exchange students included three (*Chineses, Chinese*).

6. Marta befriended several (*women, womans*) who jogged at the same time as she.

7. Jamaal watched with interest the documentary on (*spacecraft, spacecrafts*).

8. (*Louses, Lice*) are tiny, flat parasites with sucking mouthparts.

9. Do you remember the rhyme that begins, "Little Bo Peep has lost her (*sheeps, sheep*)"?

10. Looking at the two pairs of (*pliers, plierses*), I chose the pair with rubber-coated handles.

EXERCISE B In each of the following sentences, one plural noun is misspelled. Underline the misspelled word. Then, above it, write the word correctly.

Example 1. Kevin is a mechanic who specializes in helicopters and other *aircraft*. aircrafts.

11. The city councilmans voted to table three issues until after elections.

12. Ms. Robles, the art teacher, distributed rulers and scissorses to the classes.

13. All of the park rangers wore binocularses around their necks.

14. The team of archaeologists discovered two new specieses of dinosaurs.

15. Male mooses can weigh over 1,500 pounds.

Language and Sentence Skills Practice

Review of Forming Plurals of Nouns A

15l. The singular form of a noun names one person, place, thing, or idea. The plural form names more than one. Remembering the following rules will help you spell the plural forms of nouns.

(1) For most nouns, add *s*.
(2) For nouns ending in *s, x, z, ch,* or *sh,* add *es*.
(3) For nouns ending in *y* preceded by a vowel, add *s*.
(4) For nouns ending in *y* preceded by a consonant, change the *y* to *i* and add *es*.
(5) For some nouns ending in *f* or *fe,* add *s*. For others, change the *f* or *fe* to *v* and add *es*.
(6) For nouns ending in *o* preceded by a vowel, add *s*.
(7) For most nouns ending in *o* preceded by a consonant, add *es*.
(8) The plurals of a few nouns are formed irregularly.
(9) For a few nouns, the singular and the plural forms are the same.

EXAMPLES	pen—pens	box—boxes	guy—guys	berry—berries
	sheriff—sheriffs	thief—thieves	stereo—stereos	
	hero—heroes	tooth—teeth	deer—deer	

EXERCISE   On the line following each singular noun, write its plural form.

Examples   1. leaf _____ *leaves* _____

2. reindeer _____ *reindeer* _____

1. alley _____
2. goose _____
3. stitch _____
4. half _____
5. theory _____
6. echo _____
7. jeans _____
8. roof _____
9. burglary _____
10. gas _____
11. dish _____
12. wife _____
13. mouse _____

14. house _____
15. binoculars _____
16. tomato _____
17. knife _____
18. royalty _____
19. brush _____
20. ox _____
21. strength _____
22. child _____
23. donkey _____
24. Sioux _____
25. county _____

Compound Nouns

15l. The singular form of a noun names one person, place, thing, or idea. The plural form names more than one. Remembering the following rules will help you spell the plural forms of nouns.

(10) For most compound nouns, form the plural of only the last word of the compound.

> **EXAMPLES**   toothpick—toothpick**s**   hairbrush—hairbrush**es**

(11) For compound nouns in which one of the words is modified by the other word or words, form the plural of the word modified.

> **EXAMPLES**   mother-in-law—mother**s**-in-law   president-elect—president**s**-elect

EXERCISE A   On the line following each singular noun, write its plural form.

Example 1. phonebook _____*phonebooks*_____

1. backpack _____

2. old-timer _____

3. blueberry _____

4. ex-senator _____

5. father-in-law _____

6. fingernail _____

7. justice of the peace _____

8. navel orange _____

9. maid-of-honor _____

10. Japanese American _____

EXERCISE B   In each of the following sentences, underline the correct spelling of the word in parentheses to complete the sentence.

Example 1. One of the (<u>managers-on-duty</u>, manager-on-duties) asked for Lian's help.

11. Lian folded (tablescloth, tablecloths) and placed them on the shelves.

12. One of Lian's (sister-in-laws, sisters-in-law), Amy, entered the store.

13. As she arranged the pairs of (candlesticks, candlesstick) on shelves, Lian said hello to Amy.

14. Amy was one of the two (editor in chiefs, editors in chief) that she knew.

15. Amy worked with other (Asians American, Asian Americans) on the staff of an Asian culture

magazine.

MECHANICS

Words from Other Languages

15l. The singular form of a noun names one person, place, thing, or idea. The plural form names more than one. Remembering the following rules will help you spell the plural forms of nouns.

(12) For some nouns borrowed from other languages, plurals are formed as in the original languages.

EXAMPLES   alumnus—alumn**i**   parenthesis—parenthes**es**

A few nouns borrowed from other languages have two acceptable plural forms. A dictionary lists the preferred form in English first.

EXAMPLES   formula—formula**s** *or* formul**ae**   cactus—cactus**es** *or* cact**i**

EXERCISE   Above the underlined noun in each sentence, write its plural form.

Example 1. My mom and aunt are <u>alumna</u> of the same college.
(alumnae)

1. The painting depicted three <u>seraph</u> with angelic faces.

2. Marcos printed copies of the <u>datum</u> he found on the Internet.

3. Lunar and solar eclipses are not common <u>phenomenon</u>.

4. Thea consulted several <u>index</u> before she found the information she needed.

5. To qualify for the scholarship, an applicant would have to meet several <u>criterion</u>.

6. The detective described several <u>basis</u> for his theory.

7. Which of these <u>medium</u> do you like best: radio, television, or newspaper?

8. The Hammonds planted <u>cactus</u> beneath their windows as a security technique.

9. Your research paper should prove one thesis, not two <u>thesis</u>.

10. Part of Taylor's job is to type <u>memorandum</u>.

11. For the geometry exam, I memorized five mathematical <u>formula</u>.

12. "Do you handle <u>crisis</u> well?" asked the fire chief of the job applicant.

13. Our homework is to measure the <u>radius</u> of these circles.

14. Bradley and Oscar are <u>alumnus</u> of my high school.

15. Maria consulted two of the <u>appendix</u> for further information.

16. For tomorrow's class, read the chapter on <u>bacterium</u>.

17. David placed the quotation in <u>parenthesis</u>.

18. The tiny insect had two <u>antenna</u> on its head.

19. In his psychology class, Raleigh studied several interesting <u>psychosis</u>.

20. The valentine was decorated with hearts and two <u>cherub</u>.

Numerals, Letters, Symbols, and Words Used as Words

15l. The singular form of a noun names one person, place, thing, or idea. The plural form names more than one. Remembering the following rules will help you spell the plural forms of nouns.

(13) To form the plurals of numerals, most capital letters, symbols, and most words referred to as words, add an *s* or both an apostrophe and an *s*.

    EXAMPLES   1900—1900**s** or 1900**'s**   *X*—*X***s** or *X***'s**   *hello—hello***s** or *hello***'s**

Add both an apostrophe and an *s* to form the plurals of all lowercase letters, certain capital letters, and some words referred to as words.

    EXAMPLES   *a—a***'s**   *l—l***'s**   *chair—chair***'s**

EXERCISE Above the underlined numeral, letter, symbol, or word in each sentence, write its plural form.

    Example 1. Both of the <u>pear</u> in this circular from the market are misspelled. *(pear's)*

1. Do all e-mail addresses have <u>@</u> in them?

2. The treasure map had two large, black <u>X</u> on it.

3. We are reading poetry written in England during the early <u>1800</u>.

4. Try varying your word choice instead of using so many <u>*very*</u> in your writing.

5. <u>A</u> are my favorite grade, of course.

6. Are these capital <u>O</u>, or are they zeroes?

7. Write <u>$</u> at the left of the dollar amounts.

8. Marina had dotted all her <u>*i*</u> with little hearts.

9. I counted three <u>*um*</u> as you delivered your oral report.

10. Mark all of the extra large shirts with <u>XL</u>.

11. Most of the people in my class were born in the late <u>'80</u>.

12. My aunt thinks that <u>7</u> are lucky.

13. If you use <u>*and*</u> between the items in the list, do not use commas.

14. In her typed messages, Leona uses colons and <u>)</u> to form "smiley faces."

15. The <u>*e*</u> in the Healthy Deli's sign are burned out.

16. Gilbert's <u>*hi*</u> are always friendly.

17. How many <u>*l*</u> are in *hullabaloo*?

18. Fake phone numbers are usually formed by using <u>5</u> for the first three digits.

19. In your list of goals, use <u>*</u> to begin the items.

20. The URL should begin with three <u>w</u>.

MECHANICS

Review of Forming Plurals of Nouns B

15l. The singular form of a noun names one person, place, thing, or idea. The plural form names more than one. Remembering the following rules will help you spell the plural forms of nouns.

(10) For most compound nouns, form the plural of only the last word of the compound.

(11) For compound nouns in which one of the words is modified by the other word or words, form the plural of the word modified.

(12) For some nouns borrowed from other languages, plurals are formed as in the original languages.

(13) To form the plurals of numerals, most capital letters, symbols, and most words referred to as words, add an *s* or both an apostrophe and an *s*.

EXAMPLES	footrest—footrest**s**	chief of staff—chief**s** of staff	
	medium—medi**a**	100–100**s** or 100**'s**	*T—T***s** or *T***'s**
	&—&**s** or &**'s**	*very—very***s** or *very***'s**	

EXERCISE On the line provided, write the plural form of each of the following nouns.

Examples 1. alumnus _____*alumni*_____

2. 5 _____*5s* or *5's*_____

1. # _____

2. toothbrush _____

3. 1990 _____

4. *A* _____

5. *review* _____

6. vice president _____

7. editor in chief _____

8. parenthesis _____

9. % _____

10. *i* _____

11. *hello* _____

12. *Z* _____

13. cactus _____

14. sister-in-law _____

15. stepchild _____

16. *K* _____

17. *3* _____

18. @ _____

19. phenomenon _____

20. son-in-law _____

21. *if* _____

22. grand jury _____

23. * _____

24. 1700 _____

25. *P* _____

Numbers

15m. Spell out a number that begins a sentence.

> **EXAMPLE** **Four thousand thirty** people bought tickets to the concert series.

15n. Spell out a *cardinal number*—a number that states how many—that can be expressed in one or two words. Otherwise, use numerals.

> **EXAMPLES** The **twenty-eight** delegates represented **two thousand voters.**
>
> I believe that **4,030** people bought tickets to the concert series.

15o. Spell out an *ordinal number*—a number that expresses order.

> **EXAMPLE** This is my **fourth** hike up to the summit of Mount Whitney. [not *4th*]

15p. Use numerals to express numbers in conventional situations.

> **EXAMPLES** Room **34**   **10** percent   **56** Elm St.   July **12, 2000**   **8:30** A.M.

EXERCISE Each sentence contains two choices in parentheses. Underline the choice that completes the sentence correctly.

Example 1. <u>(Thirty-six,</u> 36) students are in my homeroom class.

1. The population of our town is *(twenty-five thousand, 25,000)* people.

2. Thanksgiving occurred on the *(27th, twenty-seventh)*.

3. My address is *(Eighty-seven, 87)* West Mapleshade Lane.

4. This is the *(tenth, 10th)* poem by Langston Hughes that I have analyzed.

5. *(Five thousand dollars, $5,000)* seems too high a price for that car.

6. The seminar will be held in the conference room in Room *(5, Five)*.

7. At the campground were *(twenty-nine, 29)* guides and 242 campers.

8. My sister's birth date is December *(twenty-five, 25)*, 1992.

9. I'll meet you after school at *(three fifteen, 3:15)*.

10. The Girl Scout troop sold over *(eight hundred, 800)* boxes of cookies.

Language and Sentence Skills Practice

353

Words Often Confused A

Review the Words Often Confused covered on pages 391–392 of your textbook for information on the correct spelling and usage of the following terms:

affect, effect   all together, altogether   brake, break
all ready, already   altar, alter   capital, capitol
all right

EXERCISE Underline the word in parentheses that correctly completes the meaning of each sentence below.

Example 1. During the test, I didn't let distractions (affect, effect) my concentration.

1. I didn't feel (all together, altogether) safe, so I asked for an escort to my car.

2. If you see debris or an animal in the road, you should (brake, break) the car.

3. The nap had a good (affect, effect) on my mood.

4. My bruised shin soon felt (all right, allright) after I applied an ice pack.

5. The boys were (already, all ready) full, so we skipped the last course.

6. Hartford is Connecticut's (capital, capitol).

7. The club members were (already, all ready) to elect a new president.

8. His snide remarks (affected, effected) my opinion of him.

9. A rounded dome complements the (capital's, capitol's) classic lines.

10. Is he sure that he'll raise enough (capital, capitol) for the business venture?

11. I have (already, all ready) been to the dentist for my six-month checkup.

12. At the front of the church were the organ, the (altar, alter), and the pulpit.

13. Once you've gathered your laundry (altogether, all together), we'll go to the laundromat.

14. "The contract will become void if you (altar, alter) it," said the lawyer.

15. The sign in the store said, "If you (brake, break) it, you buy it."

16. "We are (altogether, all together) happy to have you with us this weekend," said Grandma.

17. I use sunscreen to prevent some of the damaging (affects, effects) of the sun's rays.

18. The painting depicted a knight in armor kneeling at an (altar, alter).

19. The birthday cake and punch are (already, all ready), but the decorations are not finished.

20. Five-year-old Trina printed her name in large (capital, capitol) letters.

MECHANICS

Words Often Confused B

Review the Words Often Confused covered on pages 392–394 of your textbook for information on the correct spelling and usage of the following terms:

choose, chose   *consul, council, counsel*   *desert, desert, dessert*

coarse, course   *councilor, counselor*   *formally, formerly*

complement, compliment

EXERCISE   Underline the word in parentheses that correctly completes the meaning of each sentence below.

Example 1. We'll skip (*desert, dessert*) so we won't be late to the movie.

1. In my sewing (*coarse, course*), we are making quilt squares.

2. The City Arts (*Consul, Council, Counsel*) is petitioning the city for more funds.

3. The union president (*formally, formerly*) worked as fork lift operator.

4. Yesterday in shop class, I (*choose, chose*) my next project.

5. Most colleges have (*councilors, counselors*) available to help students adjust to college life.

6. The French (*consul, council, counsel*) in the United States held a press conference.

7. The Sahara (*desert, dessert*) is huge: it covers about 3,500,000 square miles.

8. I meant to (*complement, compliment*) you on your eloquent speech.

9. Which of your poems will you (*chose, choose*) as your contest entry?

10. Of (*coarse, course*) we will pick you up from the airport.

11. "Who would (*desert, dessert*) a cute puppy like this one?" said Josephine.

12. This evening, the mayor will (*formally, formerly*) announce his intention to run for office again.

13. The (*coarse, course*) pathway hurt the soles of my bare feet.

14. Bettina's (*council, counsel*) was this: prioritize homework and quit the part-time job.

15. Stark black does not (*compliment, complement*) everyone's complexion.

16. I would like the fruit parfait for (*desert, dessert*).

17. As an elective, I signed up for a (*coarse, course*) in screenwriting.

18. "Will the (*councilors, counselors*) approach the bench," directed Judge Jazaar.

19. When Clark fell ill, Polly (*chose, choose*) Brent as her new partner for the duet.

20. Given the situation, what would you (*council, counsel*) me to do?

Language and Sentence Skills Practice

MECHANICS

Words Often Confused C

Review the Words Often Confused covered on pages 394–395 of your textbook for information on the correct spelling and usage of the following terms:

hear, here   loose, lose   moral, morale

its, it's   miner, minor   passed, past

lead, led, lead

EXERCISE   Underline the word in parentheses that correctly completes the meaning of each sentence below.

Example 1. As part of the remodeling project, all (lead, <u>led</u>) pipes are being replaced.

1. Let's stop (hear, here) at this restaurant for a seafood dinner.

2. The brawny (miner, minor) wielded a pick and shovel.

3. If we (loose, lose) this game, we won't qualify for the playoffs.

4. We feel (its, it's) unnecessary to dress formally for dinner.

5. It is not a (miner, minor) crime for a soldier to desert the military.

6. The (moral, morale) of the story is, "The person who stands for nothing will fall for anything."

7. I can (hear, here) some church bells in the distance.

8. Who (lead, led) the band as they marched in the Fourth of July Parade?

9. "Do you know anything about the nanny's (passed, past)?" asked Corie.

10. Mr. Wharton will (lead, led) the orchestra on the concert tour.

11. Is this pipe made of steel or (lead, led)?

12. Team (moral, morale) was high after the pep rally.

13. When I apologized to Arturo, he said, "We won't dwell in the (passed, past)."

14. Bob has a habit of jingling the (loose, lose) change in his pocket.

15. The heavy wrought-iron gate sagged on (it's, its) hinges.

16. Who said, "You can (lead, led) a horse to water, but you can't make it drink"?

17. Kareem turned on his left turn signal and then (passed, past) the car in front of him.

18. Tory, a doll collector, stores each doll in (it's, its) original packaging.

19. The party can truly begin now that the band is (hear, here).

20. If you (lose, loose) my phone number, just check the phone book.

Words Often Confused D

Review the Words Often Confused covered on pages 395–397 of your textbook for information on the correct spelling and usage of the following terms:

peace, piece	*quiet, quite*	*stationary, stationery*
personal, personnel	*shone, shown*	*than, then*
principal, principle		

EXERCISE From the choices in parentheses, underline the correct word to complete each sentence.

Example 1. Roll out the pie crust; *(than, then)*, place it in the bottom of the pie plate.

1. I keep my pens and *(stationary, stationery)* in the desk.

2. Tara was careful not to drive faster *(than, then)* the speed limit.

3. At the back of the store was a door labeled "*(Personnel, Personal)* Only."

4. Our *(principal, principle)* spoke about honesty and hard work.

5. They bolted the cabinet to the floor to make the cabinet *(stationary, stationery)*.

6. LuAnn mended the hem on her dress with a *(peace, piece)* of clear tape.

7. The film festival has *(shone, shown)* two films by a university student team.

8. That night, the stars *(shone, shown)* brightly in the clear sky.

9. The *(principal, principle)* ingredients of the bread are flour, baking soda, salt, and shortening.

10. The sidewalks, coated with a thin veneer of ice, were *(quiet, quite)* slippery.

11. Domingo marked the envelope, "*(Personal, Personnel)* and Confidential."

12. Andrew's voice was *(quiet, quite)* but authoritative.

13. First we'll attend the lecture, and *(than, then)* we'll go to the reception.

14. Tonight's lecture will be shorter *(than, then)* last night's.

15. Abby felt a sense of *(piece, peace)* about the decision she had made.

16. Eric never backs down from his *(principals, principles)*.

17. The air was so still that each leaf of the tree was perfectly *(stationary, stationery)*.

18. James prepared an agenda for the meeting of company *(personal, personnel)*.

19. Steve installed the new computer game, and *(than, then)* he rebooted his computer.

20. After the treaty was signed, *(peace, piece)* prevailed.

Language and Sentence Skills Practice

Words Often Confused E

Review the Words Often Confused covered on pages 397–398 of your textbook for information on the correct spelling and usage of the following terms:

their, there, they're   waist, waste   who's, whose
to, too, two   weather, whether   your, you're

EXERCISE From the choices in parentheses, underline the correct word or word group to complete each sentence.

Example 1. Kay and Phil aren't here; I think (their, there, _they're_) hiking in the hills.

1. If the (weather, whether) is fair, we're going on a hike.

2. (Who's, Whose) dog is that?

3. The dog is going on the hike, (to, too, two).

4. I don't know (weather, whether) I can hike ten full miles.

5. (Who's, Whose) carrying a canteen or bottle of water?

6. In case of an emergency, I've got a cell phone clipped to my (waist, waste).

7. The day is (to, too, two) hot to go without a hat.

8. Make sure that (your, you're) hiking boots are laced securely.

9. We wouldn't want anyone (to, too, two) trip over loose laces.

10. Dylan and Jordan have both brought (their, there, they're) compasses.

11. If (your, you're) all ready, we'll start the hike now.

12. For the first mile, we'll walk in single file rather than (two by two, to by to, too by too).

13. As you know, all (waist, waste) paper should be "packed out"—that is, carried back out of the wilderness in your backpack or pockets.

14. We should pause and wait for Cindy and Fiona; (their, there, they're) lagging behind.

15. (Your, You're) going to enjoy the view from the top of the highest hill.

16. At regular intervals, sip water (weather, whether) you feel thirsty or not.

17. Anyone (who's, whose) not tired can continue on to the next hilltop.

18. If you are (to, too, two) tired for more hiking, you can rest here until we come back.

19. You will have regained (your, you're) strength by the time we're ready to hike home.

20. You can wait for us over (their, there, they're) under those trees.

MECHANICS

Review A: **Spelling Rules**

EXERCISE On the line provided, combine each word with the prefix or suffix or write the plural form, as directed.

Examples 1. pre + adolescence = *preadolescence*

2. thief [plural] = _____ *thieves* _____

1. sure + ly = _____

2. spy [plural] = _____

3. come + ing = _____

4. ir + reverent = _____

5. glory + ous = _____

6. belief [plural] = _____

7. co + operate = _____

8. remit + ance = _____

9. tooth [plural] = _____

10. wife [plural] = _____

11. un + necessary = _____

12. argue + ment = _____

13. dis + assemble = _____

14. donkey [plural] = _____

15. notice + able = _____

16. father-in-law [plural] = _____

17. nine + ty = _____

18. rodeo [plural] = _____

19. un + lucky = _____

20. match [plural] = _____

21. dis + agree = _____

22. marry + ing = _____

23. tomato [plural] = _____

24. box [plural] = _____

25. de + classify = _____

MECHANICS

Language and Sentence Skills Practice

Review B: Words Often Confused

EXERCISE A From the choices in parentheses, underline the correct word or word group to complete each sentence.

Example 1. LaTasha is (<u>altogether</u>, all together) pleased with her completed English paper.

1. The bride and groom stood together at the (altar, alter).

2. My brother likes science fiction better (than, then) detective stories.

3. Children learning to write often use only (capital, capitol) letters.

4. (Your, You're) not going to change my mind.

5. What are we going to have for (desert, dessert) tonight?

6. I was afraid he would (loose, lose) the money.

7. (Their, They're) planning to invite you to the party.

8. Mr. Arp has (shone, shown) us the building designed by I. M. Pei.

9. Do you know (weather, whether) cats are colorblind?

10. Her favorite (coarse, course) is history.

EXERCISE B In each of the following sentences, underline the word or word group that is used incorrectly. Above the error, write the correct word or word group to complete the sentence.

Example 1. Billie and <u>to</u> of her friends arrived at the party all together.
                two

11. The company president's personnel stationery is engraved with his initials.

12. This tire has a peace of glass embedded in its tread.

13. The effect of the magic trick was all together astonishing.

14. Whose taking you home after your soccer game?

15. In my oral report, you'll here about Emily Dickinson and the life she led.

16. Ms. Randall, is it allright if I go talk to Principal LeFevre now?

17. The consul received many complements on his political acumen.

18. During the field trip to the state capital, we took a brake to visit a water park.

19. After a noisy day at work, the minor enjoyed the peace and quiet of his cozy home.

20. I packed fruit cups for dessert since their healthier than cookies.

MECHANICS

Review C: **Spelling Rules and Words Often Confused**

MECHANICS

EXERCISE A On the line provided, combine each word with the prefix or suffix listed or write the plural form, as directed.

Examples 1. flute + ist = _____*flutist*_____

2. tributary [plural] = ____*tributaries*____

1. un + nerving = _____

2. sister-in-law [plural] = _____

3. polite + ly = _____

4. continue + ous = _____

5. *A* [plural] = _____

6. acquaint + ance = _____

7. dis + approve = _____

8. life [plural] = _____

9. nine + ty = _____

10. carry + ing = _____

11. bereave + ment = _____

12. 7 [plural] = _____

13. potato [plural] = _____

14. *&* [plural] = _____

15. chief [plural] = _____

16. tune + ing = _____

17. *very* [plural] = _____

18. ax [plural] = _____

19. conceive + able = _____

20. patio [plural] = _____

EXERCISE B From the choices in parentheses, underline the correct word or word group to complete each sentence.

Example 1. The coach decided to (*altar, alter*) a few of the plays.

21. The (*moral, morale*) is "Look before you leap."

22. What character traits are necessary to (*succeed, succede*) in life?

23. (*It's, Its*) a beautiful day, isn't it?

24. These new instructions will (*supersede, superceed*) the previous ones.

25. I think that we drove (*passed, past*) the turnoff.

Review D: Spelling Rules and Words Often Confused

EXERCISE A From the choices in parentheses, underline the correct word or word group to complete each sentence.

Example 1. The coach decided to (altar, _alter_) a few of the plays.

1. The two prospectors were lost in the (desert, dessert) for several days.

2. (10,000, Ten thousand) fans filled the concert hall.

3. Can you name all the (capital, capitol) cities in the United States?

4. I chose to take an elective (coarse, course) in dress design.

5. We will need about (100, one hundred) feet of thick rope.

6. Please dress (formally, formerly) for the party.

7. Submit your job application to the (personal, personnel) department.

8. The usher has (shone, shown) the guests to their seats.

9. Only (25, twenty-five) days remain until my birthday.

10. We plan to go first to the park and (than, then) to the movies.

EXERCISE B In each of the following groups of words, one word is misspelled. Underline the misspelled word. Then, on the line provided, write the word correctly.

Example 1. beginner, <u>curateor</u>, prefix _____ _curator_ _____

11. mouses, toothbrushes, houses _____

12. monkeys, recede, rooves _____

13. interceed, immature, chiefs of staff _____

14. children, carefuly, bitterly _____

15. diservice, accede, _a's_ _____

16. proceed, exceed, conceed _____

17. boxes, useing, trapped _____

18. churchs, parentheses, diseases _____

19. receive, weight, neice _____

20. ordinarily, truly, radicaly _____

Proofreading Application: Letter of Application

Good writers generally are good proofreaders. Learn to become a careful proofreader so that you can correct errors in grammar, usage, spelling, and punctuation. Readers will have more trust in what you're communicating if you do your best to make sure that your writing is error-free.

When you are applying for a job or internship, you know that your appearance is important. When you write a letter promoting yourself for an internship or job, the text must also have a neat appearance; that is, it should be free of errors, including misspelled and misused words and numerals.

PROOFREADING ACTIVITY

The following is a letter written to the person in charge of summer interns at a large multimedia company. It contains several misspelled and misused words. Find the errors and correct them. Use proofreading symbols to make your corrections.

Dear Dr. Ashwood:

Ms. Benitez, the councilor at my high school hear in Ithaca, in-
formmed me of your summer intern program. She payd me a nice
complement by saying that I was highly qualifyed for an internship
at your company. Ms. Benitez knows my interest in multimedia. In
actuallity, its my passion. I have taken every coarse offerred in
computers and multimedia. In addition, I spend a large amount of
time createing independent multimedia projects at home. I work pre-
dominatly with AuthorPro, although its competition, Auto-Director, is
also advantagous. The latter is preferrable when the project includes
a great deal of interactivity.

I truely hope you will consider me for an internship at Creative
Media Solutions, and I beleive you will not be disatisfied with my
creativity. I look forward to hearing from you're personal office
soon.

Sincerly,

for **CHAPTER 15: SPELLING** `pages 377–400`

Literary Model: Novel

> Still, she [Henry's mother] had disappointed him by saying nothing whatever about returning with his shield or on it. He had privately primed himself for a beautiful scene. . . . But her words destroyed his plans. She had doggedly peeled potatoes and addressed him as follows: "You watch out, Henry, an' take good care of yerself in this here fighting business—you watch out, an' take good care of yerself. Don't go a-thinkin' you can lick the hull rebel army at the start, because yeh can't. Yer jest one little feller amongst a hull lot of others, and yeh've got to keep quiet an' do what they tell yeh. . . .
>
> "If so be a time comes when yeh have to be kilt or do a mean thing, Henry, don't think of anything 'cept what's right, because there's many a woman has to bear up 'ginst sech things these times, and the Lord'll take keer of us all." . . .
>
> —from *The Red Badge of Courage* by Stephen Crane

EXERCISE A After reading the excerpt aloud, write eight words that the writer has spelled using nonstandard spelling conventions. (Hint: Do not list a word more than once. Do not include words in which an apostrophe indicates that a letter has been left out. *Amongst* is an acceptable variation in the spelling of *among*.)

_____ _____

_____ _____

_____ _____

_____ _____

EXERCISE B The author used nonstandard spelling in the speech of Henry's mother but not in the narration. Why do you think he did this, and what is the result?

_____

_____

_____

_____

_____

_____

_____

Literary Model (continued)

EXERCISE C *Dialect* is a form of speech spoken by people of a particular region or who belong to a particular group. Think of a dialect you have heard in a movie, on television, or in real life. Write one or two paragraphs spoken by someone who uses this dialect. Use nonstandard spelling conventions to help represent the dialect.

_____

_____

_____

_____

_____

_____

_____

EXERCISE D

1. Will your use of nonstandard spelling conventions benefit your reader, hinder your reader, or both? Explain your answer.

   _____

   _____

   _____

2. In what types of writing would the use of nonstandard spelling conventions be effective? Explain your answer.

   _____

   _____

   _____

Language and Sentence Skills Practice

Writing Application: Letter

At times, the spelling of a word can make a big difference. For example, *taping* a box is obviously not the same as *tapping* a box. A *miner* digs coal from the ground, but a *minor* usually doesn't. Believing in a *principle* is one thing, while believing in your *principal* is another. Unfortunately, the English language contains an impressive number of words whose spelling fails to abide by logical rules—consider the simple words *busy* and *ache*. Rules do exist, though, that can help you improve your spelling. You can also work toward mastery by memorizing the spelling of the most commonly misspelled words.

WRITING ACTIVITY

The school counselor in charge of exchange students has asked you to write a letter to Rafael Lizarraga, a sophomore student who is due to arrive in your town next month. The counselor wants you to include in the letter a warm welcome to the Chilean student, as well as information about your school and community. Because Rafael's knowledge of English is basic, he will probably be looking up many of the words you use in a Spanish-English dictionary, so it's imperative that you correctly spell every word. In your letter, include at least five words from the spelling lists and at least three words from the list of words often confused.

PREWRITING   Use a cluster diagram to break the topics "school" and "community" into smaller parts. Let one idea lead to another. Keep associating, circling, and connecting until you've completely run out of ideas.

WRITING   As you write, try to put yourself in Rafael's place: that of a teenager leaving his family and everything familiar to him to spend a year in a very different country and society. Begin your letter with words that you yourself would find welcoming. Next, write one paragraph in which you describe your community and another in which you describe your school. Use information from your cluster diagram to write these two paragraphs. Close the letter by telling Rafael how much you are looking forward to meeting him and offering your services as he gets oriented to his new life.

REVISING   Read your letter to determine whether you have expressed yourself as clearly as possible in standard formal English. (Informal and slang expressions are difficult for beginning language learners to understand.) Try to revise the descriptions of your school and community, adding vivid and precise words, so that Rafael can more easily visualize the area. Be sure that you have used at least five words from the spelling lists and at least three words from the list of words often confused.

PUBLISHING   Try proofreading your letter beginning with the bottom line and moving to the top. This will help you concentrate on locating errors in spelling, grammar, and punctuation rather than focusing on the content. Print out the letter and sign it. Then, with your teacher's permission, post it on a bulletin board in your classroom.

EXTENDING YOUR WRITING

Perhaps you and your classmates will want to put the letters in a binder and offer them to your school counselors or to the local chapter of a student foreign exchange organization. The information in the letters can be of service to persons who communicate with exchange students.

Choices: Exploring Common Errors

The following activities challenge you to identify common errors in the world around you. Do the activity below that suits your personality best, and then share your discoveries with your class.

GRAPHICS

Sound System

Grammar, usage, and mechanics are to your ability to communicate what a good sound system is to your favorite music. Are you outputting DVD or Hi Fi sound? You know the difference when you hear it, but can you describe the difference? You know good writing when you read it. Now try to describe it. Think about what makes good writing. What are its qualities and variables? Get together with some friends and give these questions some discussion. When you feel that you have a valid set of qualities, turn them into knobs and dials and slides and LCD's on a sound system. Perhaps you'll need an equalizer for agreement errors. A quality antenna for clear thought and clear references might be in order as well. When your design is complete, transfer it to poster board and color it appropriately. With your teacher's permission, hang it on the wall of your classroom, and explain your design to the class.

WRITING

Make It Your Own

Find out how many different ways there are to revise a fragment into a complete sentence. First, have each person in your class write down the following sentence fragment: "after the game." Each person's job is to write a complete sentence by adding words to the beginning, middle, or end of the fragment. When everyone is finished, have each person read his or her sentence to the group. Repeat the exercise using a few fragments of your own. You could also extend this activity by using one of the sentences as the first sentence of a story. Write the sentence at the top of a piece of paper, and then pass it around the classroom, having everyone add another sentence until the story is complete.

WRITING

Common Courtesy

Write a letter to your teacher thanking him or her and telling him or her how this class has helped you understand English better. Identify the specific areas that are no longer a problem for you or the things that particularly interested you. When you have finished writing your letter, proofread it carefully and deliver it to your teacher.

WRITING

Out of Your System

You've seen plenty of sentence fragments in your reading. Right? Everybody has. So, why, you are wondering, do grammar books make such a big deal about fragments? After all, all the best writers use them. Naturally, if you want to be a good writer, you probably want to learn to use fragments. In three pages of any kind of composition, use at least one of each kind of fragment—an appositive phrase fragment, a series of prepositional phrases, an infinitive phrase fragment, a participial phrase fragment, a gerund fragment, and at least three clause fragments. Then, write a paragraph analyzing your use of fragments. Do they make your composition stronger? Explain.

ART

Stronger, Higher, Faster

If you like to draw or paint, you may be the best person to show your class how important modifiers can be. When you draw a picture of three basketball players, for example, you make it easy for others to tell which player is tall, which one is taller, and which one is the tallest. Now, pick your own set of modifiers and illustrate them, including a caption that contains any modifiers you have brought to life in your illustration.

Sentence Fragments and Run-On Sentences A

EXERCISE Identify each of the following word groups by writing above it *F* if the word group is a sentence fragment, *R* if it is a run-on sentence, or *S* if it is a complete sentence.

Example 1. *F* Although we had already eaten dinner at home.

1. You shouldn't have said that, you probably hurt her feelings.

2. I'm sure that I left my glasses on the arm of the couch.

3. The doorbell rang, the dog barked and ran to the front door.

4. When we were at the shore last summer, every morning just after the sun came up.

5. Where in the world did you find that costume?

6. She wanted to go to the movies, but everyone else wanted to go to the ice rink.

7. This puzzle has over a thousand pieces, we've been working on it for weeks.

8. Looked through six volumes of the encyclopedia.

9. Wherever the children looked, in the yard, under the furniture, in the cupboards and closets.

10. You sound a little congested, do you have a cold?

11. After we finish folding the laundry and putting it away.

12. What an elegant coat that is!

13. Please explain that again; I don't know what you're talking about.

14. On the way to school, the most amazing car, painted purple and green.

15. How many kinds of alligators and crocodiles in that zoo?

16. Next Saturday would be better for me.

17. First we rode the Ferris wheel, then we got in line for the rollercoaster.

18. Despite the weather forecast, we planned a picnic lunch.

19. Please have a seat.

20. He woke up early, ate breakfast, and read the newspaper, after that he went to work.

Sentence Fragments and Run-On Sentences B

EXERCISE On the short lines provided, identify each numbered word group as a sentence fragment *(F)*, a run-on sentence *(R)*, or a complete sentence *(S)*. Then, on the long lines provided below, rewrite the paragraph, correcting sentence fragments and run-ons.

Example [1] ___*F*___ The idea of pools where the general public can go not being new.

The idea of pools where the general public can go is not new.

_____

[1] _____ The bath houses built by the Romans, for example. **[2]** _____ Bath houses of the ancient Roman Empire have a well-known history, often different pools were kept at different temperatures. **[3]** _____ Some of the Roman bath houses with shops, libraries, and sports facilities. **[4]** _____ Built the largest one in Rome when Emperor Caracalla ruled. **[5]** _____ Wherever the Romans went, they established such bath houses, one in England gave the town its name, Bath. **[6]** _____ A practical location because of the area's natural hot springs. **[7]** _____ Long after the fall of the Roman Empire, English people enjoyed the public pools. **[8]** _____ Baths and public pools exist in many parts of the world today, they are very popular in Japan. **[9]** _____ Both in Budapest, Hungary, and in Moscow, the capital of Russia. **[10]** _____ Pools attract people in any location, they are a good place to chat, do informal business, or just relax.

_____

_____

_____

_____

_____

_____

_____

_____

_____

_____

_____

COMMON ERRORS

Subject-Verb Agreement A

EXERCISE A In each of the following sentences, underline the verb in parentheses that agrees in number with its subject.

Example 1. Neither Renata nor her sister *(is, are)* going to the dance on Friday night.

1. Two of our cats and our dog *(were, was)* presents from my uncle and aunt.

2. Not one of our animals *(is, are)* very well-behaved.

3. The colors in that painting *(appears, appear)* particularly vibrant in this light.

4. My cousin and I usually *(ride, rides)* bikes on Saturday.

5. Which one of these sweaters *(go, goes)* with this pair of pants?

6. Both the park near the river and the baseball field *(is, are)* owned by the city.

7. Either James or Nigel *(come, comes)* from Australia.

8. *(Have, Has)* either of them ever visited New Zealand?

9. None of the children *(remembers, remember)* all of his or her telephone number.

10. My class *(is, are)* studying the formation of rivers and lakes.

EXERCISE B In each of the following sentences, cross out any verb that does not agree with its subject, and write the correct form of the verb above the incorrect form. If all the verbs in a sentence are correct, write *C* above the sentence.

Example 1. Either Jessica or Kai ~~practice~~ *practices* piano for two hours every day.

11. You must be thinking about Jessica; Kai plays the violin.

12. How do she find the time to practice that much?

13. Both she and her brother wakes up early every morning to practice.

14. Do her brother play an instrument, too?

15. He takes violin lessons with Kai, but he also enjoys practicing with his sister.

16. Neither Jessica nor her brother mind the practice time.

17. One of their grandmothers—their mother's mother—are a professor of music at the university.

18. The whole family, including their other brother and both parents, have musical talent.

19. Have either Jessica or anyone else in her family ever played in public?

20. None of them play professionally, but all of them belong to music groups.

Subject-Verb Agreement B

EXERCISE A In each of the following sentences, decide whether the underlined verb agrees in number with its subject. If the verb form is incorrect, cross it out, and write above it the correct form. If the verb is already correct, write *C* above it.

Example 1. Each of the houses on that block ~~are~~ *is* painted a different color.

1. The book that I borrowed last month <u>is</u> overdue.

2. Unless he <u>get</u> up too late, Ralph usually walks to school.

3. Neither Russell nor his brothers <u>has</u> ever been on an airplane.

4. One of his brothers <u>want</u> to be a pilot.

5. Both my grandfather and his brother, my great-uncle Bill, <u>live</u> in Fargo.

6. They used to be farmers, but neither of them <u>farm</u> any longer.

7. Miguel, together with Alicia and Heather, <u>have</u> prepared a slide show.

8. The layout on these pages of the newspaper <u>look</u> too crowded to me.

9. Most of the children in that elementary school <u>live</u> in this neighborhood.

10. <u>Are</u> either the pool in Garrison Park or the pool in Stacy Park open yet?

EXERCISE B In each of the following sentences, circle the subject of the underlined verb. Then, if the verb does not agree in number with its subject, write the correct form of the verb above the incorrect form. If the verb already agrees, write *C* above it.

Example 1. The mother of those boys is upset because (both) of them <u>was</u> *were* playing in the street.

11. The rehearsal will not begin until all of the musicians <u>have</u> taken their seats.

12. One of the trombone players and one of the clarinetists <u>is</u> missing.

13. If seventy-five percent of the eggs <u>hatches</u>, how many chicks will we have?

14. Marissa, along with several of her classmates, <u>volunteer</u> at the children's hospital.

15. The price of avocados <u>have</u> varied a lot over the past year.

16. Spaghetti and meatballs <u>is</u> my father's favorite dish.

17. If the majority of the club <u>don't</u> want to meet next month, then we'll cancel the meeting.

18. The highlight of the banquet <u>were</u> the awards.

19. Two fifths of my allowance <u>go</u> into my savings account.

20. How many pieces of chicken <u>do</u> we need for the picnic?

COMMON ERRORS

Pronoun-Antecedent Agreement A

EXERCISE A   In each of the following sentences, circle the antecedent of the pronoun in parentheses. Then, underline the pronoun in parentheses that agrees with the antecedent.

Example 1. Every (student) in the class has to finish (*their*, <u>*his or her*</u>) project by next Friday.

1. Some people say that dogs come when you call (*it*, *them*), but cats take a message and get back to you later.

2. One of the girls in my gym class twisted (*their*, *her*) ankle on the stairs.

3. The members of the concert band will arrive early to tune (*its*, *their*) instruments.

4. How long has the United States had (*their*, *its*) present system of government?

5. Every citizen should exercise (*their*, *his or her*) right to vote.

6. Anyone who is entering a project in the science fair should set up (*his or her*, *their*) display.

7. If we work together with the ninth-graders to raise the funds (*themselves*, *ourselves*), we won't have to ask our parents for so much money for the trip.

8. Reggie and Clara reminded (*themselves*, *himself or herself*) that the last bus would leave at 6:00 P.M.

9. If they miss that bus, one of them will have to call (*his or her*, *their*) parents for a ride.

10. Unless we can use the darkroom, we won't be able to develop (*our*, *their*) photographs.

EXERCISE B   In each of the following sentences, cross out any pronoun that does not agree with its antecedent. Then, write the correct pronoun above the incorrect pronoun. If the sentence is already correct, write *C* above it.

Example 1. The new camera club has already elected ~~their~~ *its* officers.

11. All three runners from our school have finished her races.

12. My dog Dusty, who was one of a litter of seven puppies, is sleeping in her doghouse.

13. Clay's younger brother and sister always have peanut butter sandwiches in his or her lunches.

14. Not everyone has turned in his or her permission form yet.

15. Most of the books looked interesting, but it cost too much.

16. I prefer to use molasses because their taste is stronger and more distinctive.

17. The encyclopedia is on the shelves over there; which volumes of it do you need?

18. Rachel, who shares a room with two of her sisters, really enjoys her company.

19. According to my father, when he and his brother were young, he both liked spinach.

20. A search party located the boys in the morning, after they had looked for them all night.

HOLT HANDBOOK | Fourth Course

Pronoun-Antecedent Agreement B

EXERCISE Complete each of the following sentences by writing a pronoun that agrees with its antecedent.

Example 1. We need to repair these stone walls before one of _____ *them* _____ collapses.

1. I need the scissors, but I can't remember where I left _____.

2. Anyone who hasn't decided on a topic needs to make _____ decision.

3. Both Clarence and his brother keep _____ in good condition.

4. My grandparents rode in the camper, and my cousin drove _____ car for them.

5. One of our dogs enjoys _____ bath, but the other runs away when it's time

   for a bath.

6. Despite _____ fatigue, the hikers set up camp and cooked a simple meal.

7. Let the bread cool on a rack after you take _____ out of the oven.

8. The booster club members met _____ fund-raising goal.

9. Measure two thirds of a cup of milk and mix _____ into the batter.

10. When the ten o'clock news comes on, _____ may have a story about the

    regional track meet.

11. The soccer team was disappointed that _____ did not make a single goal.

12. I won't make that pasta and casserole again; none of the guests seemed to like

    _____.

13. Rowena took her little brother to the barber shop to have _____ hair cut.

14. Either Michael or Fernando hopes to become a doctor when _____ grows up.

15. According to my count, only about thirty percent of the plastic containers we collected are

    recyclable; maybe we should count _____ again.

16. Please ask those people over there if one of them left _____ umbrella in the

    auditorium.

17. All of the members have agreed to bring _____ photographs.

18. None of the boys would admit that _____ had broken the window.

19. The judge asked the jury if _____ needed more time to reach a decision.

20. Please get the bag of groceries out of the car and put _____ on the table.

Language and Sentence Skills Practice

Pronoun Forms A

EXERCISE A In each of the following sentences, underline the correct pronoun in parentheses.

Example 1. No one on my team runs faster than (*him*, *he*).

1. Mr. Jeffers asked us, Tranh and (*I*, *me*), to join your group.

2. Neither of (*we*, *us*) tap dance fans can even do the two-step.

3. All of the other girls on the golf team have had more practice than (*she*, *her*).

4. It is (*they*, *them*) who are making a mistake they will regret.

5. The sudden screeching of an owl startled the new scouts and (*he*, *him*).

6. The Nobel Prize will be awarded to four other scientists and (*she*, *her*) this year.

7. My parents always like to know (*who*, *whom*) else is invited to the party.

8. Leo's manager gave Jenna and (*he*, *him*) a lesson about the cash register.

9. Your friends claim that you are a better cook than (*I*, *me*).

10. Mrs. Wong, Coach Wood, and (*she*, *her*) have agreed to serve as sponsors.

EXERCISE B In each of the following sentences, cross out any incorrect pronoun and write the correct pronoun above it.

Example 1. She and ~~me~~ are the only students who finished the test early.

11. Do you know whom is rehearsing on the stage this afternoon?

12. The salesclerk showed my mother and I at least ten pairs of shoes.

13. Us tenth-graders are already looking forward to graduation.

14. My family and me have visited over twenty national parks.

15. We were supposed to meet Clarissa and Mario at the movies, but we didn't hear from they in time.

16. The chores were divided among David, Kevin, and he.

17. Whomever wants to work on the mural should wear old clothes on Friday.

18. Take Ms. Simmons and he these papers when you go to the office.

19. The woman who designed the winning float in the parade is her.

20. To who should the students turn in this application, and by when?

Pronoun Forms B

EXERCISE In each of the following sentences, underline the correct pronoun in parentheses. Then, identify the use of the pronoun by writing above it *S* for *subject*, *PN* for *predicate nominative*, *DO* for *direct object*, *IO* for *indirect object*, *OP* for *object of a preposition*, or *A* for *appositive*.

                                   A

Example 1. My best friends, Tammy and *(her, she)*, gave me a surprise party on my birthday.

1. *(Whom, Who)* wants to help make posters this weekend?

2. Please show *(us, we)* drama students the plans for the new auditorium.

3. Four of my cousins, Rich, Steve, Karen, and *(he, him)*, are older than I am.

4. Nadia couldn't remember whether she had invited Carol and *(she, her)* to the party.

5. The most cheerful person in our class is *(her, she)*.

6. The coach asked three members of the team—Nick, Calvin, and *(me, I)*—to stay after practice for a few minutes.

7. Next summer, my father will teach my brother and *(I, me)* how to drive a car.

8. LaShonda didn't think the tomatoes looked ripe, so she didn't buy any of *(they, them)*.

9. Either *(she, her)* or her grandmother does most of the family's grocery shopping.

10. After *(them, they)* pick up their clothes, we will take the children to the park.

11. What Simone and *(she, her)* planned to wear to the costume party was a big secret.

12. After we ran into Celie and Carl outside the restaurant, we went inside and sat with *(him or her, them)* for a few minutes.

13. Are the women who own the landscaping business *(them, they)*?

14. *(Them, They)* and my brothers have gone to the same summer camp every year.

15. Didn't your grandmother ask you to mow the lawn for *(she, her)*?

16. The people you wanted me to call and remind about the meeting are *(who, whom)*?

17. Kristin, Maxine, Lena, and Tom are some of the students *(who, whom)* should be asked to help.

18. Tell Nate or *(I, me)* the combination to your locker so that one of us can bring your books home for you.

19. After the dance performance, my parents gave flowers to my sister and *(me, I)*.

20. Please draw Sam and *(I, me)* a map to your house.

COMMON ERRORS

Clear Pronoun Reference A

EXERCISE   On the lines provided, rewrite the following sentences, correcting any inexact pronoun references. If a sentence is already correct, write *C* on the line.

Example 1. I didn't want a second helping of spaghetti, which no one at the table could believe.

No one at the table could believe that I didn't want a second helping of spaghetti.

1. Before Ann and Miriam started their research, she had to sharpen her pencils.

_____

2. Whenever the sky looks that threatening, it usually means we can expect a bad thunderstorm.

_____

3. My brothers like to jump on the trampoline, which is why they are always at Neil's house.

_____

4. In the newspaper article, it did not say when the parade will start.

_____

5. My aunt and uncle told my parents that they would not be able to go to the concert.

_____

6. In my school, they like to have an assembly every Friday morning.

_____

7. According to the report I heard, teenagers and young adults are not getting enough calcium.

_____

8. My father told my brother that he needed to get the car washed.

_____

9. If we want to be on time, that means we'd better leave in the next ten minutes.

_____

10. Julie repeated the instructions to Cynthia until she was sure that she could do the problem.

_____

Clear Pronoun Reference B

EXERCISE On the lines provided, rewrite the following sentences, correcting any inexact pronoun references. If a sentence is already correct, write *C* on the line.

Example 1. On the sign outside the store, it said "No dogs allowed."

The sign outside the store said "No dogs allowed."

1. Raul admired sketches of buildings, which is why he thought of being an architect.

_____

2. In the fourteenth chapter, the author explains about red and white blood cells.

_____

3. The bank apologized for the inconvenience, but this was no comfort to the clients in line.

_____

4. Even though rain was predicted, it didn't stop them from counting on this picnic.

_____

5. The specialist and the patient discussed the problems she had been having.

_____

6. On the radio, they said the price of gasoline is going up again.

_____

7. For the choir's first selection, it was a medley of spirituals.

_____

8. The visiting authors talked to the students about their writing.

_____

9. Rosanne reminded Matty to choose a recipe that she would find easy to prepare.

_____

10. By the time Cletus got the clothes off the line, it had already started raining.

_____

COMMON ERRORS

Verb Tense

EXERCISE A   In each of the following sentences, determine whether the underlined verb is in the correct tense. If the tense of the verb is incorrect, write the correct form of the verb above the incorrect form. If the tense of the underlined verb is already correct, write *C* above it.

arrive
Example 1. When you arrived at the theater, please look for us.

1. Last Friday night, we had gone to the game after we ate dinner.

2. By this time next week, we will have finished our review of geometric solids.

3. When we visited the Bahamas last summer, we have seen some amazing fish.

4. Despite the advances that medical science has made, much research into the causes of cancer
   remained to be done.

5. If the train leaves at 4:00 p.m., we will have arrived before dark.

6. When she calls, I had already begun to cook dinner.

7. I have removed the hinges and sanded the door, so now I was ready to paint.

8. The dog had dug a hole under the fence and has escaped from the yard.

9. Before the alarm begins to ring, I was already up and dressed.

10. On Saturday mornings, we usually eat a late breakfast, run errands, and have done chores.

EXERCISE B   The verb tenses in the following paragraph are used inconsistently and illogically. Underline any verb that is in the incorrect tense, and write the correct form of the verb above it.

live
Example   [1] The Basques are a group of people who will have lived on both sides of the

border between France and Spain.

[11] The Basque area in the western Pyrenees Mountains will undergo political change in recent times. [12] Even though King Juan Carlos began to return Spain to democratic rule in 1975, the Basque inhabitants would want independence. [13] In 1980, the people of this unique region are voting overwhelmingly for self-government. [14] Spain decides to grant them home rule. [15] The Basque inhabitants, with their distinct culture and language, would have wanted home rule for a long time.

Verb Forms A

EXERCISE In each of the following sentences, underline the incorrect verb form and write the correct form above it.

Example 1. None of the students had *spoken* ~~speaked~~ to the teacher about the homework assignment.

1. At the bookstore, I choosed a biography and two books of poetry.

2. By the time we reached the station, our train had already leaved.

3. Please sit the vase of flowers in the middle of the dining room table.

4. The team was disappointed because they had losed the game.

5. I could have buyed three new sweaters for the amount of money that jacket cost.

6. She would have enjoyed the campout more if she had brung her scarf and hat.

7. The children slowly drug the toboggan up the hill.

8. I would have ate more of my lunch, but I ran out of time.

9. That old dog has been laying in the shade all day.

10. By tonight, I will have wrote more than ten pages of my paper.

11. I wish my mother had talked to me before she throwed my old shoes away.

12. All night long, the wind from the ocean blowed strongly.

13. Before my grandfather could became a U.S. citizen, he had to pass a test.

14. Nicholas and his sister have swam in this lake before.

15. My family seeked advice from our mechanic when we wanted to buy a new car.

16. The horse must have ran away during the night.

17. How many times do you think we have rode this bus to school in the past two years?

18. I couldn't hear her very well, but I think that's what she meaned.

19. Ray turned on the news to find out if the temperature had raised.

20. The girls had already send the pictures to their grandparents.

COMMON ERRORS

Language and Sentence Skills Practice

Verb Forms B

EXERCISE A On the line provided, write the correct past or past participle form of the verb given.

Example 1. *take*   By next year, Berto will have _____*taken*_____ his driver's test.

1. *begin*   Six weeks ago, Berto and Salim _____ a driving class.

2. *drive*   The two friends have _____ on freeways and narrow roads.

3. *forget*   Once Salim observed, because he had _____ his learner's permit.

4. *become*   Both sophomores have _____ quite confident of their skills.

5. *go*   Berto won't discuss the day he almost _____ through a red light.

6. *give*   As his older sister, I have _____ him plenty of advice.

7. *speak*   Yesterday, the instructor _____ highly of him to our parents.

8. *ride*   I have _____ with him, and I must admit he's careful.

9. *swear*   He and his friend Salim have _____ to improve the reputation of

teenage drivers.

10. *get*   I know I was happy when I _____ my license.

EXERCISE B In each of the following sentences, underline the base form of the verb that will complete the sentence correctly. Then, on the line provided, write the correct form of the verb.

Example 1. *lie, lay*   Malcolm's sunburn proved he had _____*lain*_____ in the sun too long.

11. *rise, raise*   Every morning, just before the sun _____, our rooster crows.

12. *sit, set*   I never _____ my alarm clock.

13. *lie, lay*   Even on Sundays, when most people _____ in bed a little longer, I

am up at the crack of dawn.

14. *lie, lay*   Last Sunday, I _____ my head back down, and covered my ears.

15. *rise, raise*   We have _____ chickens, ducks, and geese for many years.

16. *sit, set*   Whenever we _____ in the yard, the chickens come to visit.

17. *rise, raise*   When my little brother chased one of the geese, it _____ its wings.

18. *sit, set*   The hens are usually _____ on their eggs.

19. *lie, lay*   One of the hens _____ her eggs under our porch.

20. *sit, set*   Don't _____ your lemonade down; the ducks will drink it.

COMMON ERRORS

Comparative and Superlative Forms A

EXERCISE A In each of the following sentences, underline the correct form of the adjective or adverb in parentheses.

Example 1. This fireworks display is (*impressiver, more impressive*) than last year's was.

1. Which of your two neighbors have you known (*longer, longest*)?

2. She always finished her work (*more quickly, quicklyer*) than anyone else.

3. His brother has some of the (*more interesting, most interesting*) fish I've ever seen.

4. None of the students, including Jorge, is (*ready, readier*) for the test.

5. (*Mucher, More*) work remains to be done in that area.

6. These are some of the (*most aggressive, more aggressive*) mosquitoes we've encountered all summer.

7. Unfortunately, (*manier, many*) children in the United States are not covered by health insurance.

8. Samantha did a lot (*well, better*) on her test than she thought she would.

9. It's too bad that he had to leave the game early because he didn't feel (*better, well*).

10. In high school we have (*more, manier*) classes that last longer than an hour.

EXERCISE B In the following sentences, underline any double comparison or other error in the use of comparative and superlative forms of modifiers. Then, write the correct form above the incorrect usage.

Example 1. Someday I will explore the most deepest parts of the ocean.
deepest

11. Believe it or not, the world ocean—called that because all oceans are connected—is the most largest region on earth.

12. Many find its scenery more spectacularer than any landscape.

13. Learning that seventy percent of the earth's surface is water, people are more respectfuller of the world ocean.

14. If Mount Everest were submerged in the most deep part of the ocean, its peak would be a mile below the surface.

15. In the future, gooder research of ocean life may help solve the problem of food shortages.

Comparative and Superlative Forms B

EXERCISE A In each of the following sentences, underline the correct form of the adjective or adverb in parentheses.

Example 1. Of these four puppies, which do you like *(better, best)*?

1. *(More, Most)* trees in our yard still have their leaves.

2. What is the *(least, lowest)* offer you will accept for the car?

3. He usually doesn't hear *(worse, badly)*, but he has an ear infection.

4. That little girl just told me the *(delightfulest, most delightful)* story!

5. She couldn't decide whether she liked the coat or the jacket *(best, better)*.

6. When the peaches are *(ripe, more riper)*, we will pick our own at a nearby orchard.

7. I wish I had heard *(much, more)* music, but I had to leave early.

8. The discussion this afternoon will be *(more informal, informaller)* than yesterday's

discussion was.

9. Can you solve this puzzle in the *(fewer, fewest)* possible moves?

10. These potato pancakes taste *(weller, better)* than the ones I ate last week.

EXERCISE B In the following sentences, underline any double comparison or other error in the use of comparative and superlative forms of modifiers. Then, write the correct form above the incorrect usage.

Example 1. This talk show host's stories are even more *sillier* than his jokes are.

11. I agree; this is probably the most boringest show I've seen in a long time.

12. We should spend least time watching TV.

13. Well, some programs are a lot more better than this one is.

14. Why are some of the people on television paid mucher money than others?

15. You and I did watch a gooder series about space exploration recently.

Misplaced Modifiers

EXERCISE On the lines provided, rewrite the following sentences to correct the misplaced modifiers. You may need to rearrange or add words to make the meaning of a sentence clear.

Example 1. I unintentionally put the pen into my shirt pocket that was leaking.

_____ *I unintentionally put the pen that was leaking into my shirt pocket.* _____

1. Singing an ancient spiritual song, the tourists listened to the old people of the village.

_____

2. Vast and calm, we watched the sun set over the Pacific Ocean.

_____

3. The crowd cheered as the runner rounded the bases, stomping and whistling loudly.

_____

4. The hurricane finally hit the coast that had been stalled out in the ocean.

_____

5. Twitching its tail and meowing hungrily, the man placed a saucer of food in front of the kitten.

_____

6. The woman gave one of the cones to a man, who had bought two ice cream cones.

_____

7. As we walked among the trees, we could hear the songs of the birds, towering and ancient.

_____

8. Rolling down the hill backwards, the man ran after his car.

_____

9. When she fell off the tricycle, the woman comforted the little girl.

_____

10. The purple martin house is now occupied by sparrows that we put up last fall.

_____

Dangling Modifiers

EXERCISE On the lines provided, rewrite each of the following sentences to correct the dangling modifier. You may need to rearrange or add words to make the meaning of a sentence clear.

Example 1. After an exciting day at the amusement park, dinner at home was relaxing.

After an exciting day at the amusement park, we had a relaxing dinner at home.

1. While waiting in line, the music started.

_____

2. Before visiting my grandparents, the flat tire had to be fixed.

_____

3. To teach someone to drive, patience and a calm manner are important.

_____

4. When sledding down the big hill near my house, a rock was in the path of the sled.

_____

5. Prepared and well-rested, the final exam in geometry was not at all difficult.

_____

6. Leaving through a gate that someone had left open, the road was blocked by the cows' passage.

_____

7. Determined to unravel the mystery, all the clues were re-examined.

_____

8. Hurrying through the crowd as the final whistle blew, the train pulled out of the station.

_____

9. As a stranger in the city, the one-way streets and traffic circles were confusing.

_____

10. Weary from days of traveling under the hot desert sun, the oasis provided shade and water.

_____

COMMON ERRORS

HOLT HANDBOOK | Fourth Course

Misplaced and Dangling Modifiers

EXERCISE Each of the following sentences contains a dangling or misplaced modifier. On the lines provided, rewrite each sentence so that its meaning is clear.

Example 1. The hikers were prepared to take photos of butterflies walking along the path.

Walking along the path, the hikers were prepared to take photos of butterflies.

1. After next week our supervisor selected two trainees to assume regular duties.

_____

2. While reaching for the second prize, the first place trophy was knocked over by Pete.

_____

3. To achieve a higher grade on finals, steady learning throughout the term is wise.

_____

4. After being left in disrepair, we found the cabin roof let in rain and wind.

_____

5. Aunt Lyla saw a poodle on her way to the dentist.

_____

6. Allison posted her report card on the refrigerator, full of self-confidence.

_____

7. Walking the dogs in the park on Sunday afternoon, it began to rain hard.

_____

8. Repainted from top to bottom, the neighbors admired the historic cottage.

_____

9. The principal said there was too much trash on the floor over the loudspeaker.

_____

10. Having filled out the application, an interview with a supervisor was set up.

_____

COMMON ERRORS

Double Negatives and Other Errors

EXERCISE A　In the following sentences, eliminate any double negatives by crossing out incorrect words and writing the correct forms above them if necessary.

Example 1. I couldn't see ~~no one~~ *anyone* around to help me.

1. We were so tired that we couldn't barely put one foot in front of the other.

2. There weren't no sandwiches left by the time I got through the cafeteria line.

3. That store doesn't accept no employment applications by telephone.

4. She looked for graph paper everywhere in the house, but she didn't find none.

5. Jerome didn't want to read neither of those books for his report.

6. My mother said that we can't go swimming in the river no more.

7. Don't tell me you haven't never eaten Italian food!

8. Why didn't no one remember to bring a camera?

9. Wasn't nobody available to unlock the gymnasium doors?

10. The little boys were so excited that they couldn't hardly sleep the night before the trip.

EXERCISE B　On the lines provided, rewrite each of the following sentences to correct any double negatives and other errors in usage.

Example 1. There wasn't hardly anybody on the beach early this morning.

　　　Hardly anybody was on the beach early this morning.

11. Ain't nobody come up with that idea before.

_____

12. We can't bag no more trash until the trucks haul this load away.

_____

13. Losing her temper, my little sister said, "Can't nobody tell me what to do!"

_____

14. Don't you want no second helping of these mashed potatoes?

_____

15. The streets were so confusing that we couldn't scarcely tell which way to turn.

_____

Standard Usage A

EXERCISE A In each of the following sentences, underline the correct word or words in parentheses.

Example 1. The cat was (setting, <u>sitting</u>) on the table, licking its whiskers.

1. Despite the hours she spent studying, she did (real, really) (bad, badly) on the exam.

2. Could you (loan, lend) me five dollars until the weekend?

3. There are (alot, a lot) (fewer, less) clouds in the sky than there were earlier today.

4. He (use, used) to repair his guitar (hisself, himself).

5. From (they're, their) discussion during class, she (inferred, implied) that everyone agreed with her position.

6. The story of my grandfather's (immigration, emigration) from Russia has been passed down for generations.

7. Naomi's mother said that she would (learn, teach) us two girls how to weave.

8. (Whom, Who) were you calling on the telephone?

9. The movie (what, that) I told you about is (suppose, supposed) to start at eight o'clock.

10. Some books, such as *Uncle Tom's Cabin* and *The Jungle*, have (affected, effected) social change.

EXERCISE B On the lines provided, rewrite each of the following sentences to correct any errors in usage.

Example 1. Matt decided to try and remember whether he might of loaned his bike to James.
    Matt decided to try to remember whether he might have loaned his bike to James.

11. She ought not to of turned off the alarm clock, but she was kind of tired this morning.

_____

12. The reason she can't hardly keep her eyes open is because she stayed up late last night.

_____

13. We probably should of planted less flowers and more vegetables this year.

_____

14. A number of students was standing in the hallway like they didn't have nowheres to go.

_____

15. Without they catch a later train, they don't have but two hours to tour the museum.

_____

COMMON ERRORS

Standard Usage B

EXERCISE A In the following sentences, underline the words that are used incorrectly or informally according to the rules of standard English usage. Then, write the correct usage above the incorrect usage.

supposed to have
Example 1. We were <u>suppose to of</u> been there an hour ago.

1. The candy and trinkets were divided between the triplets.

2. You will burn up less calories walking than jumping rope.

3. Beside American history and chemistry, Mia studies algebra.

4. Being that it is noon, lunch hour begins now.

5. In Shakespeare's works are many illusions to mythology.

6. That there dog doesn't like the mail carrier.

7. She read where the tickets would go on sale at seven o'clock in the morning.

8. He would of called, but he was already late.

9. Don't he know that the moon affects the tides?

10. Do you think you can get this strawberry jam stain off of my shirt?

EXERCISE B On the lines provided, rewrite the following paragraph, correcting any words or phrases used incorrectly or informally according to the rules of standard English usage.

Example [1] Are you inferring that he don't really want a job?

 Are you implying that he doesn't really want a job?

[11] I would not of believed what my friend Ike wore to his job interview if I had not seen him with my own eyes. [12] Beside a tuxedo with plaid lapels, he wore a top hat whose brim was bent. [13] He looked like he might of been going to a prom during the days of Charles Dickens! [14] I told him that wearing those kind of clothes for an interview at the ice cream shop could backfire some, but my warning had no affect on him. [15] Hopefully, he learned his lesson, but he is still looking everywheres for a place to earn money this summer.

_____

_____

_____

_____

_____

for **CHAPTER 16: CORRECTING COMMON ERRORS**   *pages 266–85*

Capitalization A

EXERCISE A In each of the following sentences, circle any letter that should be capitalized but is not.

Example 1. Do you want to go out for (c)hinese or (i)talian food with (a)unt (r)ita and (u)ncle (n)ick?

1. jean lives with her family in the hancock arms apartments on forty-fifth street.

2. mom and dad's business advisor, uncle raymond, developed the advertising campaign.

3. greta read me an article about buddhist monasteries in tibet.

4. Most passenger trains in the u.s., such as the *sunset limited*, are run by amtrak.

5. Everyone in the ecology club voted for a trip to the atlantic coast.

6. classes at tubman high school begin august 30, but the next monday, labor day, is a holiday.

7. "I asked dad," reggie began, turning to look at frank, "if he could take us fishing at lake jefferson."

8. visitors to yosemite and yellowstone national parks have the opportunity to see some of the most beautiful areas of the american west.

9. your parents or grandparents probably remember exactly where they were when they heard that president john f. kennedy was assassinated on november 22, 1963.

10. Every year on halloween, our radio station replays orson welles's adaptation of h.g. wells's novel *The War of the Worlds*.

EXERCISE B Most of the sentences in the following paragraph contain capitalization errors. Circle any letter that should be capitalized and draw a slash (/) through any letter that should be lowercase. If the capitalization in a sentence is correct, write *C* above the sentence.

Example [1] (O)n (j)uly 15, the /Morning /Edition of the newspaper carried an apology and a correction from the /Editor, (j)ames (w)ylie.

[11] The *gracy city gazette* always apologizes for its errors. [12] The article we printed on tuesday, "on with the festival!," was not entirely accurate. [13] We misquoted the dates for the peaches and cream festival. [14] a parade will kick off festivities on july 29. [15] Gracy City council members will lead the way to the norwegian Pioneer memorial monument in lincoln park. [16] They will also hold groundbreaking ceremonies for the new gracy memorial hospital after the parade. [17] Festival activities will continue through the third of August. [18] we hope this clears up any inaccurate information printed by this Newspaper. [19] Please accept editor wylie's apologies for earlier errors. [20] Most of all, don't forget to join your neighbors for all the Summer fun!

Language and Sentence Skills Practice

COMMON ERRORS

Capitalization B

EXERCISE   In each of the following sentences, circle any letter that should be capitalized and draw a slash (/) through any letter that should be lowercase.

Example 1. did you ask dr. fishbein or her Dental Assistant about your toothache during your appointment last friday?

1. Mom and dad always watch *meet the press* and *washington week in review* on Sunday mornings.

2. Simms & sons, on Fifty-Seventh street, is a Company that specializes in restaurant furniture.

3. In *The westing game,* a novel by ellen raskin, the lyrics of "America The Beautiful" provide clues to the Mystery.

4. "Ladies and Gentlemen," the speaker began, "we must let the Mayor and City Council know exactly how we feel about the plans to put a Natural Gas pipeline through our neighborhoods."

5. In england, boxing day, the day after christmas, is the traditional day to exchange gifts.

6. That airline does not fly to New Mexico's Capital, santa fe.

7. Our neighbor, dr. pat kelly, has a ph.d. degree in american history, not an m.d. degree.

8. The university of texas at austin and the university of michigan in ann arbor have Tens of Thousands of students.

9. does mr. keaton expect us to read this whole chapter, "the westward expansion," in one night?

10. I didn't see that Program last tuesday because our town does not have an nbc affiliate.

11. The audience waited while senator bates organized her notes and adjusted the microphone.

12. The cats, persephone and demeter, were named after characters in Ancient Greek Myths.

13. The north star, polaris, appears to be almost directly above the north pole.

14. When you reach the Intersection of broadway and san pedro street, turn right, or east.

15. The vcr isn't working, so I guess we'll have to listen to cds.

16. Send your film to p.o. box 11122, seattle, wa 99002; you'll receive your pictures and a free roll of film in about Two Weeks.

17. Does the museum of modern art have any Summer internships for High School students?

18. Unless you live in the southern hemisphere, you won't be familiar with Constellations such as the southern cross and centaurus.

19. The defense lawyer refused to comment about judge mewhirter's ruling.

20. "In case of an Emergency," the notice read, "Please call 911 to reach ems or the police."

Commas A

EXERCISE In each of the following sentences, insert commas where necessary.

Example 1. Mr. Wilson, would you initial my schedule change, please?

1. Do you want to walk to school tomorrow morning or should we sleep a little later and catch the bus?

2. This recipe calls for nuts raisins and chocolate chips.

3. On Tuesday October 24 at 4:00 p.m. the junior class will assemble in the auditorium.

4. No I appreciate the invitation but I've already made plans for Saturday night.

5. Whenever I see a rainbow I recall my grandmother's stories about leprechauns and their pots of gold.

6. That man Jesse's uncle works for one of the airlines in Dallas Texas.

7. Ms. Branter who teaches physical education classes coaches the soccer and volleyball teams.

8. Many people celebrated the end of the millennium on December 31 1999 but others insisted upon waiting until December 31 2000.

9. He wanted to go skateboarding with his friends of course but he hadn't finished his chores.

10. According to her sister Marty is applying to Georgia Tech Texas A&M and LSU.

11. That was my best broad jump so far Dave.

12. My grandmother who is over seventy gets up every morning at six o'clock walks three miles and then goes for a swim at the YMCA pool.

13. Unfortunately one of our scheduled speakers Dr. F. E. Maxwell Jr. can't make it today.

14. He apparently missed his connection and is now waiting in the airport in Raleigh North Carolina until the airline can find him a seat on another flight.

15. The crisp clear fall weather was invigorating.

16. Celie despite her cold insisted on running in the 10K race.

17. "Elias we don't have enough money to buy another car" his father explained "and unless you saved money you couldn't afford the gasoline not to mention the insurance."

18. Imelda and Esmeralda my twin nieces will start school next year in the fall.

19. The rehearsals are scheduled for Wednesday December 6 and Friday December 8.

20. After we finish our exams in June we're all planning a trip to the beach.

Language and Sentence Skills Practice

Commas B

EXERCISE In each of the following sentences, insert any missing commas and draw a slash (/) through any unnecessary commas.

Example 1. My father's older brother, my uncle Steve, and his partner/are going to show us how to change a flat tire.

1. Camila, and her mother Sra. Alcocer will be preparing all the food for the party.

2. We have games this Friday and Saturday next Friday and Saturday and I believe the following, Friday as well.

3. According to the weather forecast the storm, will reach our area in the middle of the night sometime after midnight.

4. Cassie's address is 1339 Milam Street Apartment 12-B and her phone number is 604-7490.

5. Although he is almost never late for school he overslept, this morning.

6. Next weekend I am going camping with Nate my best friend, since elementary school.

7. On Thursday and Friday the performances of *Fiddler on the Roof* will begin at seven o'clock but on Saturday the curtain goes up at eight o'clock.

8. Please take this flyer to the front office ask Ms. Jameson, to approve it and make thirty copies for the class.

9. My dogs whose names are Wolfie and Bear are huge but gentle.

10. The concert despite the fact that all the tickets were sold out was cancelled.

11. Fortunately we will be able to get our money back but the process will take several weeks.

12. Mom if you have a few minutes could you please show me how to sew this button on?

13. My grandparents who became U.S. citizens only a few years ago never forget to vote.

14. In the dim flickering light of the candles the children's eyes shone, as they opened their gifts.

15. "Everyone in the class" Mr. Martin said "except for Nelson Glenn and Christine has turned in a permission slip for the field trip."

16. The Customer Service Department I believe has an 800-number so the call will be free.

17. I have classes, at 9:00 and 10:30 lunch at 12:05 and a meeting after school today.

18. None of the materials on that cart including the magazines may be checked out.

19. She brought a notebook, and a tape recorder to the interview, she had scheduled.

20. There is one item, in that catalog, item number 7767 the rain jacket that would be very useful.

Semicolons and Colons

EXERCISE In each of the following sentences, insert colons and semicolons where appropriate.

Example 1. When you're in Ireland, be sure to include the following on your itinerary : the *Book of Kells*, which is housed at Trinity College , the Ring of Kerry, a scenic route in the western part of Ireland , and of course, Blarney Castle.

1. The flight leaves at 1 30 P.M. it arrives in Paris at 7 45 A.M. the next day.

2. When you are at the office supply store, please pick up the following supplies for my science fair project a tri-fold display board, two clear report covers, and a package of graph paper.

3. Some of the relatives at my family reunion came from as far away as Honolulu, Hawaii Anchorage, Alaska and Portland, Maine.

4. You can't buy both the boots and the shoes you'll have to choose one or the other.

5. Bettina introduced us to everyone in her family her mother and father, who came to the United States from Germany when they were in their 20's her brother Ralf, who owns a catering business and her sister Margaret, who is still in elementary school.

6. The castle was begun in 1294 and occupied off and on for the next two centuries it was conquered and burnt about 1500.

7. My brother plays the piano I take guitar and flute lessons.

8. My father is a man of many talents he is an accomplished amateur golfer, an avid gardener, and a published poet.

9. Aaron seldom watches television he says he has better things to do.

10. Please look in the cupboard and tell me whether we need any of these items from the grocery store tomato soup, peanut butter, macaroni, vegetable oil, and crackers.

COMMON ERRORS

Quotation Marks and Other Punctuation A

EXERCISE A In the following sentences, insert quotation marks where necessary.

Example 1. "Nadia!" Rita shouted. "Did you hear about the skating party?"

1. What skating party? asked Nadia, turning to face her friend. When? Where?

2. Let me look at my notes, said Rita, and I'll tell you all the details.

3. Rita continued, Oh, here they are! This backpack has so many pockets I can never find anything.

4. You were saying . . . ? prompted Nadia.

5. Everyone should meet at Marilyn's house at four o'clock on Saturday, Rita said.

6. Unfortunately, Rita, said Nadia with a sigh, there's a little problem.

7. What kind of problem? asked Rita. The rink isn't expensive, and you can rent skates there.

8. Nadia sighed again and said in a whisper, I don't know how to skate.

9. Oh, that's all right! Rita said. You'll catch on fast, and we can all help you.

10. Do you really think so? asked Nadia. Well then, I can't wait!

EXERCISE B On the lines provided, rewrite each of the following sentences, underlining any words that should be italicized and inserting quotation marks, apostrophes, hyphens, dashes, parentheses, brackets, and ellipsis points where necessary.

Example 1. Do you want to borrow my copy of The Old Man and the Sea or Daniels copy?

Do you want to borrow my copy of The Old Man and the Sea or Daniel's copy?

11. Well, let me see. Im sure this is the right direction, said Cecily, looking at her compass.

_____

12. I think it was about 10:00 pm, said the witness. I know that because he the defendant always walked his dogs around the block at that time.

_____

13. Only the sopranos not I are able to reach the high notes in The Star Spangled Banner.

_____

14. During President Clintons first term in office 1993 1997, the Republicans won control of the US House of Representatives.

_____

15. Everyone in Ms. Cranfields literature class has to read Shakespeares Julius Caesar.

_____

COMMON ERRORS

Quotation Marks and Other Punctuation B

EXERCISE On the lines provided, rewrite the following dialogue, correcting the punctuation and capitalization. Be sure to start a new paragraph when the speaker changes.

Example [1] What did you do this weekend asked Kevin, as he and Carl were walking to school.

"What did you do this weekend?" asked Kevin, as he and Carl were walking to school.

[1] Nothing much I guess, said Carl [2] Nothing at all? [3] Not one single thing? [4] You must have done something! [5] Well, the basement flooded, and we spent most of the weekend mopping up water said Carl. [6] You call that nothing! exclaimed Kevin. [7] How did that happen? [8] The plumber he's my brother in law was working on some old cast iron pipes Carl began And he forgot to shut off one of the water lines. [9] You wouldn't have believed the mess! [10] There was a foot maybe even two feet of water in the basement by the time we shut the water off.

_____

_____

_____

_____

_____

_____

_____

_____

_____

_____

_____

_____

_____

_____

_____

_____

_____

_____

COMMON ERRORS

Apostrophes

EXERCISE In each of the following sentences, insert apostrophes where necessary.

Example 1. Maria's aunts' names are Clara and Bella.

1. She wont be able to come with us to tonights dance performance.

2. In a little over two hours, we can be packed and ready to leave for Grandma Joness house.

3. We shouldnt have tried to take this test without a good nights sleep.

4. Didnt I tell you we should have gone to sleep before two o clock in the morning?

5. In the late 1990s, many Americans bought large cars, even though smaller cars mileage ratings were better.

6. The Gonzalezes ranch is in New Mexico, near its border with Texas.

7. The newspapers political editor came to the journalism classes awards banquet.

8. Well meet at the Smiths house; then Saras dad will take us to the movies.

9. The companys president will take you to the conference room on the buildings second floor.

10. Thats an incredibly long kite tail; its at least forty or fifty feet long!

11. Carlas family gave the landlord one months notice before they moved out of the apartment.

12. Dont you agree it's a beautiful morning?

13. My mother always says, "Mind your *p*s and *q*s," but she cant tell me the origin of the saying.

14. Well, my fathers favorite saying is "Cross all your *t*s and dot all your *i*s."

15. Three schools representatives to the District Student Council met to discuss their concerns about the school boards plans.

16. The dogs leashes are on a hook in the closet; Guss leash is the long green one.

17. Nows the time to ask for your parents help.

18. Well all go together in Nathans brothers car.

19. The roads sharp curves and potholes make it an inexperienced drivers worst nightmare.

20. Hes just gotten his learners permit, and his sisters husband is teaching him to drive.

All Marks of Punctuation Review A

EXERCISE On the lines provided, rewrite each of the following sentences, underlining any word that should be italicized and inserting appropriate punctuation marks.

Example 1. Key West Florida is closer to Cuba about 90 miles than it is to the Florida mainland about 100 miles

Key West, Florida, is closer to Cuba (about 90 miles) than it is to the Florida mainland

(about 100 miles).

1. Key West the last of the Florida Keys is connected to the mainland by the Overseas Highway

_____

2. In 1905 when Henry Flagler 1830 1913 decided to extend the railroad to Key West Key West was Floridas most populated city

_____

3. It was also the United States closest deep water port to the proposed Panama Canal

_____

4. During the seven year long construction period hurricanes threatened the project several times at one time over four thousand men were working on the rail route

_____

5. Many native born Key Westers a person born on the two by four mile island is called a Conch pronounced konk are descended from early residents who salvaged shipwrecks.

_____

6. When the cry Wreck ashore went up everyone would rush out to see what could be salvaged

_____

7. One of Key Wests well known residents was the author Ernest Hemingway 1899 1961 who owned a house on the island from 1931 until his death

_____

8. Today the Hemingway House is among the islands most popular tourist attractions

_____

9. While he lived in Key West Hemingway wrote several novels including For Whom the Bell Tolls and short stories such as The Short Happy Life of Francis Macomber

_____

10. Hemingway owned nearly fifty cats todays visitors still look for those cats descendants especially the six toed ones which are easy to spot

_____

Language and Sentence Skills Practice

All Marks of Punctuation Review B

EXERCISE Proofread the following letter for correct use of end marks, commas, semicolons, colons, apostrophes, hyphens, dashes, parentheses, quotation marks, and italics. Add or delete punctuation as needed.

Example [1] Please bring the following to the meeting: tickets, money, and questions.

[1] 1420 Winston Ave Apt 12

[2] Gwyneth TX 77091

[3] February 10 2002

[4] Mysteries Unlimited Club

4000 B Academy Blvd

Denver CO 80602

[5] Dear Sir or Madam

[6] Since June 10 1998 I have been a member of Mysteries' Unlimited. [7] In your last, club newsletter you invited members to send in their original mysteries, for possible publication [8] I have been writing stories for several years but Ive never submitted anything for publication [9] Im enclosing a copy of my story Broken Glasses [10] The storys setting is Exeter England I grew up there, so the setting is depicted accurately! [11] A cabdriver disappears without a trace except for his' broken glasses The narrator is Glenda a self confident schoolgirl about my age who lives across the street from the missing driver [12] After finding the glasses in the street Glenda pursues additional clues loud music screeching tires and flashlights at midnight [13] Although she is painfully, shy she interviews at least twenty five people friends neighbors and customers of the cab driver in her effort to find him [14] She contacts the police of course but most of them she does make one friend on the police force dismiss her well founded worries as the product of an over active imagination [15] Arent they embarrassed when the girl solves the mystery [16] Can you guess how [17] By the way the story contains no violence or weapons

[18] Please consider, publishing my original story in your annual anthology (Best Mysteries). [19] I have enclosed a self addressed stamped envelope for your reply

[20] Sincerely

Francine Gomez

Spelling A

EXERCISE A In each of the following sentences, two words are underlined. If a word is misspelled, write the word correctly above it. If a word is spelled correctly, write *C* above it.

            concede *C*
Example 1. Finally, the team had to <u>conceed</u> <u>defeat</u>.

1. If you finish early, <u>procede</u> to the next section of the test <u>immediately</u>.

2. Either you <u>believe</u> in the <u>movement</u> or you don't.

3. City <u>taxes</u> rarely go for building music <u>studioes</u>.

4. Insect larvae are sometimes found underneath <u>leafs</u>.

5. The <u>bookkeeper</u> has an <u>accurate</u> record of the bank deposits.

6. After she read the poem, an appreciation of literary <u>beauty</u> <u>siezed</u> her.

7. Scientists often report any <u>modifications</u> to their <u>theories</u>.

8. <u>Roofs</u> in those <u>countrys</u> are made of natural materials.

9. Those youngsters' manners are <u>aweful</u>, and they are always <u>disobeying</u> their parents.

10. Don't get in an <u>argument</u> about whose <u>achievement</u> was the greatest.

EXERCISE B In each of the following sentences, underline any misspelled word and write the correct spelling above it.

     Seven   *calves*
Example 1. 7 miles into the race, the muscles in my <u>calfs</u> began to ache.

11. I think that television show is overated.

12. The exhibit contained artifacts from an ancient buryal site.

13. My brother's collection of pennys is truly amazeing.

14. He was disatisfied with the service he had received at the restaraunt.

15. Unfortunatly, I don't understand these chemical formula.

16. The questionaire was the 4th one she had answered in as many days.

17. The blizzard knocked down the power lines and blanketted the town in snow.

18. Twelvth-grader's in our school take a class trip every spring.

19. My sister-in-laws are both sopranoes, and my brothers are bass's.

20. At the zoo, I especially enjoyed seeing the wolfs, the kangaroos, and the deers.

COMMON ERRORS

Spelling B

EXERCISE In each of the following sentences, underline any misspelled word and write the correct word above it.

Example 1. After we finished sewing the costumes, we ~~died~~ them. *dyed*

1. When he forgets to cross his *t*s, they look just like his *l*s.

2. After a satisfiing lunch, we all took a nap.

3. Sharon was dismaied when she realized she had missed the rehearsal on Wednesday.

4. My great grandfather founded his business shorttly after he came to the United States.

5. Let me check my calendar; I beleive I have a practice that afternoon.

6. There are basicly only two solutiones to this problem.

7. She had been coughhing for dais and her voice sounded hoarse.

8. His costume was the winer for "Best Character from History."

9. Please post notics on the bulletin boards so that everyone will know about tonight's meeting.

10. Wayne is a consciencious student; he is always studiing.

11. The batter should have reachd the consistency of sour cream or yogurt.

12. My family tryed to get a room at the motel, but there were no vacancys.

13. The superintendent of schools has substantial teaching expereince.

14. In the part of the county that is outside the city, the sheriff is the cheif law enforcement officer.

15. I recieved a pamphlet explaining the summer programs availlable for high school students.

16. An extraordinary traffic jam outside the stadium causeed us to be late for the tournament.

17. Saddly, he has a tendency to exaggerate thinges.

18. As the hot-air balloones ascended, the crowd cheerred.

19. I have looked in every concievable place, but I still can't find my journal.

20. Despite the freezeing temperatures, the ski trip was unforgetable.

Words Often Confused

EXERCISE A In each of the following sentences, underline the word in parentheses that correctly completes the sentence.

Example 1. Did you (*chose, choose*) the pasta or the stew at lunch?

1. Has your family decided what (*rout, route*) to take on the drive to Anchorage?

2. Except for a few (*miner, minor*) errors, Shima's report is excellent.

3. Job openings are posted on the (*personnel, personal*) director's bulletin board.

4. Native peoples of the (*plains, planes*) continued to move westward.

5. Citizens of the world hope for (*piece, peace*) among all nations.

6. To boost team (*morale, moral*), Coach Van Winkle ran laps, too.

7. Do you think having the garage sale was a (*waste, waist*) of time?

8. William doesn't know (*whether, weather*) to ask Ms. Ling for a retest.

9. The dome on the state (*capital, capitol*) is being cleaned.

10. Their use of (*coarse, course*) language during the formal dinner made a poor impression.

EXERCISE B In each of the following sentences, underline any misused word and write the correct word above it. If all the words in a sentence are used correctly, write *C* after the sentence.

Example 1. I have an appointment with the career *councilor* this afternoon. [counselor]

11. He wasn't aware that the moon effects the tides on earth.

12. One of this political party's principals is that all meetings should be open to the public.

13. The motion to except the engineering company's contract past unanimously.

14. Don't stomp on the brake pedal; press it calmly and steadily.

15. She was formally an attorney in private practice, but now she owns a bookstore.

16. Their trying to give you a complement.

17. Whose planning to submit an application to the personal department?

18. In the dark tunnel, the lights on the minors' helmets shown eerily.

19. The path lead to a quite picnic area.

20. Did you here the guide's talk about the history of the capital building?

Spelling and Words Often Confused

EXERCISE In each of the following sentences, underline each misspelled or misused word and write the correct word above it.

> *break*
Example 1. Annie hadn't meant to <u>brake</u> the window.

1. My grandparents recently sold the house they had owned for 42 years.

2. They have all ready packed everything; the house looks desserted.

3. Occasionally, I here sirens in the night.

4. In the passed, she had always enjoyed family re-unions.

5. You should try a peace of the banana bread; its really delicious!

6. Everytime we loose a game, our moral plummets.

7. Days in the desert sun must have effected his thinking.

8. During the bicycle maintenance class, we were shone how to adjust breaks and fix a flat.

9. You're parents don't like to waist money.

10. In my expereince, surprise partys are alot of fun.

11. Last Tuesday, our state senator gave us a personnel tour of the capitol.

12. The commencement ceremony will include a speech by a famous alumni.

13. On the 2nd Wednesday of every month, the nieghborhood association meets.

14. Do any of there friends or aquaintences work for that company?

15. At the end of they're feild trip to the museum, all the sophomores bought souvenirs.

16. A single, magnificent painting of a pack of wolfs was the dominant object in the room.

17. One of our requirments for graduation is a grammar coarse.

18. Did she loose her sunglasses or merely missplace them?

19. One characteristic of many succesful athletes is self confidence.

20. Its allright; I know you must have been extremly fatigued after the race.

COMMON ERRORS

Review A: **Usage**

EXERCISE A If a sentence contains a subject-verb or pronoun-antecedent agreement error, underline the incorrect word and write the correct word or words above it. If the sentence is already correct, write *C* after it.

                     know

Example 1. Few people knows the truth.

1. Thailand, unlike many other Asian countries, were never a European colony.

2. For 15,000 years Aboriginal Australians have used the boomerang to hunt for its food.

3. Tigers that stalk humans is rare.

4. A designer of Italian automobiles often has formal art training in their background.

5. The Chinese people evaporated seawater in wide heated pans to get salt.

6. Sue don't know that the Hebrew word *shalom* mean "peace."

7. Dr. Martin Luther King, Jr., advocated nonviolent action to make a nation correct their injustices.

8. Some of the inhabitants of Quebec speaks French and English equally well.

9. Its mild climate and spectacular scenery make the Riviera a popular destination.

10. No one chose to write their report about the brief war between England and Argentina in 1982.

EXERCISE B Rewrite each of the following sentences, correcting any errors in the use of modifiers.

Example 1. Always sensibly dressed, the weather never worries her.

     She never worries about the weather, for she is always sensibly dressed.

11. Being that I plan to go into engineering, excellent math skills are required.

_____

12. Its sirens blaring and its lights flashing, the children watched the fire engine speed by.

_____

13. Counting all the leftovers, more apples than oranges were found to have been eaten.

_____

14. Dim but twinkling, the most young boy looked out his bedroom window at the first star.

_____

15. That was one of the most poignant and more touching stories than any I've read.

_____

COMMON ERRORS

Review B: Mechanics

EXERCISE   Rewrite the following sentences, correcting any punctuation and capitalization errors.

Example 1. I couldnt believe what I read, about truffles the other day exclaimed Kanisha.

"I couldn't believe what I read about truffles the other day!" exclaimed Kanisha.

1. What in the world are truffles Kim asked?

_____

2. Well her friend said theyre a fungus that looks a little like mushrooms they grow underground and some people consider them a great delicacy

_____

_____

3. Wanting to know more, Kim asked How do truffle hunters know where the truffles are?

_____

4. "Not easily answered Kanisha" In France pigs are trained to sniff them out

_____

5. "I suppose" Kim said shaking her head that a handful of truffles must be incredibly expensive

_____

6. Kanisha had also learned the following, about truffles that they usually grow, around the roots of trees especially Oaks, that they may be as small as a pea or as large as an orange and that they first became popular near the end of the 15th Century

_____

_____

7. The main french *truffières* truffle grounds are in Périgord and Vaucluse.

_____

8. Some People are sensitive to the scent of truffles others look for other signs small yellow flies that hover over the ground for example that truffles are below the surface

_____

_____

9. Truffles a member of the genus, Tuber have been prized as food since ancient times!

_____

10. If youre ever offered the chance to eat truffles even a tiny piece try them theyre wonderful

_____

Review C: **Usage and Mechanics**

EXERCISE On the lines provided, rewrite the following letter, correcting any errors in usage and mechanics.

> **Example** One rainy, Saturday afternoon I decided to write a letter to my freind, Marcy who
> have moved to Albuquerque right before school begun
>
> *One rainy Saturday afternoon, I decided to write a letter to my friend Marcy, who had*
>
> *moved to Albuquerque right before school began.*

January 13 2001

dear Marcy

Its been a long time since I had wrote an old fashioned letter but I wanted to use the stationary my Grandmother give me for my birthday Next time Ill e-mail you that's alot more faster While waiting for the rain to stop a letter to a friend is a good way to get back in touch with them Ive been fine how are you doing All of your Classmates particularly Renata Christopher and Sandra sayed to say hi Renata told me to tell you Im quoting her exactly Save a place for me at the university of new mexico maybe you too could be roomates

guess what Ms Jimenez shes the teacher in biology II is from new mexico says the sandia mountains are absolute beautiful especially at sunrise and sunset Maybe ill try and visit you someday and see it for myself Until than send me some pictures

Are you still planing to visit during the holidays Let me know well have a party

Always Your Friend,

Lynn;

_____

_____

_____

_____

_____

_____

_____

_____

_____

_____

_____

_____

Language and Sentence Skills Practice

Proofreading Application: E-mail

Good writers are generally good proofreaders. Readers tend to admire and trust writing that is error-free. Make sure that you correct all errors in grammar, usage, spelling, and punctuation in your writing. Your readers will have more confidence in your words if you have done your best to proofread carefully.

Experienced writers sometimes use sentence fragments and, rarely, run-on sentences to create a certain effect, particularly in works of fiction. However in a business letter or e-mail, you should not include fragments and run-ons in your writing, as these may confuse your reader and create a negative impression.

PROOFREADING ACTIVITY

The following is an e-mail request to a chamber of commerce for information. Find and correct any run-on sentences and sentence fragments. Use proofreading symbols to make your corrections.

```
TO:       webmaster@fresnocc.org

SUBJECT:    Tourist Information

   My family will be visiting Fresno next month, it will be our

first time there. I offered to research your fair city. So that our

six-day stay will be as interesting and entertaining as possible.

   It is an ideal place for me to visit I like old railroad depots.

I read that the Santa Fe Depot in Fresno was constructed in 1896.

Also, think William Saroyan is a fascinating writer, and I read that

a museum highlights his works. In that same museum I would expect to

find information about the Forty-Niners who settled around Fresno

during the California gold rush, is that true?

   My interest was piqued by a mention of the Shin-Zen Friendship

Gardens, would you please send information about this? Then we can

decide. Whether we want to go there. Also, what are the exact dates

in October of the Big Fresno Fair? Hopefully, when we are in Fresno.

   Thank you in advance for your assistance in making our visit to

Fresno a great one.
```

Literary Model: Poem

It is in the small things we see it.
The child's first step,
as awesome as an earthquake.
The first time you rode a bike,
wallowing up the sidewalk.
The first spanking when your heart
went on a journey all alone.
When they called you crybaby
or poor or fatty or crazy
and made you into an alien,
you drank their acid
and concealed it.
· · · · · · · · ·

Later,
when you face old age and its natural conclusion
your courage will be shown in the little ways,
each spring will be a sword you'll sharpen,
those you love will live in a fever of love,
and you'll bargain with the calendar
and at the last moment
when death opens the back door
you'll put on your carpet slippers
and stride out.

—from "Courage" by Anne Sexton

EXERCISE A   Write *S* to the left of the first word of each complete sentence in the two stanzas above. Write *F* to the left of the first word of each sentence fragment. Write *R* to the left of each run-on sentence.

EXERCISE B

1. Why do you think Sexton uses fragments to describe some of the remembered "small things" that show courage?

_____

_____

_____

2. Why do you think Sexton uses a run-on sentence in the final stanza to express her prediction for the future?

_____

_____

_____

From "Courage" from *The Awful Rowing Toward God* by Anne Sexton. Copyright © 1975 by Loring Conant, Jr., Executor of the Estate of Anne Sexton. All rights reserved. Reprinted by permission of **Houghton Mifflin Company.** Electronic format by permission of **Sterling Lord Literistic, Inc.**

Literary Model (continued)

EXERCISE C   Write a poem about memories and expectations. Use sentence fragments, complete sentences, and run-on sentences to help you express what you want to say about each.

_____

_____

_____

_____

_____

_____

_____

_____

_____

_____

_____

_____

EXERCISE D   Describe how your use of complete sentences, sentence fragments, and run-on sentences helps reinforce your poem's message. Use specific details from your poem in your answer.

_____

_____

_____

_____

_____

_____

_____

_____

_____

_____

for **CHAPTER 16: CORRECTING COMMON ERRORS**   page 110–455

Writing Application: Test

WRITING ACTIVITY

It is time to change roles. Instead of taking a test that evaluates your knowledge of key language skills, you are going to create one for someone else to take. Carefully go over the items in the list that appears at the beginning of Chapter 16. As stated in the first paragraph, these are key skills and concepts that many writers often find problematic. These items are also the grammar, usage, and mechanics topics that you will evaluate in the test you are going to create. You will write a passage, consisting of one or two paragraphs, that includes errors to be identified. You will need to make a checklist of the skills and concepts you are testing, with each item in the list followed by how many of that type of error you have incorporated into the passage. You will provide the student taking your test with an adapted version of the checklist, which he or she will use as a test-taking aid. Keep track of the errors you are incorporating. This will facilitate your creating the answer key.

PREWRITING   Decide on the topic of your passage; it should be one that you can easily write one or two paragraphs about. You may want to consult your checklist before making the final decision. Your task will be to write a passage that you will have to deliberately craft with certain types of language and constructions (so that errors are included). It may be that some topics lend themselves more readily than others to such writing.

WRITING   When you begin to write the passage, you may discover that it is difficult to incorporate all of the different types of common errors. Use your checklist to help you create a passage with at least one of each type of error. Remember to create an answer key, as well as a copy of your checklist that will be used by the student taking the test.

REVISING   Set aside your test for a while. Then, take it as if you were seeing it for the first time. Use the checklist as a student taking the test would to make sure that all the errors indicated on the checklist appear in the test.

PUBLISHING   Proofread your test to be sure that you have not unintentionally included errors not listed on the checklist. You do not want to confuse the test-taker! Then, create two copies of your test and checklist and one of the answer key. Give a copy of the test and checklist to a classmate, and ask him or her to complete the test. Grade it using the answer key.

EXTENDING YOUR WRITING

Present your teacher with the clean copy of the test and checklist, plus the answer key, for future use. You may wish to create two or three more tests covering different topics. Be sure to provide your teacher with an answer key for each test.

Identifying Sentence Fragments

EXERCISE A Decide whether the following groups of words are sentence fragments or complete sentences. If the word group is a sentence fragment, write *F* on the line provided. If the word group is a sentence, write *S*.

Example ___*F*___ **1.** Everyone slang at least once in a while.

_____ **1.** New words are constantly entering the world's languages.

_____ **2.** Do not last very long.

_____ **3.** Most people know of at least a few slang expressions.

_____ **4.** Slang terms by small groups of people.

_____ **5.** Are part of languages only in a limited sense.

_____ **6.** Do become generally popular?

_____ **7.** Like a hit song, a new slang word's acceptance almost overnight.

_____ **8.** Because slang terms fade into oblivion.

_____ **9.** Many people can name slang expressions that are no longer used.

_____ **10.** The slang of children greatly from that of their grandparents' generation?

_____ **11.** Most people do not slang terms in formal conversations.

_____ **12.** Slang popular in the 1800s completely unfamiliar to many people today.

_____ **13.** For instance, most people would not understand an invitation to join a *rout*, a fashionable social gathering.

_____ **14.** Was once a slang term for a large party.

_____ **15.** When a word endures.

_____ **16.** Slang terms in personal conversation.

_____ **17.** That slang terms have a long history of use in informal speech?

_____ **18.** Until another slang term becomes popular.

_____ **19.** No one would use it today.

_____ **20.** Most languages fairly permanent slang expressions.

SENTENCES

Language and Sentence Skills Practice

Identifying Sentence Fragments (continued)

EXERCISE B Decide what is missing from each of the following groups of words. If the subject is missing, write *SUB* on the line provided. If the verb is missing, write *V* on the line provided. If both a subject and a verb are present but no complete thought is expressed, write *I* for *incomplete*.

Example _*SUB*_ **1.** At many schools can provide career guidance.

_____ **21.** Many high school students about their future careers.

_____ **22.** Are researching opportunities and setting career goals.

_____ **23.** Word-processing programs for students.

_____ **24.** Which is one of the most essential office skills.

_____ **25.** A word-processing course helpful to college-bound students?

_____ **26.** Because most college professors do not accept handwritten essays.

_____ **27.** In large cities, specialized schools specific kinds of vocational training.

_____ **28.** Provide performing arts high schools for future entertainers.

_____ **29.** Emphasize training in the sciences while covering traditional academic course work.

_____ **30.** If a student attends one of these science high schools.

_____ **31.** When the school instituted a yearly poll of students' career choices.

_____ **32.** Was designed to meet students' needs.

_____ **33.** Some courses internship programs to give students hands-on experience.

_____ **34.** Which is very helpful in making a career decision.

_____ **35.** If students are asked to fill out a questionnaire.

_____ **36.** Can meet with professionals from different fields.

_____ **37.** Do offer a series of career nights to investigate a specific field?

_____ **38.** Students and teachers with professionals about writing, traveling, and meeting deadlines.

_____ **39.** May have a hard time deciding which seminar to attend.

_____ **40.** Perhaps a job with diversified responsibilities good for many students.

SENTENCES

Revising Phrase Fragments

EXERCISE A Revise each of the following phrase fragments to make it a complete sentence. You may add the fragment to a complete sentence or develop the fragment into a complete sentence by adding a subject, a verb, or both a subject and verb. Write the revised sentences on the lines provided.

Example 1. to visit one of the most exciting cities in the world

Jenna is anxious to visit one of the most exciting cities in the world.

1. in New York City

_____

2. equipped with cameras and guidebooks

_____

3. taking public transportation

_____

4. the New York subway system

_____

5. to see the Statue of Liberty

_____

6. interested in getting some exercise

_____

7. to avoid getting lost

_____

8. looking at the skyline

_____

9. of the tall buildings

_____

10. a center of theater productions

_____

Revising Phrase Fragments (continued)

EXERCISE B Revise each of the following phrase fragments to make it a complete sentence or develop the fragment into a complete sentence by adding a subject, a verb, or both a subject and a verb. Write the revised sentences on the lines provided.

Example 1. a group of divers from Woods Hole, Massachusetts

The warm waters of the Caribbean beckoned to a group of divers from

Woods Hole, Massachusetts.

11. in the Caribbean

_____

12. to dive into the ocean

_____

13. to learn more about corals

_____

14. trained in undersea exploration

_____

15. by experienced divers

_____

16. a living organism

_____

17. surrounded by multicolored fish

_____

18. an expert at identifying various species

_____

19. on some rocks

_____

20. of life under the sea

_____

414

Revising Subordinate Clause Fragments

EXERCISE A Each of the following items contains a subordinate clause fragment and an independent clause. Correct each subordinate clause fragment by linking it to the independent clause. You may need to change some punctuation and capitalization. Write your revisions on the lines provided.

Example 1. Stories of people can inspire us. Who have overcome difficulties.

Stories of people who have overcome difficulties can inspire us.

1. Alice Walker was born in 1944. Who was the youngest of eight children.

   _____

2. She had an unfortunate accident. When she was eight years old.

   _____

3. She was blinded in one eye. When she was shot by a BB gun.

   _____

4. Even though the resulting scar made her self-conscious. She did not let it control her life.

   _____

5. Walker believed she could accomplish almost anything. If she set her mind to it.

   _____

6. Jaime Escalante became famous for his success in teaching underprivileged students at

   Garfield High School in Los Angeles. Where he was a math instructor.

   _____

7. Escalante knew he could reach these students. Whose potential he recognized.

   _____

8. Although it was not easy. Escalante demanded excellence from his students.

   _____

9. So many of his students passed an exam in calculus that testing officials had them take

   another, more difficult test. Which they also passed.

   _____

10. Wherever he taught. Escalante's message was the same: "Believe in your dreams."

   _____

SENTENCES

Language and Sentence Skills Practice

Revising Subordinate Clause Fragments (continued)

EXERCISE B Decide whether the following word groups contain subordinate clause fragments. If the word group contains a subordinate clause fragment, use proofreading symbols to join the subordinate clause to the independent clause. You may need to change some punctuation and capitalization. If the word groups are already complete sentences, write *C* on the line provided.

Example _____ **1.** My sister and I love to study animals. That are unusual.

_____ **11.** Hummingbirds have a high metabolism. Which keeps their hearts beating at the incredible rate of 1,260 times per minute.

_____ **12.** A hummingbird's heart is 2.4 percent of its body weight. Which typically is 3 grams.

_____ **13.** Even when it is at rest. A hummingbird takes 250 breaths every minute.

_____ **14.** Though they are tiny. These birds have incredible stamina.

_____ **15.** A male ruby-throated hummingbird's wing beats have been registered at 78 times per second. When he is in ordinary flight.

_____ **16.** Koalas are marsupials, mammals like kangaroos and opossums. That have bags or pouches for their young.

_____ **17.** At birth, a koala is only one inch long. It will stay in its mother's pouch for seven to nine months.

_____ **18.** When the young koala is strong enough to leave the pouch. It may still stay with its mother for as long as two years.

_____ **19.** Koalas are sometimes called "koala bears." Although they are not bears.

_____ **20.** The name *koala* is an aboriginal word meaning "one who does not drink." Koalas drink very little because they eat eucalyptus leaves, which contain a lot of water.

SENTENCES

Using Subordinate Clauses in Sentences

EXERCISE A Revise each of the following subordinate clause fragments to make it a complete sentence. You may need to change punctuation and capitalization. Write the revised sentences on the lines provided.

Example 1. because the common cold is hard to cure

Because the common cold is hard to cure, it is better to prevent it if possible.

1. that vitamin C can help prevent colds

_____

2. who wants to avoid the common cold

_____

3. if people drink plenty of citrus juice

_____

4. because citrus drinks are refreshing

_____

5. while grapefruit juice is yellow or pink

_____

6. although tangerine juice tastes good

_____

7. as long as they are very cold

_____

8. because lemonade can be high in sugar and calories

_____

9. since many citrus drinks are high in vitamin C

_____

10. that they should drink eight glasses of water each day

_____

SENTENCES

Using Subordinate Clauses in Sentences (continued)

EXERCISE B Revise each of the following subordinate clause fragments to make it a complete sentence. You may need to change punctuation and capitalization. Write the revised sentences on the lines provided.

Example 1. which enable a person to move comfortably in different social circles

Good manners, which enable a person to move comfortably in different social circles,

are easily learned.

11. because no one is born with good manners

_____

12. if good manners are thoroughly learned

_____

13. although it may be considered old-fashioned

_____

14. unless there is a valid reason

_____

15. when people use good manners

_____

16. who has learned not to interrupt another's conversation

_____

17. which include telephone etiquette

_____

18. that would be helpful to co-workers

_____

19. who represent the company

_____

20. when people are treated with respect

_____

SENTENCES

Identifying and Revising Fragments

EXERCISE A Decide whether the following pairs of word groups contain fragments. If the pair of word groups contains a fragment, use proofreading symbols to make the fragment a complete sentence. You may need to change punctuation and capitalization. You may also need to add or change words. If both word groups are already complete sentences, write *C* on the line provided.

Example _____ **1.** Before contact with Europeans, The Incas had an advanced civilization.

_____ **1.** Before the Spanish conquest in 1532. The Inca empire dominated the Andes Mountains region.

_____ **2.** An emperor who demanded strict obedience ruled the land. All business was run by the state.

_____ **3.** The sick and elderly were clothed and fed, and people were subjects of the state. Which could draft citizens for its projects.

_____ **4.** The Inca farmed the mountainsides, terracing the landscape and irrigating the crops, and they were brilliant engineers. Whose roadways were connected by ferries and bridges.

_____ **5.** Their construction of the city of Machu Picchu is an example. Of their skill with tools like the plumb bob and the wooden roller.

EXERCISE B Each of the following items contains a fragment and an independent clause. Correct each fragment by linking it to the independent clause. You may need to change punctuation and capitalization. You may also need to add or change words. Write your revisions on the lines provided.

Example 1. Ankara is an ancient city. That archaeologists believe dates from the Stone Age.

Ankara is an ancient city that archaeologists believe dates from the Stone Age.

6. The city's architecture reflects various influences. Roman, Byzantine, and Ottoman in origin.

_____

7. Ankara's commercial center is in the old section of the city. That grew along the slope of the citadel.

_____

8. The new section boasts hotels, theaters, and restaurants. Which is much like city centers in other cities.

_____

SENTENCES

Identifying and Revising Fragments (continued)

9. Dominated by imposing government buildings and foreign embassies. Ankara is also home to cultural and educational institutions.

   _____

10. Replacing Istanbul. Ankara became the capital of Turkey in 1923.

    _____

EXERCISE C Use proofreading symbols to make each of the fragments in the following word groups a complete sentence. You may need to change punctuation and capitalization. You may also need to add or change words.

Example 1. Clara Barton had been shy; however, her desire to help others changed her behavior.

When she grew older,

11. During the Civil War. She saw that the soldiers lacked food and medical supplies.

12. She received donations to offset critical shortages. After placing a newspaper advertisement.

13. She became involved with a charitable organization when she worked behind German lines during the Franco-Prussian War. The International Red Cross.

14. She began a five-year struggle to persuade people that the United States should have its own branch of the society. Returning to the United States.

15. The American Red Cross collects donated blood, but it has also been actively engaged. With aid to refugees, the exchange of prisoners of war, and disaster relief.

Revising by Correcting Run-on Sentences

EXERCISE A Use proofreading symbols to correct each of the following run-on sentences by using the method of revision indicated in parentheses.

Example 1. During the 1950s and 1960s, many people believed that all agricultural chemicals were safe⁄ *⁀; however,* many of these chemicals proved to be harmful to the environment. (Use a semicolon with a conjunctive adverb and a comma.)

1. An environmentalist named Rachel Carson studied the effects of these chemicals, she published her findings in the book *Silent Spring*. (Use a coordinating conjunction.)

2. Eventually Carson's book was translated into many languages laws were passed around the world to protect the environment. (Form two sentences.)

3. Like Carson, Joy Adamson was interested in the environment, she concentrated her efforts on the habitat of the African lion. (Use a semicolon.)

4. A lion cub named Elsa became famous when Adamson published her experiences in the book *Born Free*, the book was made into a popular film. (Use a coordinating conjunction.)

5. Both Carson and Adamson emphasized the importance of our relationship with nature these women overcame obstacles to obtain the world's respect for their causes. (Form two sentences.)

EXERCISE B Some of the following groups of words are run-on sentences. Use proofreading symbols to revise each run-on sentence to make it one or more complete sentences. You may have to change punctuation and capitalization. You may also need to add, delete, or change words. If the word group is already a complete sentence, write *C* on the line provided.

Example _____ **1.** The Grand Canyon is immense⁄ it is over 250 miles long, parts of the canyon are 18 miles wide, *and* some portions are more than a mile deep.

_____ **6.** The canyon is astonishingly beautiful some of Earth's history is recorded in its walls.

_____ **7.** Crystallized and twisted rocks lie at the bottom of the canyon's inner gorge, they are estimated to be about two billion years old.

_____ **8.** Above those rocks, the geologic record continues layer by layer rocks dating from the Mesozoic Era, 245 to 66.4 million years ago, have been eroded away.

_____ **9.** Oddly enough, creation of the canyon began in relatively recent geologic times, no more than six million years ago, when the Colorado River undertook its current course.

SENTENCES

Revising by Correcting Run-on Sentences (continued)

_____ **10.** The river may be responsible for the depth of the canyon, rain, wind, temperature, and chemical erosion helped to create its width.

EXERCISE C Use proofreading symbols to revise each of the following run-on sentences to make one or more complete sentences. You may have to change punctuation and capitalization. You may also need to add, delete, or change words.

Example 1. Long and narrow, Chesapeake Bay washes the coasts of Maryland and Virginia its location and history are significant.

11. The upper section of Chesapeake Bay runs through Maryland, the lower bay separates a section of Virginia from the rest of the state.

12. Among the oldest historical sites along the bay are Yorktown and Jamestown these cities were early colonial settlements.

13. Captain John Smith of Jamestown gave the bay the American Indian name *che-sep-ack* the word means "country on a great river."

14. During the War of 1812, the Chesapeake Bay was controlled by the British, they were able to land a ground force, march on the White House, and set it on fire.

15. The Civil War's famous battle between two ironclad ships took place in Hampton Roads, the battle was fought between the *Monitor* and the *Merrimack*.

SENTENCES

Correcting Fragments and Run-on Sentences

EXERCISE A Use proofreading symbols to correct the fragments and run-on sentences in the following items. You may have to change punctuation and capitalization. You may also need to add, delete, or change words.

Example 1. If you have "an albatross around your neck," You are burdened.

1. A famous poem by Samuel Taylor Coleridge, *The Rime of the Ancient Mariner*, is based on an old superstition. That killing an albatross brings bad luck.

2. A large ocean bird. The albatross may follow a ship for days at a time.

3. With a favorable wind. The albatross flies at a rate of one hundred miles per hour.

4. More than eleven feet from tip to tip. The wingspread of the albatross wider than that of any other bird.

5. The body of an albatross is relatively small, for example, it may be no more than nine inches wide.

6. A male albatross is white with black wingtips, the female's neck and back are dappled with brown.

7. Seventeen species of albatross have been identified, most spend their time in tropic seas.

8. Sits on the water to eat, feasting on squid, fish, and garbage from ships.

9. The range of the albatross is extensive, the black-footed species may travel anywhere along the Pacific coast and has been sighted as far north as Alaska.

10. The Antarctic islands are remote and barren, but they are the preferred nesting area. For the albatross.

SENTENCES

Correcting Fragments and Run-on Sentences (continued)

EXERCISE B Use proofreading symbols to correct the fragments and run-on sentences in the following items. You may have to change punctuation and capitalization. You may also need to add, delete, or change words.

Example 1. There are many versions of the story of King Arthur one of the best is *The Once and Future King* by T.H. White.

11. Part myth, part history. The story of King Arthur is based on a Celtic legend.

12. The historical elements are difficult to authenticate. In all the tales about Arthur.

13. Arthur was born in dangerous circumstances, Merlin took him to be raised by Sir Ector.

14. Arthur's true identity would be revealed if he successfully completed a task. A task that only the rightful king could complete.

15. Plunged into a stone. A great sword could be removed only by the person who was meant to be king.

16. To prove their worthiness, many strong knights attempted to remove the sword, nevertheless, all failed.

17. Sent back to get a sword for Sir Kay. Arthur pulled the sword from the stone.

18. Sir Kay recognized the sword and took credit for pulling it from the stone. Admitting later that it was Arthur who had removed the sword.

19. Arthur pulled the sword from the stone a second time. To prove that there had been no mistake.

20. Arthur took the sword, he was acknowledged as Britain's rightful king.

SENTENCES

Revising Fragments and Run-on Sentences

EXERCISE A Correct the fragments and run-on sentences in each of the following items. You may have to change punctuation and capitalization. You may also need to add, delete, or change words. Write the revised sentences on the lines provided.

Example 1. The Seven Wonders of the World continue to fascinate people. Even though most of them no longer exist in their original splendor.

Even though most of them no longer exist in their original splendor, the Seven Wonders of the World continue to fascinate people.

1. The Hanging Gardens of Babylon were a series of terraces filled with tropical plants and flowers. Whose extraordinary beauty is lost in the past.

_____

2. After the forty-foot ivory and gold statue of Zeus at Olympia had endured for ten centuries. It disappeared, too.

_____

3. Tradition tells us. That the temple of Artemis at Ephesus was destroyed by fire.

_____

4. Exactly what happened to the Mausoleum at Halicarnassus is unclear, still, relics of it are displayed in the British Museum.

_____

5. The Colossus of Rhodes was a bronze statue. Whose height ancient historians estimate to have been 105 feet.

_____

6. The Colossus was toppled by an earthquake in 224 B.C. Having stood for about 1,500 years.

_____

7. The great lighthouse at Alexandria was also felled by an earthquake it was thought to be the model for modern lighthouses.

_____

8. The single exception to these losses is the remarkable endurance of the Egyptian pyramids. The only wonders to remain into the modern era.

SENTENCES

Revising Fragments and Run-on Sentences (continued)

9. Although they are the oldest of these ancient sites. The pyramids continue to withstand the rigors of time.

_____

10. Not all lists of the Seven Wonders of the World are the same. The most commonly listed sites.

_____

EXERCISE B   Revise the following paragraphs to correct sentence fragments and run-on sentences. Change the punctuation and capitalization as necessary to make each sentence clear and complete. You may have to add, delete, or move words. Write the revised paragraphs on the lines provided.

Example   Standing upright and arranged in a circle. England's Stonehenge monument is an intriguing structure.

Standing upright and arranged in a circle, England's Stonehenge monument is an

intriguing structure.

According to archaeologists, Stonehenge was built between 3100 and 1550 B.C. the monument probably underwent three phases of construction. The first phase included a circular ditch and a ring of pits. That are known as the Aubrey Holes. In the second phase, thought to have occurred in about 2100 B.C., massive rock pillars from Wales were brought to the site, these immense stones were placed in two concentric circles. The last stage of construction was probably completed before 1500 B.C. Incredibly, thirty stones, each standing upright and weighing as much as fifty tons, were placed in a circle the circle ringed a series of stones placed in the shape of a horseshoe.

_____

_____

_____

_____

_____

_____

_____

_____

_____

SENTENCES

Combining Sentences by Inserting Words A

EXERCISE A Combine each set of sentences below by inserting the underlined word from one sentence into the other sentence. The directions in parentheses tell you when a word form should be changed. Use proofreading symbols to mark your changes.

Example 1. Many sections of the Great Wall of China have deteriorated *badly* throughout the centuries. ~~The deterioration has been bad.~~ (Add –*ly* to *bad*.)

1. The Great Wall was built <u>completely</u> by hand. The Great Wall of China is the longest structure ever built by hand.

2. Stretching along what was then China's border, the Great Wall is nearly four thousand miles long. The Great Wall ran along the <u>northern</u> border of China.

3. The Great Wall reaches a height of almost thirty-five feet at some points. This height is <u>remarkable</u>.

4. The Great Wall is made up of three components: passes, signal towers, and walls. These are <u>major</u> components of the Great Wall.

5. Located at different points along the Great Wall, passes allowed merchants, civilians, and military forces to enter and exit. The passes were located at <u>key</u> points.

6. Gate towers were often built of <u>wood</u>. Gates in the pass were guarded by soldiers in the gate tower, which was a one-to-three-story building. (Add –*en* to *wood*.)

7. Signal towers, platforms often built on hilltops, were used by the military to send messages along the wall. These platforms were built <u>high</u> to help soldiers see for long distances.

8. Soldiers would make <u>loud</u> noises with clappers or gunfire. Soldiers would use fires, lanterns, smoke signals, banners, or noises to send messages.

9. Because the Chinese took advantage of natural formations, such as mountain cliffs and gorges, not all sections of the wall were man-made. Using these <u>existing</u> formations saved time and energy.

10. The eastern section of the wall, on top of which runs a road made of brick and mortar, crosses the Mongolian Border Uplands. The Mongolian Border Uplands are a <u>mountainous</u> region.

SENTENCES

Combining Sentences by Inserting Words A (continued)

EXERCISE B Combine each set of sentences below by inserting the underlined word or words from one sentence into the other sentence. The directions in parentheses tell you when a word form should be changed. Use proofreading symbols to mark your changes.

Example 1. ~~The Panama canal was an outstanding accomplishment.~~ The Panama Canal, a sea-
way connecting the Atlantic Ocean and the Pacific Ocean, was ~~a~~ feat of engineering.
(an outstanding)

11. The Panama Canal runs through the Isthmus of Panama and is about forty miles in length
from shoreline to shoreline. The Isthmus of Panama is <u>narrow</u>.

12. For nearly ten years, thousands of laborers cleared jungles and swamps, using shovels and
dredges. The shovels and dredges were <u>steam-powered</u>.

13. The construction of the canal was supported by the president of the United States, Theodore
Roosevelt. Theodore Roosevelt was the <u>twenty-sixth</u> president of the United States.

14. After the canal's completion in 1914, a voyage by ship from New York to California was
reduced from 13,000 miles to 5,200 miles. The reduction was <u>significant</u>. (Add *–ly.*)

15. Locks—chambers that raise and lower ships to different levels—were added to the canal so
that two ships could travel in opposite directions at the same time. The chambers had <u>three</u>
<u>tiers</u>. (Delete *–s*, add hyphen between *three* and *tier*, and add *–ed* to *tiers.*)

16. With a width of 110 feet and a depth of 70 feet, however, the locks cannot accommodate supertankers or supercarriers. The supertankers and supercarriers are <u>enormous</u>.

17. The ships that use the canal are <u>commercial and military</u>. Averaging about 34 ships a day and
170 million short tons of cargo a year, the canal is a heavily used waterway.

18. Nearly 70 percent of the cargo that travels through the canal is headed to or from the United
States. The canal is <u>strategically placed</u>.

19. The United States maintained control of the canal until 1999, when Panama gained control of
the Canal Zone. Panama gained <u>regional</u> control.

20. The area is <u>important</u> both to Panama and to the United States. When Panama took control of
the canal, it gave U.S. military installations there the right to defend the area.

SENTENCES

Combining Sentences by Inserting Words B

EXERCISE A Combine the following pairs of sentences by deciding which words from one sentence should be inserted into the other sentence. Remember that there may be more than one way to combine each pair of sentences. Choose the combination you think is best. Change the forms of words or replace words as necessary. Use proofreading symbols to mark your changes.

Example 1. John Steinbeck was a novelist and short-story writer, as well as a screenwriter and
           an award-winning
playwright. ~~He was an award-winning author.~~

1. Steinbeck, who is best known for his powerful descriptions of ordinary people, had once wanted to write romances. In fact, Steinbeck's original goal was to write romances.

2. Steinbeck once worked as a fruit picker. Before Steinbeck became a successful author, he supported himself as a construction worker, journalist, and deckhand.

3. In 1962, Steinbeck won the Nobel Prize for literature, which showed the world's respect for his work. The Nobel Prize is a prestigious award.

4. *The Grapes of Wrath*, Steinbeck's first major novel, depicts the life of migrant workers and their families. Steinbeck's portrayal of migrant life is realistic.

5. Steinbeck disliked fame and tried to escape it by going to Mexico. He went to Mexico often.

6. In Mexico, Steinbeck collected marine life and collaborated with Edward F. Ricketts on *The Sea of Cortez*, a book about the fauna of the Gulf of California. Edward F. Ricketts was a biologist.

7. Steinbeck's *The Grapes of Wrath* and *East of Eden* were adapted for the theater and for motion pictures. The adaptations were successful.

8. In Steinbeck's novella *The Pearl*, the main character, Kino, is temporarily assured of a better life when he finds a pearl. The pearl is extraordinary.

9. Kino does not want to part with the pearl, but eventually he does. The pearl causes many problems for Kino and his family, so Kino throws the pearl into the sea.

10. Steinbeck had a heart attack in December of 1968 and died in his apartment. The apartment was in New York City.

SENTENCES

Combining Sentences by Inserting Words B (continued)

EXERCISE B Combine the following pairs of sentences by deciding which words from one sentence should be inserted into the other sentence. Remember that there may be more than one way to combine each pair of sentences. Choose the combination you think is best. Change the forms of words or replace words as necessary. Use proofreading symbols to mark your changes.

Example 1. The ∧brief reign of Tutankhamen, an Egyptian pharaoh, lasted about nine years.

~~Tutankhamen's reign was brief~~

11. Howard Carter and Lord Carnarvon received permission to search the Valley of the Kings for several tombs. The Valley of the Kings was a desolate place.

12. The pharaohs ruled the Egyptian dynasties. The Valley of the Kings was the burial site of most of the pharaohs of the 18th, 19th, and 20th dynasties.

13. Carter and Carnarvon found Tutankhamen's tomb in 1922. The treasure-filled tomb was filled with valuable objects.

14. When Carter entered the tomb, he found a passage that led to a series of underground rooms. The passage led to four rooms.

15. The burial place was small. Unlike the tombs of other pharaohs, Tutankhamen's burial place did not contain false doors, deep pits, and stone obstructions to discourage grave robbers.

16. Once the excavation team was inside the tomb, they found a collection of caskets, vases, parts of chariots, and statues. The caskets were covered with ornaments.

17. Tutankhamen's mummy had been buried in a solid gold coffin, which had been placed inside two coffins covered with hammered gold. The two outer coffins were made of wood.

18. One find was remarkable. The most valuable part of the treasure was a solid-gold mask that weighed twenty-two pounds.

19. Removing the mummy's wrappings, Carter's team found many gold and jeweled amulets. The wrappings provided protection for the mummy.

20. Tutankhamen's mask and other treasures from his tomb can be seen at the Egyptian Museum located in Egypt. The Egyptian Museum is located in Cairo, Egypt.

SENTENCES

Combining Sentences by Inserting Phrases

EXERCISE A   Combine the following pairs of sentences into one sentence by inserting the underlined phrase from one sentence into the other sentence. There may be more than one way to combine each pair. For some sentence pairs, the hints in parentheses will tell you when to change the forms of words and when to add commas. Use proofreading symbols to mark your changes.

Example 1. Maria Mitchell~~,~~ *an American astronomer,* was born in Nantucket, Massachusetts. ~~Mitchell was an American astronomer.~~ (Add two commas.)

1. The Mitchells had an observatory on the roof of their house. Mitchell and her father studied the stars from the observatory.

2. Mitchell noticed a strange star where none had been before. She saw the star in 1847.

3. She thought it might be a comet, so she plotted the object's coordinates. She plotted the coordinates as it moved across the sky.

4. Her father wrote a Harvard University professor a letter. He wrote a letter about Maria's discovery.

5. Father Francesco de Vico was a Catholic priest. Father Francesco de Vico noticed the same comet two days after Mitchell did. (Add two commas.)

6. The king of Denmark awarded a prize to Father Francesco. The prize was for discovering a comet through a telescope.

7. The king was unaware of Mitchell's discovery. He was unaware of her discovery at the time of the award's presentation.

8. Mitchell had to reach an agreement with the king. Mitchell received the prize a year later. (Change *reach* to *reaching*, and add a comma.)

9. Mitchell was the first woman elected to the American Academy of Arts and Sciences. She was elected in 1848.

10. From 1875 to 1876, Mitchell served as the president of the Association for the Advancement of Women. The Association for the Advancement of Women was an organization she had helped found in 1873. (Add a comma.)

Language and Sentence Skills Practice

SENTENCES

Combining Sentences by Inserting Phrases (continued)

EXERCISE B   Combine the following pairs of sentences into one sentence by inserting a phrase from the second sentence into the first sentence. There may be more than one way to combine each pair. For some sentence pairs, the hints in parentheses will tell you when to change the forms of words and when to add commas. Use proofreading symbols to mark your changes.

Example   1. Have you ever wondered who invented the Frisbee®? ~~It is~~ a plastic disk that people

   throw to their pets or to their friends, (Add a comma.)

11. One story claims that the game of Frisbee® was "invented" in the 1820s by Elihu Frisbie. Elihu Frisbie was a student at Yale. (Add a comma.)

12. Frisbie reportedly tossed a collection plate from the Yale chapel. He tossed the plate out onto the campus grounds.

13. Years later, Princeton, Dartmouth, and other colleges claimed credit for the pie-pan-tossing craze. They each insist that they invented the tossing game. (Change *insist* to *insisting*, and add a comma.)

14. Another theory is that the name originated from the empty pie tins that students would toss back and forth to one another. The pie tins were made by the Frisbie Baking Company.

15. In 1948, Walter Morrison turned the pie pan into a plastic disc. Morrison was a California building inspector. (Add two commas.)

16. Morrison marketed his disc at a time when people were fascinated with UFOs. The disc was called the "Pluto Platter." (Add two commas.)

17. The disc became very popular after Morrison exhibited it. He exhibited it at California fairs and beaches.

18. Rich Kerr and Arthur "Spud" Merlin bought the rights to the plastic disc in 1957. They bought the rights from Morrison.

19. The two toy enthusiasts changed the name of the disc to Frisbee.® They had heard some of the old pie-pan-tossing stories. (Change *had heard* to *having heard*, and add a comma.)

20. Ultimate Frisbee® and disc golf have made the sport popular. The sport is played around the world.

Combining Sentences Using Compound Subjects and Verbs

EXERCISE A Combine each of the following sets of short sentences into a single sentence. Make sure that each sentence has a compound subject, a compound verb, or both. Remember that verbs and subjects must agree in number. Write the revised sentences on the lines provided.

Example 1. Wolves are canines, like dogs. Coyotes are canines, like dogs.

Wolves and coyotes are canines, like dogs.

1. Wolves are carnivorous mammals. Coyotes are carnivorous mammals. _____

_____

2. Wolves and coyotes sometimes live alone. Wolves and coyotes always hunt for large prey in

packs. _____

_____

3. Wolves attack weaker animals, preventing overpopulation of some species. Coyotes attack

weaker animals, preventing overpopulation of some species. _____

_____

4. Coyotes are thought to mate for life. They may accept another mate if their first mate leaves.

_____

_____

5. A wolf pack consists of an adult pair and their offspring. A wolf pack usually numbers from

five to nine animals. _____

_____

6. Litter sizes vary somewhat. They normally range from five to nine pups for both wolves and

coyotes. _____

_____

7. Both male wolves and male coyotes help feed the young. Both male wolves and male coyotes

help protect secluded dens. _____

_____

8. By howling, wolves and coyotes announce territorial changes. By howling, wolves and coyotes

also call pack members together for a hunt. _____

_____

SENTENCES

Combining Sentences Using Compound Subjects and Verbs (continued)

9. Coyotes can adapt to a variety of environments. Coyotes are found in almost every state.

_____

_____

10. Diseases afflict wolves and coyotes. Parasites afflict wolves and coyotes. Both can reduce the

numbers of these predators. _____

_____

EXERCISE B Combine each of the following pairs of short sentences into a single sentence. Make sure that each sentence has a compound subject, a compound verb, or both. Remember that verbs and subjects must agree in number. Write the revised sentences on the lines provided.

Example 1. Earth is the third planet from the sun. Earth has one moon.

　　　　Earth is the third planet from the sun and has one moon.

11. Mars travels around the sun in 687 days. Mars completes one revolution every 24 hours and

37 minutes. _____

_____

12. Jupiter moves slowly around the sun. Jupiter spins rapidly on its axis, completing a revolution

every ten hours. _____

_____

13. Phobos is a moon that orbits Mars. Deimos is a moon that orbits Mars.

_____

_____

14. Four large moons orbit Jupiter. About twelve smaller moons orbit Jupiter.

_____

_____

15. Jupiter's four major moons were first seen by Galileo. Jupiter's four major moons are called

the Galilean satellites. _____

_____

SENTENCES

Combining Sentences to Create Compound Sentences

EXERCISE A Combine each pair of sentences below into a compound sentence by using a comma and a coordinating conjunction, a semicolon, or a semicolon with a conjunctive adverb and a comma. Use proofreading symbols to mark your changes.

Example 1. The city of Sydney has a large, deep harbor on Australia's southern coast. This harbor is the busiest port in the country.

1. The city of Sydney, Australia, began as a prison colony in 1788. It grew slowly until the mid-1800s.

2. Around 1800, a farmer brought the first sheep to Sydney. By 1842, many people had settled in the city because of its thriving wool industry.

3. By 1848, Sydney was no longer used as a prison colony. Its rich farmland continued to attract settlers from around the world.

4. With the discovery of gold in New South Wales in 1851, people seeking their fortune rapidly expanded the city's population. By 1891, Sydney had more than 383,000 residents.

5. Sydney remained Australia's largest city throughout the 1990s. Its area, including suburbs, is about forty-seven hundred square miles.

6. The city still has reminders of its origins as a British prison colony. Prison buildings, such as Hyde Park Barracks, which housed male prisoners, have been preserved throughout the city.

7. Many of Sydney's residents are primarily of European descent. The city's Asian population has increased greatly since the mid-1900s.

8. Because of the city's location and moderate temperatures, its residents, known as Sydneysiders, enjoy many watersports such as surfing and sailing. They also have a taste for cultural activities, including the theater, opera, and fine works of art.

9. The Sydney Opera House, located on the harbor, is a major arts center. It has a concert hall, two theaters, and rehearsal and recording studios.

10. Sydney is also home to the Australian Museum. This museum contains the largest natural history collection in Australia.

Language and Sentence Skills Practice

SENTENCES

Combining Sentences to Create Compound Sentences (continued)

EXERCISE B Combine each pair of sentences below into a compound sentence by using a comma and a coordinating conjunction, a semicolon, or a semicolon with a conjunctive adverb and a comma. Use proofreading symbols to mark your changes.

Example 1. In 1990, the National Aeronautics and Space Administration (NASA) launched the

Hubble Space Telescope. The telescope was used to study our solar system.

11. NASA's Goddard Space Flight Center in Greenbelt, Maryland, controls the telescope by radio

commands. The Space Telescope Science Institute in Baltimore, Maryland, is the telescope's

science operations center.

12. The Hubble telescope orbits Earth roughly 380 miles from the surface. Information collected is

transmitted to Earth.

13. Astronomers hoped that the Hubble telescope would be an important tool in their search for

new planets beyond our solar system. Three years after its launch, engineers found problems

with the telescope's instruments.

14. In 1993, space shuttle astronauts installed new instruments on the telescope. Additional repairs

were made in 1999.

15. The telescope has a large mirror that measures ninety-four inches in diameter. The mirror

gathers light that helps scientists study stars and galaxies.

16. The telescope contains two cameras that photograph images of objects. These cameras are

valuable because they allow astronomers to see space without atmospheric distortions.

17. These instruments allow astronomers to see images the size of the planet Pluto. They have also

discovered Charon, a satellite of Pluto.

18. The Hubble telescope has discovered evidence of black holes as far away as 50 million light

years. Astronomers using the telescope have also sighted rings of dust around stars.

19. The Hubble telescope has also found evidence of a belt of icy debris around our solar system.

The data collected from the Hubble telescope suggest that there may be 100 million comets in

this belt.

20. Another major celestial event was recorded by the Hubble telescope when fragments of the

Shoemaker-Levy 9 comet smashed into Jupiter. The images recorded by the Hubble telescope

showed detailed views of each impact.

436

Combining Sentences to Create Complex Sentences

EXERCISE A Using subordinate clauses, combine each of the following pairs of sentences into a single complex sentence. Remember that there may be different ways to combine the sentences. Change or delete words as necessary, and write your revised sentences on the lines provided.

Example 1. Cape Breton Island is an island off the coast of Canada. It is connected to Nova Scotia by a mile-long causeway.   *Cape Breton Island is an island off the coast of* *Canada that is connected to Nova Scotia by a mile-long causeway.*

1. Cape Breton Island was originally called Île Royale. It was called Île Royale when it was a French colony. _____

   _____

2. Its granite hills are considered a part of the Appalachian Highlands. Cape Breton is not part of the mainland. _____

   _____

3. The north end of the island contains forests, lakes, and high plateaus. It has been preserved as Cape Breton Highlands National Park. _____

   _____

4. Cape Breton is a center of manufacturing and mining. Its coal deposits are the largest in Canada. _____

   _____

5. Farming and deep-sea fishing are important industries to Cape Breton. Farming is primarily contained to the Margaree Valley. _____

   _____

6. The first permanent settlement was established in 1713. The French built the Fortress of Louisbourg. _____

   _____

7. Louisbourg was named for the French king Louis XIV (1643–1715). Louis XIV was also known as the Sun King. _____

   _____

8. The fortress was captured by the English in 1758 and destroyed in 1760. The ruins of the fortress are a national historic park. _____

SENTENCES

Combining Sentences to Create Complex Sentences (continued)

9. French settlers and United Empire Loyalists arrived at the end of the eighteenth century. They accounted for the majority of the population at the time. _____

    _____

10. The Scottish Highlanders began arriving in the early nineteenth century. They introduced the Gaelic language to the island. _____

    _____

EXERCISE B Using subordinate clauses, combine each of the following pairs of sentences into a single complex sentence. Remember that there may be different ways to combine the sentences. Change or delete words as necessary, and write your revised sentences on the lines provided.

Example 1. Alexander Graham Bell was a naturalized United States citizen and a teacher of the hearing impaired. He invented the telephone. *Alexander Graham Bell, who invented the telephone, was a naturalized United States citizen and a teacher of the hearing impaired.*

11. Bell was born in Edinburgh, Scotland. He left in 1870 to immigrate to Canada.

    _____

    _____

12. Bell first considered the idea for the telephone in 1874. He was working on a multiple telegraph. _____

    _____

13. The first telephone transmission of human speech was on March 10, 1876. Bell and his assistant were experimenting in their laboratory. _____

    _____

14. The Bell Telephone Company was organized in 1877. The telephone's effectiveness and potential were previously demonstrated at the 1876 Philadelphia Centennial Exposition.

    _____

    _____

15. A museum was built by the Canadian government on Cape Breton Island, Nova Scotia, the site of Bell's summer home. The museum contains many of Bell's inventions.

    _____

    _____

SENTENCES

Revising Sentences by Combining

EXERCISE A Using all of the sentence-combining skills you have learned, combine each of the following sets of sentences into a single sentence. Create new sentences by inserting words or phrases, by creating compound subjects and verbs, by creating compound sentences, or by creating complex sentences. Remember that there may be different ways to combine the sentences. Change or delete words as necessary, and write your revised sentences on the lines provided.

Example **1.** Food supplies have been one of the world's concerns as the population has increased. Food supplies are a main concern of people around the world.

Food supplies have been one of the world's main concerns as the population has

increased.

1. Drought, floods, and other natural disasters can cause famine. Famine results from the natural disasters if food supplies are destroyed or cannot be transported.

_____

_____

2. Governments are not always able to supply sufficient food to their people during natural disasters. The governments of many countries around the world know this.

_____

_____

3. About 600 million people, most of them children, suffer from malnutrition. Malnutrition is a condition caused by inadequate amounts of protein and calories.

_____

_____

4. Childhood malnutrition creates mental and physical disabilities. The effects can also be seen when a malnourished child matures. _____

_____

5. The population will continue to grow each year. The production of food will also have to increase to keep up with the demand. _____

_____

Revising Sentences by Combining (continued)

EXERCISE B Using all of the sentence-combining skills you have learned, combine each of the following sets of sentences into a single sentence. Create new sentences by inserting words or phrases, by creating compound subjects and verbs, by creating compound sentences, or by creating complex sentences. Remember that there may be different ways to combine the sentences. Change or delete words as necessary, and write your revised sentences on the lines provided.

Example 1. Amateur radio is a hobby that allows radio operators to run their own radio stations. The operators are referred to as hams. *Amateur radio is a hobby that allows radio operators, who are referred to as hams, to run their own radio stations.*

6. Radio operators number roughly one million. They transmit messages around the world. They use International Morse Code or voice to send messages.

_____

_____

7. Guglielmo Marconi was the first person to successfully transmit radio signals across the Atlantic Ocean. Marconi's transmission of radio signals in 1901 began the era of amateur radio.

_____

_____

8. As technology advanced, amateur radio-communications satellites called Oscars (Orbiting Satellite Carrying Amateur Radio) were launched into space. The amateur satellites reached space by "hitchhiking" with other satellites. _____

_____

_____

9. Some ham operators bounce signals off the moon to communicate. Others have devised ways to use their radio sets to transfer information between computers.

_____

_____

10. Amateur radio operators have played a valuable role in assisting emergency personnel. Ham operators have received recognition from world governments for their efforts.

_____

_____

SENTENCES

Revising Paragraphs by Combining Sentences

EXERCISE A   Using the sentence-combining skills you have learned, revise the following paragraphs on the lines provided. Do not change the original meaning of the paragraph. Use your judgment to decide which sentences to combine and how to combine them. Write clear, varied sentences that read smoothly.

Example 1. Roadrunners can fly. They rarely do. They prefer to run.

Roadrunners can fly, but they rarely do because they prefer to run.

1.   Roadrunners are noted for their amusing behavior. Oddly, they seem to enjoy chasing golf balls. Roadrunners live primarily on lizards and snakes. They are known to eat the fruits of cactus. They can also catch cicadas or grasshoppers. They catch them by jumping into the air. Roadrunners tolerate little contact with humans. They do not like intruders near their nests. Roadrunners are being forced into new habitats in wilder, more remote areas. This is an unfortunate development.

_____

_____

_____

_____

_____

_____

_____

2.   The U.S. Army wanted the Nez Perce to give up their land in Oregon. Chief Joseph and his people would not submit willingly to this demand. Chief Joseph was the Nez Perce leader. They refused to be forced onto a reservation. The reservation was in Idaho. Canada would be a refuge for the Nez Perce. Chief Joseph was certain of this. He led his people on a historic march. They marched to avoid involuntary relocation. The march began in the summer of 1877. It ended in surrender on October 5th because the Nez Perce were exhausted from traveling. The Nez Perce were just forty miles from freedom. They had traveled fifteen hundred miles. Their peaceful surrender earned respect for American Indians. Their gallant dignity earned respect for American Indians.

_____

_____

_____

_____

_____

_____

_____

SENTENCES

Revising Paragraphs by Combining Sentences (continued)

EXERCISE B Using the sentence-combining skills you have learned, revise the following paragraphs on the lines provided. Do not change the original meaning of the paragraph. Use your judgment to decide which sentences to combine and how to combine them. Write clear, varied sentences that read smoothly.

Example 1. Amy Tan was born in 1952. She is a Chinese American.

> *Amy Tan, a Chinese American, was born in 1952.*

3. Amy Tan's parents wanted her to become a surgeon and a pianist. Tan had other goals. She got a master's degree in linguistics. Tan then worked with disabled children. She also was a business writer. She decided that she wanted to write fiction. Tan's first novel was *The Joy Luck Club*. It was a huge success. This book was made into a movie in 1993. It focused on the relationship between four Chinese mothers and their daughters. Tan has written two more novels. The names of the novels are *The Kitchen God's Wife* and *The Hundred Secret Senses*.

_____

_____

_____

_____

_____

_____

_____

4. Deer are known to be fast runners. They are also known to be excellent swimmers. They may seem timid to humans. They are not defenseless. Their sharp hooves can deliver damaging blows. The male's antlers are formidable weapons. The antlers are branched. Deer have some exotic relatives. This is an interesting fact. Scientific evidence suggests a connection between deer and giraffes. Deer and giraffes have a common genetic past.

_____

_____

_____

_____

_____

_____

_____

Revising Sentences to Create Parallel Structure

EXERCISE A Bring balance to the following sentences by putting the ideas in parallel form. Add or delete words as necessary. Use proofreading symbols to mark your changes. If the sentence is already correct, write C on the line provided.

Example _____ **1.** After school, John's chores are cleaning his room, doing the dishes, and
~~to study~~. *studying*

_____ **1.** The process of evaluating a television documentary includes watching, listening, and to take notes.

_____ **2.** In our class discussion of *The Scarlet Letter*, we discussed the imagery, the symbolism, and where the novel was set.

_____ **3.** The travelers decided that hiking into the Grand Canyon would be good exercise and that driving by it would be boring.

_____ **4.** The student council needs volunteers to bring refreshments, to decorate, and for making posters.

_____ **5.** The heroine of the play persuades her brothers to mortgage the farm, to invest in more land, and to repair the house.

_____ **6.** Many talented performers enjoy acting, singing, and to dance.

_____ **7.** Some goals of the group are building membership, encouraging change, and to raise funds.

_____ **8.** Car owners understand the importance of keeping tires inflated, filling the gas tank, and to check the oil.

_____ **9.** At tennis camp, I had three goals: perfect my serve, improve my backhand, and win more matches.

_____ **10.** Before Dr. Monroe began her presentation, she took a moment to introduce herself, list her qualifications, and thanking us for the invitation.

Language and Sentence Skills Practice

Revising Sentences to Create Parallel Structure (continued)

EXERCISE B   Bring balance to the following sentences by putting the ideas in parallel form. Add or delete words as necessary. Use proofreading symbols to mark your changes.

Example 1. For the interview, the applicant had to prepare a résumé, write a cover letter, and researching the company.

11. In her free time, the author enjoys reading, gardening, and travels.

12. How does Keisha find the time to volunteer at the literacy center, to play volleyball, and for studying?

13. Many Europeans like to watch American television and listening to American music.

14. The map shows that the Mississippi River begins at Lake Itasca and flowing into the Gulf of Mexico.

15. My parents try to instill in us three main qualities: compassion, intelligence, and being independent.

16. The senator decided to give up her seat in the Senate and running for president.

17. When we go to the lake for the weekend, we enjoy swimming, hiking, camping, and to barbecue.

18. Many students find that getting into college is relatively easy but to adjust to college life is more difficult than they had thought it would be.

19. They want to contribute by donating money and to volunteer some time.

20. My goals are to work, to study, and self-sufficiency.

SENTENCES

Revising Stringy Sentences

EXERCISE A   Revise each of the following stringy sentences. Break the stringy sentence into two or more shorter sentences, turn an independent clause into a subordinate clause, or turn an independent clause into a phrase. Write the revised sentences on the lines provided.

Example 1. Frédéric Auguste Bartholdi was a French sculptor, and he was born in 1834, and he died in 1904. _Frédéric Auguste Bartholdi, a French sculptor, was born in 1834 and died in 1904._

1. Bartholdi designed the Statue of Liberty, and he used elements of the Egyptian pyramids and his mother's face as a model. _____

_____

2. The statue was completed in France in 1884, and it had to be carefully crated in sections, and it had to be shipped to the United States, and then it had to be reassembled.

_____

_____

3. The Statue of Liberty is more than 150 feet high, and its original cost was $400,000, but the cost of its 1986 restoration was $230 million. _____

_____

_____

4. The statue's torch is about 305 feet above the ground, and its flame is lit at night by the reflected light of sixteen lamps around its rim, and it is gold-covered.

_____

_____

5. The statue holds a tablet, and the tablet is in her left arm, and the tablet is engraved with the date of the Declaration of Independence in Roman numerals.

_____

_____

SENTENCES

Revising Stringy Sentences (continued)

EXERCISE B Revise each of the following stringy sentences. Break the stringy sentence into two or more shorter sentences, turn an independent clause into a subordinate clause, or turn an independent clause into a phrase. Write the revised sentence on the lines provided.

Example 1. The Underground Railroad was actually aboveground, and it was not really a

railroad, but it was a system to help enslaved people escape to free states or to

Canada. *The Underground Railroad was actually aboveground and was not really a*

railroad. It was a system to help enslaved people escape to free states or to Canada.

6. The railroad had "conductors," and they made sure that "packages" traveled safely between

"stations" throughout the long journey, and these "packages" were fugitive slaves.

_____

_____

7. On their way to freedom, some fugitives pretended to be on errands for their masters, and

others wore disguises, and men dressed as women, and women dressed as men.

_____

_____

8. Many ministers and farmers volunteered to work on the Underground Railroad; however,

former slaves helped to run it, too, and everyone involved was courageous and resourceful.

_____

_____

9. Harriet Tubman helped hundreds of people reach freedom, and she was well known on the

Underground Railroad, and she made many dangerous trips to the South to rescue slaves.

_____

_____

10. Abraham Lincoln was president of the United States during the Civil War, and he issued the

Emancipation Proclamation in 1863, and he hoped that the proclamation would help bring

slavery and the war to an end. _____

_____

_____

SENTENCES

Revising Wordy Sentences

EXERCISE A Decide which of the following sentences are wordy and need revision. If a sentence is wordy, revise it to reduce the wordiness. Use proofreading symbols to mark your changes. If a sentence does not need revision, write C on the line provided.

Example _____ **1.** My report will be completed ~~in a timely and expeditious manner.~~ *on time*

_____ **1.** At this point in time, I would like to announce that I am ready to commence presenting my report.

_____ **2.** My report is five hundred words, thereby exceeding the required length set forth by my instructor.

_____ **3.** In the event that I am unable to read the entire report in the allotted period of time today, I will finish going through its contents tomorrow.

_____ **4.** My report provides many insights into what it is like to be an astronaut.

_____ **5.** An astronaut is someone who takes a spaceflight out into space.

_____ **6.** Because there is a complete lack of gravitational pull in space, astronauts experience weightlessness during spaceflight out in space.

_____ **7.** Since there are so many astronauts, I would like to focus my report on one in particular.

_____ **8.** Sally Ride is a famous astronaut who is a popular favorite of many people.

_____ **9.** The reason I am embarking on a detailed exposition of Sally Ride is that I am interested in female astronauts who have been in the space program.

_____ **10.** Sally Ride was the first woman astronaut in the U.S. space program to orbit the earth.

SENTENCES

Revising Wordy Sentences (continued)

EXERCISE B Some of the following sentences are wordy. If a sentence is wordy, revise it to reduce the wordiness. Use proofreading symbols to mark your changes. If a sentence doesn't need revision, write C on the line provided.

Example _____ **1.** The Wright brothers invented the airplane ~~and they created a machine that could fly.~~

_____ **11.** Kill Devil Hill, a narrow strip of land that is located near Kitty Hawk, North Carolina, was the site of their first experiments in 1900 at the beginning of the twentieth century.

_____ **12.** The brothers made four successful flights at Kitty Hawk on December 17, 1903.

_____ **13.** These pioneer flights were witnessed and seen by only five people, one of whom photographed a flight just at the moment the plane left the ground.

_____ **14.** Not very many newspapers at all were interested in the historic flights, and some printed false, incorrect information in their stories.

_____ **15.** The Wright brothers' invention remained unnoticed for the next five years without much attention.

_____ **16.** The two brothers, who continued with their efforts despite the lack of attention, believed that airplanes would one day be used to carry mail and passengers and hoped planes could prevent and prohibit war.

_____ **17.** In 1913, a year after Wilbur contracted and succumbed to typhoid fever, Orville Wright received the Collier Trophy for his invention of a useful apparatus used to balance airplanes automatically.

_____ **18.** For their contributions to aeronautics, the Wright brothers were elected in the year 1965 to the Hall of Fame of Great Americans, which is situated in New York City.

_____ **19.** Wilbur was the older of the two brothers, and he was four years older than Orville.

_____ **20.** Orville didn't expire until 1948, which was a total of thirty-six years after his older brother's death.

SENTENCES

for **CHAPTER 18: WRITING EFFECTIVE SENTENCES**   pages 481–82

Varying Sentence Beginnings

EXERCISE A Revise the following sentences by varying their beginnings. Use the instructions in parentheses to determine whether the sentence should start with a single-word modifier, a phrase, or a subordinate clause. Add or delete words as necessary to make the sentence sound better. Write your revised sentences on the lines provided. Hint: The words that you should use according to the instructions are underlined.

Example 1. The unique art of producing stained glass is frequently associated with the decoration of houses of worship. (single-word modifier)

Frequently, the unique art of producing stained glass is associated with the decoration

of houses of worship.

1. The earliest known complete stained-glass windows are thought to be those of the Augsburg Cathedral in Germany, which date from the eleventh or twelfth century. (phrase)

_____

_____

2. Artisans specializing in stained glass began trying to achieve the effects of oil painting in the 1400s. (phrase) _____

_____

3. Enamel pigments made painting on glass as easy as painting on canvas in the sixteenth century; however, critics thought this development was unfortunate. (subordinate clause)

_____

_____

4. Stained-glass art later depended on more difficult coloring techniques, which included firing the glass at low temperatures to "fix" the paint. (single-word modifier)

_____

_____

5. Advocates for the art of stained glass believed that stained glass should be distinct from oil painting and encouraged a return to traditional methods of coloring glass during the Gothic revival of the nineteenth century. (phrase)

_____

_____

SENTENCES

Varying Sentence Beginnings (continued)

EXERCISE B   Revise the following sentences by varying their beginnings. Use the instructions in parentheses to determine whether the sentence should start with a single-word modifier, a phrase, or a subordinate clause. Add or delete words as necessary to make the sentence sound better. Write your revised sentences on the lines provided.

Example 1. The ancient Greeks proposed the first scientific explanations of the earth's composition, but the ancient Greeks blended fact, superstition, and guesswork in their scientific explanations. (phrase)

Blending fact, superstition, and guesswork, the ancient Greeks proposed the first scientific explanations of the earth's composition.

6. Herodotus, a Greek historian, studied marine fossils and then concluded that the earth had once been completely covered by water. (subordinate clause)

_____

_____

7. Strabo, a Greek geographer, wrote in his multivolume *Geography* in 7 B.C. that volcanoes and earthquakes were partially responsible for the rising and sinking of land masses. (phrase)

_____

_____

8. The Romans later wrote detailed works on geology, using knowledge of their extensive empire's varied terrain. (single-word modifier)

_____

_____

9. Pliny the Younger unintentionally promoted the science of geology in a letter about his uncle's death when he described the catastrophic eruption of Mt. Vesuvius in A.D. 79. (phrase)

_____

_____

10. Little scientific advancement took place for six hundred years until the Islamic physician Avicenna published his findings in the eleventh century. (subordinate clause)

_____

_____

Revising a Paragraph to Create Variety

EXERCISE A Using what you have learned about combining sentences and varying structure, revise the following paragraph to improve sentence style. Correct stringy and wordy sentences. Vary sentence beginnings, and add or delete words as necessary. Write your revised paragraph on the lines provided.

Example Frank Lloyd Wright was an American architect. He was a gifted architect. He designed commercial buildings and homes.

Frank Lloyd Wright was a gifted American architect who designed commercial buildings

and homes.

Wright liked his buildings to complement the landscape. He was a pioneer. He created open floor plans. He eliminated traditional room divisions. He was able to bring nature indoors. Many of Wright's designs became famous. The Guggenheim Museum in New York City is considered one of his boldest works. It contains a floor-to-ceiling spiral ramp. Wright's design for the Marin County Civic Center in California is also adventurous, and it connects three hills with a series of nine structures, and it was completed in the year 2000. Wright died in 1959. His architectural genius lives on. Many of his buildings have been preserved as museums. His contributions to architecture were extraordinary.

_____

_____

_____

_____

_____

_____

_____

_____

_____

_____

_____

_____

_____

_____

SENTENCES

Language and Sentence Skills Practice

Revising a Paragraph to Create Variety (continued)

EXERCISE B Using what you have learned about combining sentences and varying structure, revise the following paragraph to improve sentence style. Correct stringy and wordy sentences. Vary sentence beginnings, and add or delete words as necessary. Write your revised paragraph on the lines provided.

Example Flying a kite is a popular form of recreation for many people. It is popular around the world. Kites do not really serve a purpose anymore. They do not serve a useful purpose.

Although flying a kite is a popular form of recreation around the world, kites do not

really serve a useful purpose anymore.

Kites are older than any other form of aircraft. They are named after an elegant bird. The Chinese made the first kites some two thousand years ago. They attached bamboo pipes to paper kites. They did this to frighten their enemies. The sound of the wind whistling through the pipes was eerie. The sound made the enemies retreat. Scientists have used kites for research, and military personnel have used kites for research, and kites have been used by scientists and military personnel for centuries. Kites are flown in Japan during a festival. These kites are taller than people. The festival is more than four hundred years old.

_____

_____

_____

_____

_____

_____

_____

_____

_____

_____

_____

_____

_____

_____

_____

_____

_____

SENTENCES

Manuscript Form

When writing a paper, it is important to follow a manuscript style in order to present information in a neat and organized way. Here is one common manuscript style.

Margins

Leave a one-inch margin on the top, sides, and bottom of each page.

Pagination

One-half inch from the top of each page, include a header in the upper right-hand corner. The header should include your last name followed by the page number.

Indention

Paragraphs should be indented half an inch; set-off quotations should be indented an inch from the left margin (five spaces and ten spaces, respectively, on standard typewriters).

Heading

On the title page of your paper, include a heading one inch from the top of the page. The heading should include your full name, your teacher's name, the course name, and the date (day, month, year). Double-space between each line of your heading.

Title

On the title page of your paper, include the title of your paper. Double-space between the heading and the title. Center the title and capitalize the appropriate letters. Double-space between the title and body of your paper.

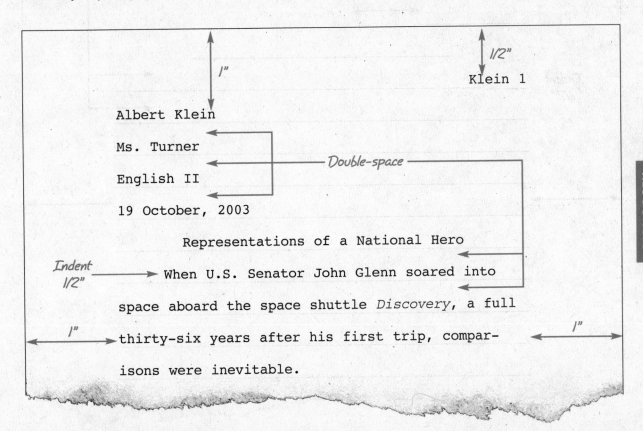

RESOURCES

Language and Sentence Skills Practice   **453**

Manuscript Form (continued)

EXERCISE The following passage is excerpted from a paper written on November 13, 2003, by Paula Delano, a student in Mr. Brown's English II class. Fill in the blanks with the appropriate information to complete the title page according to the guidelines on the previous page.

Title: The Killing of the Coral Reefs

First Paragraph: Are coral reefs "the forgotten rain forests of the sea"? When biologist Clive Wilkinson chose that subtitle for a book on the world's coral reefs, he made a dramatic point. People protest the damage done to tropical rain forests and their rich resources; yet coral reefs, an equally vital resource, suffer similar damage. While some causes are natural, human action causes most coral reef destruction, a problem having serious consequences for life on earth.

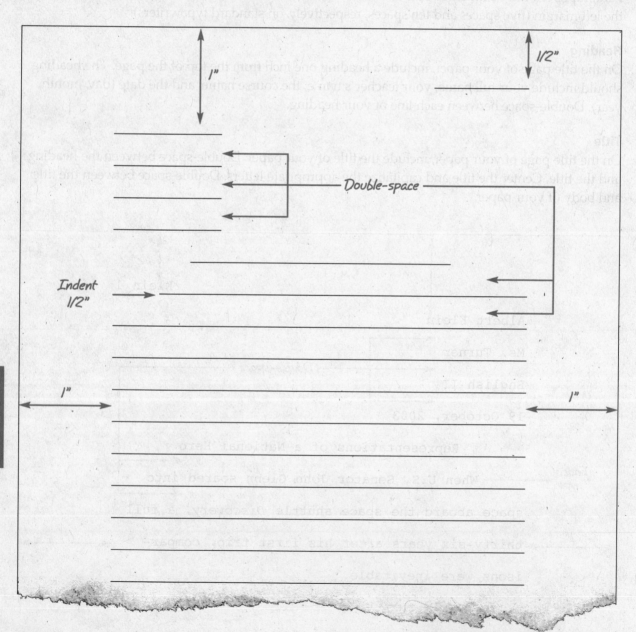

RESOURCES